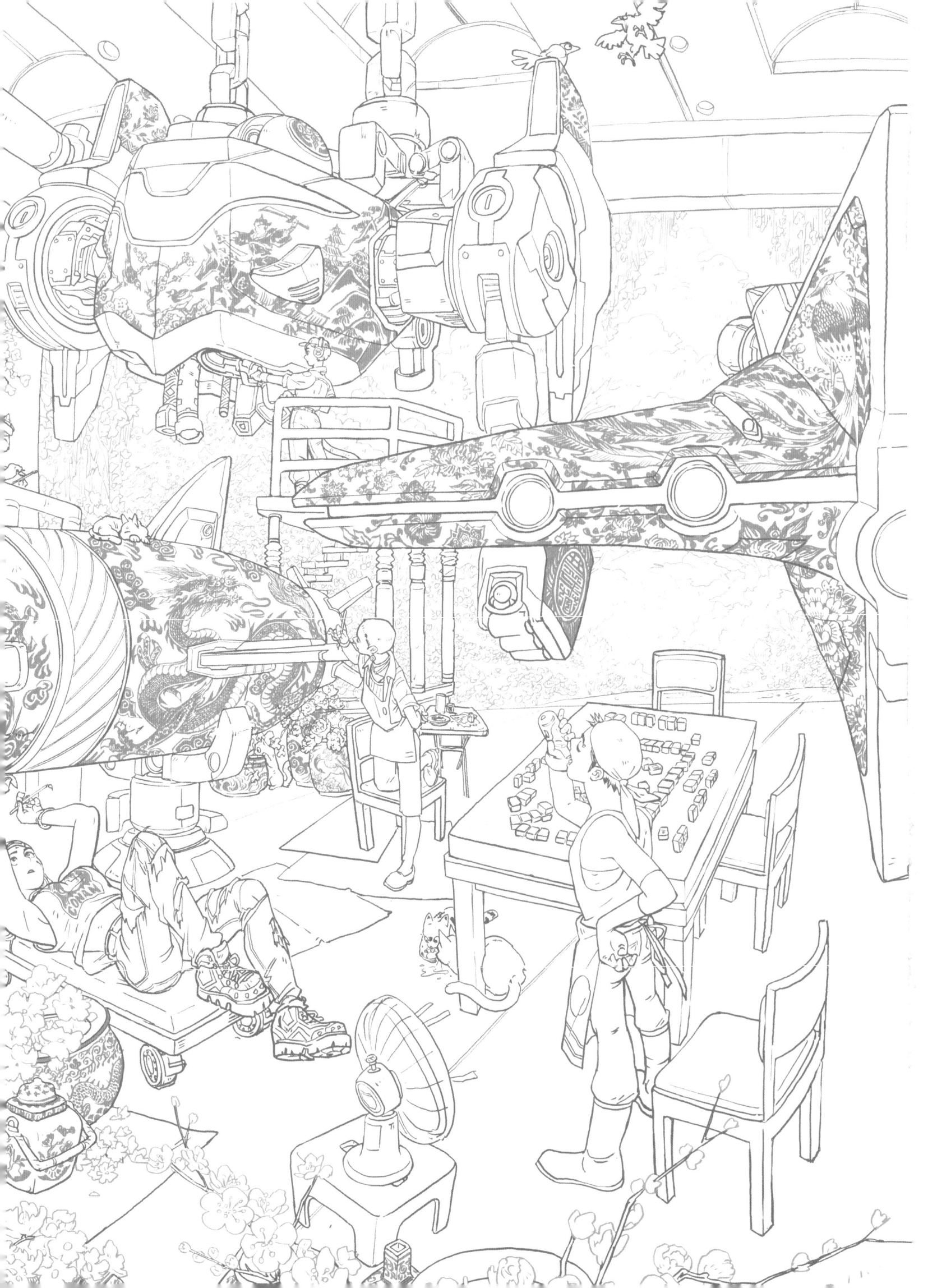

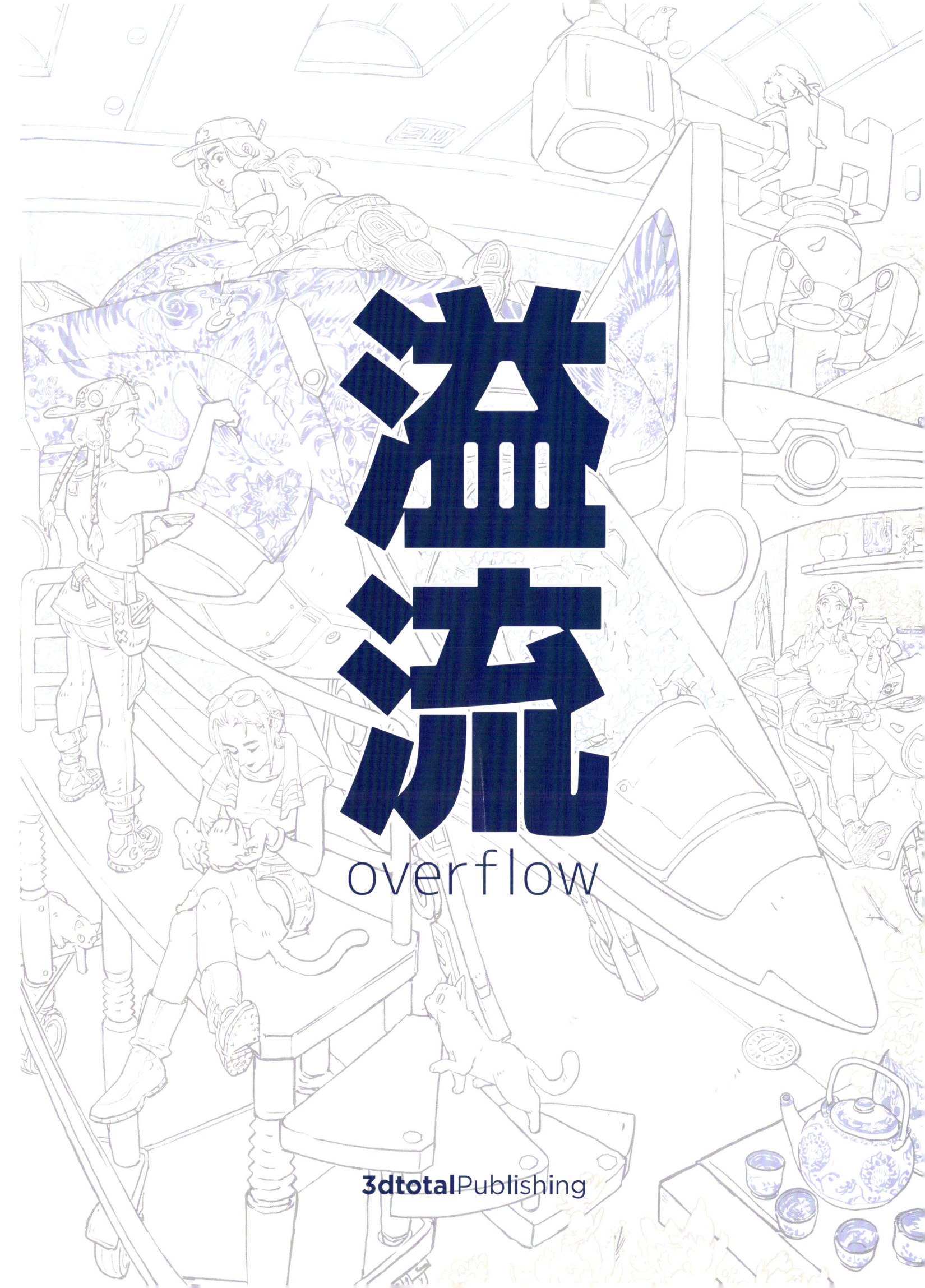

溢流
overflow

3dtotal Publishing

3dtotalPublishing

Correspondence: **publishing@3dtotal.com**
Website: **store.3dtotal.com**

Every effort has been made to ensure the credits and contact information listed are present and correct. In the case of any errors that have occurred, the publisher respectfully directs readers to **store.3dtotal.com/pages/information** for any updated information and corrections.

Thoughts and opinions expressed in this book belong to the author and not the publisher.

First published in the United Kingdom, 2025, by 3dtotal Publishing.

Address: 3dtotal.com Ltd,
29 Foregate Street, Worcester,
WR1 1DS, United Kingdom.

Hard Cover ISBN: 978-1-915992-17-8

Printed and bound in China
by C&C Offset Printing Co., Ltd

Visit **store.3dtotal.com** for a complete list of available book titles.

Editorial Project Manager: Rhiannon Joseph
Lead Editor: Samantha Rigby
Lead Designer: Joseph Cartwright
Studio Manager: Simon Morse
Managing Director: Tom Greenway

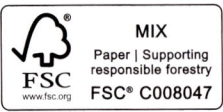

FSC
MIX
Paper | Supporting
responsible forestry
www.fsc.org   FSC® C008047

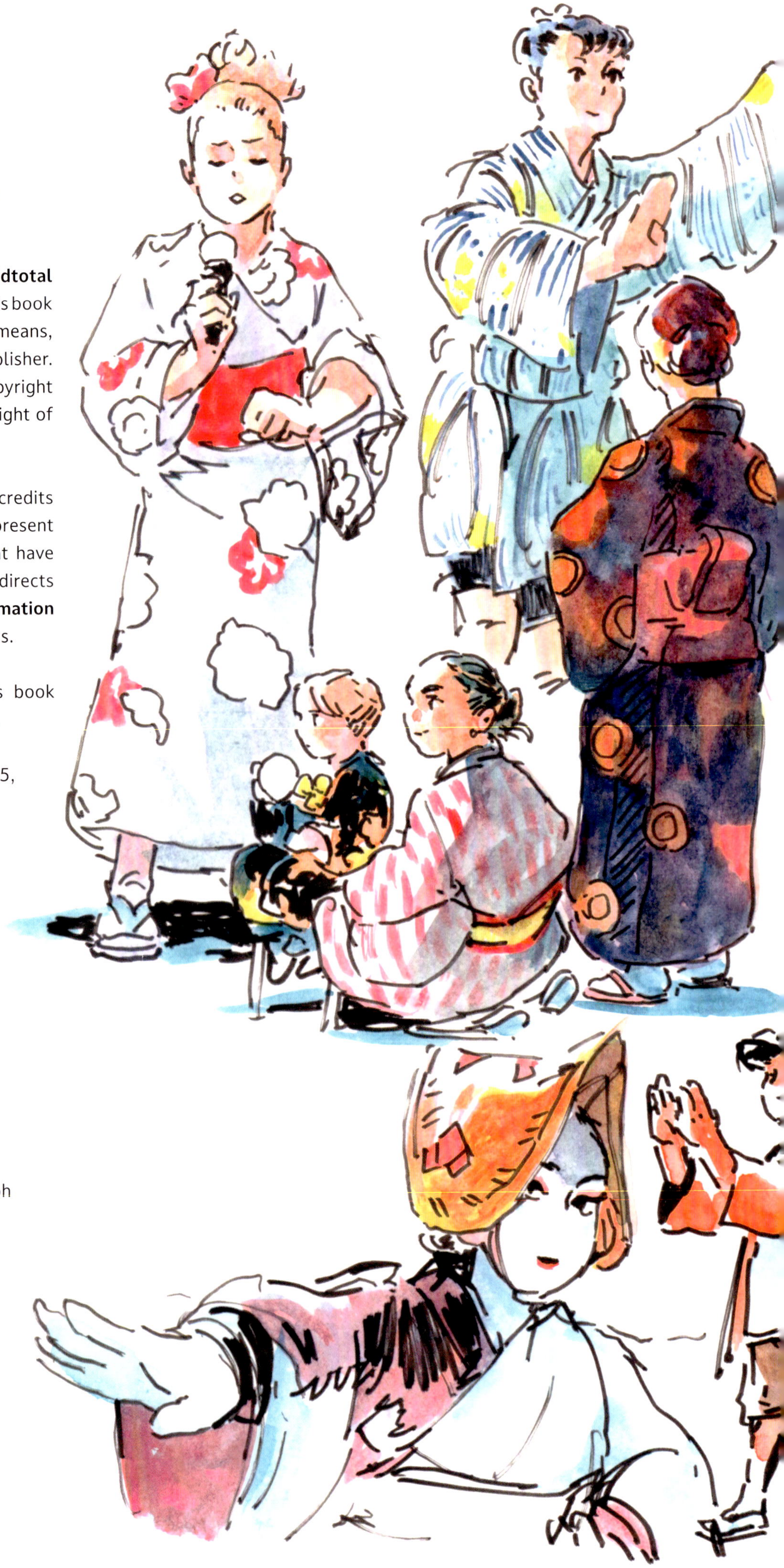

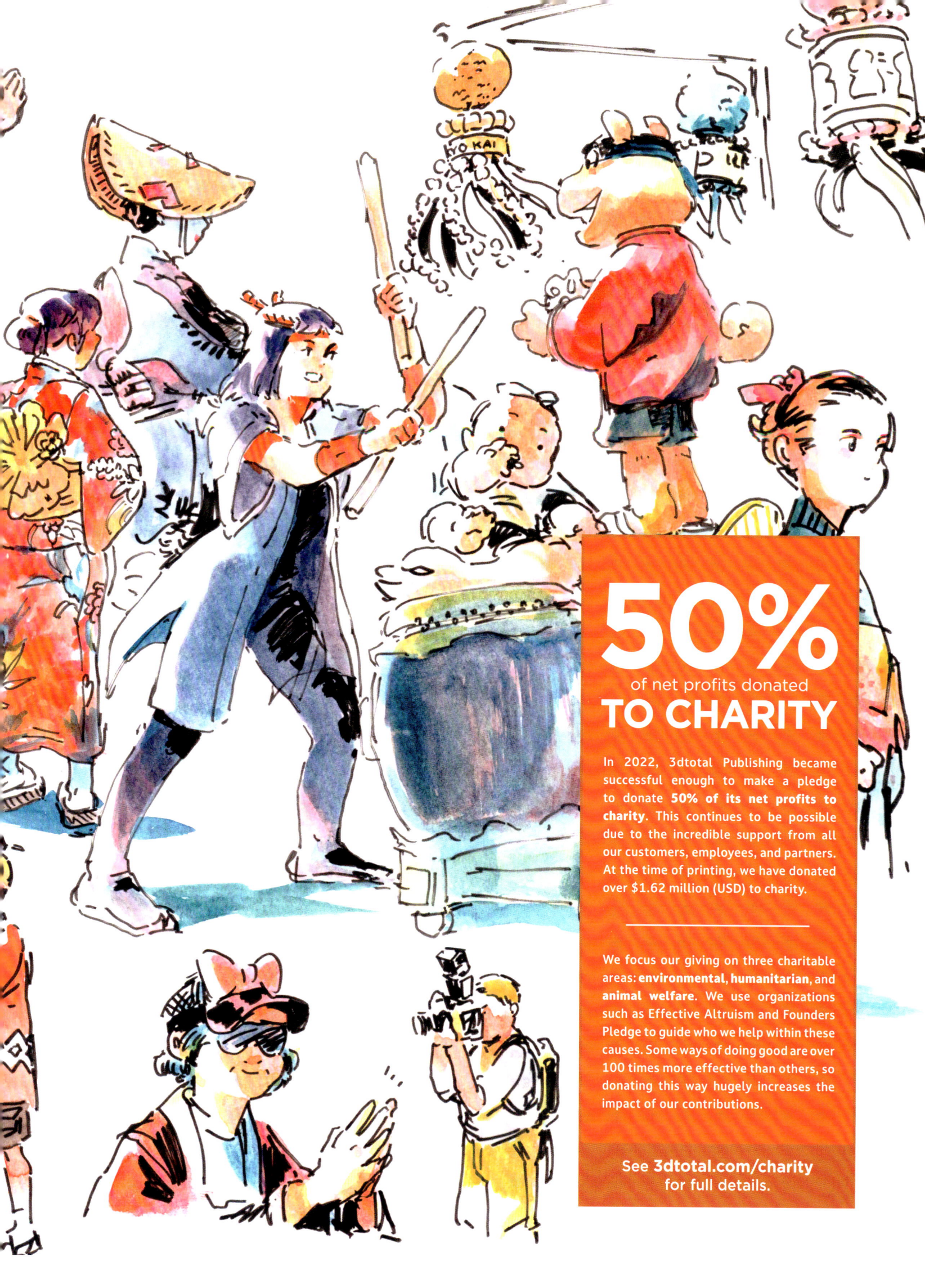

50%
of net profits donated
TO CHARITY

In 2022, 3dtotal Publishing became successful enough to make a pledge to donate **50% of its net profits to charity**. This continues to be possible due to the incredible support from all our customers, employees, and partners. At the time of printing, we have donated over $1.62 million (USD) to charity.

We focus our giving on three charitable areas: **environmental**, **humanitarian**, and **animal welfare**. We use organizations such as Effective Altruism and Founders Pledge to guide who we help within these causes. Some ways of doing good are over 100 times more effective than others, so donating this way hugely increases the impact of our contributions.

See **3dtotal.com/charity**
for full details.

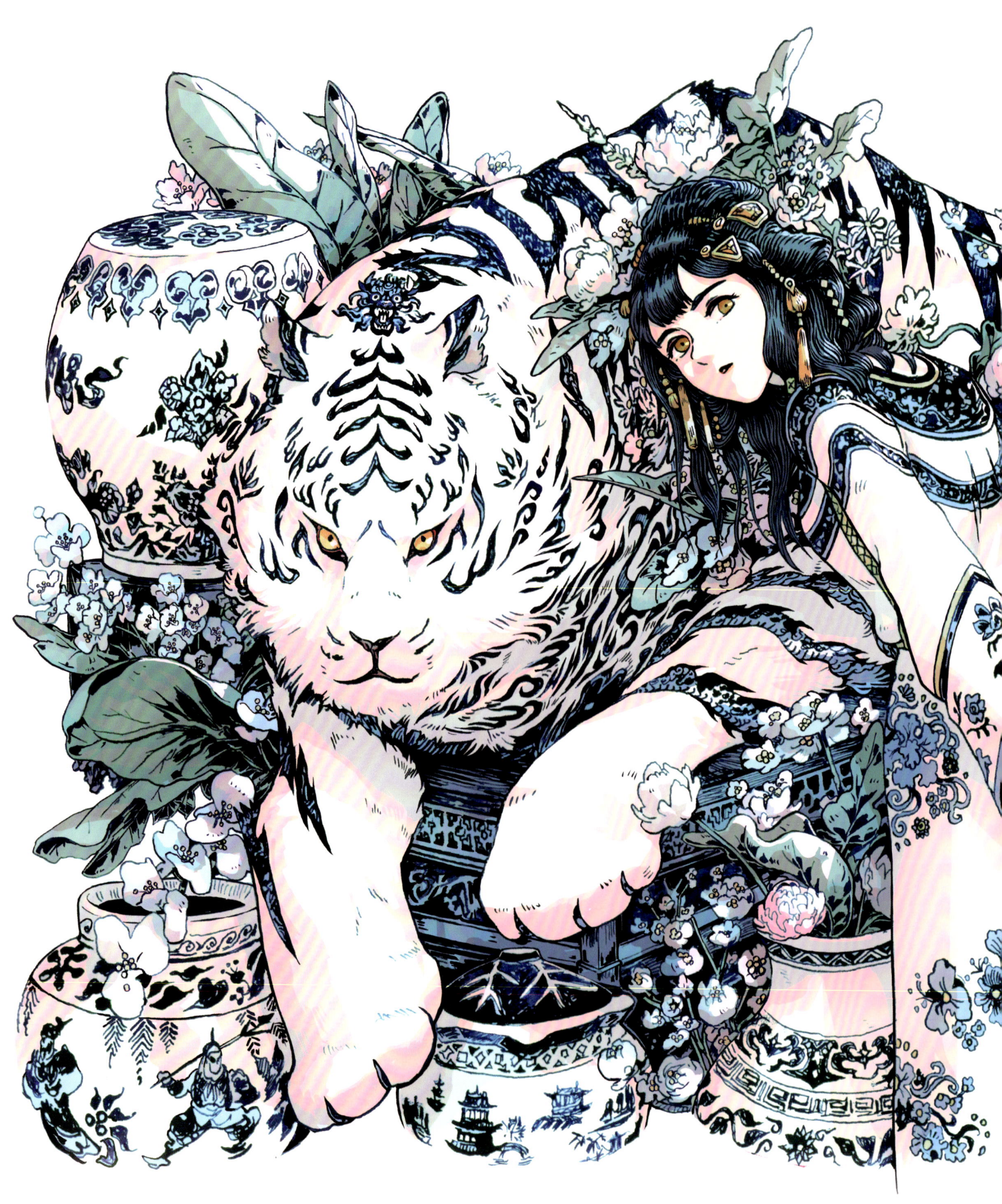

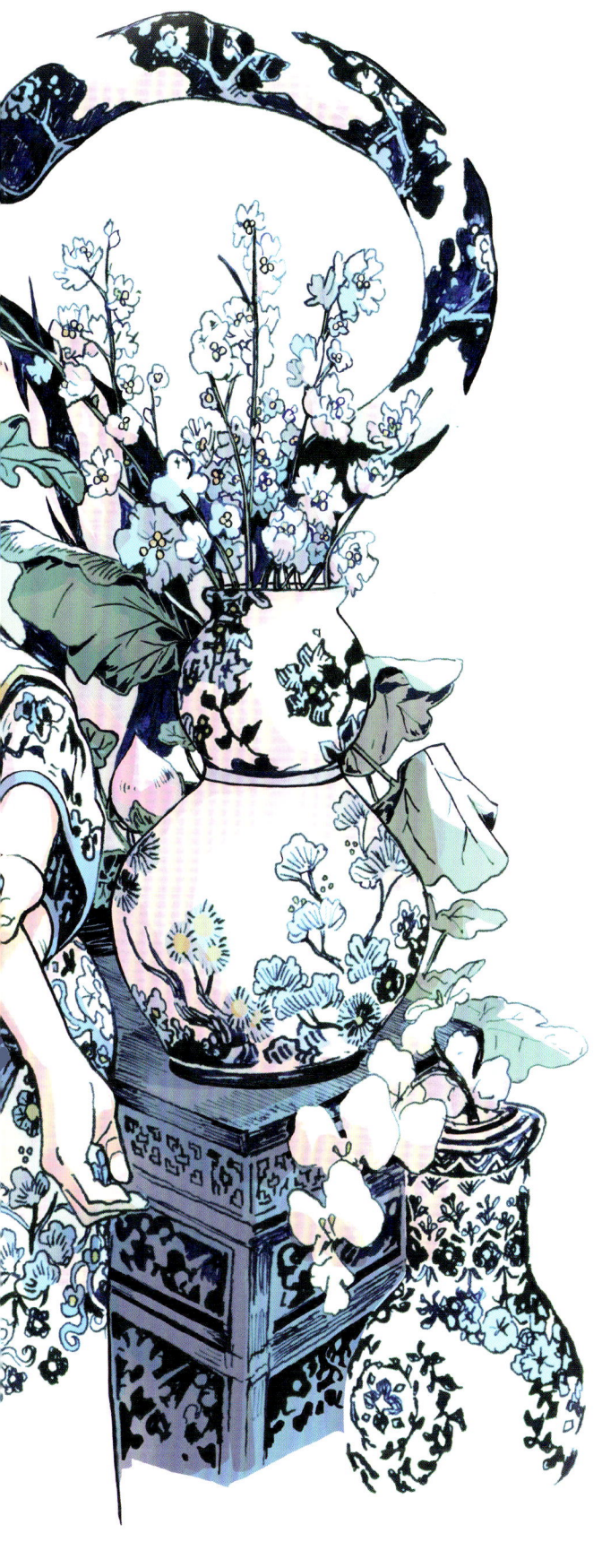

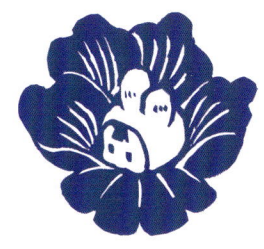

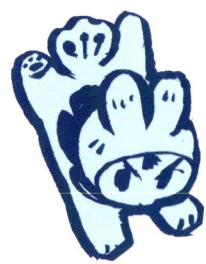

Dedicated to my son Conan Kho, who you'll find throughout this book as a little bunny guy. He's my favourite.

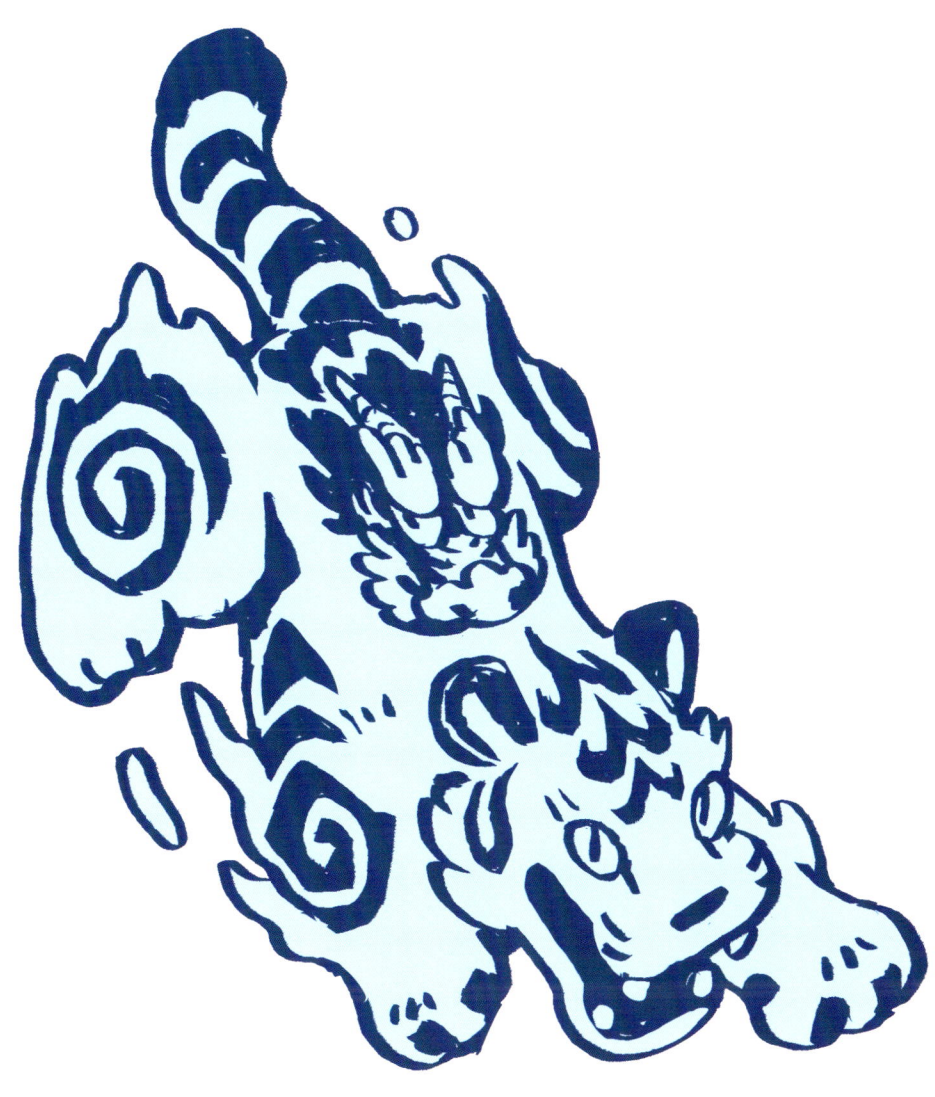

My name is Bryce Kho and I'm an illustrator and concept artist. I like to draw big, bustling scenes that make me feel like I'm somewhere nice.

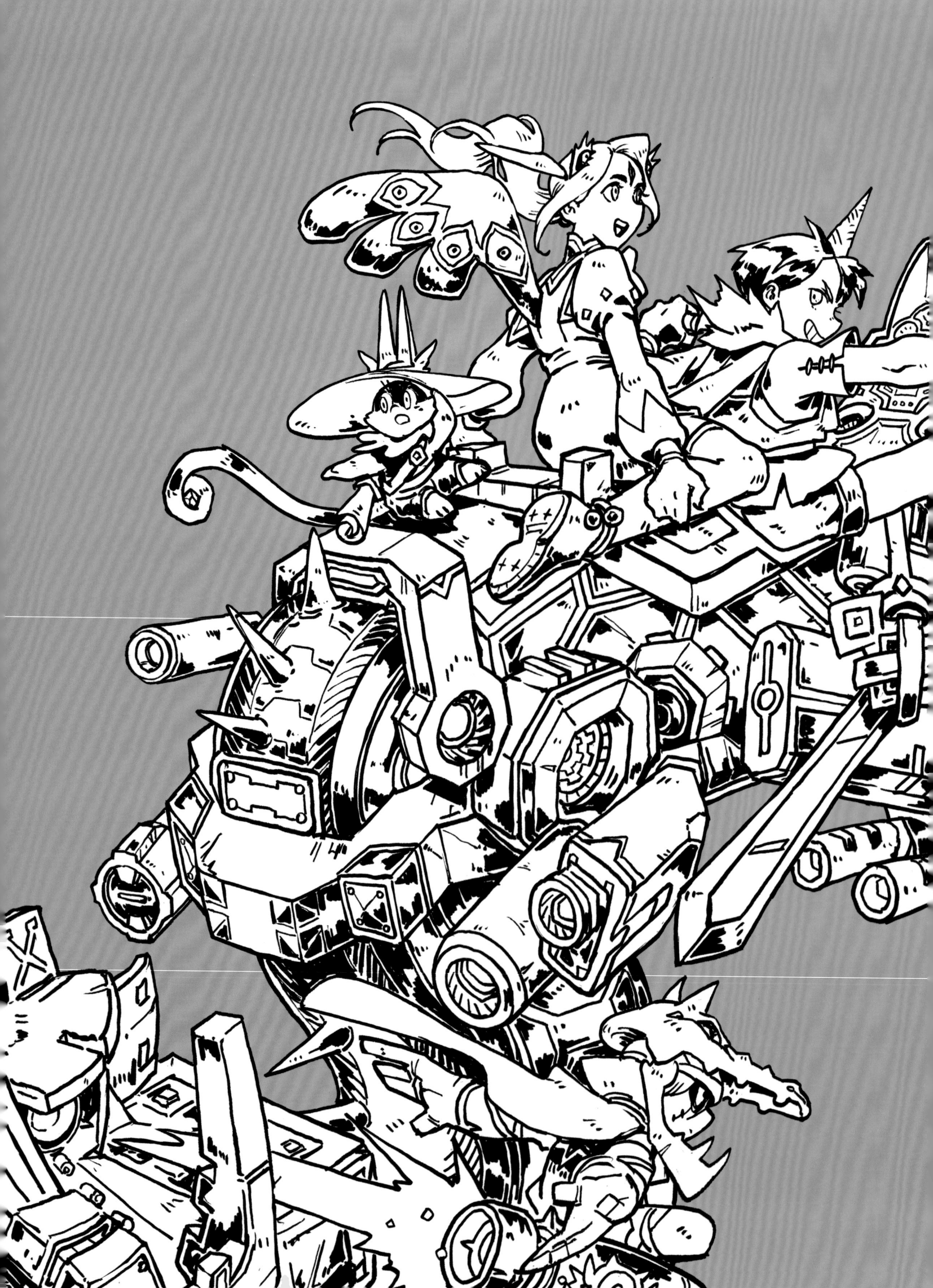

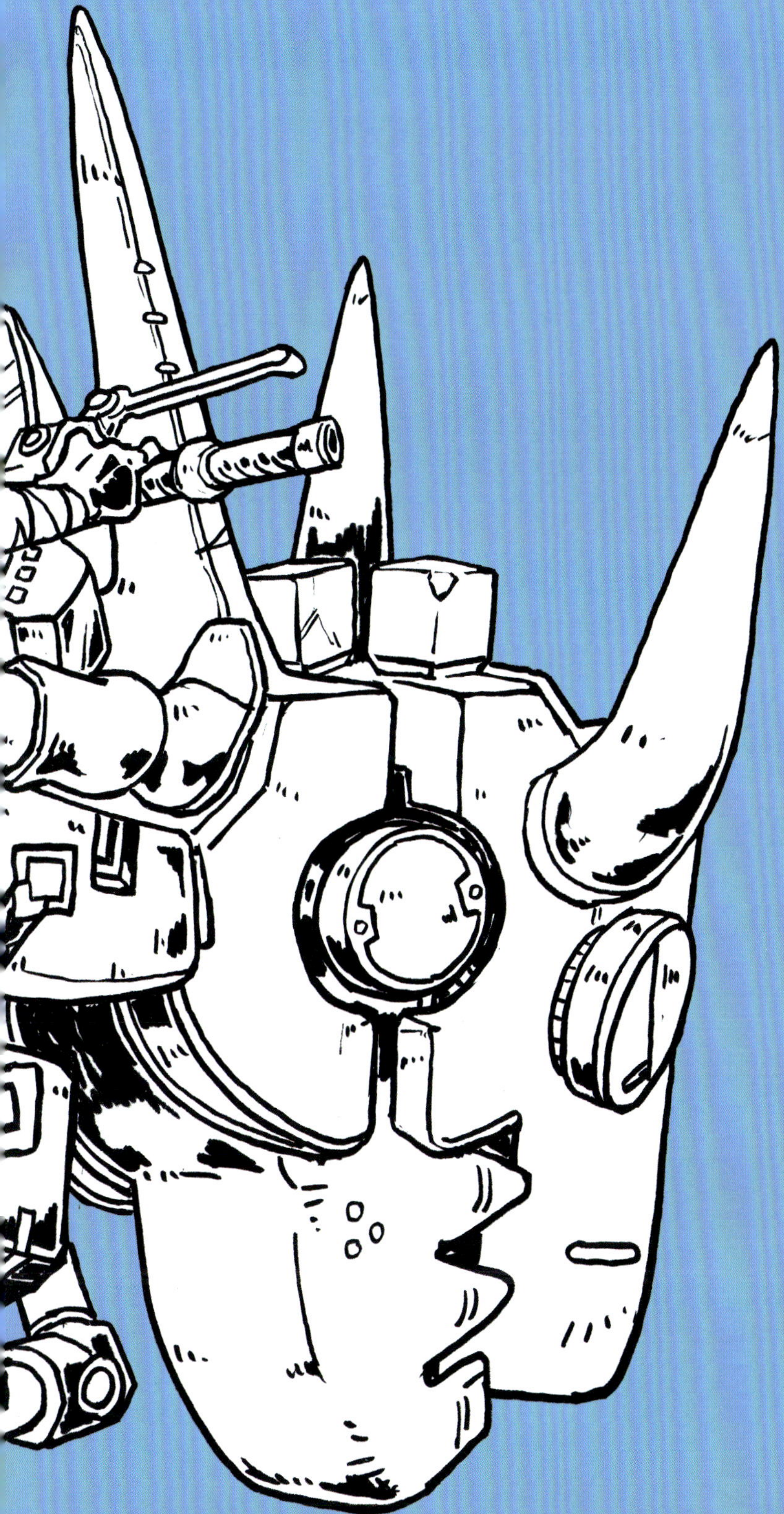

PHILOSOPHY

哲学

Looking back, the origin story of my artistic approach began in an environment where art was viewed as a hobby and not a profession. Since my father instilled the core belief that I should never become an artist, I viewed artwork as a means and not an end.

'Yes, my art might not have any value, but perhaps I could use my skills to create something else that does.'

It might sound a bit harsh or sad to an outsider, but this has always been my reality. Now, I view it through the lens of two particularly valuable lessons …

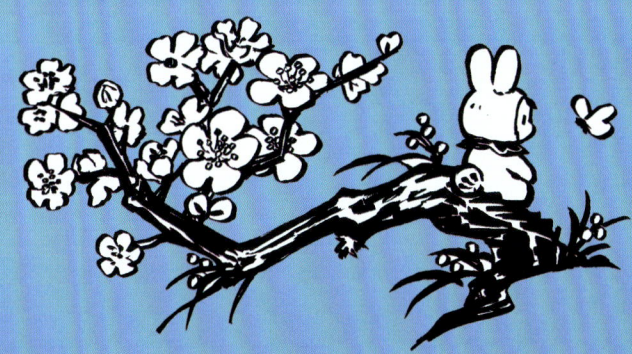

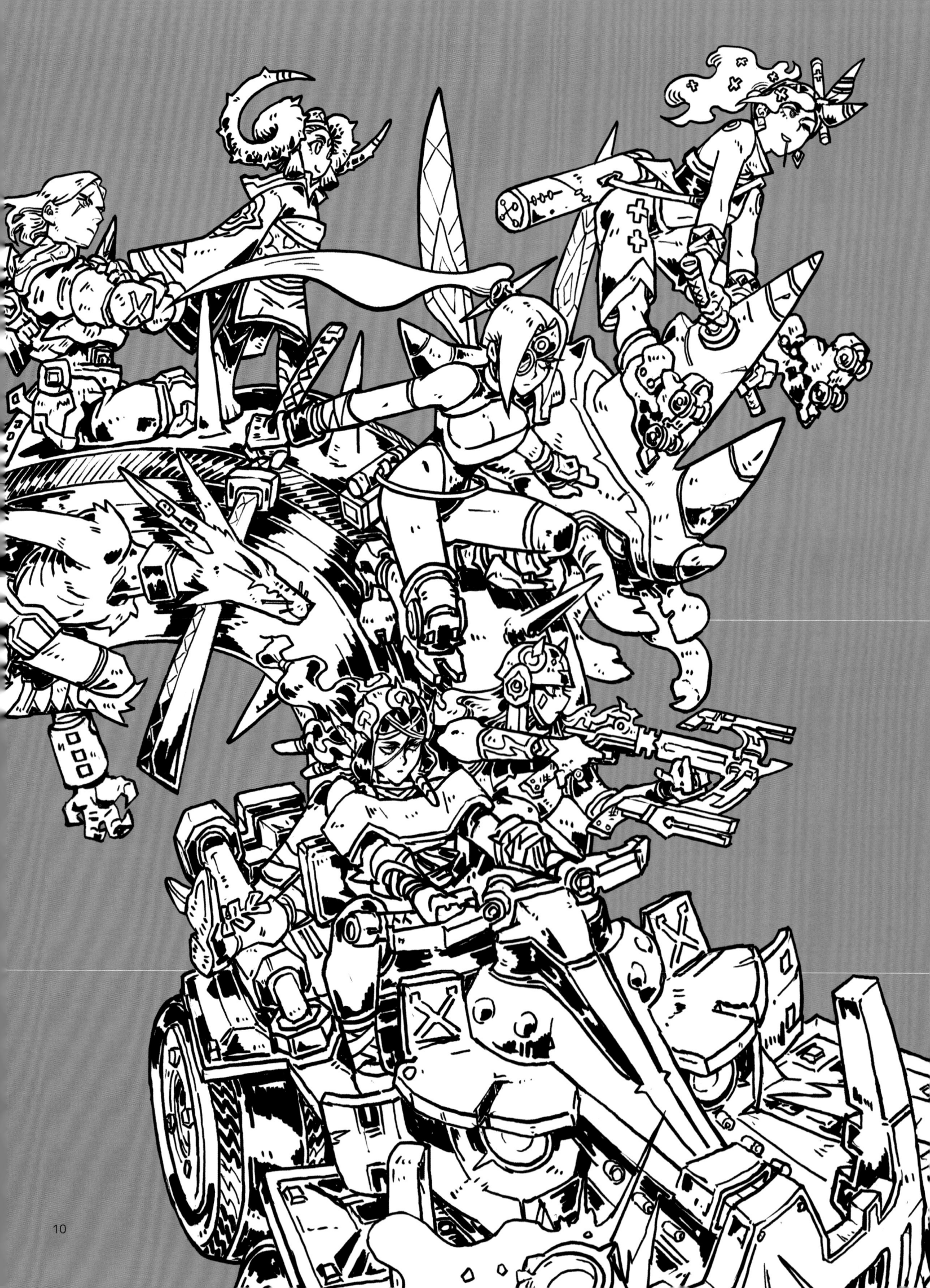

Lesson 1: Treat art like a game. Do it for the experience. Do it to see how far you can go. Do it because it's fun. I tell myself there is no practical point to it other than to spread joy, for me or others. There is no one to impress. No one actually cares what I'm doing. Therefore, it's just for me. Whatever I need to tell myself to feel less pressure while drawing, whether it's true or not, is the framework I create to give myself the freedom to keep drawing. This is a single-player game for me and there is only one goal: get better and level up.

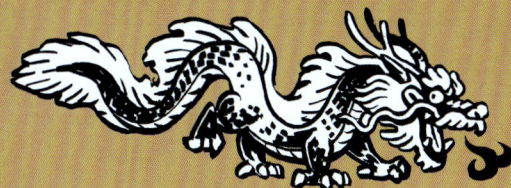

Lesson 2: The artwork must do something, say something, or be useful to someone. This may seem to contradict lesson one, but I try to maintain both mindsets to keep me creating. Of course, lesson two is a personal rule and there are plenty of artists I adore who don't necessarily agree – a beautiful flower need not explain itself. Still, from my own point of view, I feel I must infuse value into my artwork for it to have worth. This means I don't feel satisfied with what I'm creating unless it somehow also accomplishes a secondary goal: becoming a game asset, conveying a concept for a character in a story, telling a story itself, or any number of things.

DO IT TO SEE HOW FAR YOU CAN GO

TREAT ART LIKE A GAME – DO IT FOR THE EXPERIENCE

Now that I'm older, I feel that I have mostly come to terms with my identity as a fully fledged artist. It is, after all, what I do for a living, how I pay the bills. Truthfully, though, a part of me still feels a need to justify myself whenever I'm asked what I do, as if no one would believe I could be an artist without more explanation. In a way, I'm still the same child who thinks all this art stuff is just what I'm doing as a hobby until I get a real job. This book is my way of fully articulating what it means for me to be an artist – what it has taught me, what I find worthwhile, and where I want to go next.

One of the most pivotal moments in my artistic journey was in 2014 when I saw Kim Jung Gi draw during a live demo at San Diego Comic-Con. The gist of the talk can be found online on any of his YouTube videos, where he teaches structure, perspective, and cutting into forms as a way to understand how to draw. The thing that stood out to me that day was not necessarily the practical lessons, but rather what changed in me. It was the act of watching someone with the ability to live out what I'd thought was an impossible dream: playfully and freely drawing from the imagination. Of course, I did my best to integrate his lessons into my understanding, but the framework he set up was the real key – the idea that I had to draw for *understanding* rather than practice.

For the next four years, I began to take this premise seriously. Seeing that Kim Jung Gi could reach such great heights as a mere mortal made me wonder if it was a possibility for me, too. At the time, I was already going to figure-drawing classes regularly as a hobbyist, but I saw it as a way to turn off my brain and copy what I was seeing without thinking too hard. Seeing Kim Jung Gi changed that.

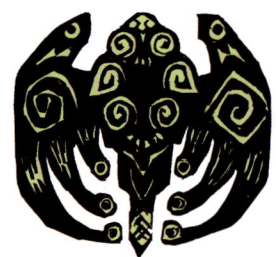

I began to challenge myself. Rather than just working on my ability to translate what was in front of me onto the page (something I still think is insanely valuable, as it teaches coordination and control), I began to wonder if I could draw from seeing *and* understanding. I started experimenting with moving around more in the room, viewing what was in front of me as volumes and shapes instead of lines and gradients.

Could I draw the model in front of me as if I were standing somewhere else? From the other side, perhaps? From below, or above? Kim Jung Gi could if he were here, but how would he do it? He proved to me that there was a whole different level to the game of drawing, and I wanted to experience what having that sort of skill would feel like.

During the talk Kim Jung Gi gave at San Diego Comic-Con, there was a person who asked him how he drew so effortlessly. Gi jokingly responded, 'Can't you see the lines I'm tracing?' Everyone laughed. But I noticed him tracing his fingers over where he would draw next, and something in me knew that he was serious, at least a little. Realistically, you couldn't draw as fluidly or seamlessly as he was demonstrating unless you actually did, in fact, see it in your head super clearly.

Then, one night at a figure-drawing class like any other (usually Mondays in downtown Los Angeles at sessions hosted by Gallery Girls – oh, how I would look forward to Mondays just for the promise of getting to relax after work by drawing), I had a breakthrough.

The moment didn't seem special at first. In retrospect, I had been gradually working my way towards it for months. I had those brief moments where things were just going well and 'flowing'. My wife later told me about flow states – those moments when you're just grooving and things feel like they're effortlessly falling into place.

But this moment was different. It was exciting. And it is burned into my memory.

I couldn't see the model's left arm because it was posed behind her back. Yet, instead of guessing or sketching to figure it out, I thought about my volumetric understanding of her arm as a cylinder and was able to visually project that image onto the page. It's hard to describe because it was different to any other moment I had experienced in my twenty-six years of drawing – it was a different sensation in my head, even. Somehow, I could see what I wanted to draw projected onto the page.

I didn't just see the general shape or a vague image in my head, separate from the real world. I could see the lines themselves transparently overlaid onto the page. Kim Jung Gi wasn't joking – he really was tracing. But the lines were invisible to everyone else because they only existed in *his* mind's eye. As for me, I could finally see what he was talking about. It wasn't for very long and it wasn't very clear, but I could really see it.

KIM JUNG GI WASN'T JOKING – HE REALLY WAS TRACING. BUT THE LINES WERE INVISIBLE TO EVERYONE ELSE ...

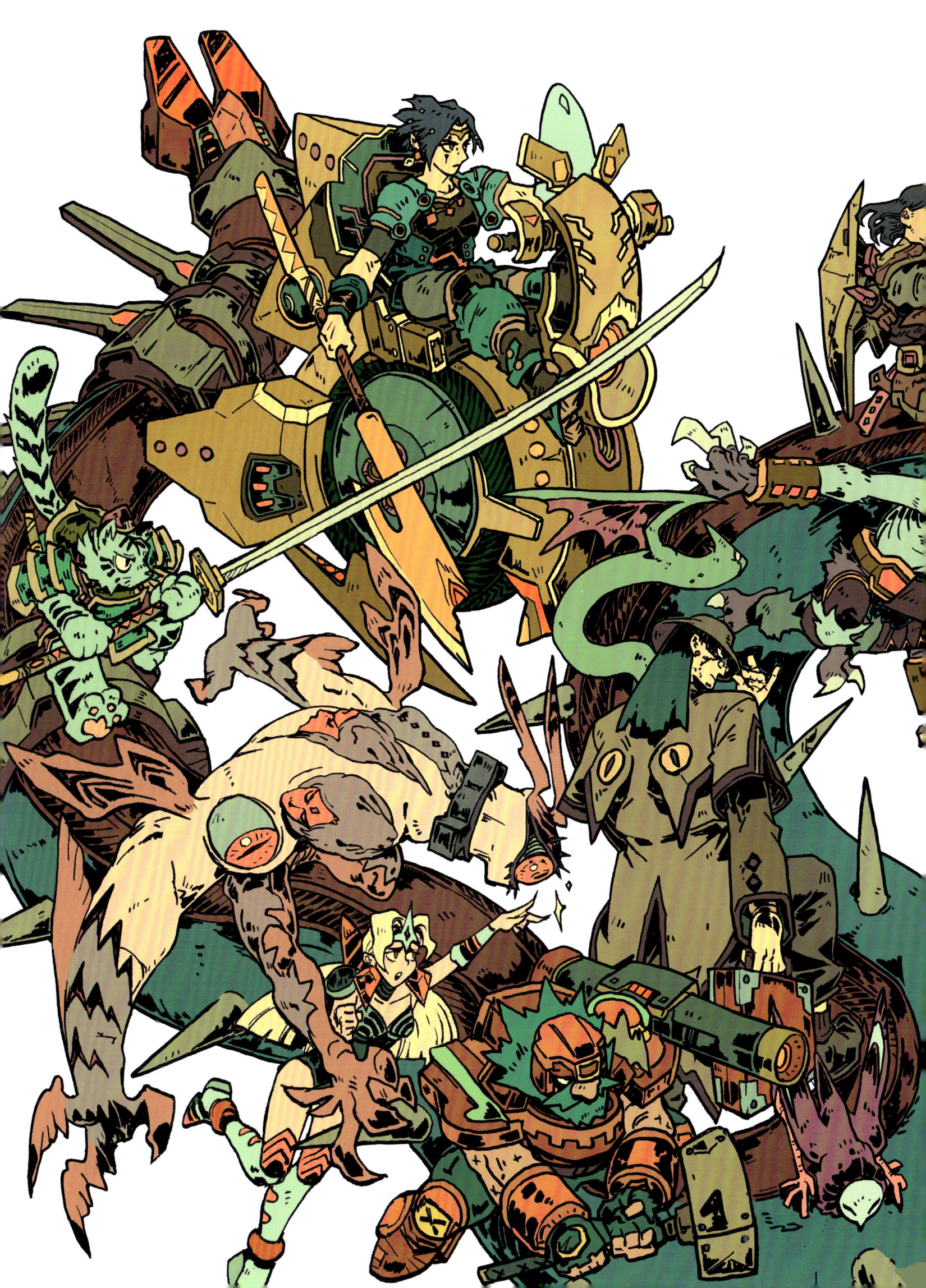

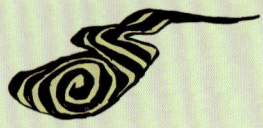

Since that moment, I've been chasing the same sensation, the same flow. It feels like clarity combined with intense focus and peacefulness, all at once. I definitely don't have it all the time, and when I do have it, it feels like the difference between having the light switched on versus off. However, I've got better at tapping into it. It feels like a superpower because it's the dream skill I always wanted, but it's also frustratingly finicky.

Sometimes, I'll draw for a whole day and not feel it. Other days, I can be basking in the flow for hours, even to the drawing's completion. Now that I've tasted it, I know I want more.

***Overflow*, the title of this book, is a reference to that pursuit.**

It's also a reference to how I want my own completed works to feel. It's my desire to make artwork that brims with life, atmosphere, and emotion, enough to overwhelm a viewer until they get lost in the worlds I've imagined. It's what I look for in art that I'd want to hang on my own walls. And so, I feel my artwork must also achieve such goals to be worthy of someone's wall space; it's what I strive for.

The rest of this book explores the process I use to achieve this overflowing sensation. In fact, my entire process is pretty much laid out here, from figure drawing to creating thumbnails, to dealing with the fact there's only a one-in-ten chance of an illustration actually connecting with an audience. To the aspiring artists who want to know how the sausage is made, I say gathering the raw ingredients is just as important as the cooking itself. To everyone else, thank you for coming and I hope you enjoy the work.

> ## IT FEELS LIKE CLARITY COMBINED WITH INTENSE FOCUS AND PEACEFULNESS

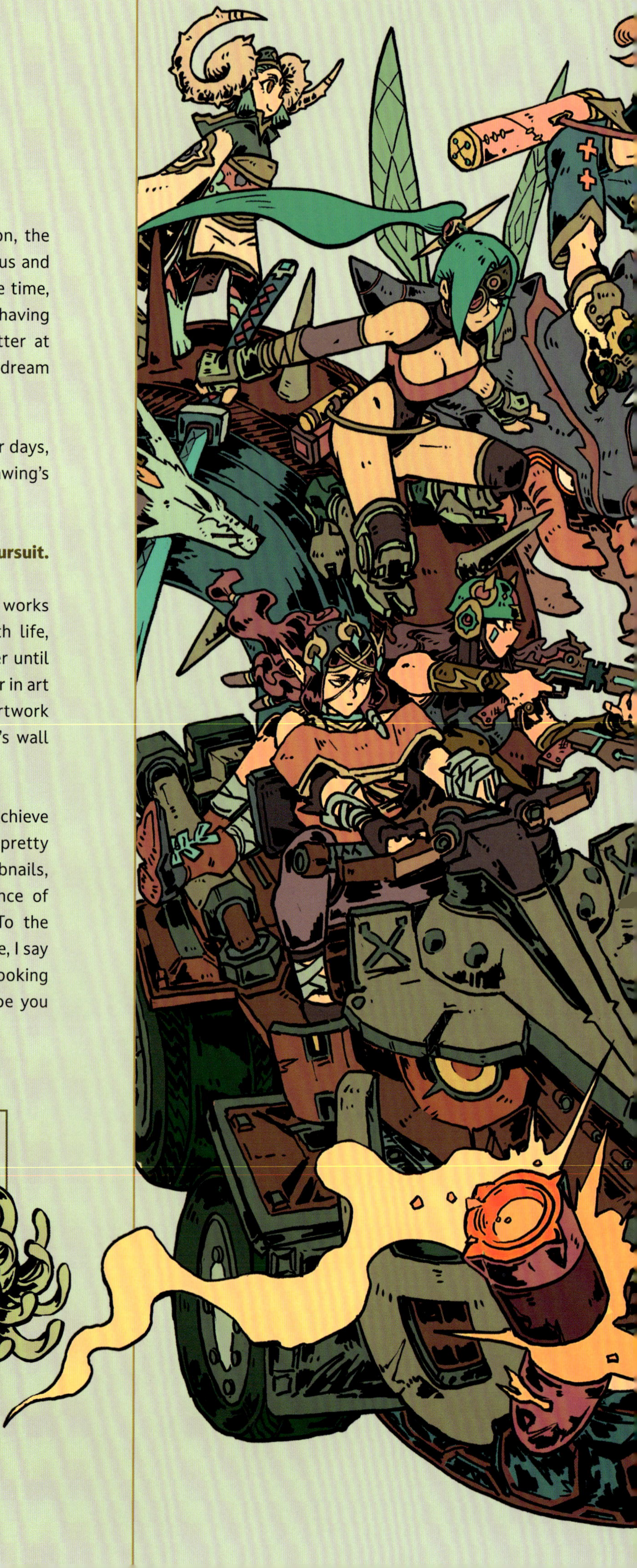

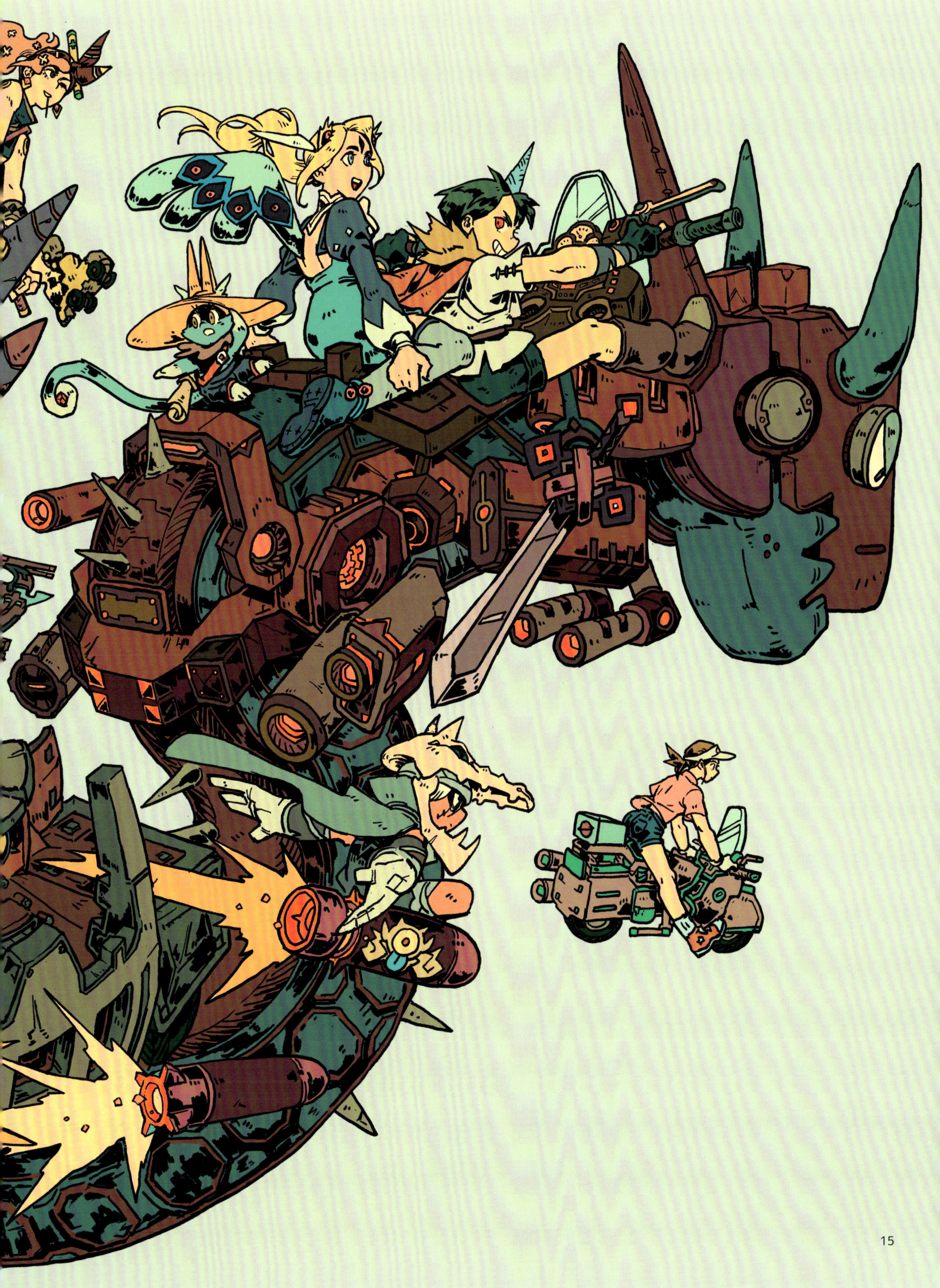

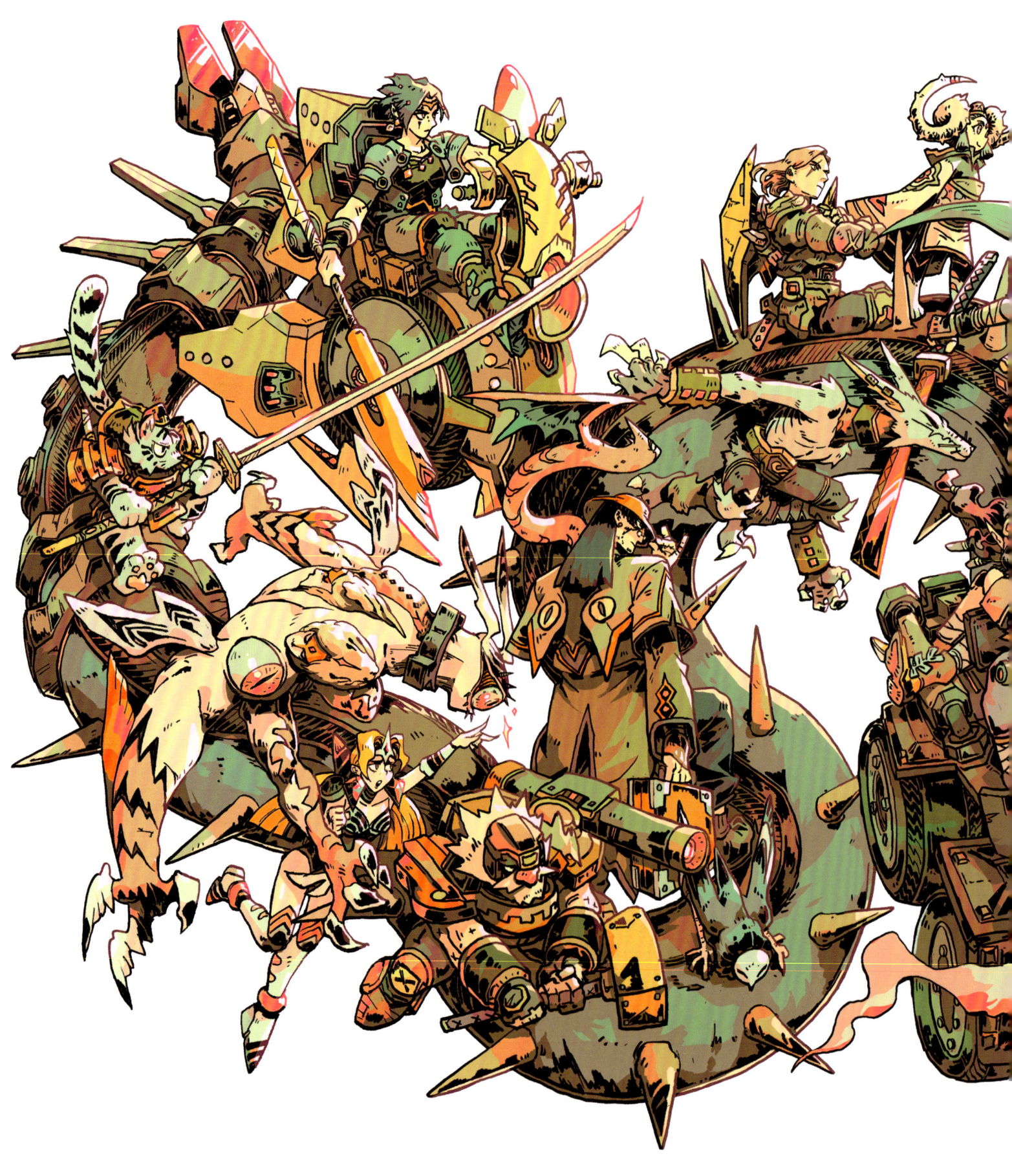

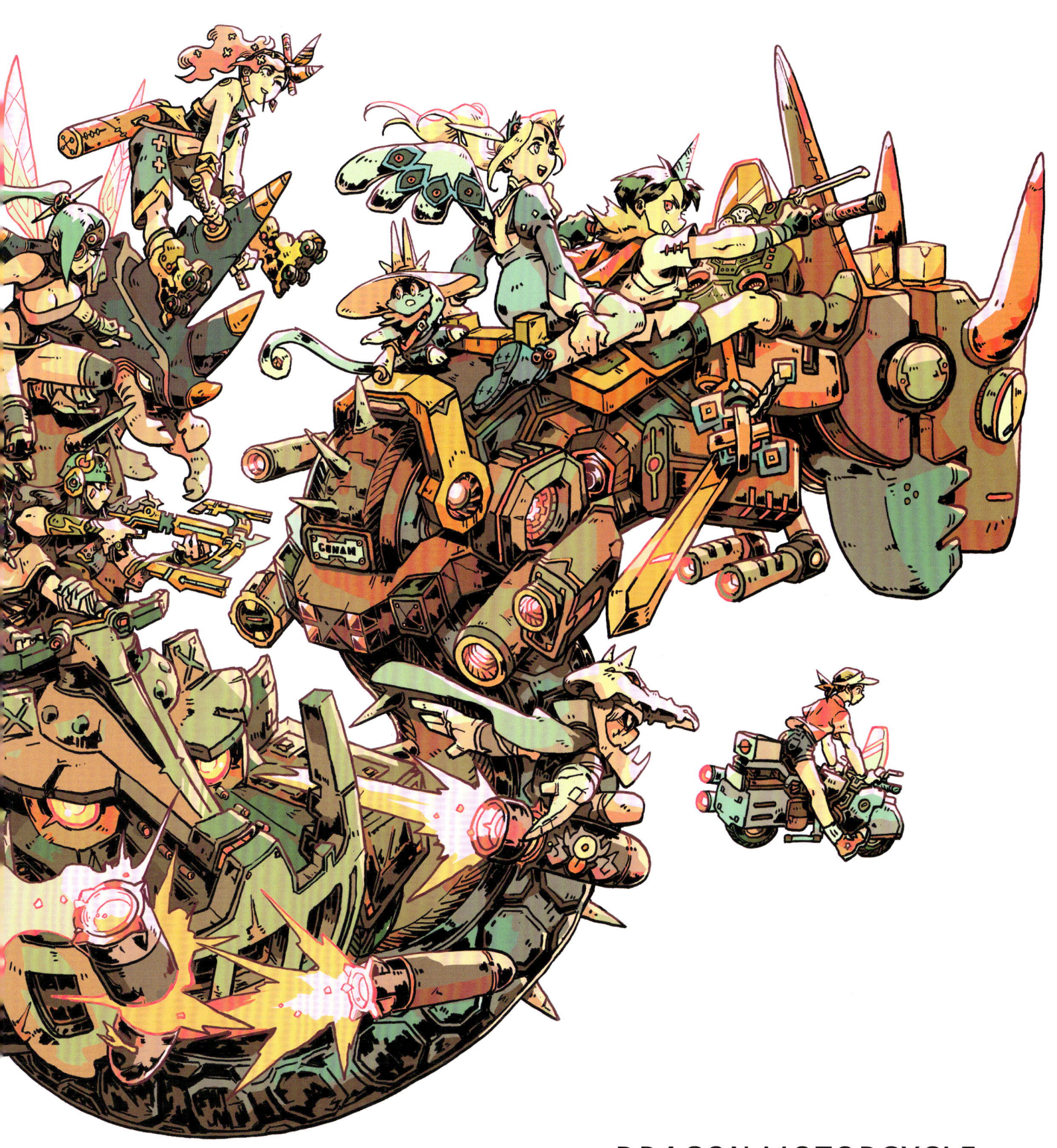

DRAGON MOTORCYCLE

ANATOMY

游刃

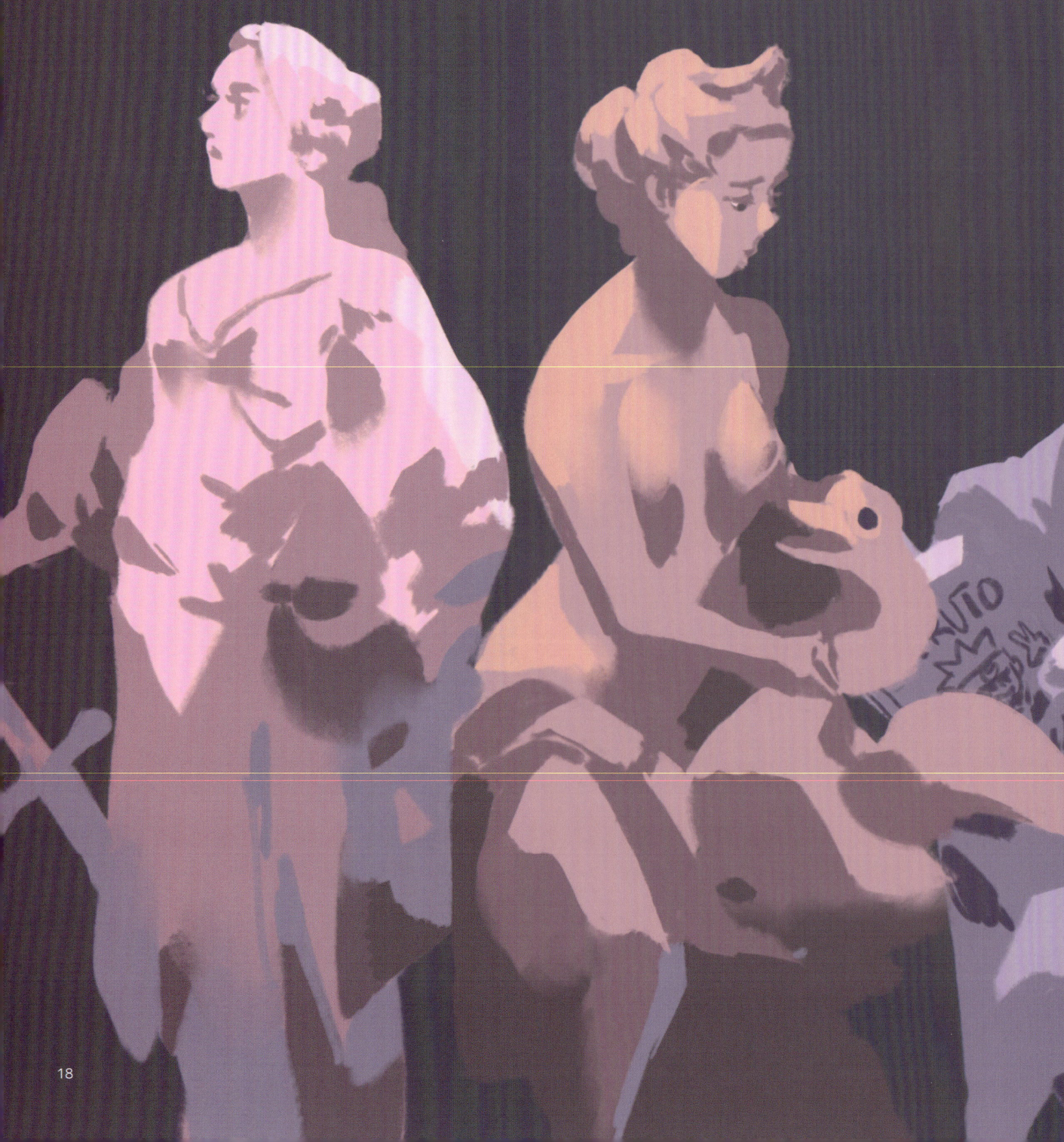

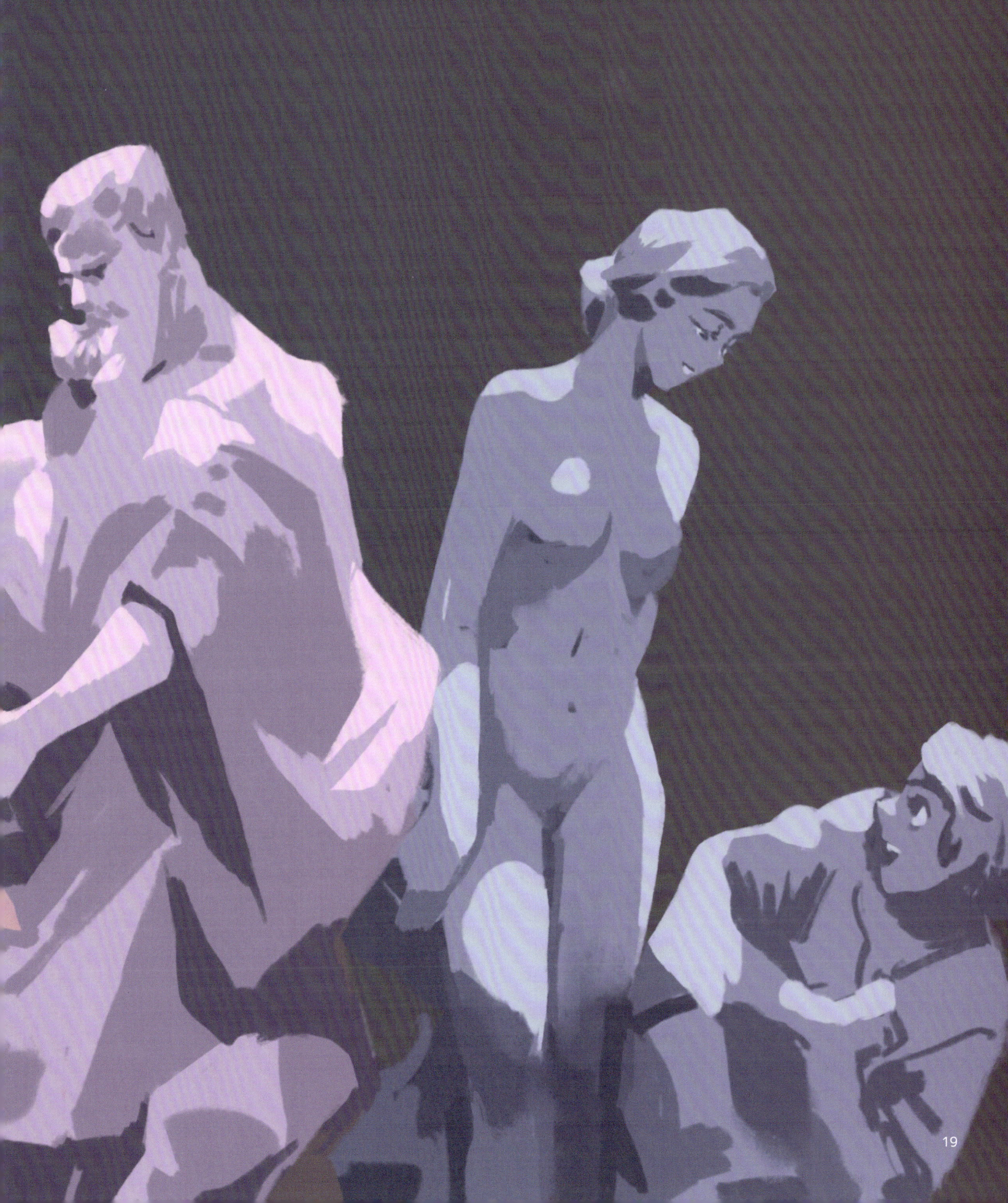

CHILDHOOD
BASICALLY THE SAME GUY

Ever since I was a little kid, I knew I wanted to do something creative. Now, as an adult, it's still shocking to me that the older I get, the more life seems to push me back to who I was back then.

My earliest memories include me impressing everyone at preschool with my *X-Men* drawings, or coming home and drawing *Ninja Turtles* with my mom. My dad brought home a giant stack of used printer paper from his office that I would regularly pull from to draw on.

I remember the first comic I ever drew, *FIGHT OR DIE*, had a cover showing the Earth inside a soldier's mouth, flames burning behind him. The five main characters were Muscle Guy, Reptile Guy, Reptile #2, Laser Guy, and Mike. 'Why Mike?' my dad had asked, puzzled.

'Because … Mike,' I replied. I was like, four years old. The point is: I've always drawn, as far back as I can remember.

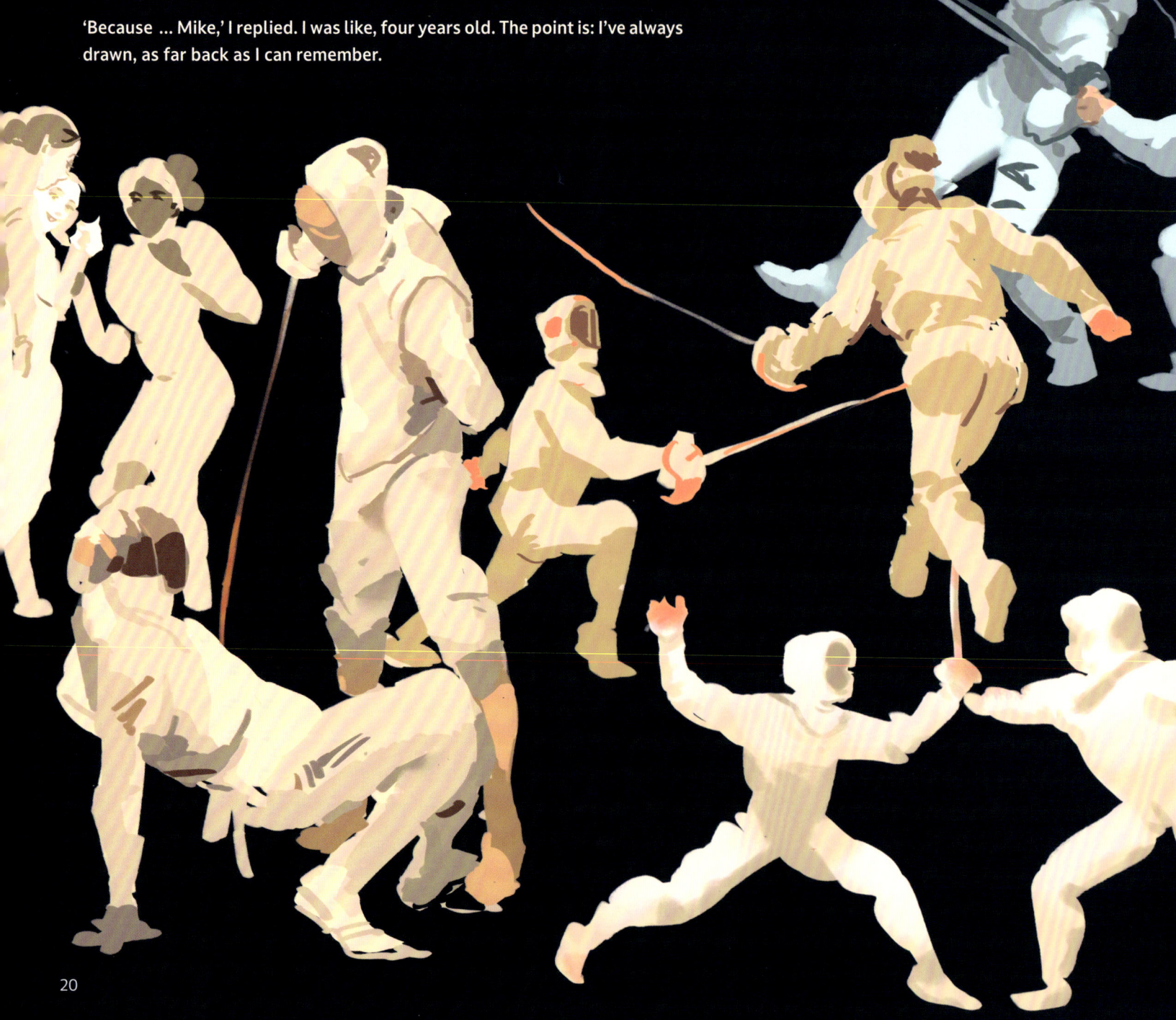

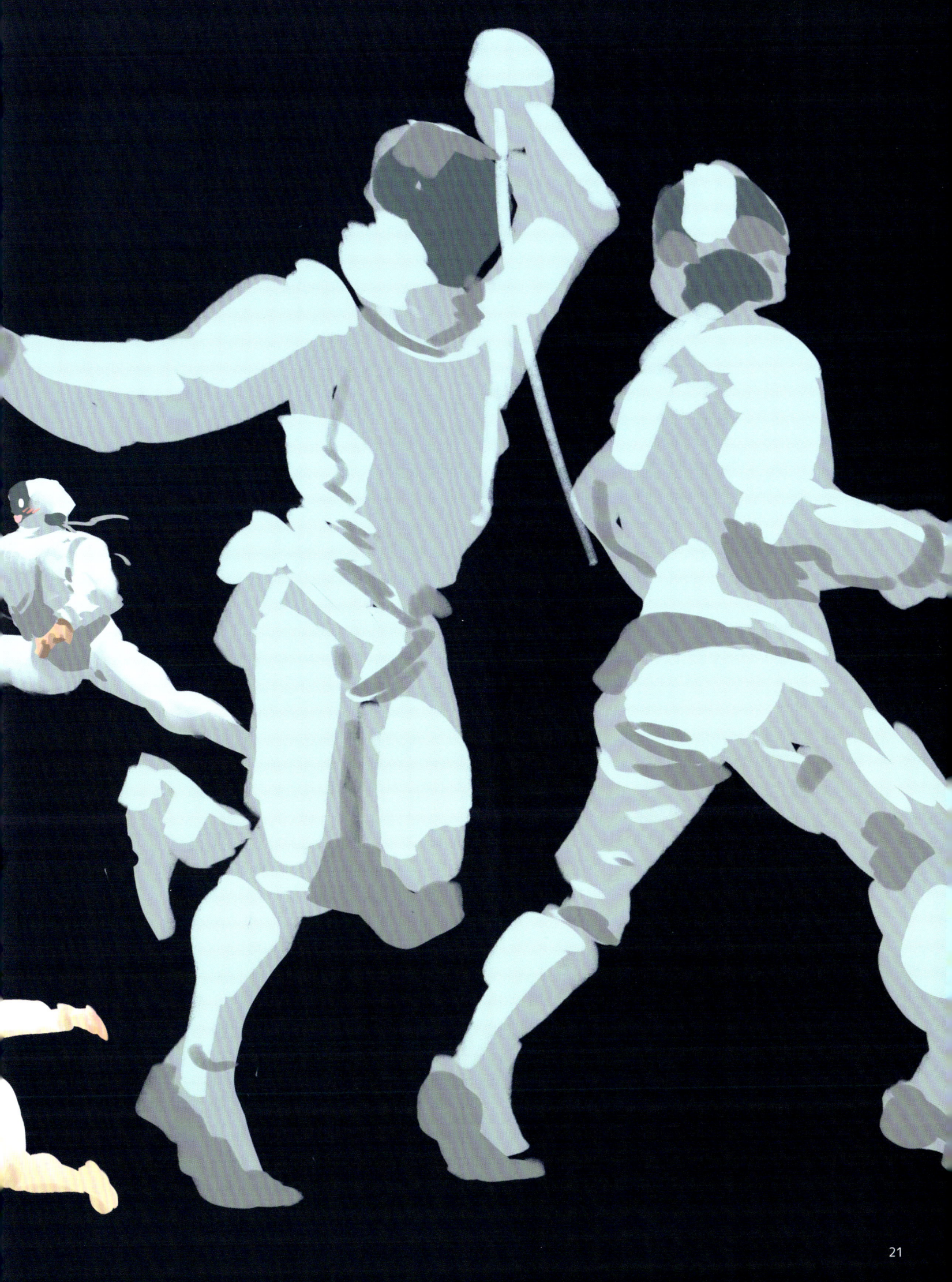

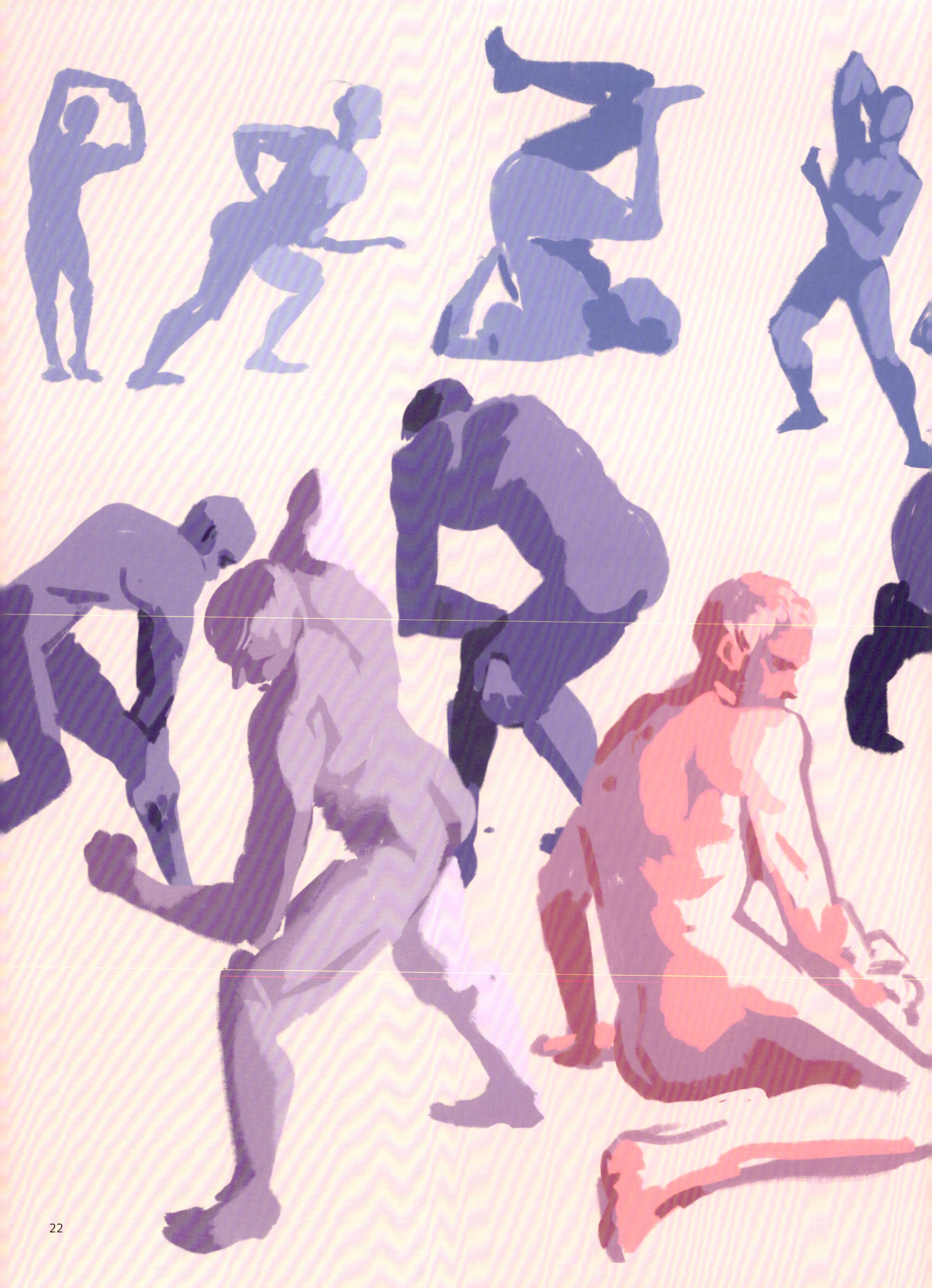

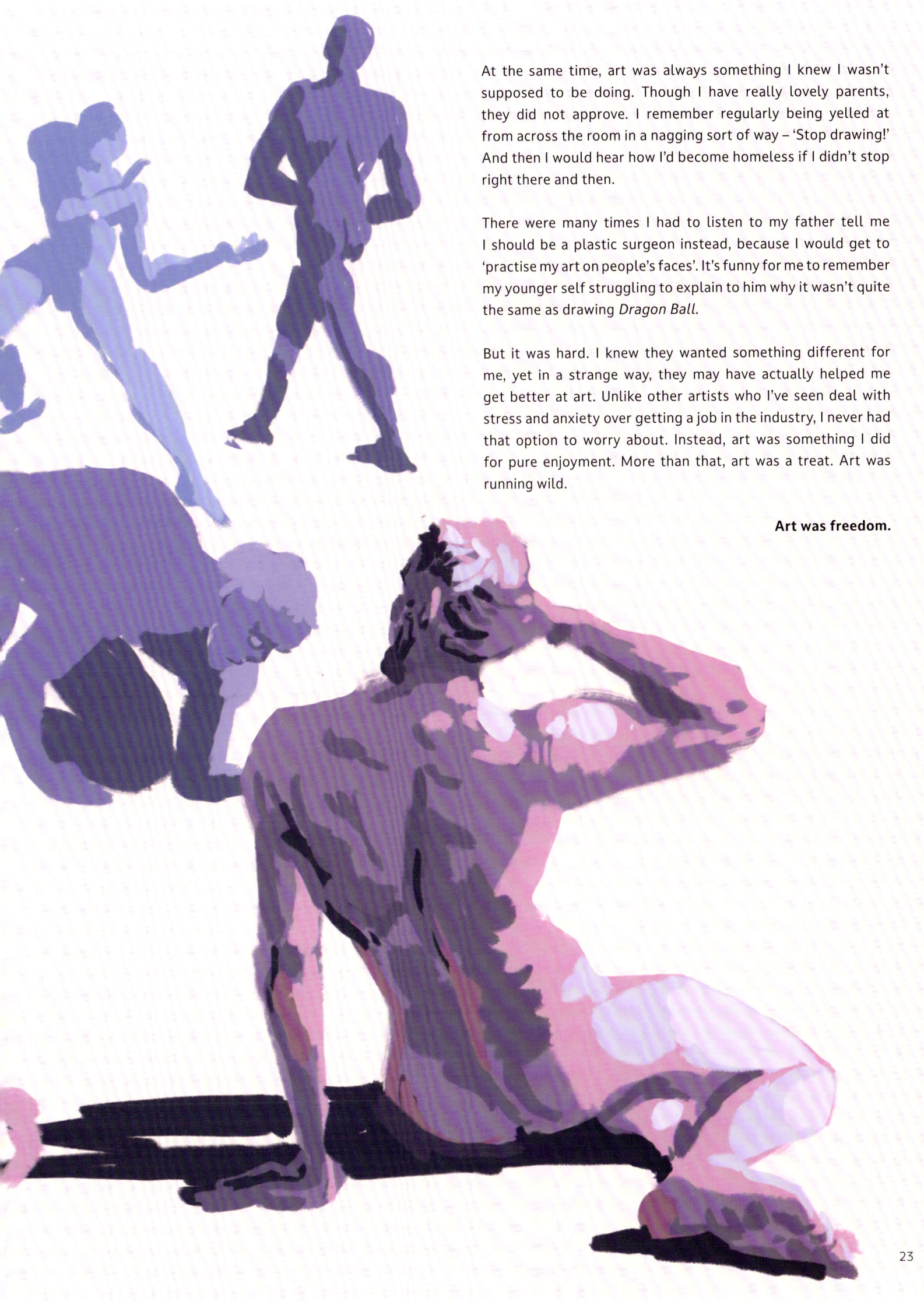

At the same time, art was always something I knew I wasn't supposed to be doing. Though I have really lovely parents, they did not approve. I remember regularly being yelled at from across the room in a nagging sort of way – 'Stop drawing!' And then I would hear how I'd become homeless if I didn't stop right there and then.

There were many times I had to listen to my father tell me I should be a plastic surgeon instead, because I would get to 'practise my art on people's faces'. It's funny for me to remember my younger self struggling to explain to him why it wasn't quite the same as drawing *Dragon Ball*.

But it was hard. I knew they wanted something different for me, yet in a strange way, they may have actually helped me get better at art. Unlike other artists who I've seen deal with stress and anxiety over getting a job in the industry, I never had that option to worry about. Instead, art was something I did for pure enjoyment. More than that, art was a treat. Art was running wild.

Art was freedom.

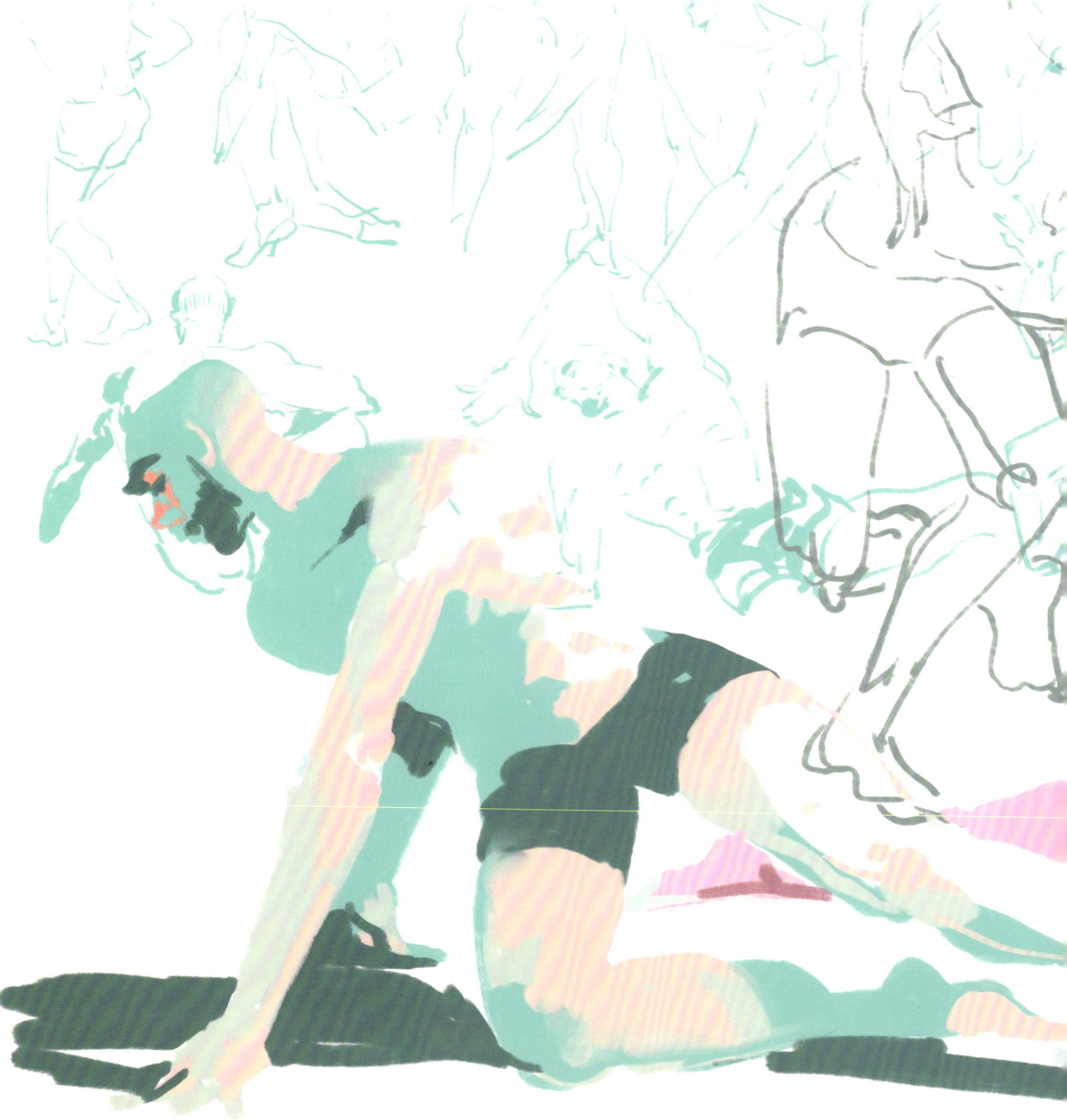

Now that I'm an adult and a working artist, I feel like one of the secret ingredients for my success has been to reinhabit my five-year-old self. Whether it's character design or fan-art illustrations, I've continually found the most success by channelling the sense of play and joy that I had as a child.

After struggling for so long in my twenties trying to be an adult – someone other than *me* – it's honestly mind-boggling to find that the key to my success is reconnecting with my inner child. At the end of the day, what audiences, customers, and everybody else really want is usually the same thing: to feel as happy as they were as kids.

By the way, I say all of this not because I want to say *I told you so* to my parents. As a new parent myself, I fully understand

ONE OF THE SECRET INGREDIENTS FOR MY SUCCESS HAS BEEN TO REINHABIT MY FIVE-YEAR-OLD SELF

the fear and concern that they had for me. I say all this because I think it could be important for other artists who are trying to get work or figure out what their art should represent – the answer to their struggles might be the same as mine. Whatever it is you loved about art growing up, it might be precisely what your art needs now.

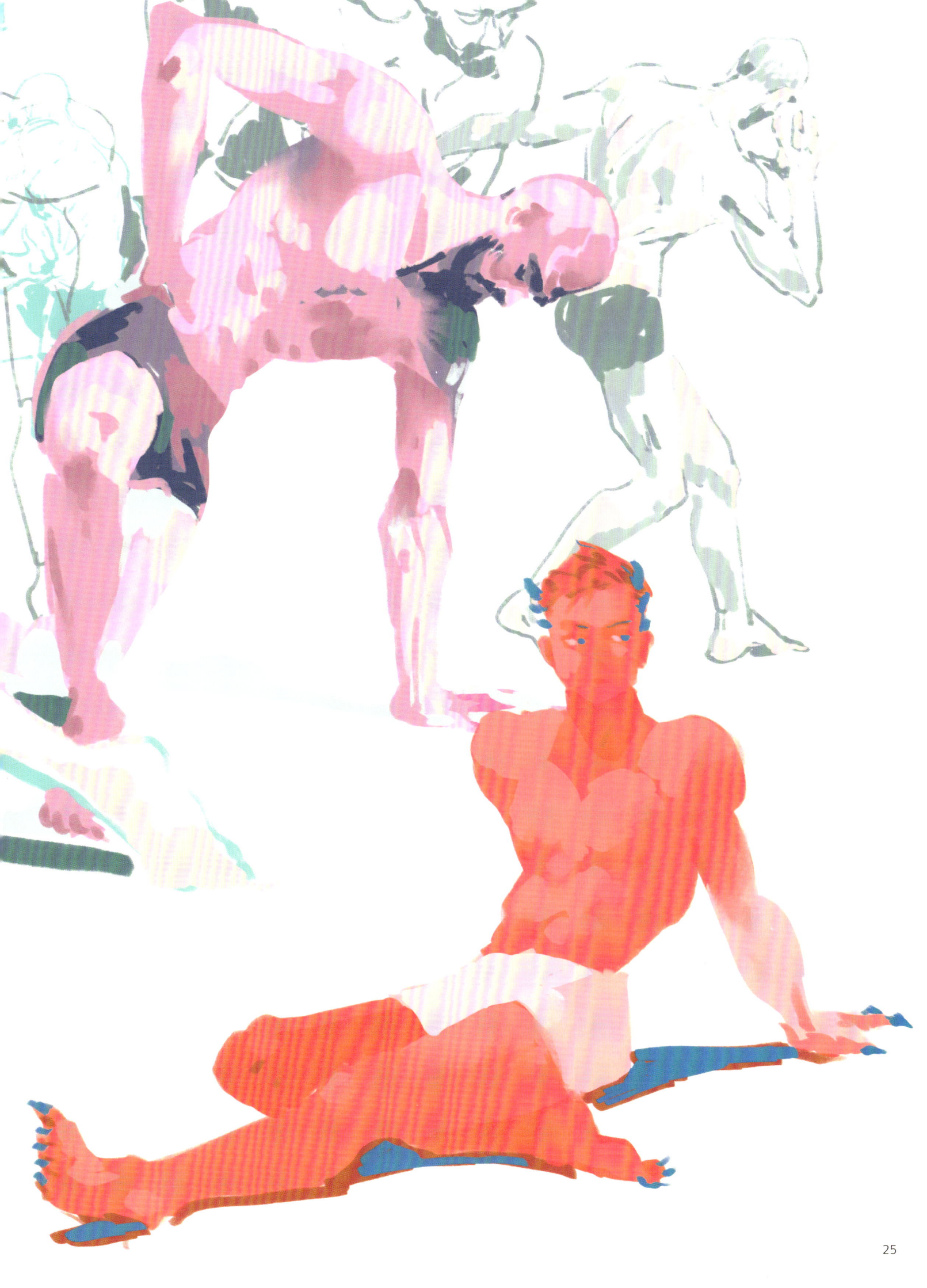

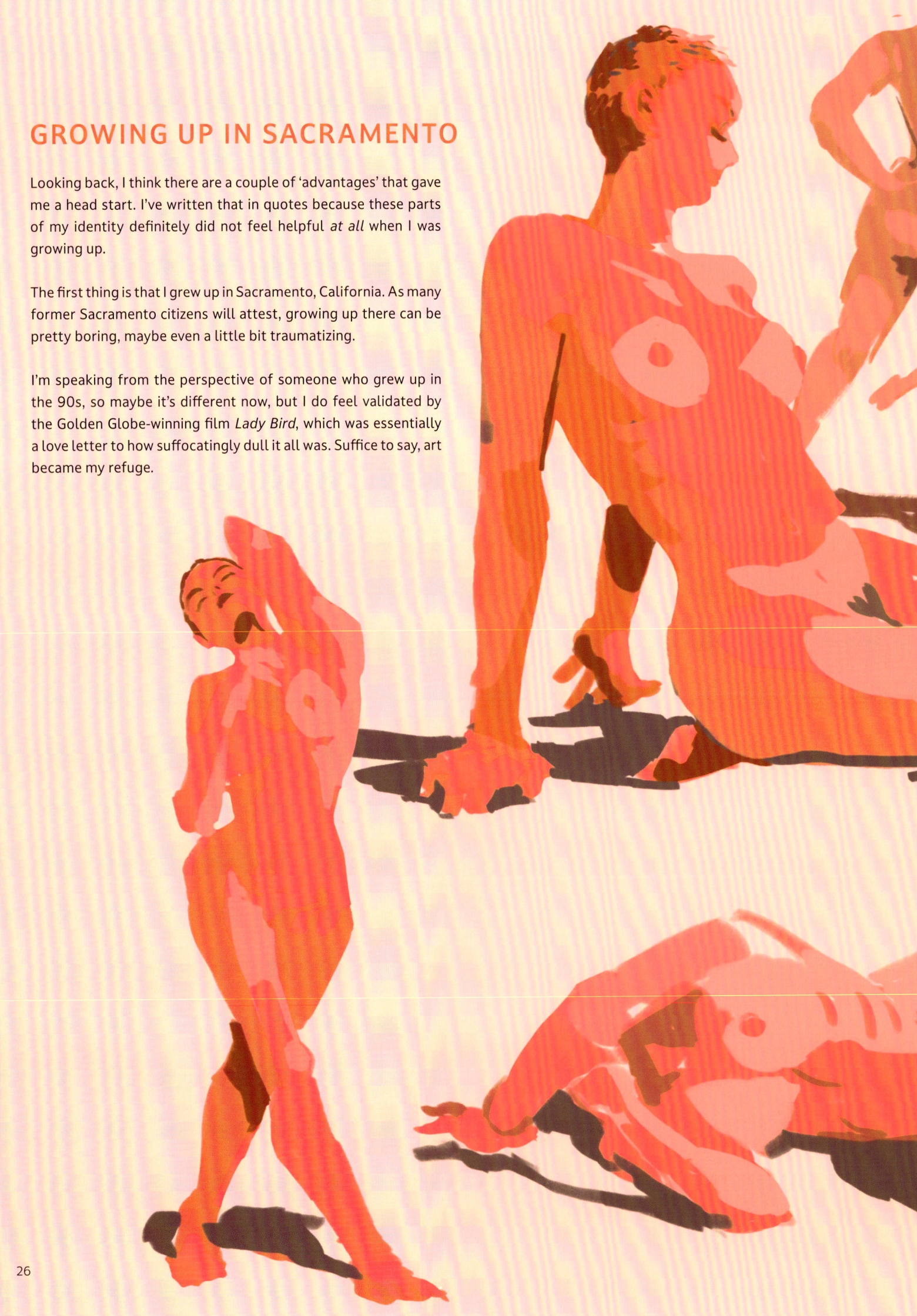

GROWING UP IN SACRAMENTO

Looking back, I think there are a couple of 'advantages' that gave me a head start. I've written that in quotes because these parts of my identity definitely did not feel helpful *at all* when I was growing up.

The first thing is that I grew up in Sacramento, California. As many former Sacramento citizens will attest, growing up there can be pretty boring, maybe even a little bit traumatizing.

I'm speaking from the perspective of someone who grew up in the 90s, so maybe it's different now, but I do feel validated by the Golden Globe-winning film *Lady Bird*, which was essentially a love letter to how suffocatingly dull it all was. Suffice to say, art became my refuge.

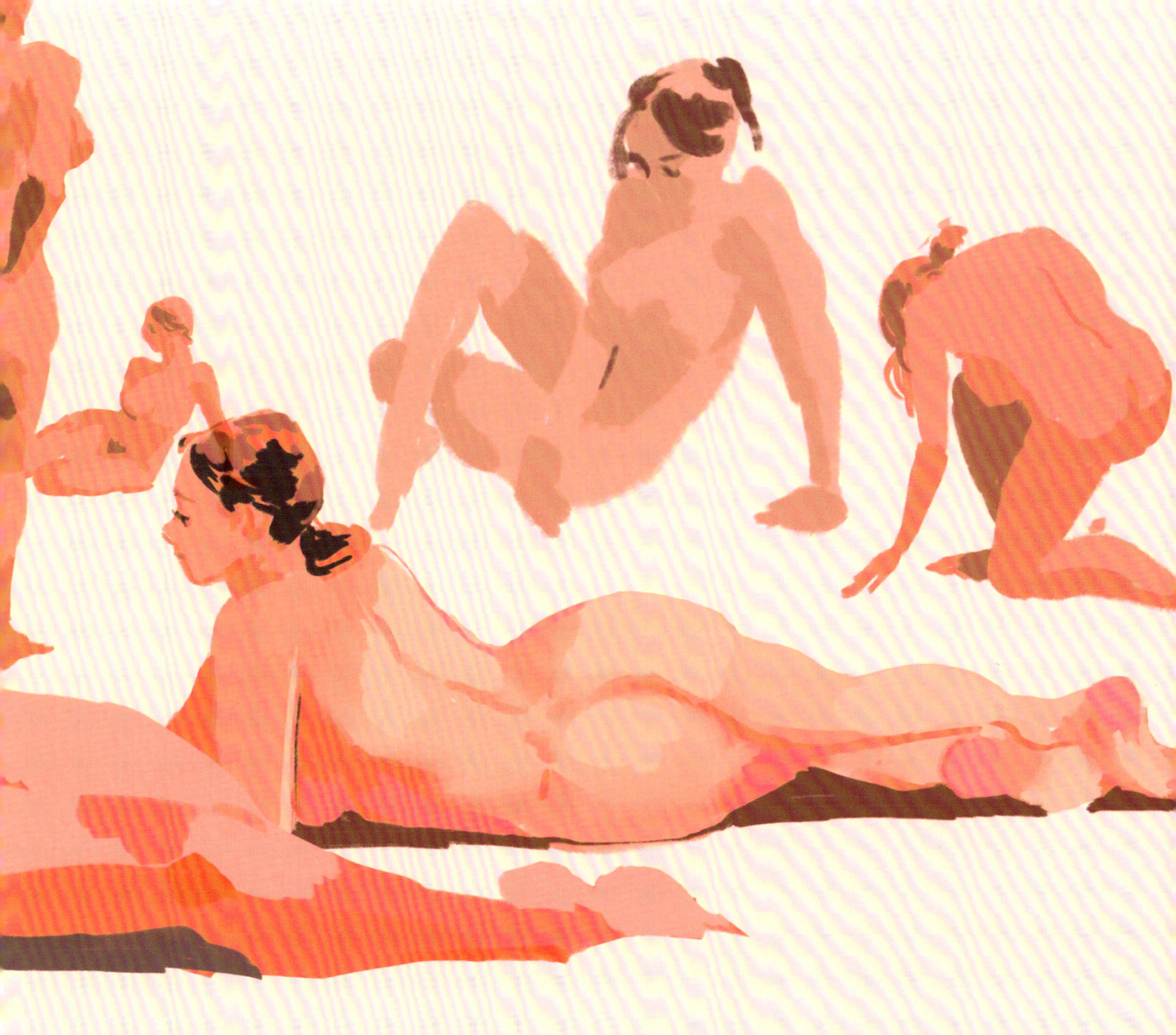

THERE'S SOMETHING UNIQUELY CHARACTER-BUILDING ABOUT HAVING TO RELY ON YOURSELF

In high school, I wanted to live in the worlds depicted by anime and manga, and being stuck in Sacramento meant that I had to use my imagination a-freaking-lot. Now that I live in Los Angeles, I can see the advantage of being surrounded by other artists pushing each other to grow and do better, but there's also something uniquely character-building about having to rely on yourself.

The answers you find are more personal. Feeling like a weirdo among your peers sucks, but it's also the sort of experience that helps a person discover themselves. Introspection rarely happens when you're just having fun, but those deep, personal conversations you have with yourself are sometimes the 'spice' that flavours your artwork later. I was definitely over-seasoned for this reason. Not salty at all about it.

DYSLEXIA SUPERPOWER

The second 'advantage' I had (and still have) was dyslexia. Basically, my eyes have trouble processing text but are great at understanding visuals. Where everyone else has separate word-processing software in their brains for reading, it's as though I can only use Adobe Photoshop for everything. It's a wonderful and powerful piece of software, but boy is it awful for handling a lot of text.

After talking to other artists and friends about how their brains work, I've also realized that when I read, or even just think about most things, I see everything in my head visually. It's not crystal clear per se, but if I have to read something, I experience it in the same way someone would who's watching a movie. This might sound cool, but sometimes that pacing can be *very* slow.

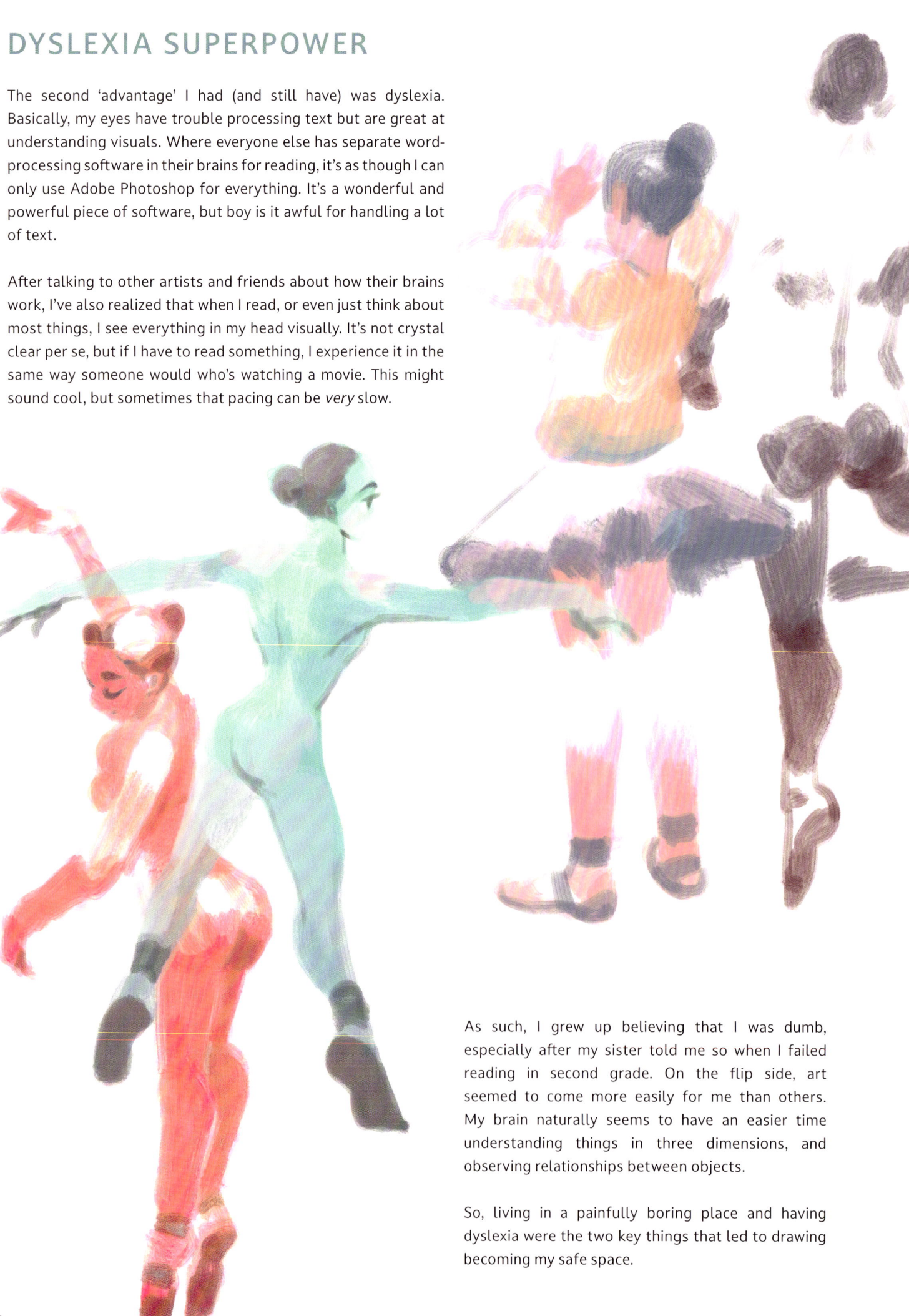

As such, I grew up believing that I was dumb, especially after my sister told me so when I failed reading in second grade. On the flip side, art seemed to come more easily for me than others. My brain naturally seems to have an easier time understanding things in three dimensions, and observing relationships between objects.

So, living in a painfully boring place and having dyslexia were the two key things that led to drawing becoming my safe space.

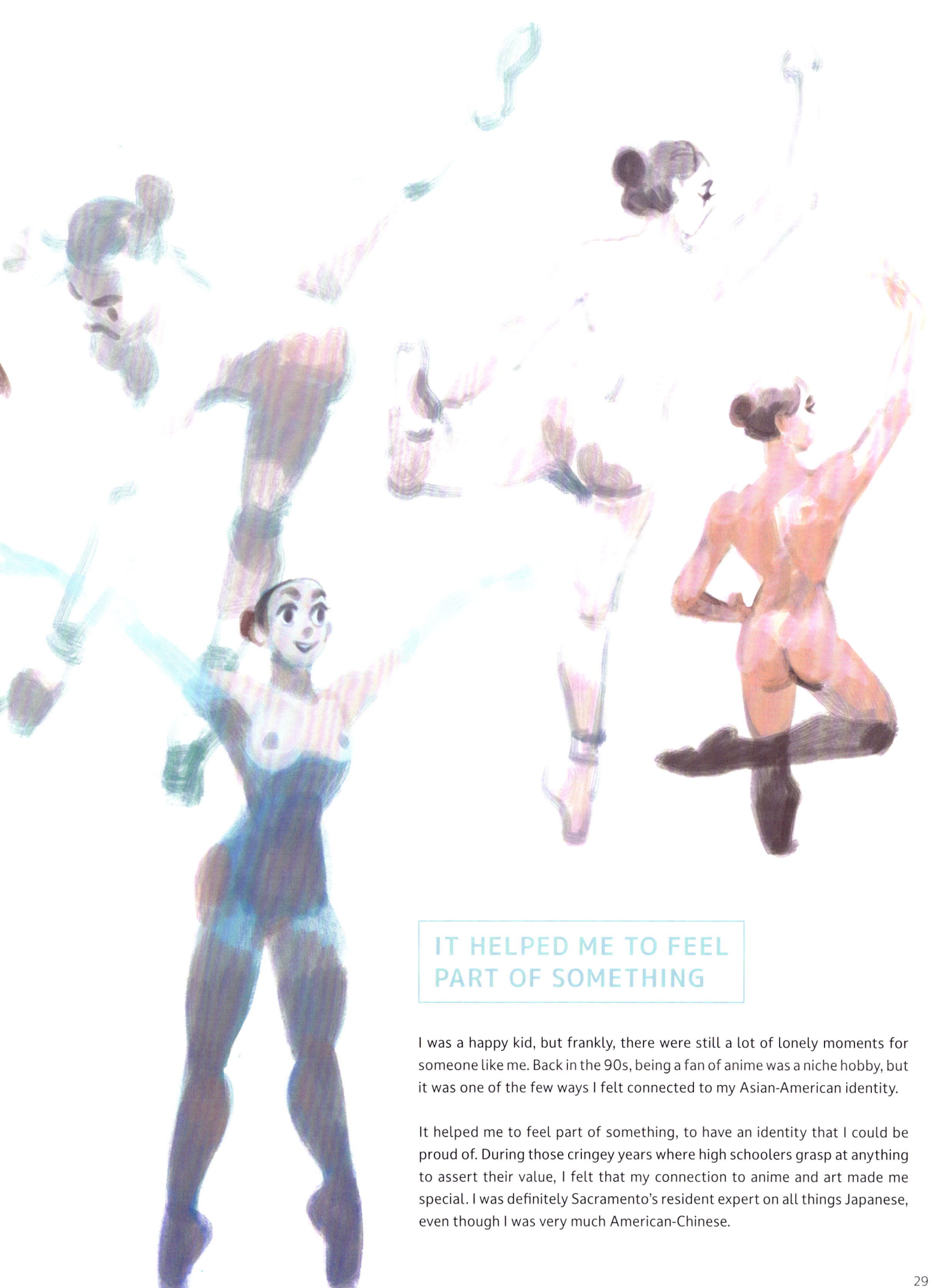

IT HELPED ME TO FEEL PART OF SOMETHING

I was a happy kid, but frankly, there were still a lot of lonely moments for someone like me. Back in the 90s, being a fan of anime was a niche hobby, but it was one of the few ways I felt connected to my Asian-American identity.

It helped me to feel part of something, to have an identity that I could be proud of. During those cringey years where high schoolers grasp at anything to assert their value, I felt that my connection to anime and art made me special. I was definitely Sacramento's resident expert on all things Japanese, even though I was very much American-Chinese.

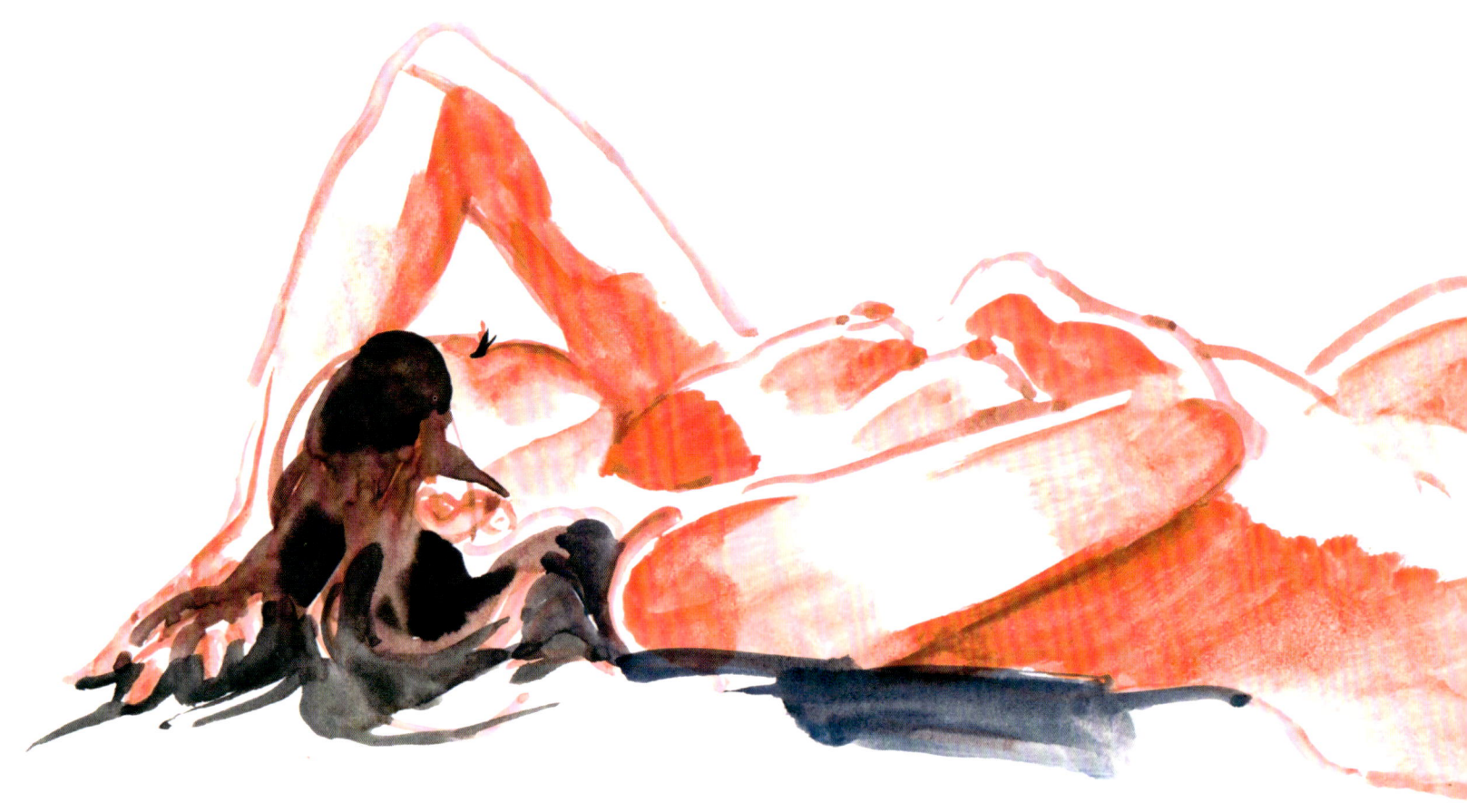

I WAS SO HUNGRY TO MEET AND TALK WITH OTHER PEOPLE ABOUT ART; TO HAVE THAT COMMUNITY

As with many creatives I've met over the years, I was known as 'the artist' on my high-school campus, which shows how uncommon it was to be into art at that age. The mantle was both a blessing and a curse. It was an identity that had status, but it was also isolating.

I was so hungry to meet and talk with other people about art; to have that community. That desperation is what led me to seek out other artists online and to throw myself into my work, trying to gain the appreciation of others on DeviantArt. Prior to this, I was someone who rushed through my artwork impatiently – I have a core memory of my father critiquing my sloppiness. But because I so desperately wanted to find community with other artists, I became determined to make more ambitious artwork that would gain attention. When those efforts were rewarded and my art garnered some popularity, it was a high that I wanted to keep chasing.

However, the adrenaline of getting praise from others gradually lost its charm. It was exhausting to feel so needy for approval. One of the main reasons I stopped drawing once I entered college was that I felt that I needed to let go of this part of my ego. I took a long pause from these bigger, more ambitious illustrations.

That initial ambition was the foundation for the artist I would become as an adult, nearly a decade later. But when I returned to that mode of drawing, I was a shell of my former, bright-eyed self. I decided not to care what others thought, instead giving myself the base assumption that they wouldn't like what I was creating. Stripping away this part of my ego left me free to pursue my art. Not for fame, but mostly as a challenge to myself, to see how much more ambitious I could get.

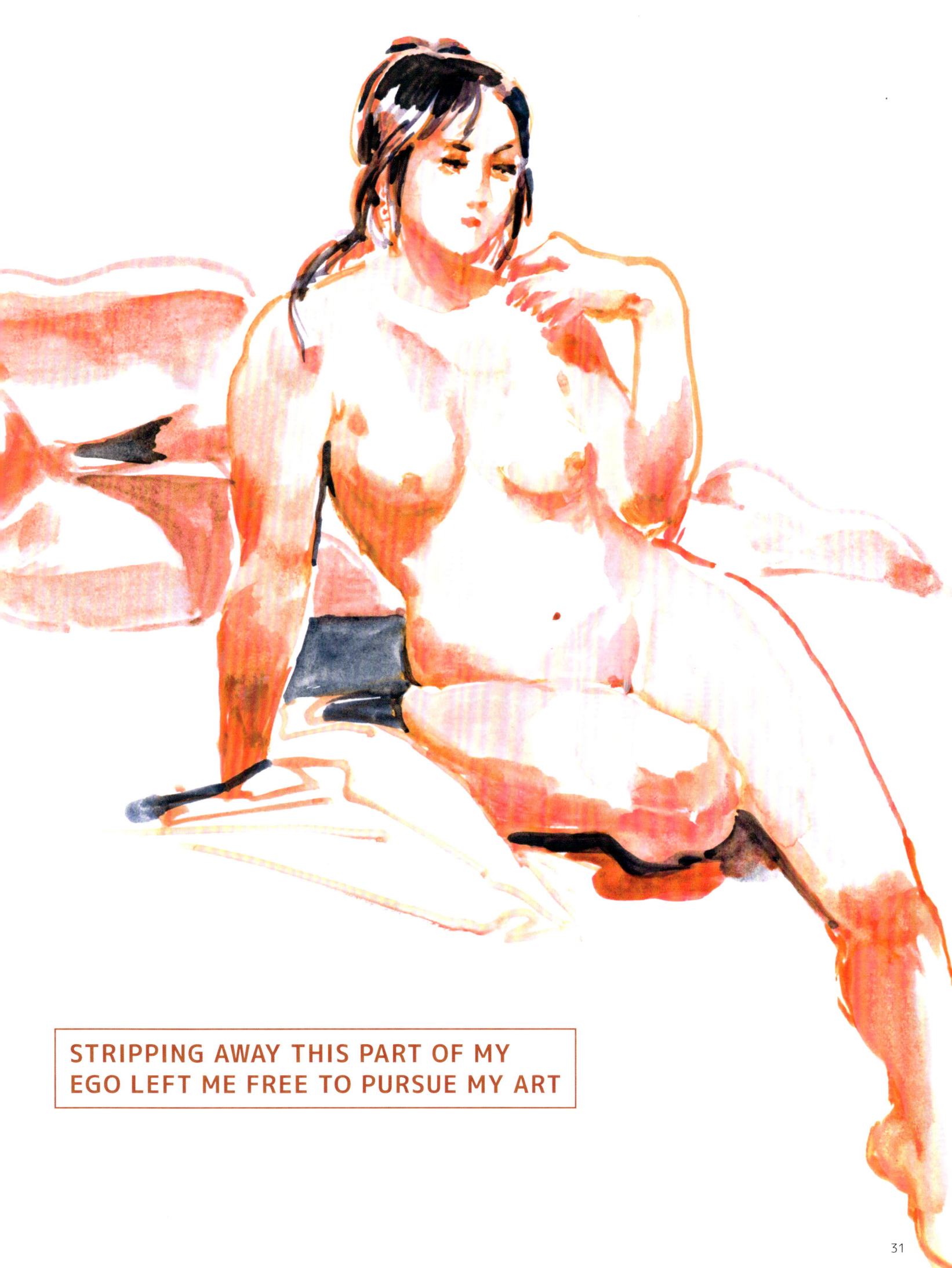

STRIPPING AWAY THIS PART OF MY
EGO LEFT ME FREE TO PURSUE MY ART

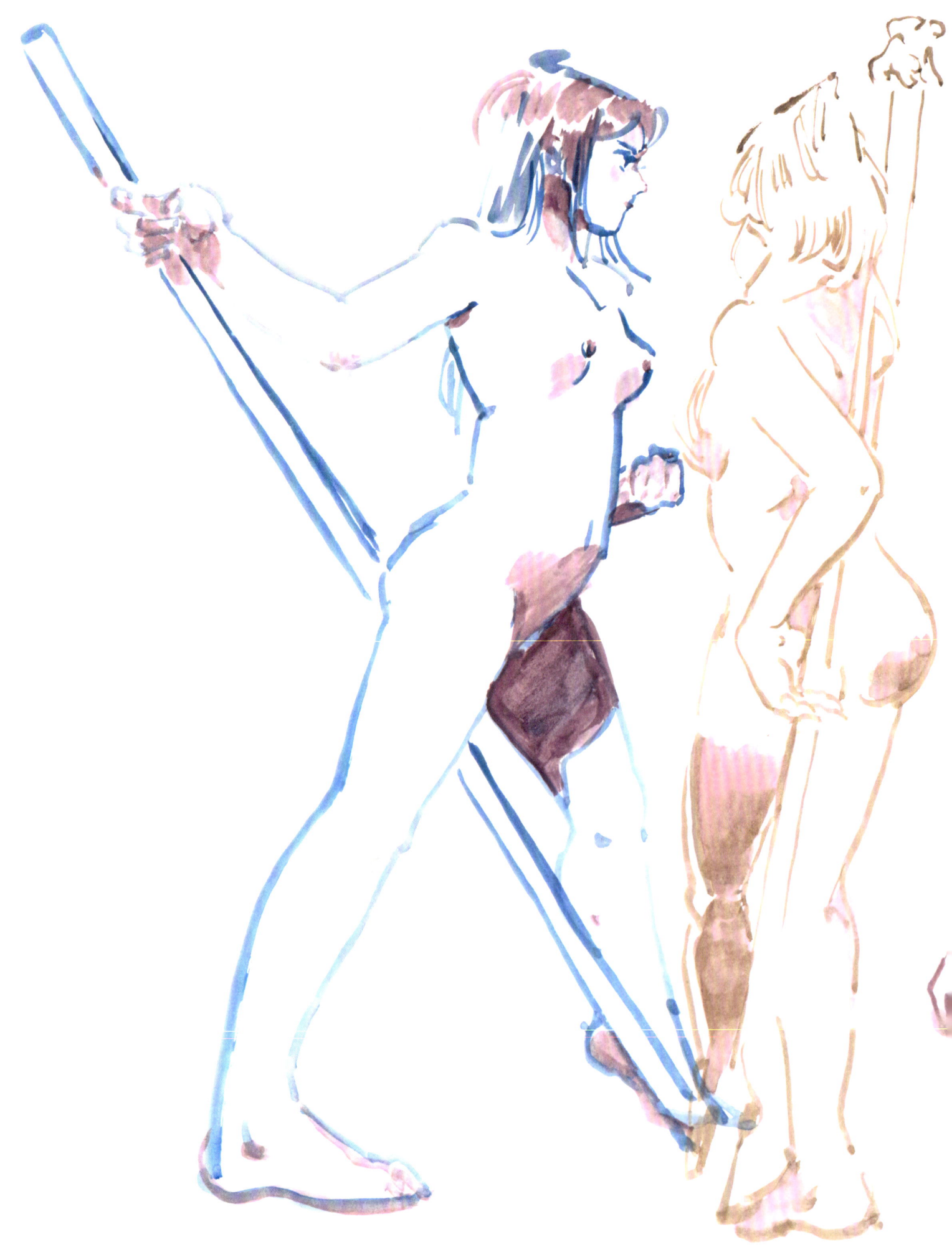

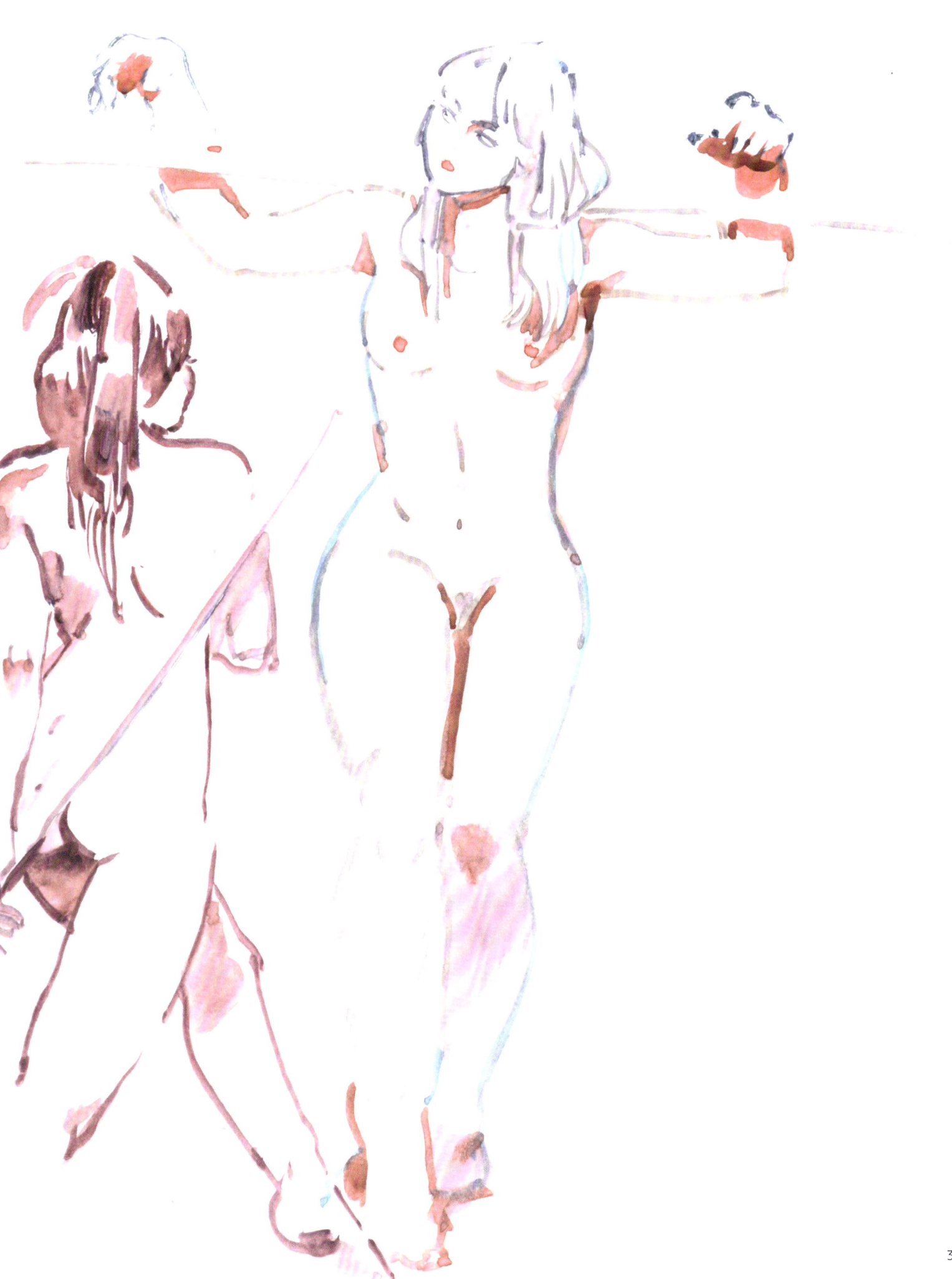

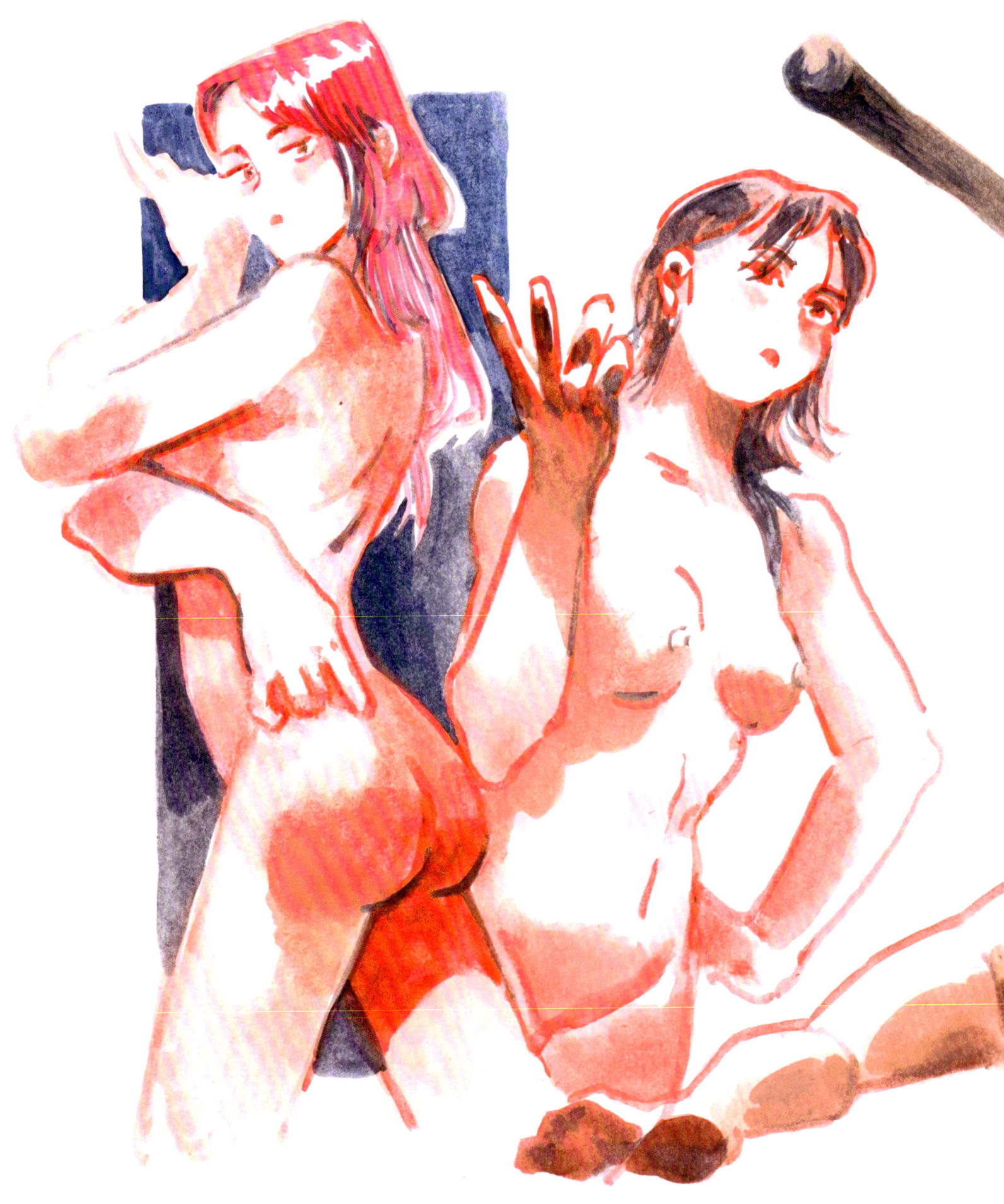

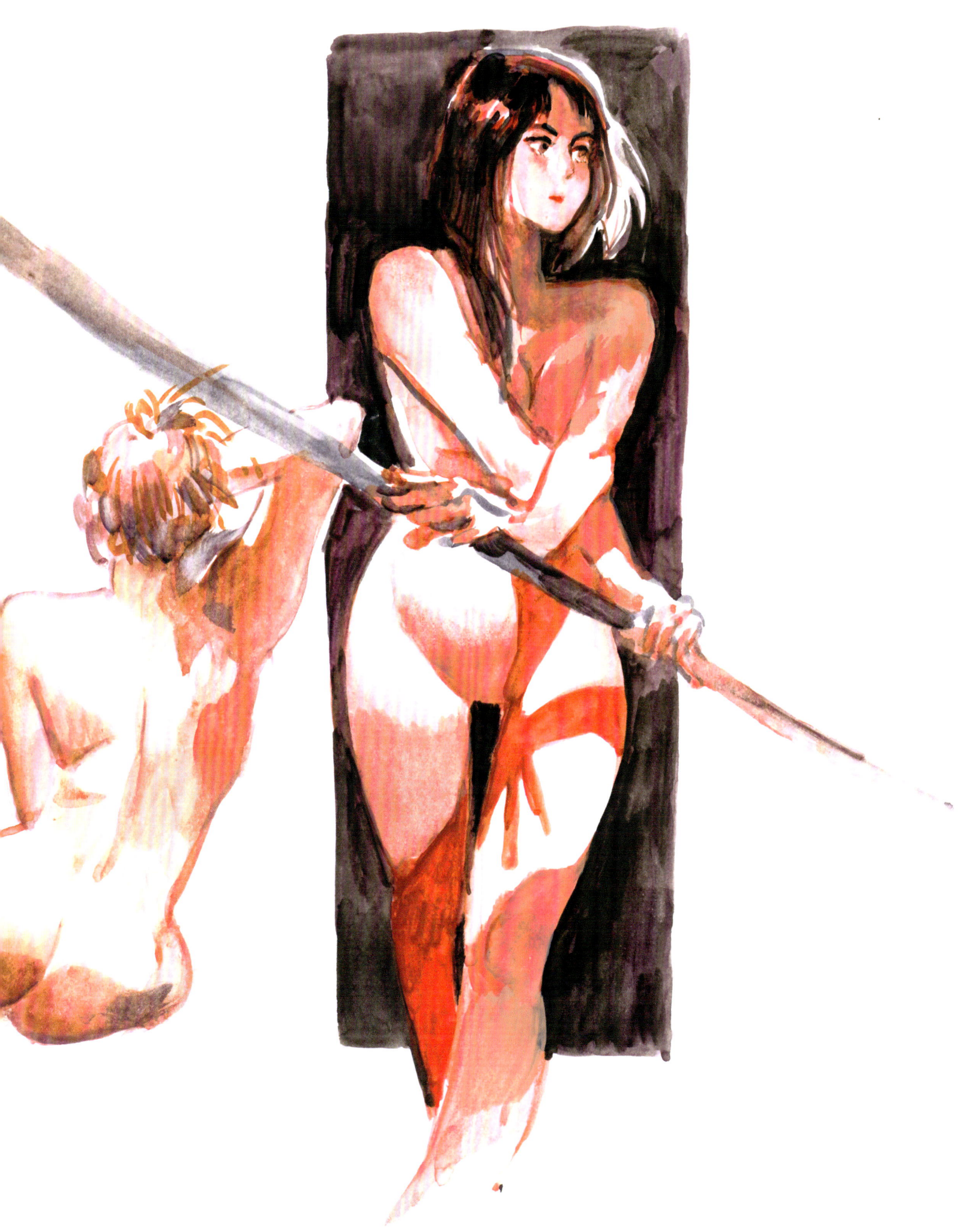

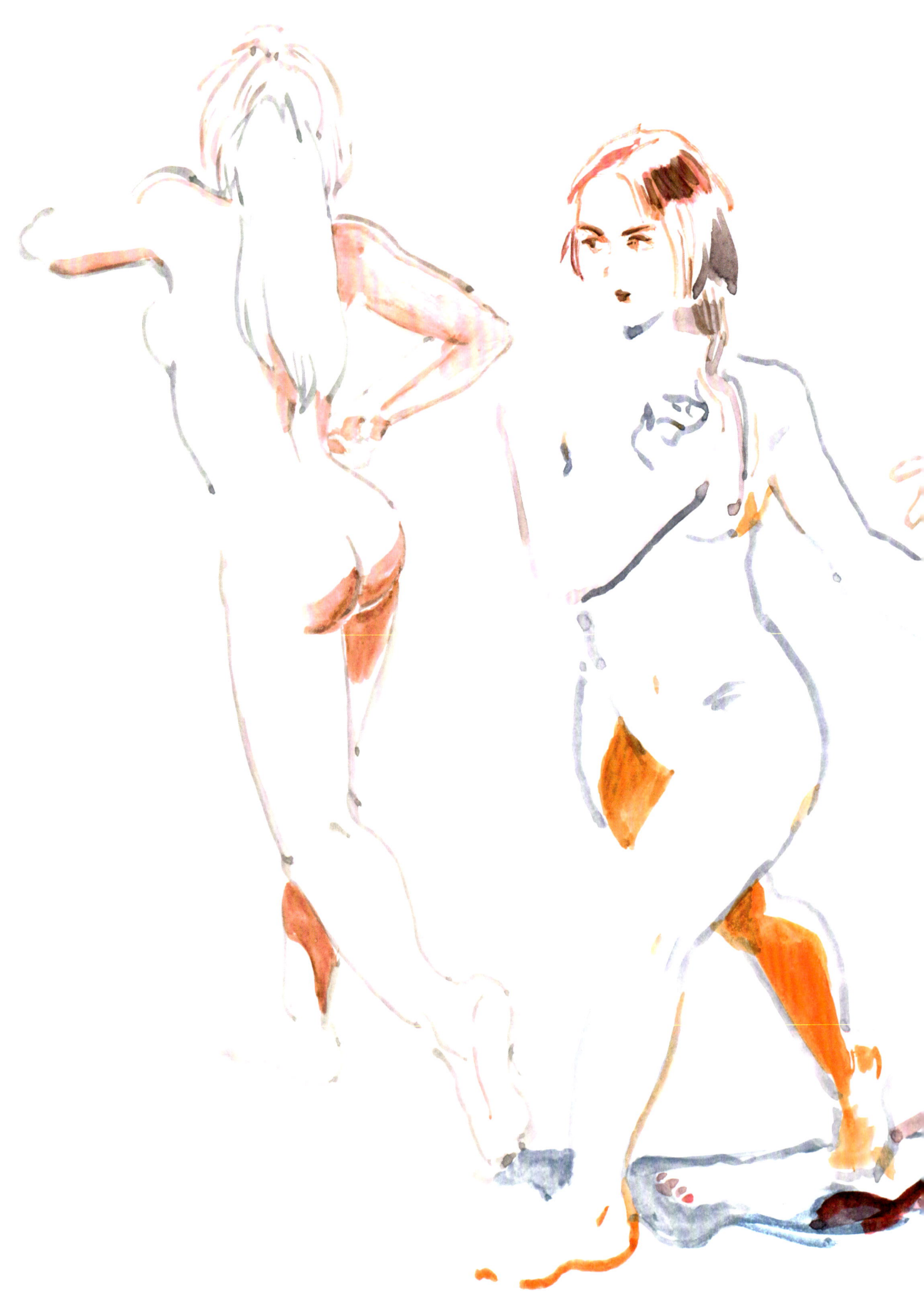

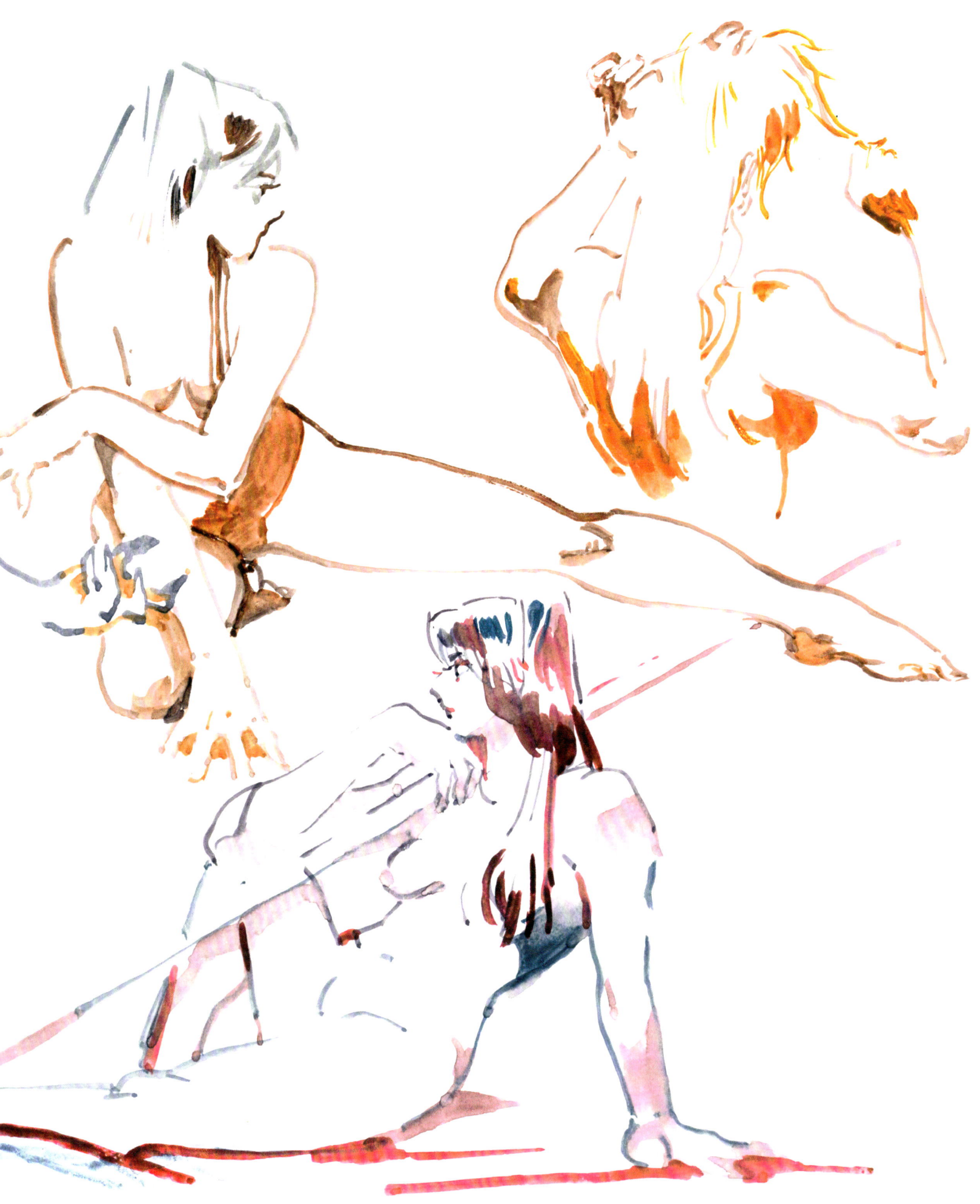

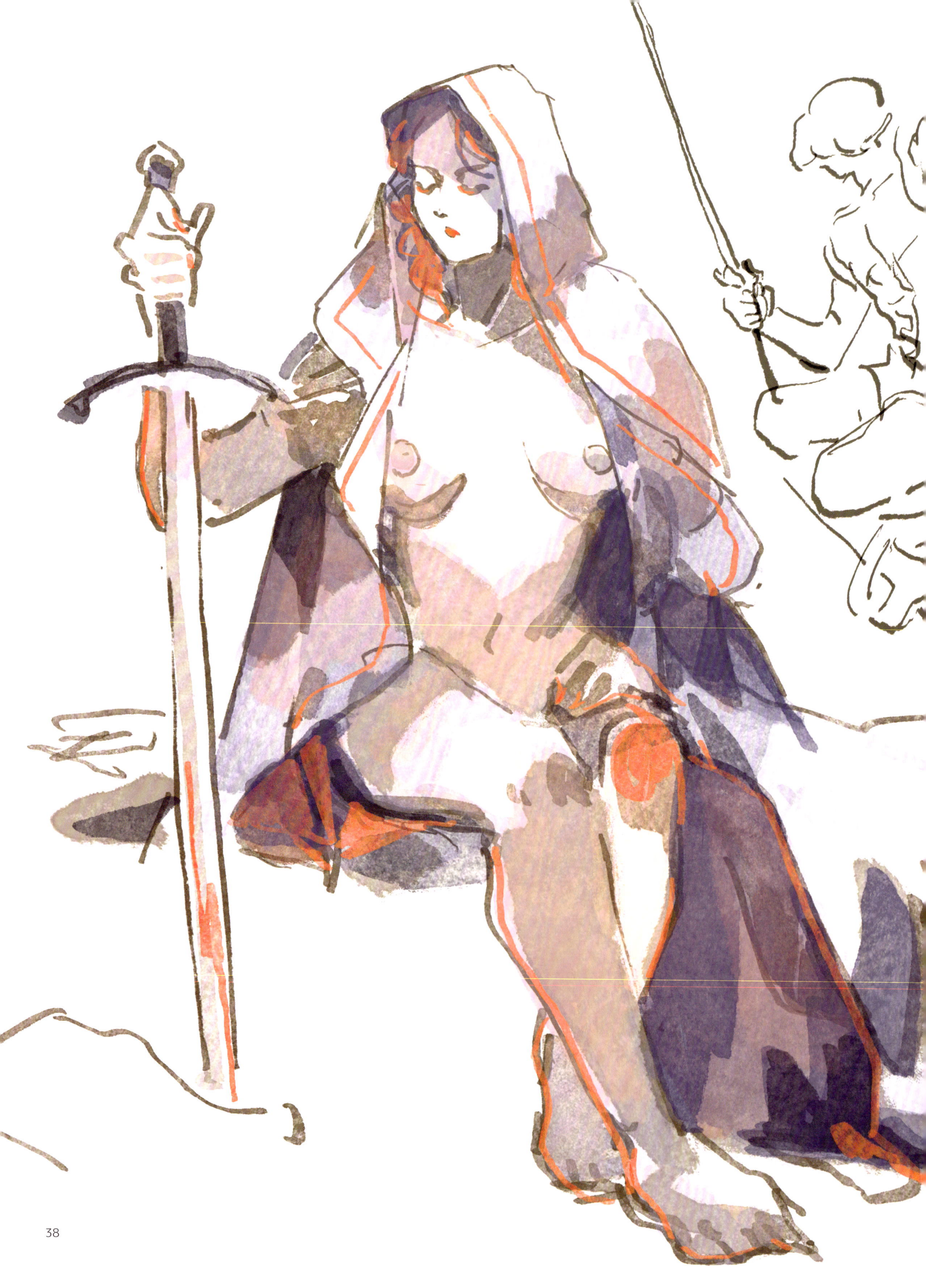

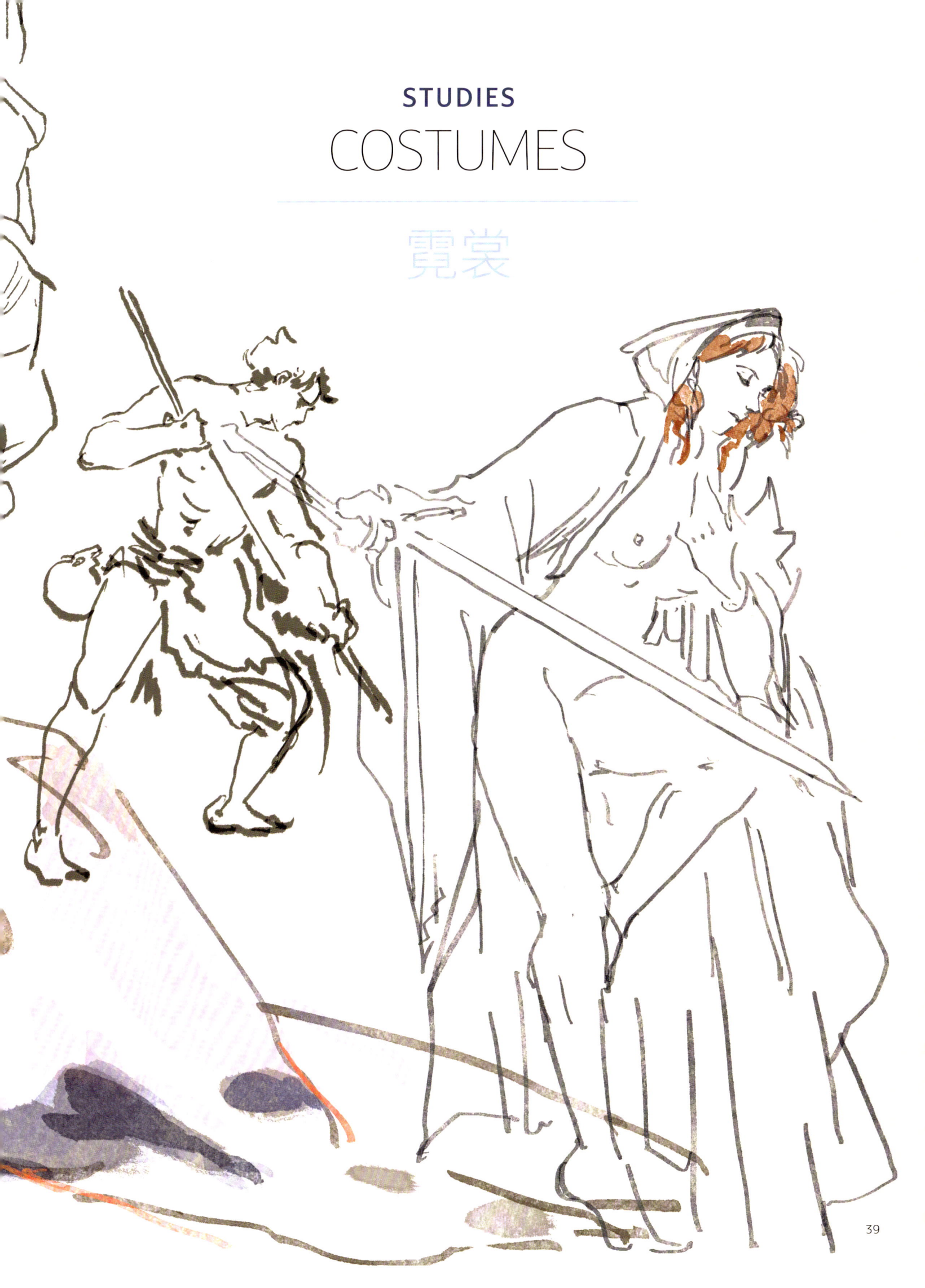

EARLY INFLUENCES
PERSONALLY, I BLAME MY COUSIN

Everything started with *Sonic* and *Ninja Turtles* when I was three years old. I have my cousin to thank for that. Honestly, I could probably just have him write this section because I basically copied everything about him that I thought was cool.

After that came *X-Men*, *Dragon Ball*, *Record of Lodoss War*, *Rurouni Kenshin*, *Akira*, and *Vampire Hunter D*. Game wise, he got me hooked on *Super Mario*, *Zelda*, *Street Fighter*, *Metal Gear*, and *Final Fantasy*. Thank you, Kevin <3

It wasn't until around middle school that I started to really develop my own taste. The shows with the biggest impact on me were *Evangelion*, *Cowboy Bebop*, and *FLCL*. I also began to appreciate individual artists around that time.

I would study Akira Toriyama for *Chrono Trigger* and *Dragon Ball Z*, Tetsuya Nomura for *Final Fantasy VII*, and almost all of the Capcom artists, but especially Akiman, Kinu Nishimura, and Falcoon. I filled a whole sketchbook with pencil studies of the oil paintings from the *Capcom Design Works* art book. I learned a lot with that sketchbook!

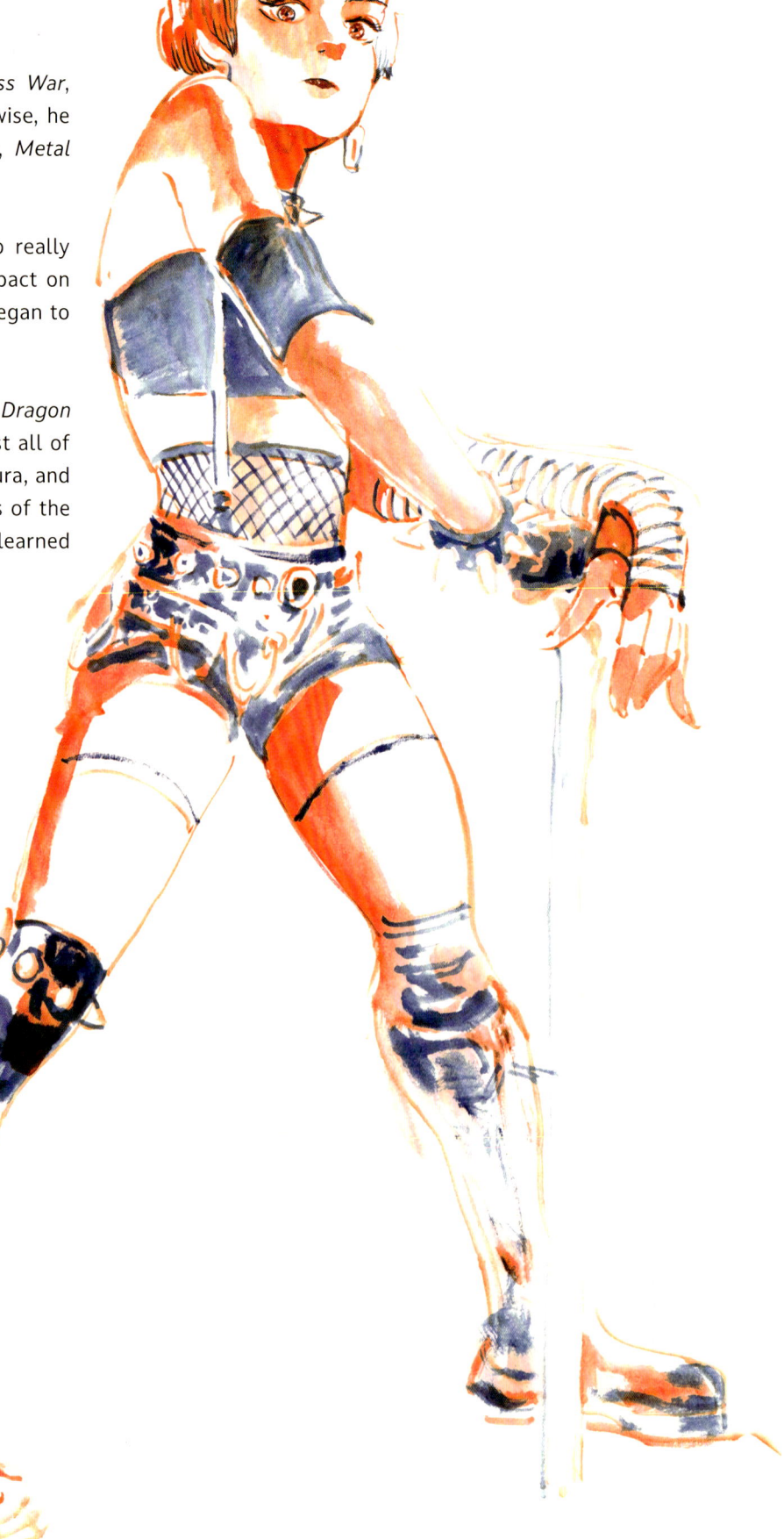

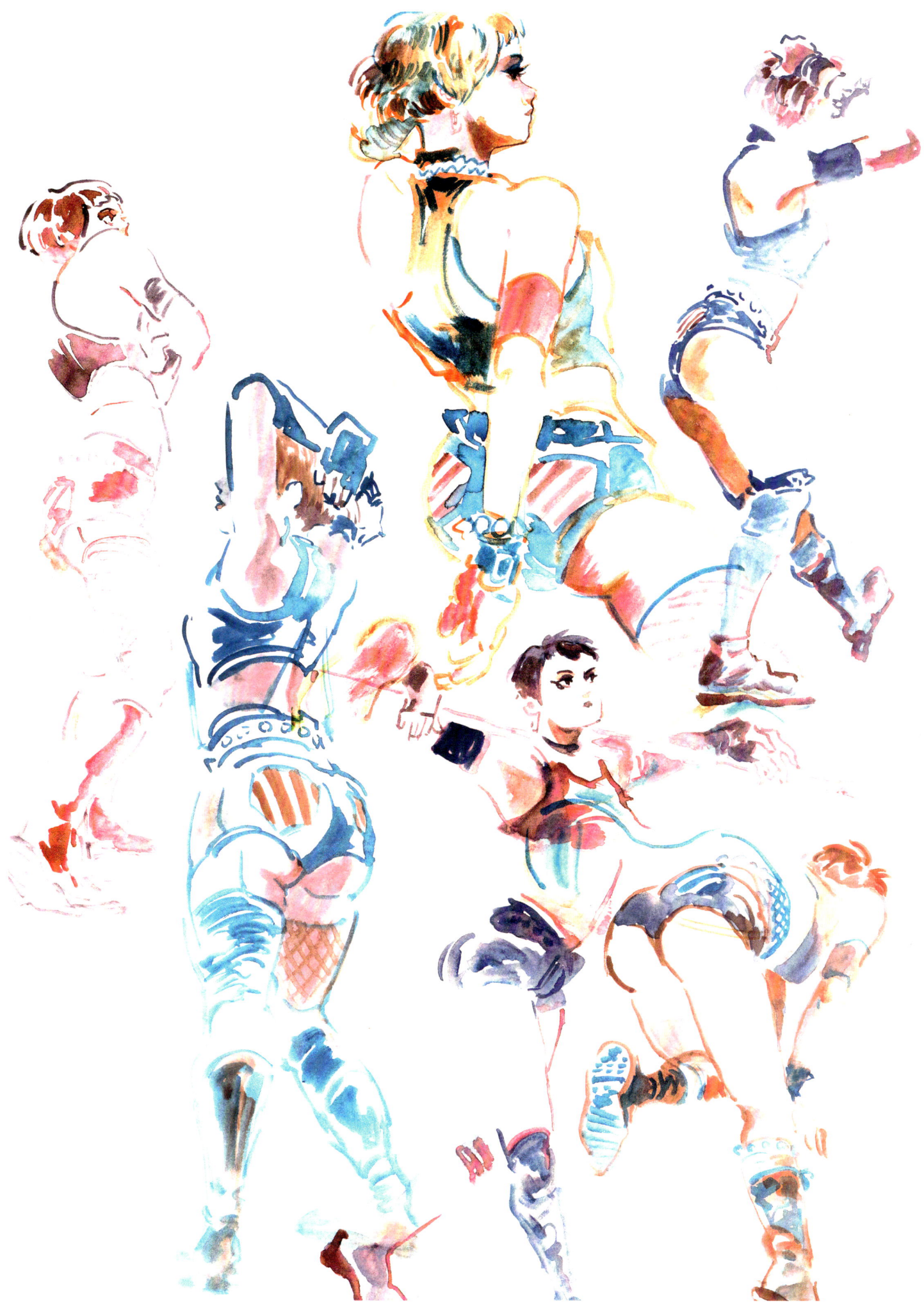

FIRMWARE UPDATES

The fun thing about how I used to study these artists is that, in a way, it's almost like my base firmware. What I mean by firmware is the part of your brain that has your earliest understanding of how to draw. I don't mean the foundations of a more classically trained artist, but rather the caveman monkey brain of someone just starting to figure out how to make art they actually like. Think of the things that you'd draw over and over on the margins of your school planner. Think cringey anime eyes. When I'm really tired, I can see my own firmware coming back out as I fall into old habits from my high-school days.

This firmware is based more on memorization than understanding – it can't be manipulated because it's more like a stamp than anything else.

During the pandemic, when my wife and I would do drawing study sessions of various artists we admired, it occurred to me that this firmware could be updated. By doing studies of other artists' work, in which we would redraw their work and then try to imitate their style when drawing a new photo reference, I felt I learned a lot very quickly.

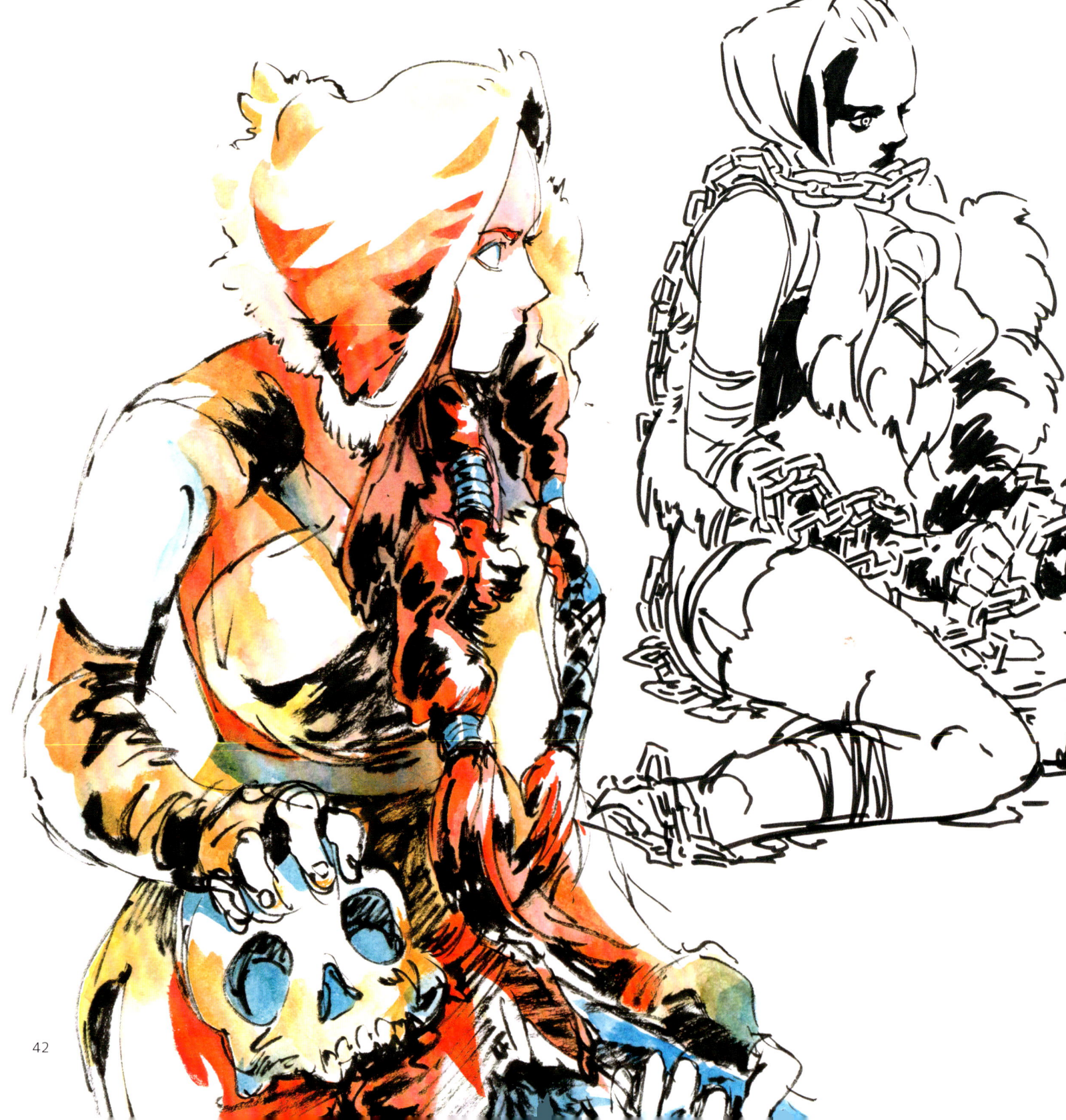

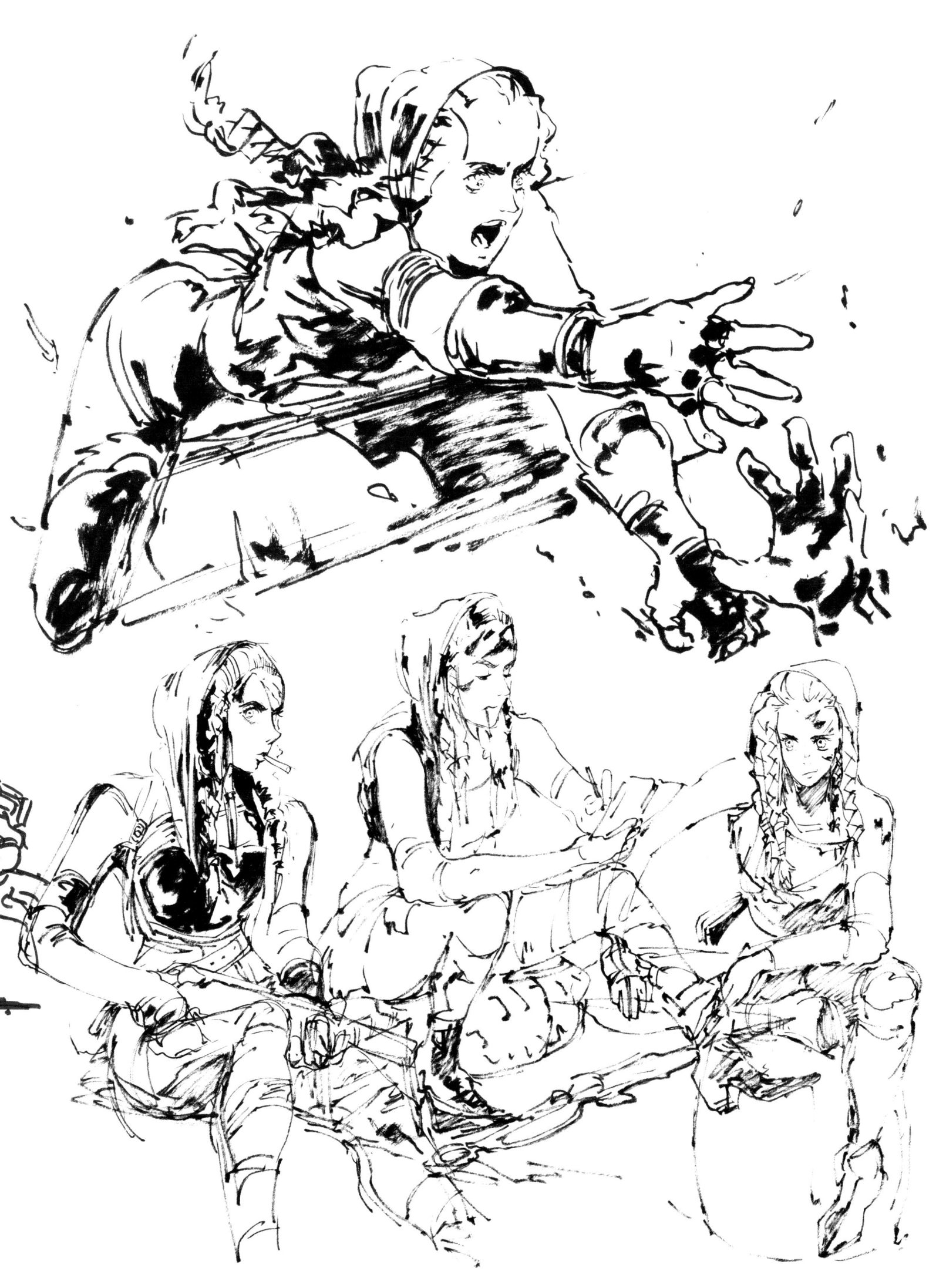

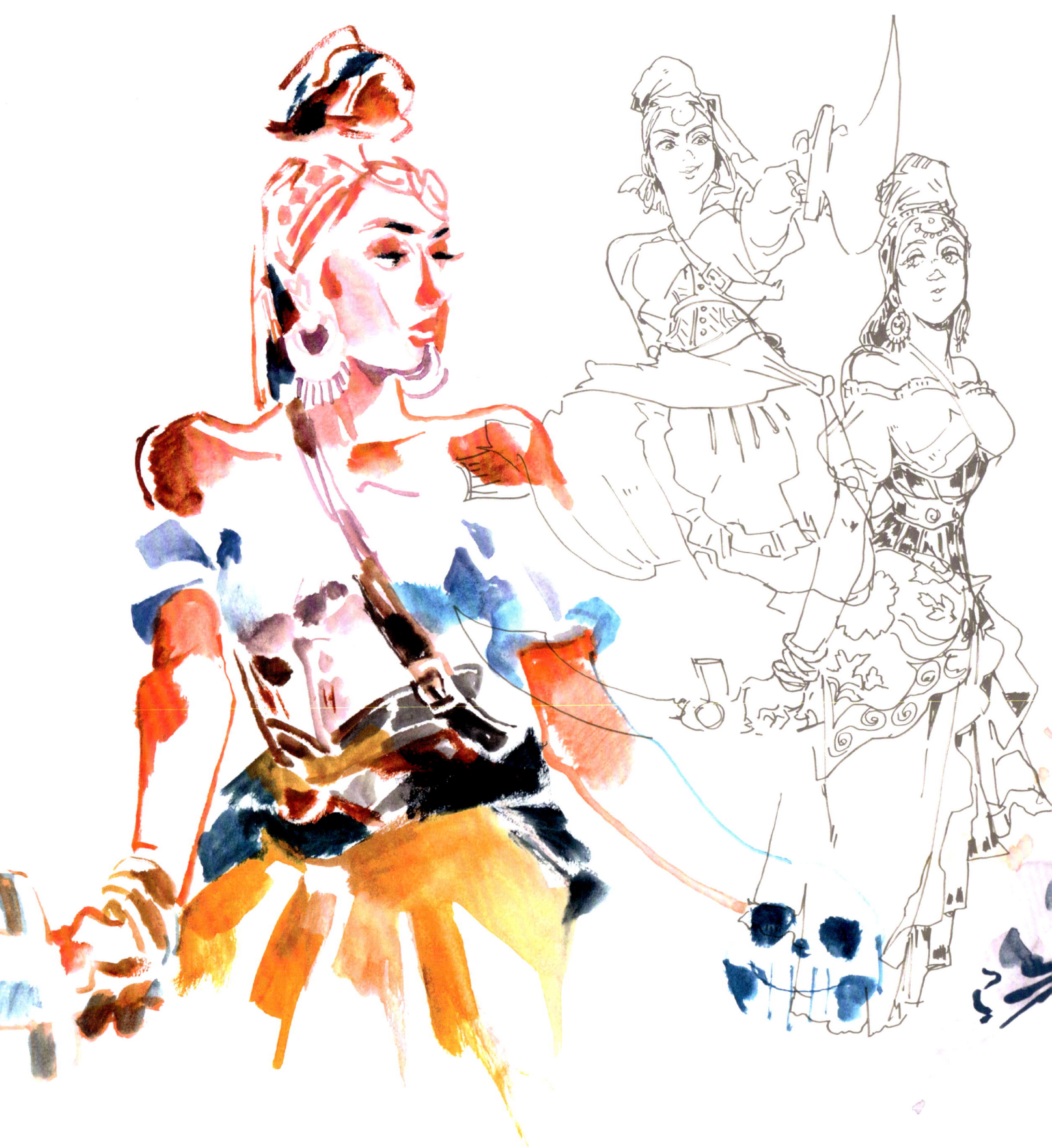

The most impactful session for me was studying the work of Keiko Murayama, an amazing artist who has worked for Pixar and won an Annie for her work on *Carmen Sandiego*. The way she draws hands and feet was particularly interesting to me, so studying her work for even just a few hours really helped with my anatomy, especially fingers in certain positions. Keiko often uses fingernails to help reveal the direction more clearly and succinctly than anything I had previously tried.

She may have taken a long time to come to that realization, but it was made plain to me simply through this method of study. Those kinds of eureka moments are precious!

After our session studying Keiko was over, I realized it felt like I hadn't touched that side of my brain since high school. It was refereshingly enlightening. Perhaps it's quite obvious to say, but sometimes studying art feels like such a vague pursuit, where most of the time is spent doing things we're already good at. But this felt different.

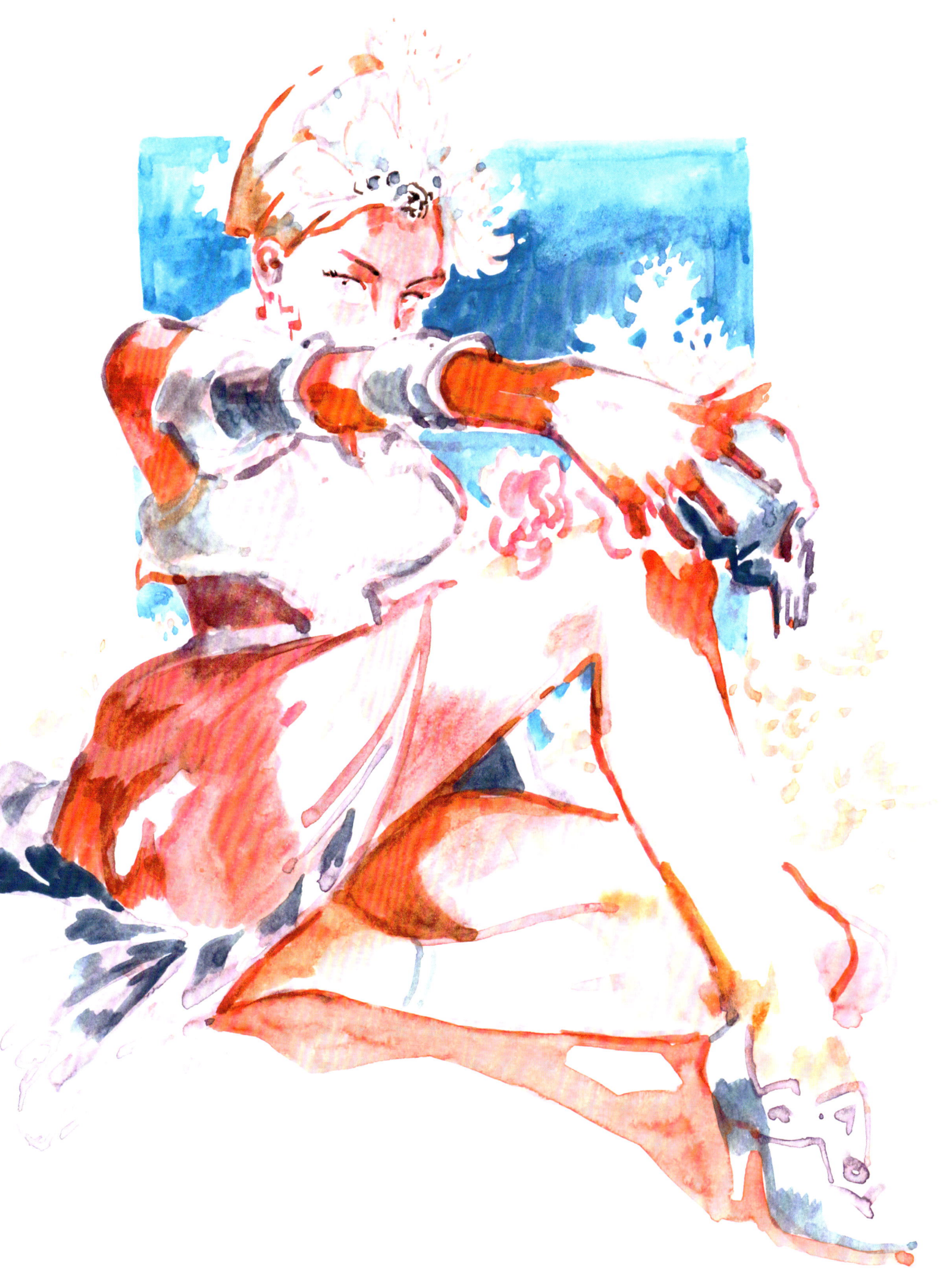

When I draw now, it's either for work or to relax. It's almost never a time to focus on my weaknesses. I think we can only find our weak spots by looking closely at artwork that can achieve things ours cannot. By studying those things directly, we can learn the most.

I definitely don't want to sound like I'm advocating for copying another artist's work. Rather, I'd like to remove some of the stigma about artists always needing to reinvent the wheel, as if we have to constantly assert our originality. Phooey! Nonsense. Learn what you can, how you can. There's enough fear involved in practising art as it is.

Embrace your influences; embrace your inner child. They need a hug, so give them one. Too many of us get worn down by life and give up drawing because we feel self-conscious or ashamed. Draw because you enjoy it. Learn because it's fun.

EMBRACE YOUR INFLUENCES; EMBRACE YOUR INNER CHILD

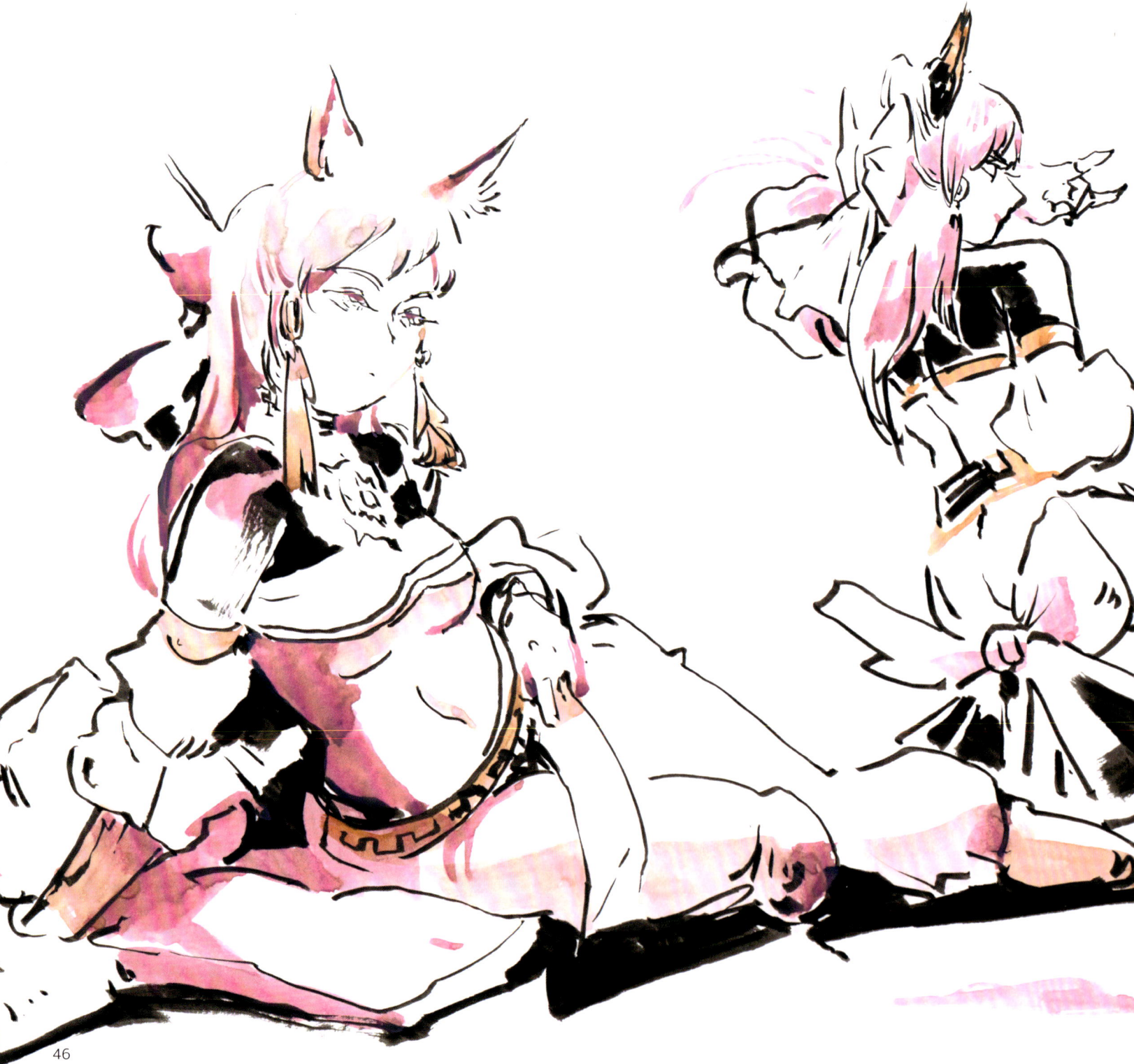

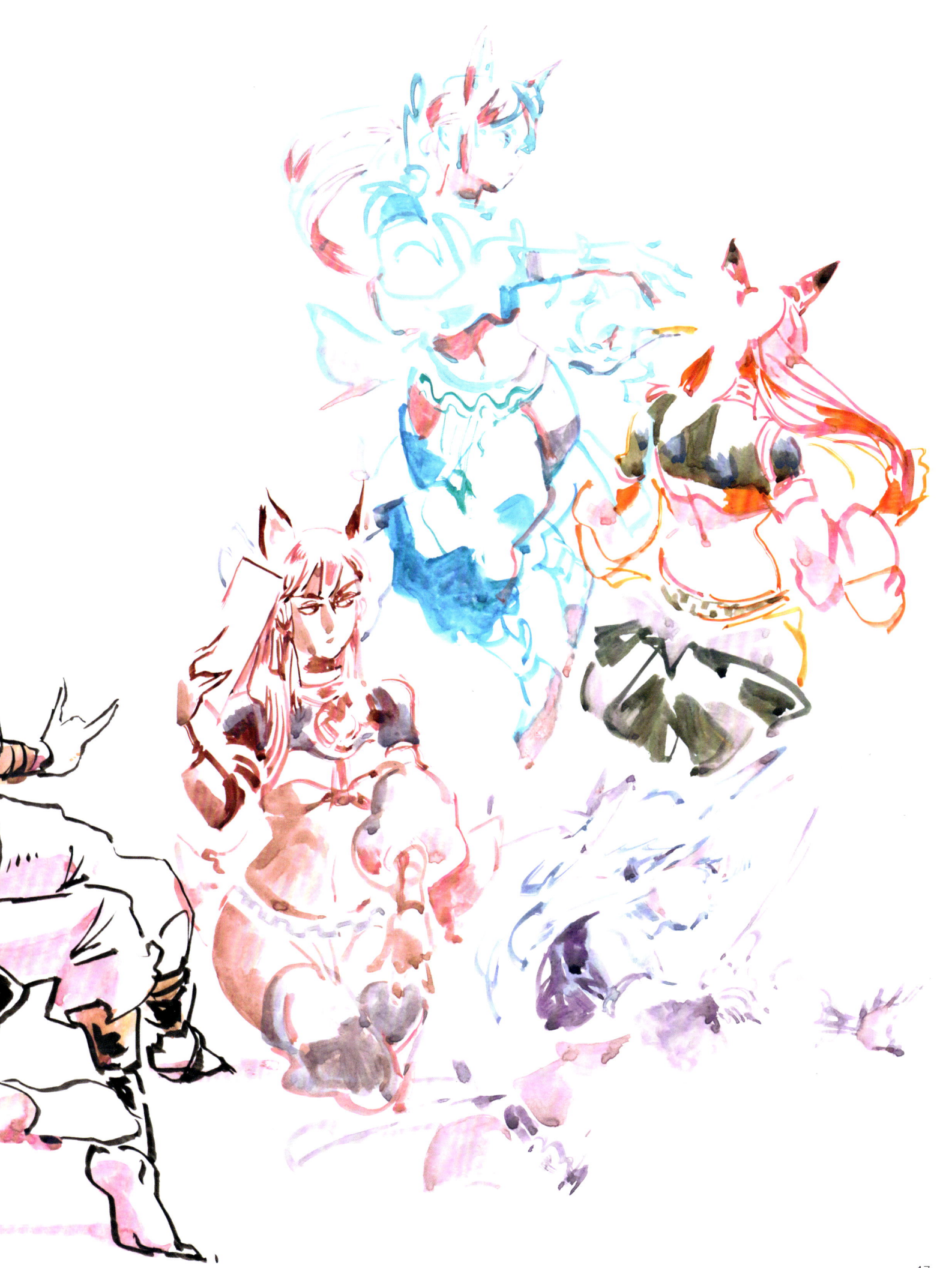

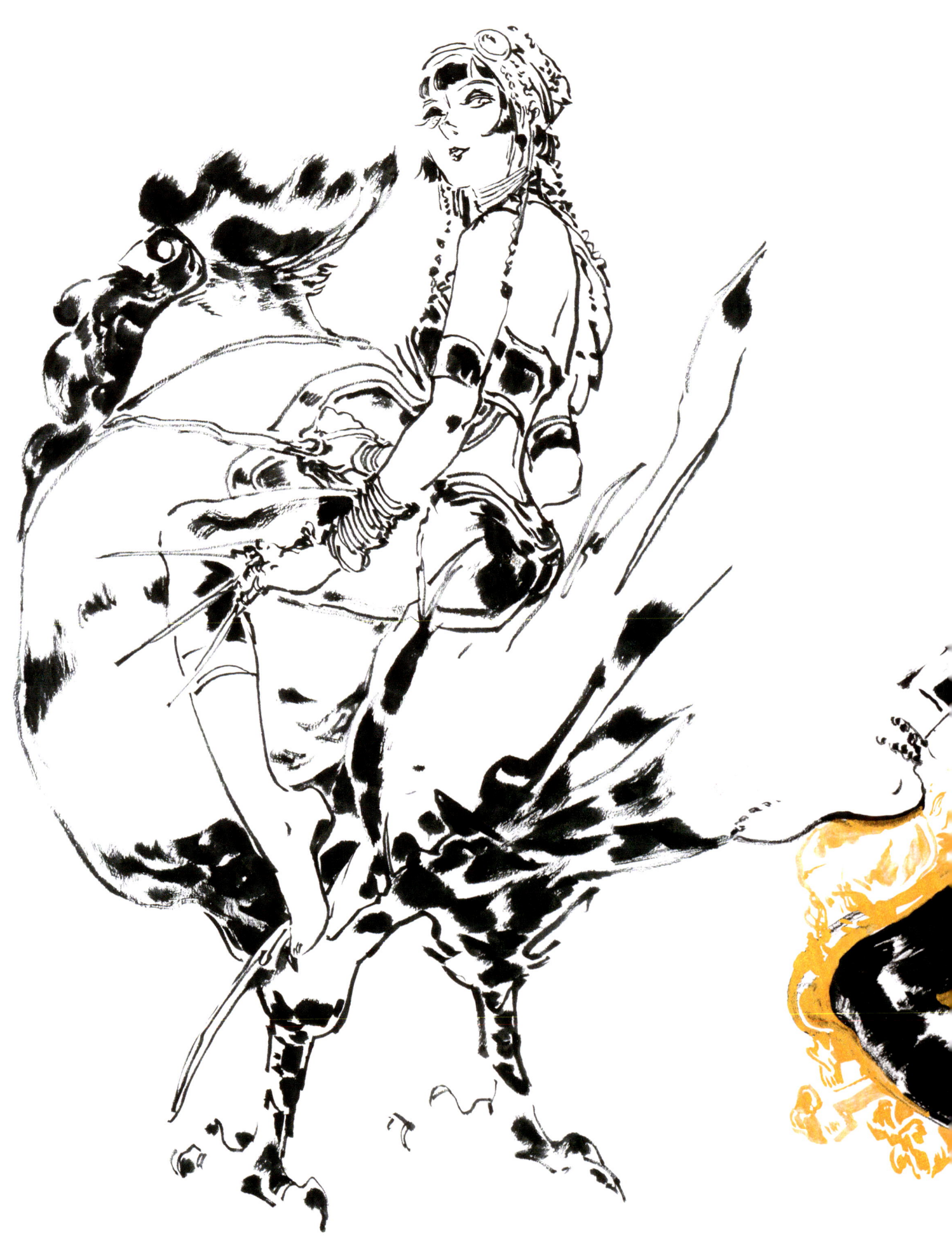

COLLEGE
FROM GAMES TO FILM...

There was a period when I considered becoming a manga graphic novelist and heading straight into it after graduating from school. But at that age, I was too scared and believed what my parents taught me about life being impossible as an artist. So I tried to be smart and think about emerging industries with jobs that could somehow still utilize my art.

I went to college at the University of California, San Diego with the intention of studying computer science and art, thinking that it could eventually lead to a job in video games, but that dream quickly disappeared. Advanced math courses were prerequisites

before we even got to the game stuff, and I felt like I was already struggling in my second quarter. Although I would later find out this was not true at all, it felt like I just didn't have what it took. So, continuing the trend of trying to do art without doing art, film-making sounded promising.

It seemed palatable enough to my parents because it's an industry with a very high-perceived value – famous celebrities, award shows, big salaries, and so on. At the start of my second year, I switched programmes.

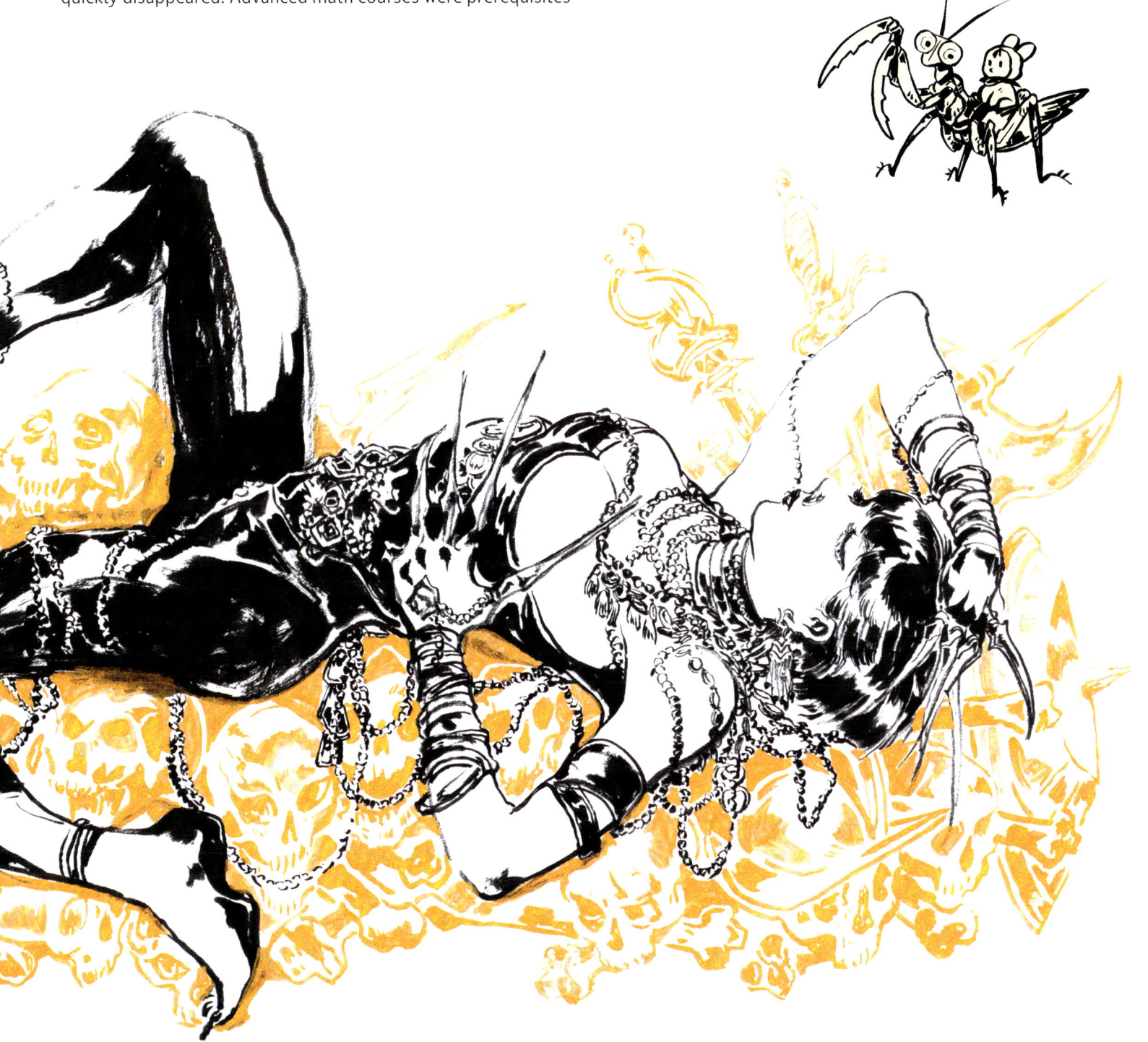

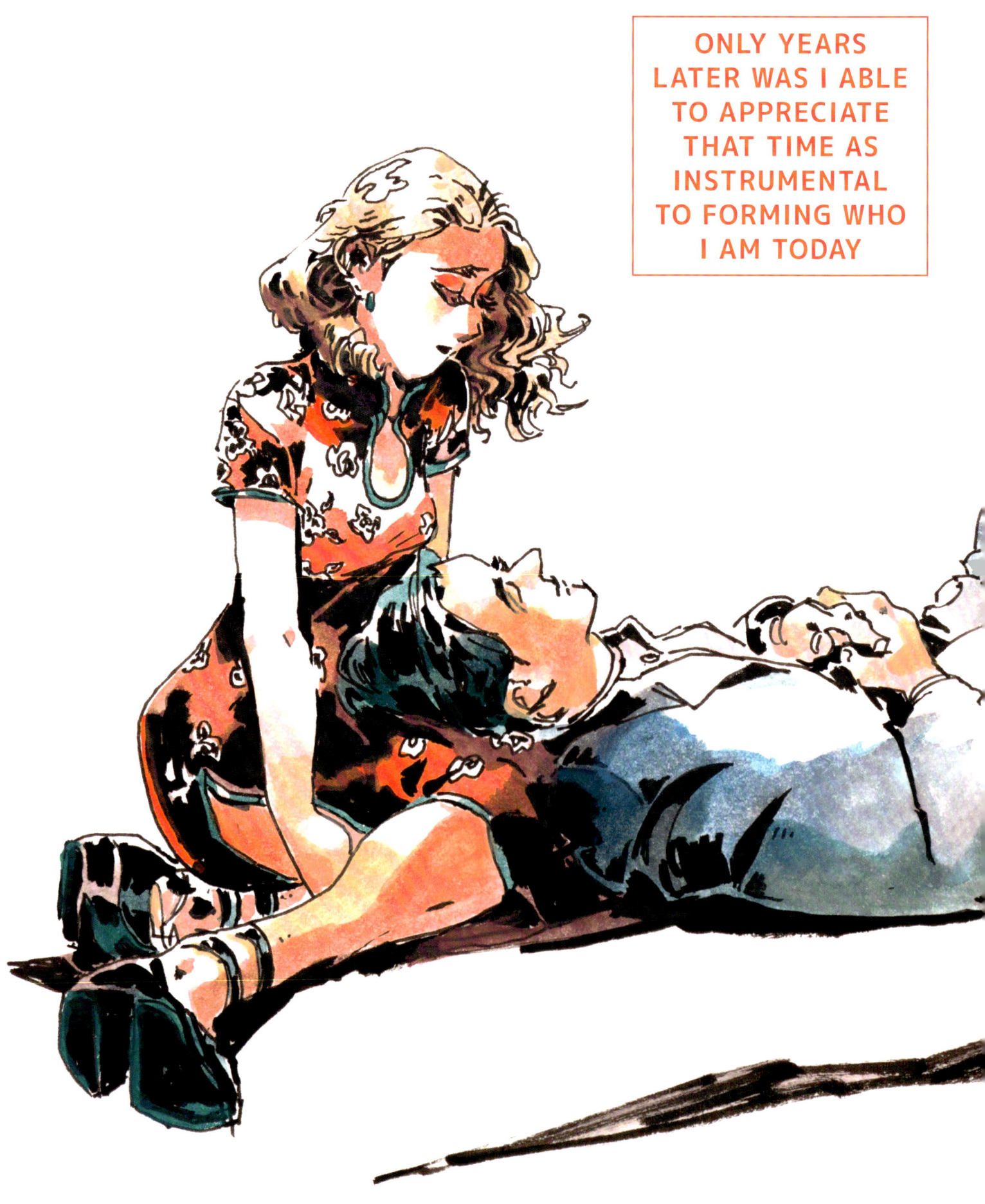

ONLY YEARS LATER WAS I ABLE TO APPRECIATE THAT TIME AS INSTRUMENTAL TO FORMING WHO I AM TODAY

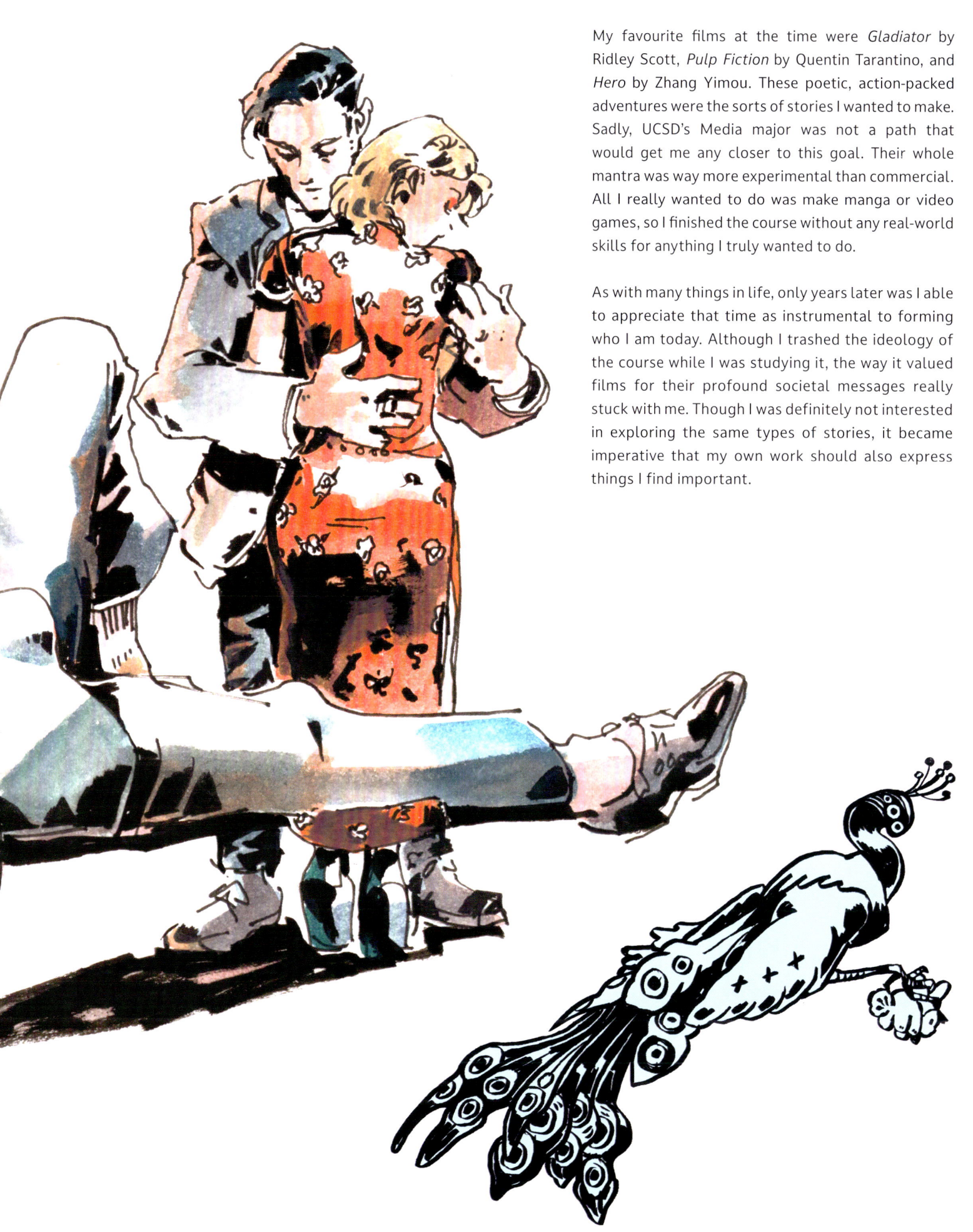

My favourite films at the time were *Gladiator* by Ridley Scott, *Pulp Fiction* by Quentin Tarantino, and *Hero* by Zhang Yimou. These poetic, action-packed adventures were the sorts of stories I wanted to make. Sadly, UCSD's Media major was not a path that would get me any closer to this goal. Their whole mantra was way more experimental than commercial. All I really wanted to do was make manga or video games, so I finished the course without any real-world skills for anything I truly wanted to do.

As with many things in life, only years later was I able to appreciate that time as instrumental to forming who I am today. Although I trashed the ideology of the course while I was studying it, the way it valued films for their profound societal messages really stuck with me. Though I was definitely not interested in exploring the same types of stories, it became imperative that my own work should also express things I find important.

STORY STORY STORY!

After finishing undergrad, I went to the University of Southern California to gain some real-world skills in their graduate film-production programme. There, I learned a lot about how to tell stories and create short films. The biggest idea the course instilled in me was the belief that good film-making was always about maximizing the amount of storytelling. This would be something I continued to obsess over. Everything else – the world-building, acting, visuals, anything that might wow an audience – was all for nothing if it didn't help develop the story. I came to appreciate how every detail in a film could say something in service of the main idea. That thinking found its way into how I approached my maximalist illustrations.

Still, as you already know, film would not be my long-term career. Though I excelled in the jobs I got while in school and felt confident about my abilities, I also knew that it was going to be a long road to reach the point of working on the type of projects I wanted, especially in a creative capacity. Judging by how rare it was for my peers to find happiness in their work, it felt as unlikely as winning the lottery.

However, I didn't really have any other options, so I began mentally steeling myself for that long journey to potential job satisfaction. But everything was about to change, seemingly out of nowhere.

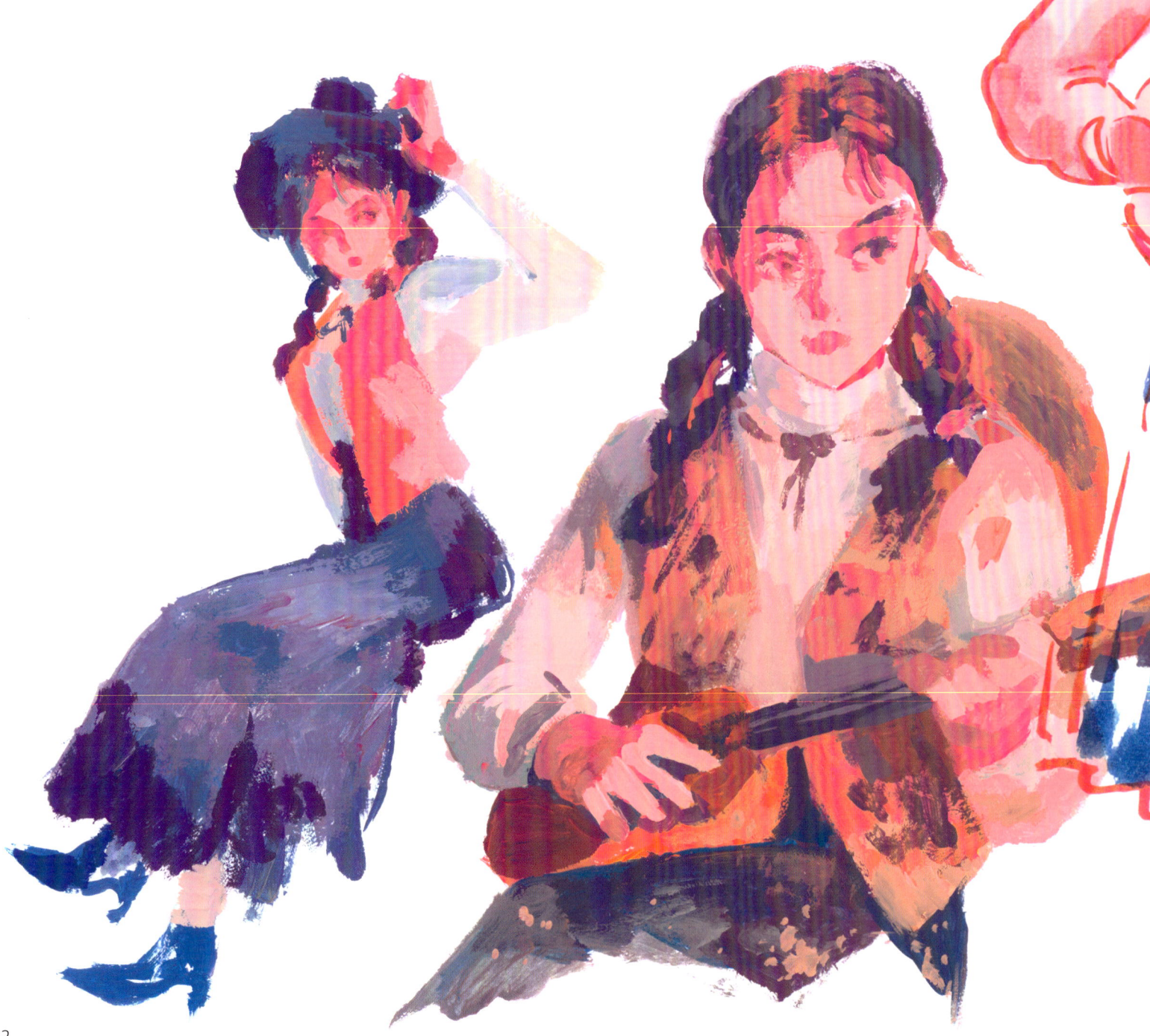

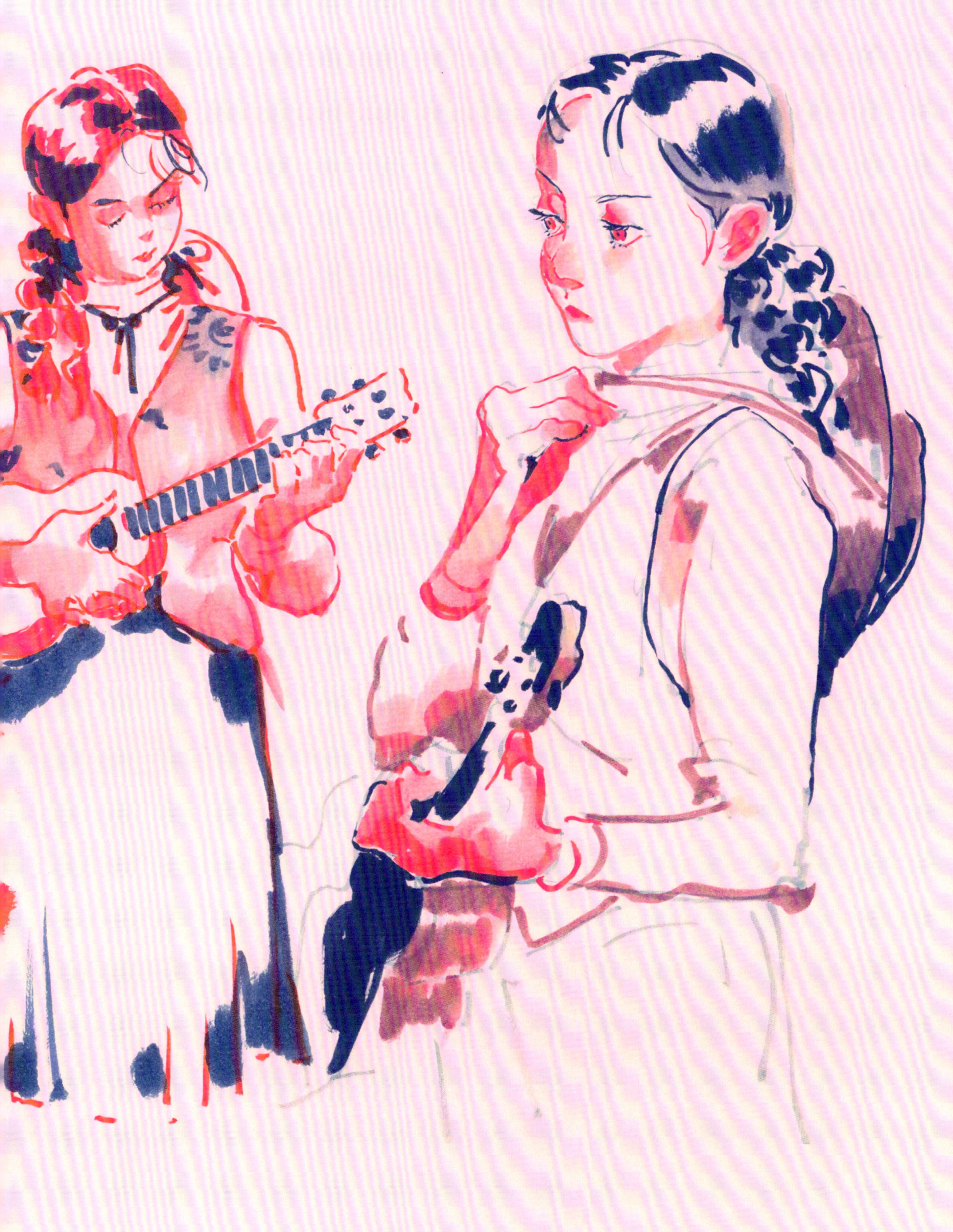

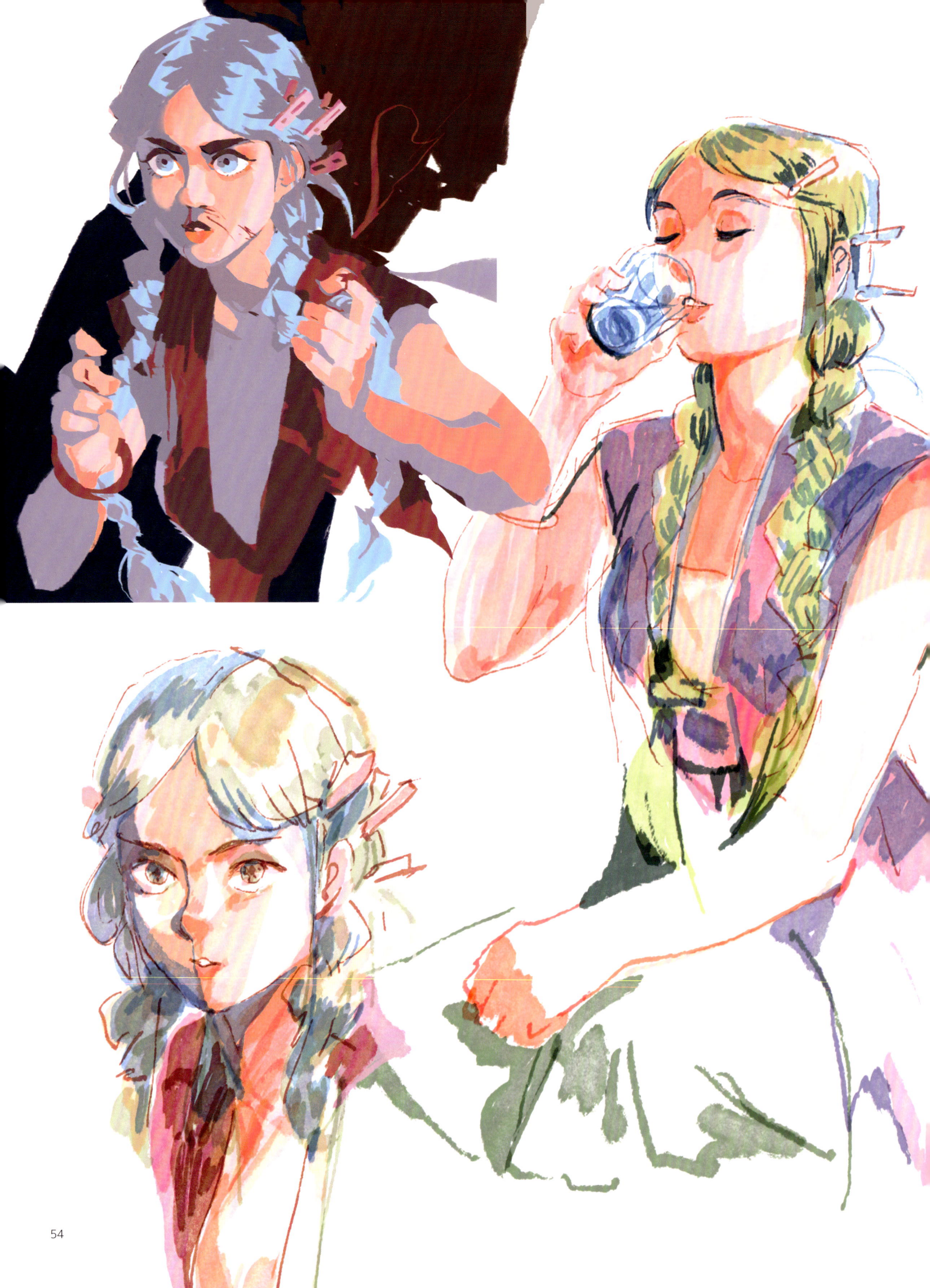

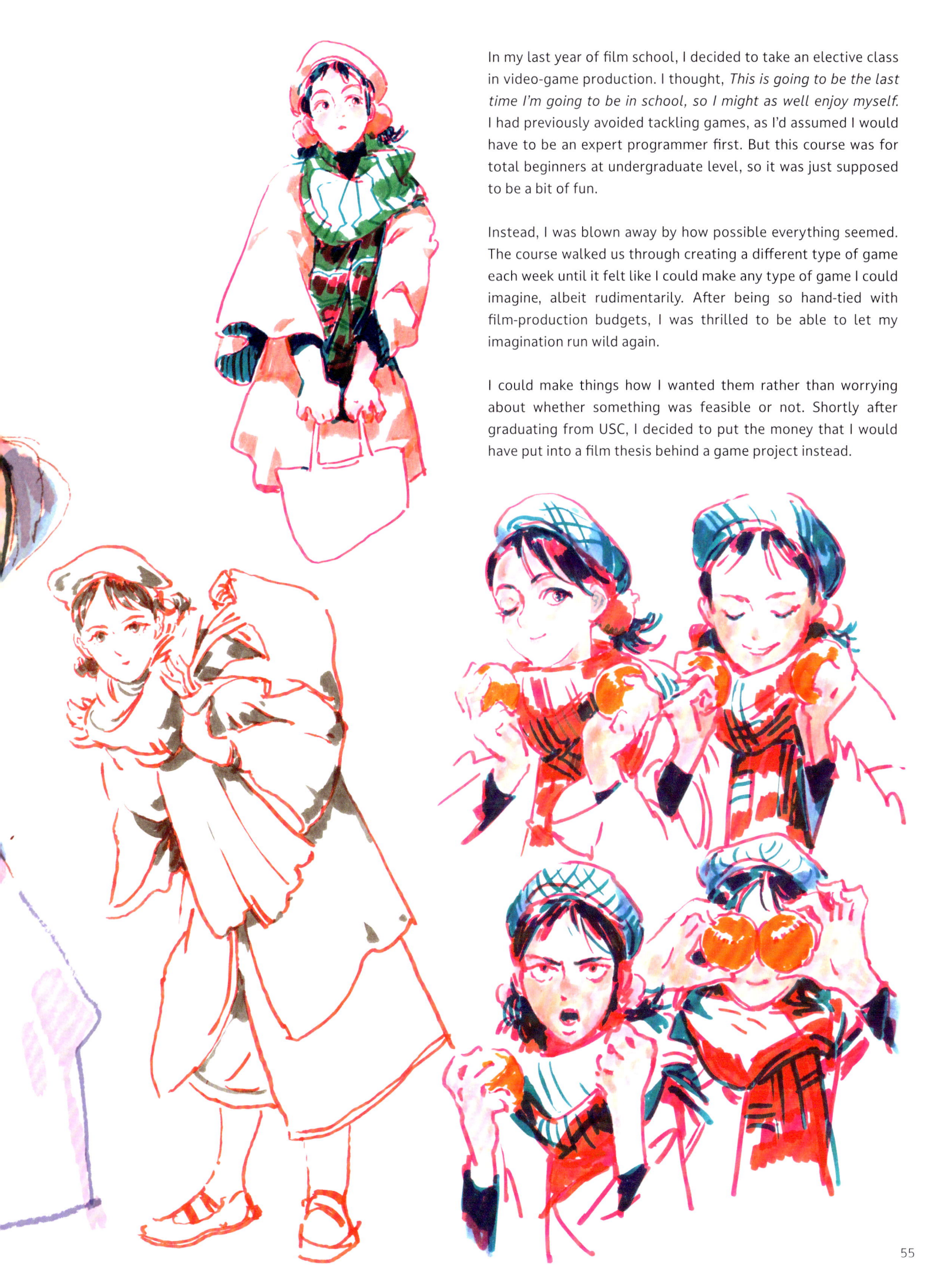

In my last year of film school, I decided to take an elective class in video-game production. I thought, *This is going to be the last time I'm going to be in school, so I might as well enjoy myself.* I had previously avoided tackling games, as I'd assumed I would have to be an expert programmer first. But this course was for total beginners at undergraduate level, so it was just supposed to be a bit of fun.

Instead, I was blown away by how possible everything seemed. The course walked us through creating a different type of game each week until it felt like I could make any type of game I could imagine, albeit rudimentarily. After being so hand-tied with film-production budgets, I was thrilled to be able to let my imagination run wild again.

I could make things how I wanted them rather than worrying about whether something was feasible or not. Shortly after graduating from USC, I decided to put the money that I would have put into a film thesis behind a game project instead.

NAVIGATING DIFFERENT CAREER PATHS
...AND FROM FILM TO GAMES

The name of the game project I spent the next four years of my life working on was *Aegis Defenders*. I made the first prototype while in a USC class, where my teacher and director of the first two *Uncharted* games, Richard Lemarchand, told me that I was onto something special.

My team, four people including myself, were able to raise $150,000 on Kickstarter and everything felt like a whirlwind of success. But that glow didn't last very long. Though we had hoped it would only take two years to finish, it would actually take four, and they were the hardest four years of my life.

Everyday, I woke up at 5 am and worked into the night. I worked so hard during that time that it nearly broke me. Without the help of my sister, Kristen, who left her senior engineer job at PopCap Games to take over as engineer, and worked for free for the final two years, we would have never been able to finish. Through sheer grit, we managed to release *Aegis Defenders* in 2018 on Playstation 4, Nintendo Switch, and PC.

The game itself did decently, especially considering it was our first game ever. We won a Gold Award from *Famitsu*, received several 9s from medium-sized press outlets, and even made it onto a 'top ten most underrated games' list.

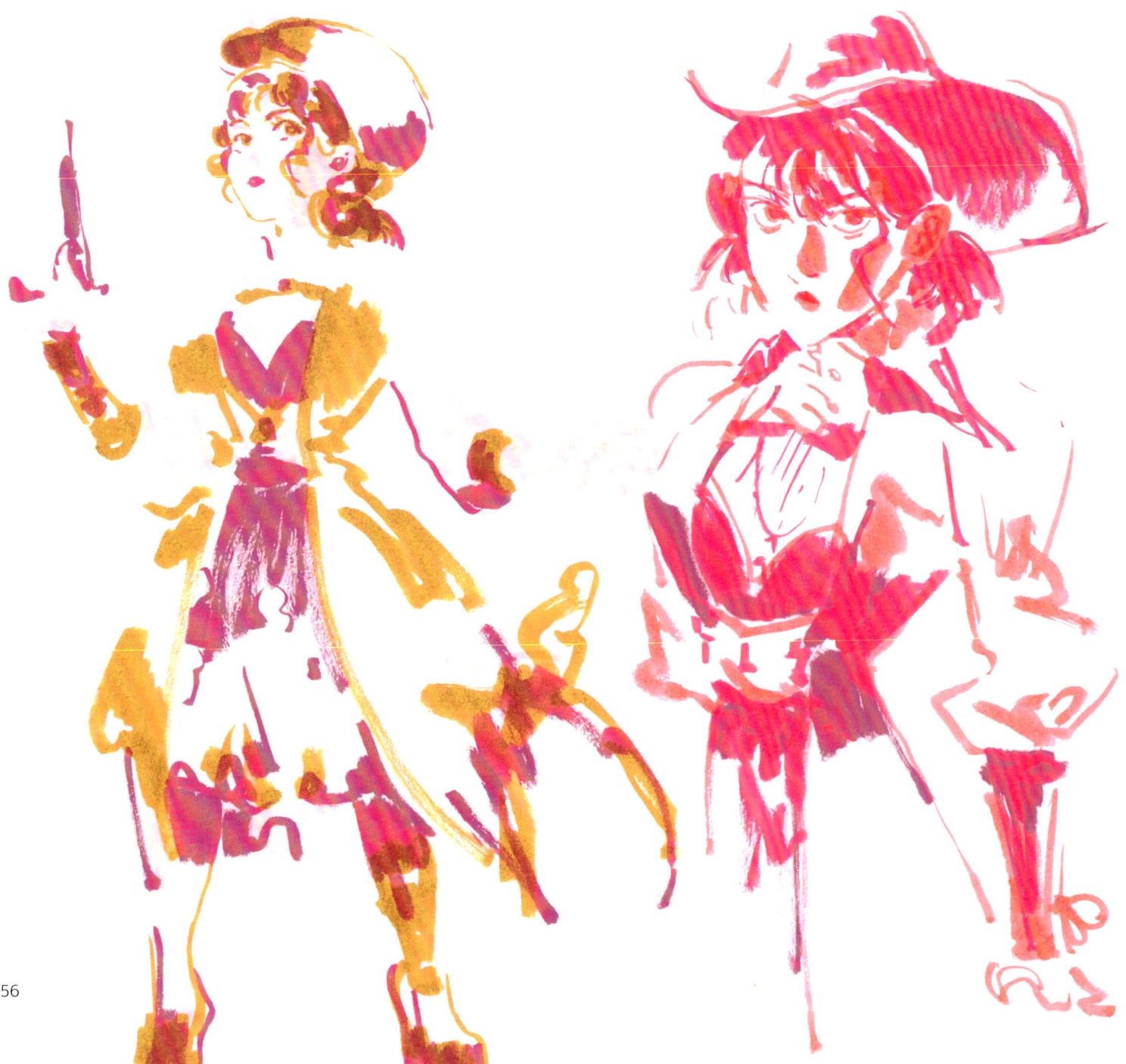

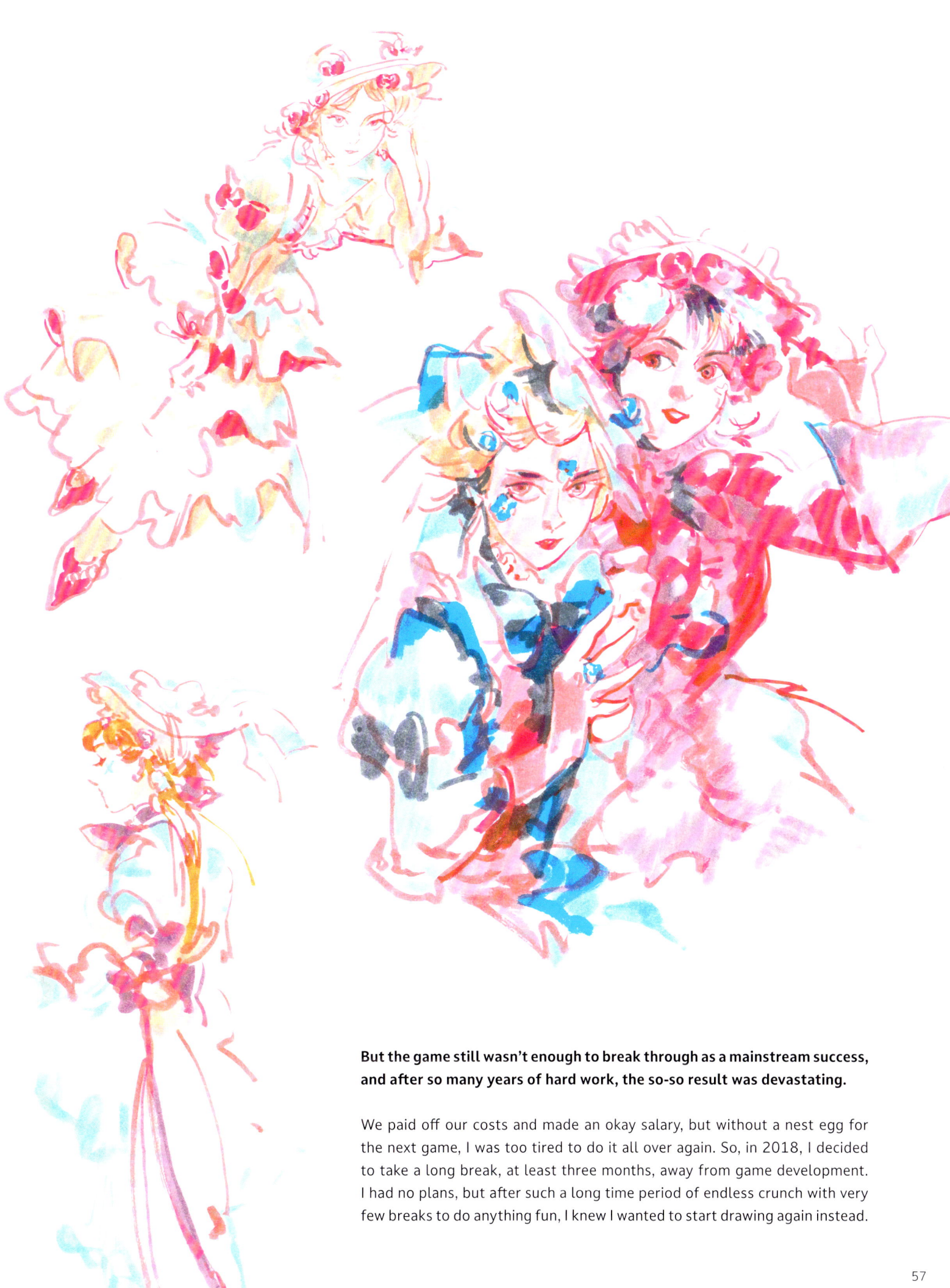

But the game still wasn't enough to break through as a mainstream success, and after so many years of hard work, the so-so result was devastating.

We paid off our costs and made an okay salary, but without a nest egg for the next game, I was too tired to do it all over again. So, in 2018, I decided to take a long break, at least three months, away from game development. I had no plans, but after such a long time period of endless crunch with very few breaks to do anything fun, I knew I wanted to start drawing again instead.

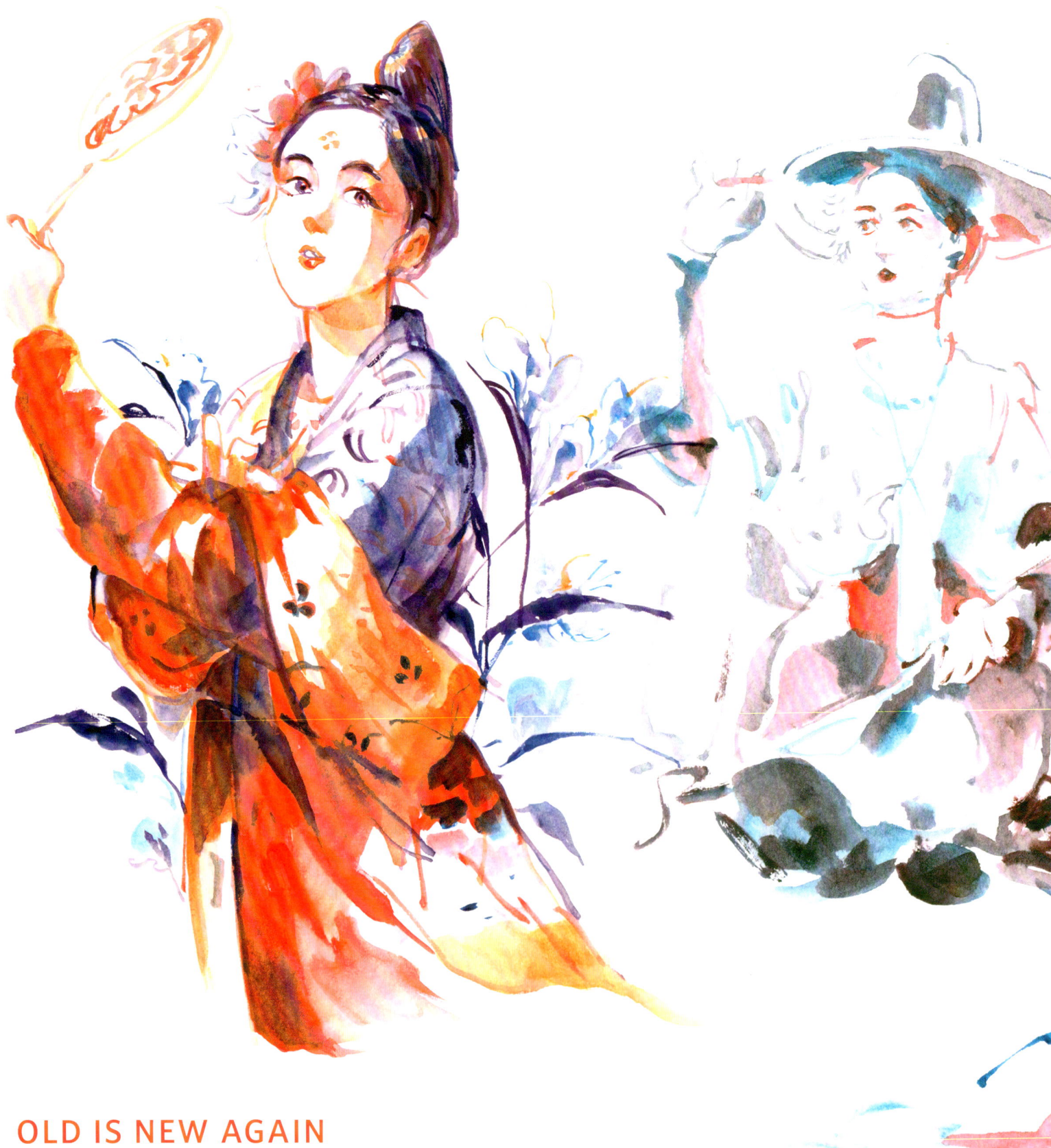

OLD IS NEW AGAIN

During this break from employment, I would go to cafés every day, maybe meet up with a friend, and just draw. It was rejuvenating and I felt like I was finally becoming a whole person again. Although being unemployed had its emotional ups and downs, I look back on that time as a real gift. With no pressure to do anything in particular, it was like I was a kid again, and I drew with childlike enthusiasm. The hardest part was creating a routine within my wide-open days, but I found that structure through Inktober, an online drawing challenge hosted in October. Each day of that month, a drawing prompt is posted by the organizers, and artists around the world interpret the theme in their own way. I participated in the event and treated it seriously; almost like a full-time job. Thanks to the daily prompts, I learned that my drawings didn't need to represent me – they could just express whatever that particular day's theme was.

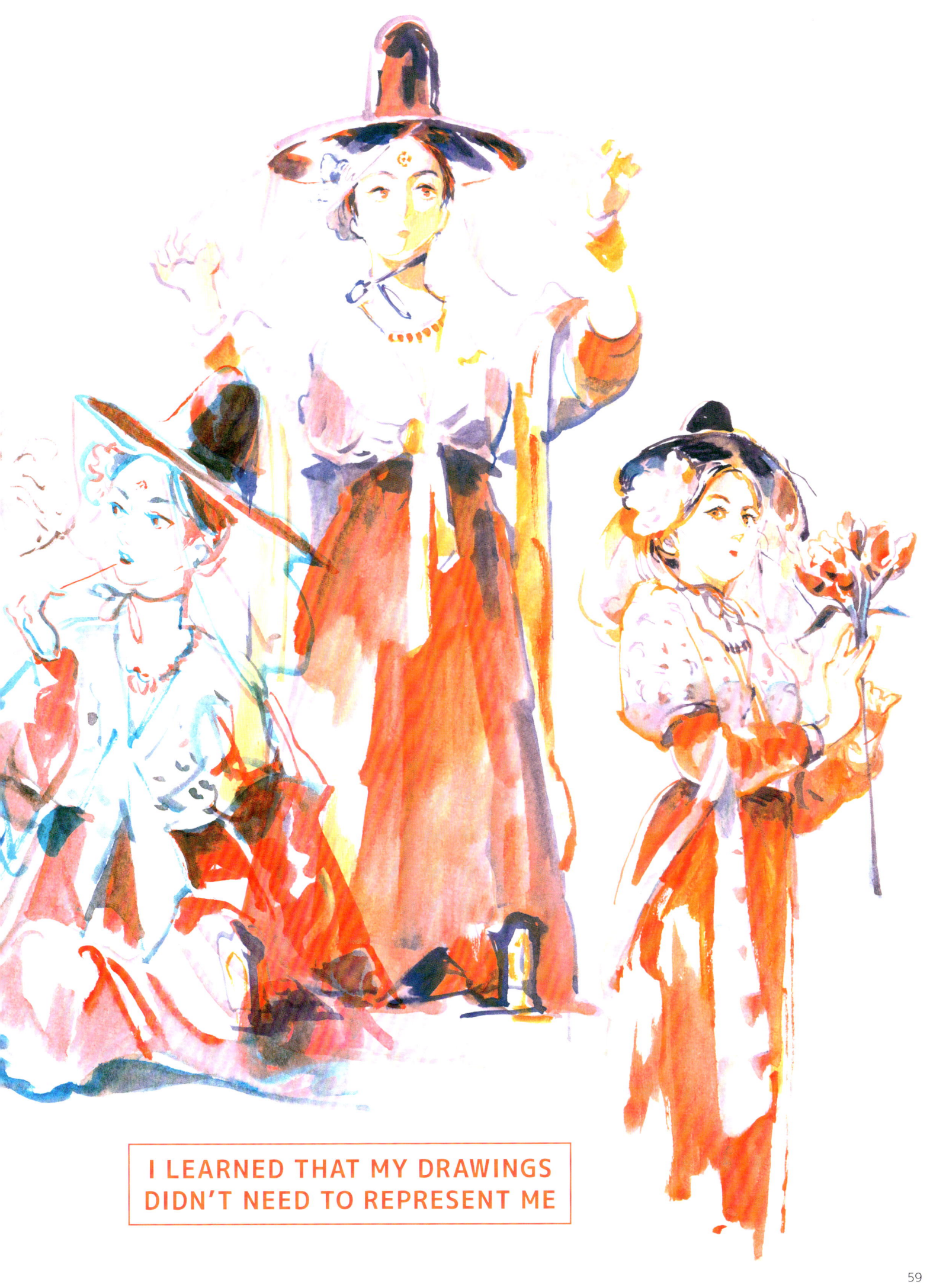

I LEARNED THAT MY DRAWINGS
DIDN'T NEED TO REPRESENT ME

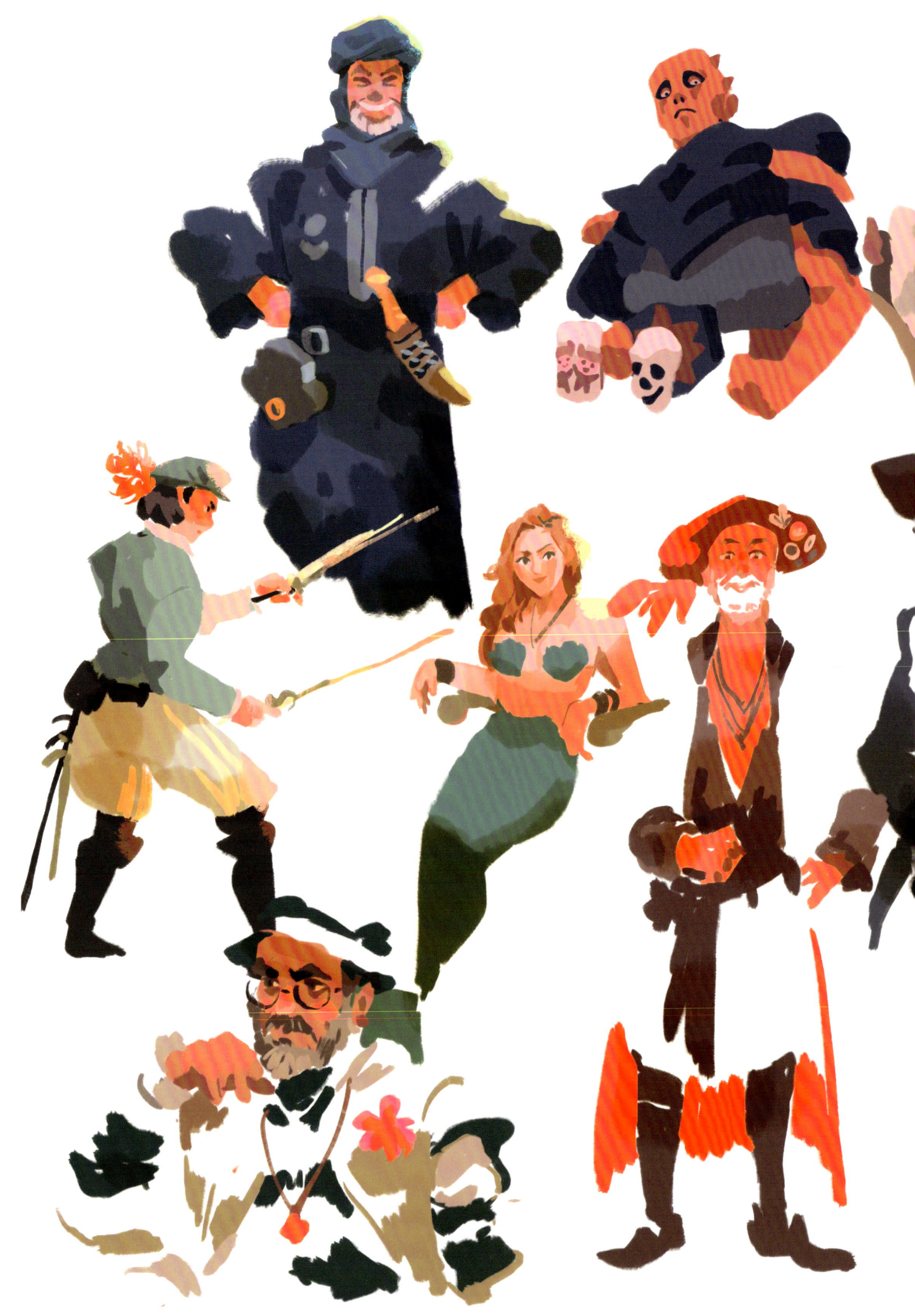

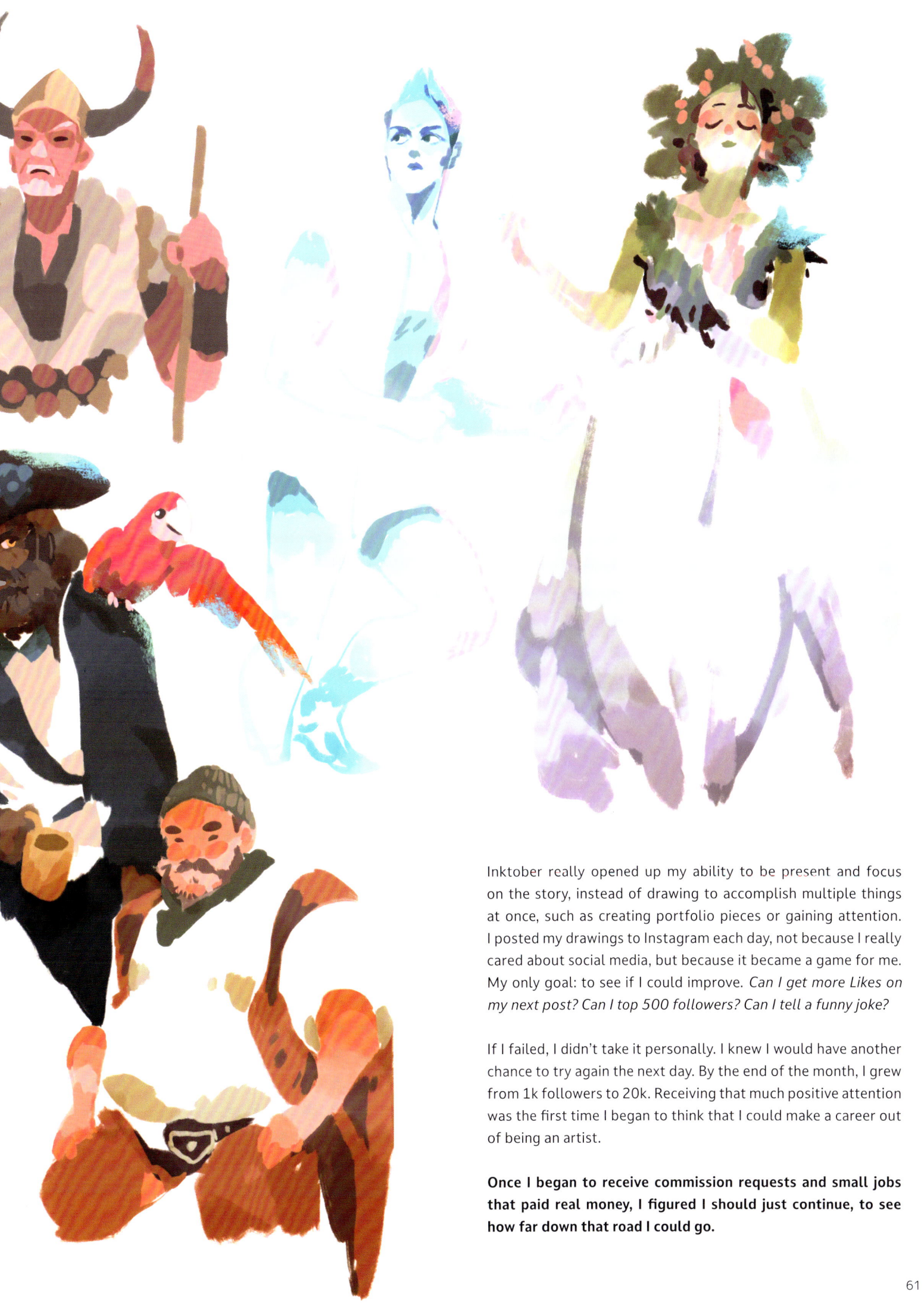

Inktober really opened up my ability to be present and focus on the story, instead of drawing to accomplish multiple things at once, such as creating portfolio pieces or gaining attention. I posted my drawings to Instagram each day, not because I really cared about social media, but because it became a game for me. My only goal: to see if I could improve. *Can I get more Likes on my next post? Can I top 500 followers? Can I tell a funny joke?*

If I failed, I didn't take it personally. I knew I would have another chance to try again the next day. By the end of the month, I grew from 1k followers to 20k. Receiving that much positive attention was the first time I began to think that I could make a career out of being an artist.

Once I began to receive commission requests and small jobs that paid real money, I figured I should just continue, to see how far down that road I could go.

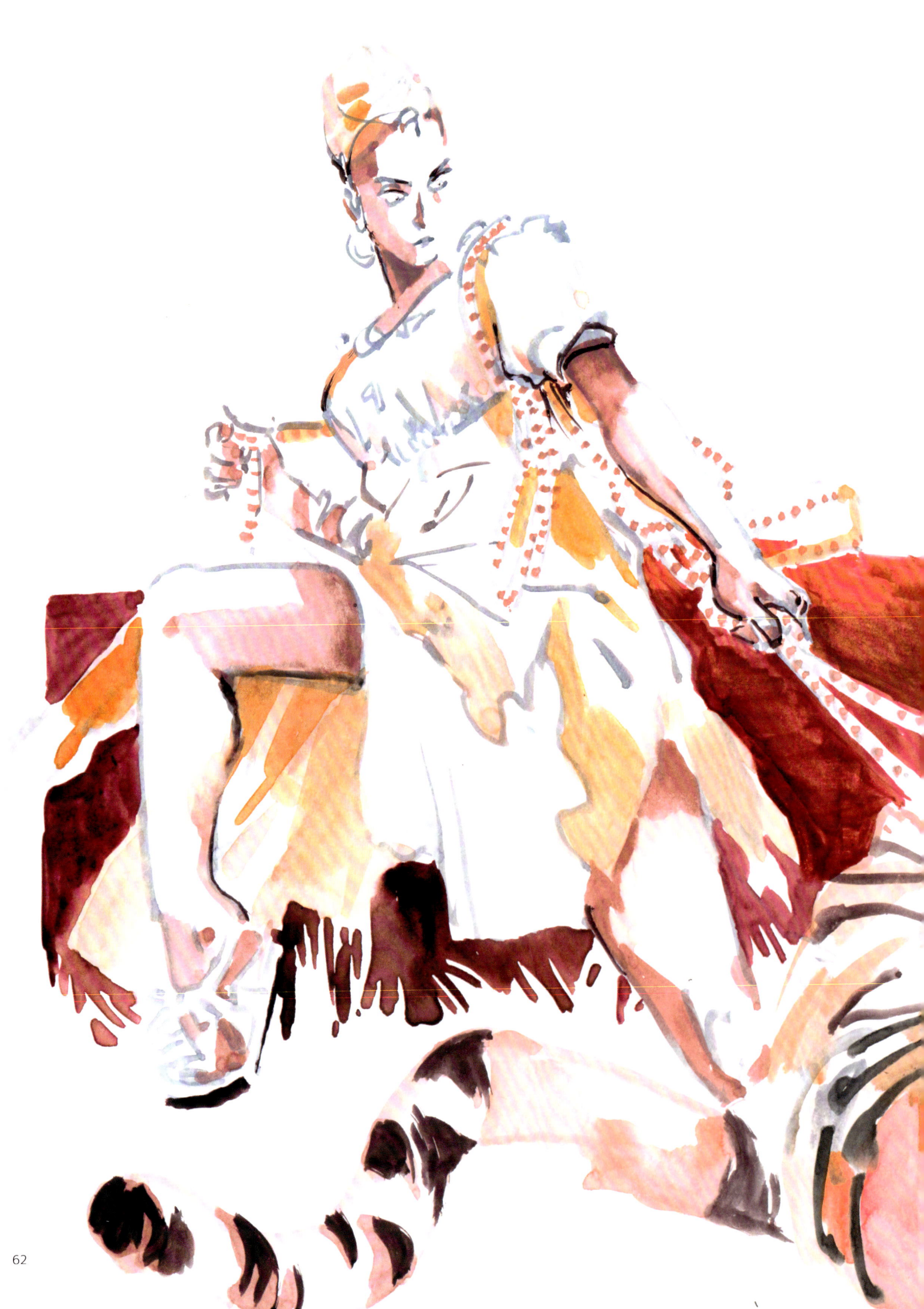

Still, things didn't go so smoothly at first. I spent a good while taking odd jobs from anyone who would commission me, while also applying for jobs, trying to break into the animation industry. My lucky break eventually came from my *Aegis* connections. I was recommended for a job that involved drawing the key art for a game called *The Messenger* by Sabotage Studio.

However, after that first job was completed, I didn't immediately join the studio. Instead, I spent the next couple of years continuing to work on another indie project – a game that would never see the light of day. If I had been younger, I think this would have felt like a really bitter end for that project, but somehow, the fact that I had struck out again didn't seem to bother me.

Perhaps my skin had simply toughened, but I think after I turned thirty, I just felt more at peace with the fact that I was who I was. Sort of like, *This is all I've got, so might as well make it work*. I was done being mad at myself for not being something I wasn't, and that feeling extended to the project's success or failure as well. I stopped worrying about what was outside of my control and just threw myself at what I could actually do to keep improving.

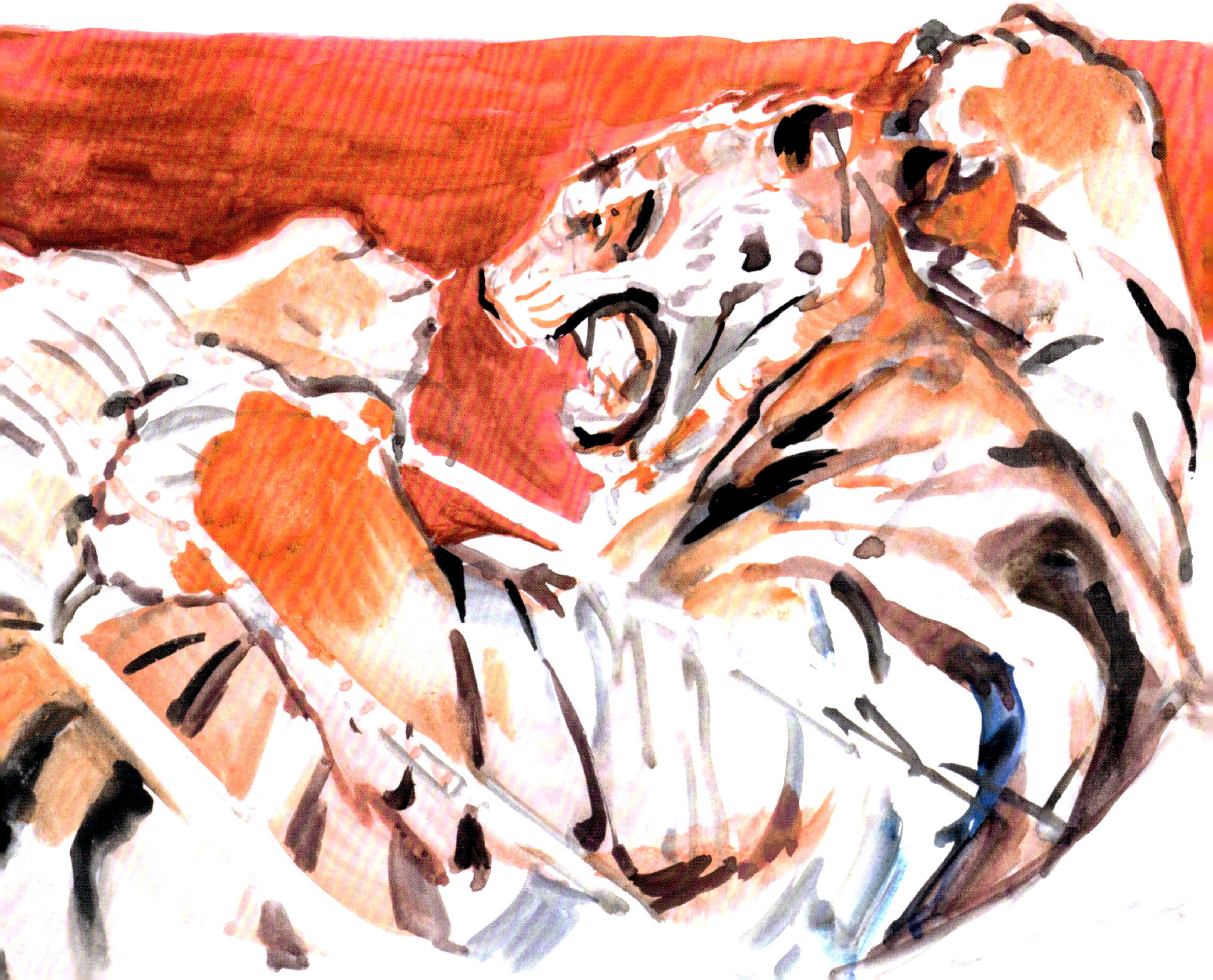

THIS IS ALL I'VE GOT, SO MIGHT AS WELL MAKE IT WORK

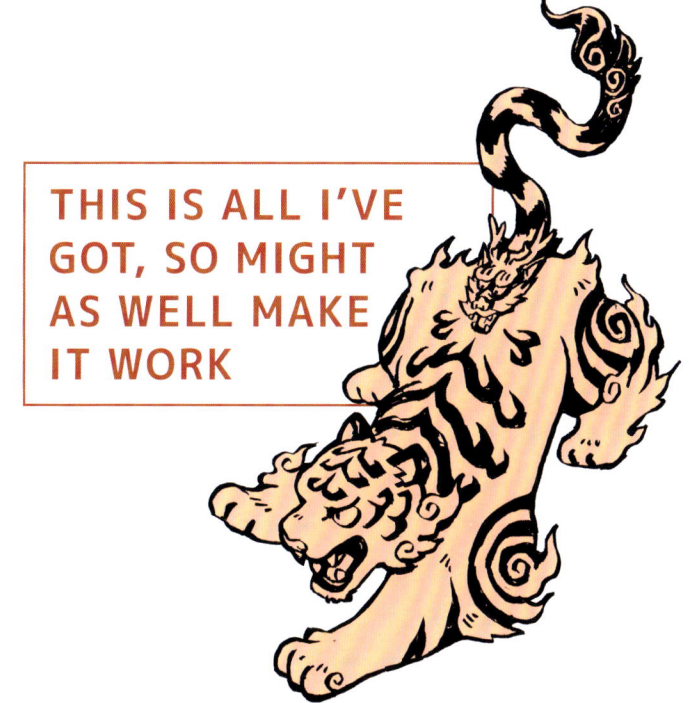

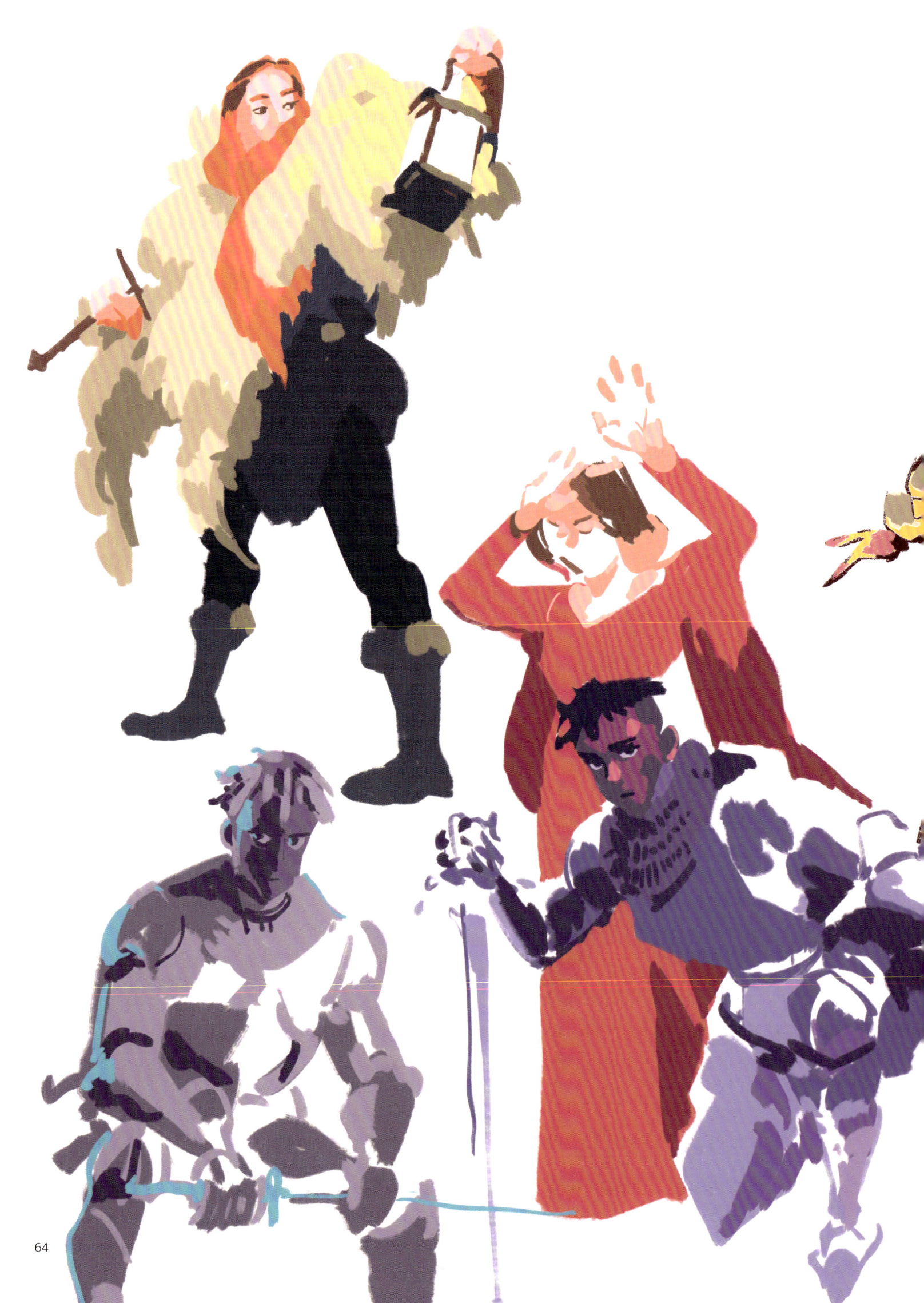

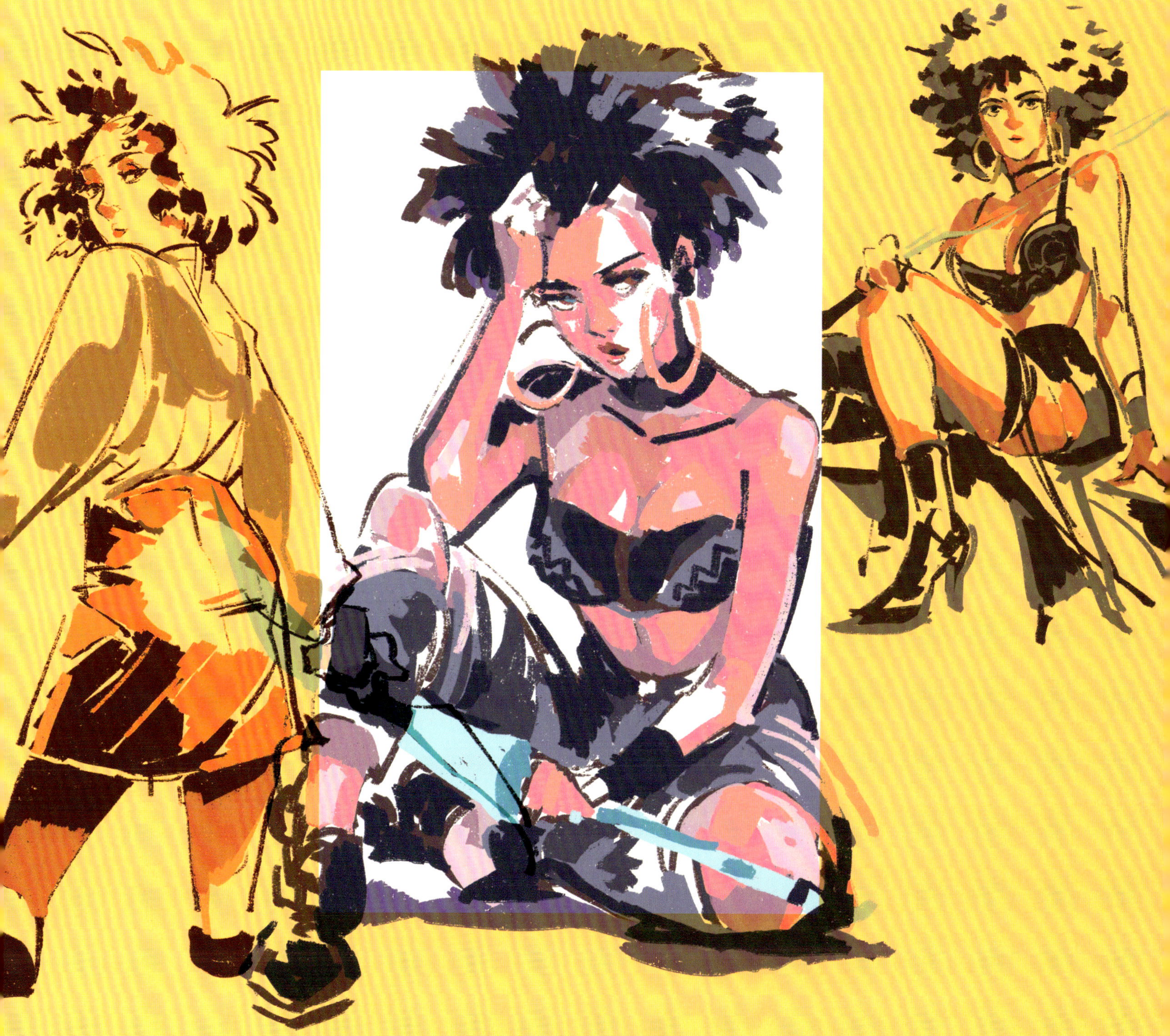

THE PRESENT

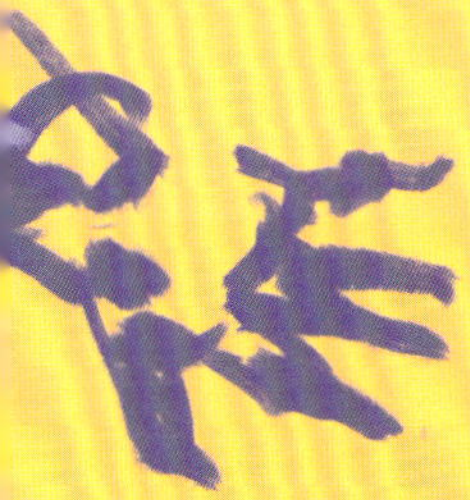

Shortly after that, Sabotage reached out to me to collaborate on *Sea of Stars* as their illustrator and concept artist. We had built up a rapport from working together on *The Messenger* and so it was an easy decision to take the job, mostly to just keep working with good people.

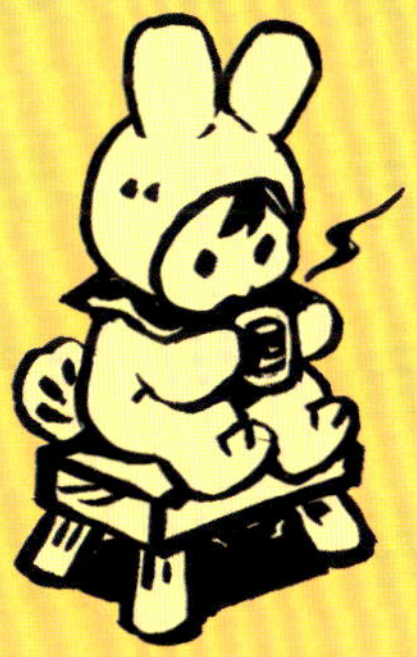

That project, which would eventually win Indie Game of the Year in 2023 at The Game Awards, had every element required for success that I knew was missing from projects I had worked on up to that point. The company culture, management, vision, talent, budget, room for creativity… all equally crucial components.

It was a recipe for success – a healthy work environment with talented, hardworking people led by a strong, unified vision. Nothing surprising if you think about it, but somehow exceedingly rare. I decided that from that time on, I would always try to put myself in that sort of environment.

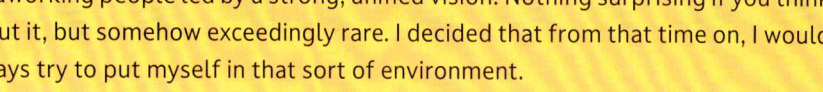

65

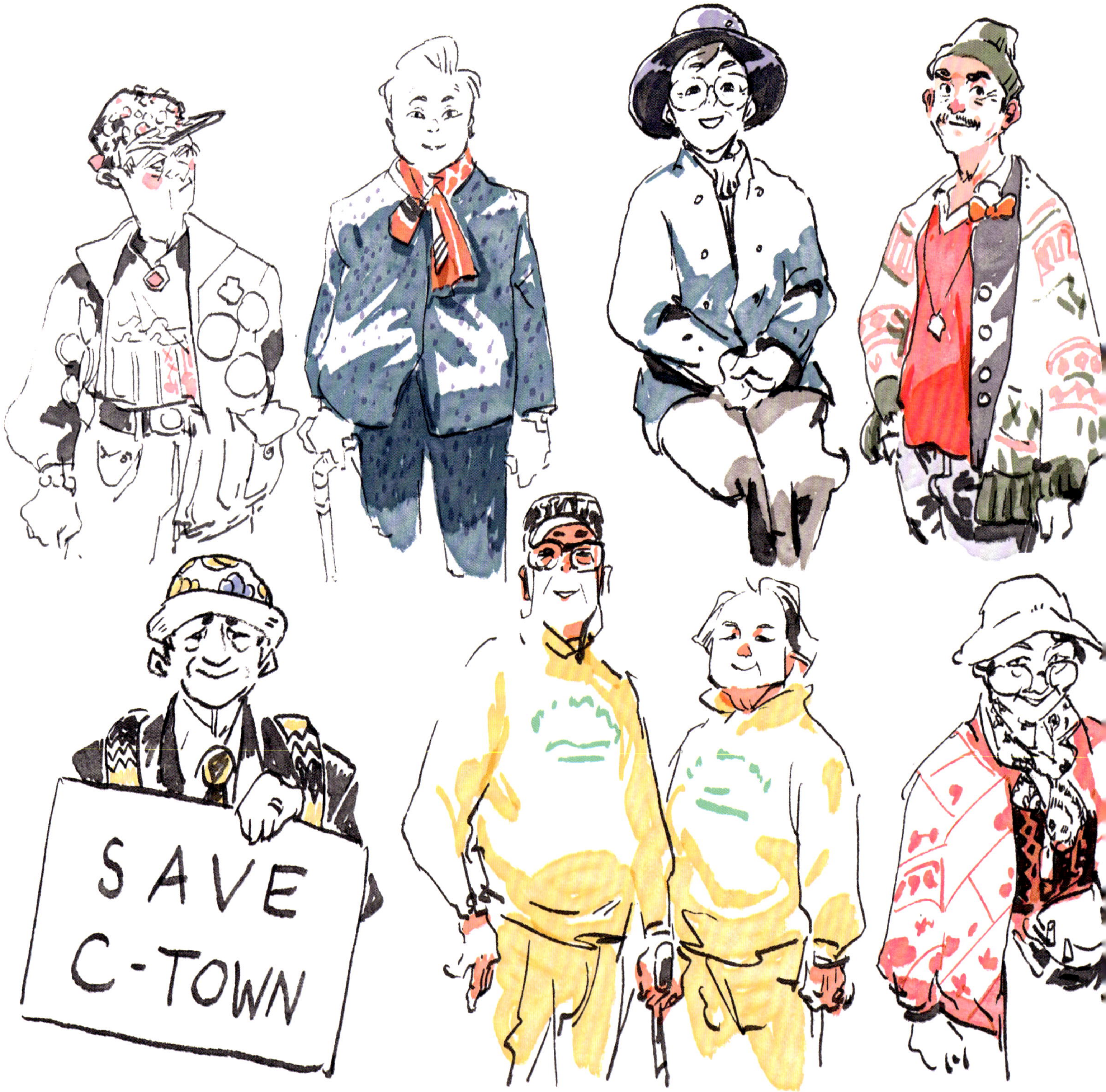

For this next phase of my career trajectory, I had to make a big choice: go full-time as a concept artist for Sabotage, or continue as a part-timer so that I could keep exploring my own personal goals. I knew a full-time job was more comfortable and less risky, but if you can't tell by now, I am a bit of a risk-taker.

The life event that made this decision the hardest for me was meeting Kris Kehasuk at LightBox Expo 2019, where I saw him thriving as a convention artist. Seeing Kris run a business where he was able to support others, all while drawing whatever he wanted … it was too tempting not to try.

IF YOU CAN'T TELL BY NOW, I AM A BIT OF A RISK-TAKER

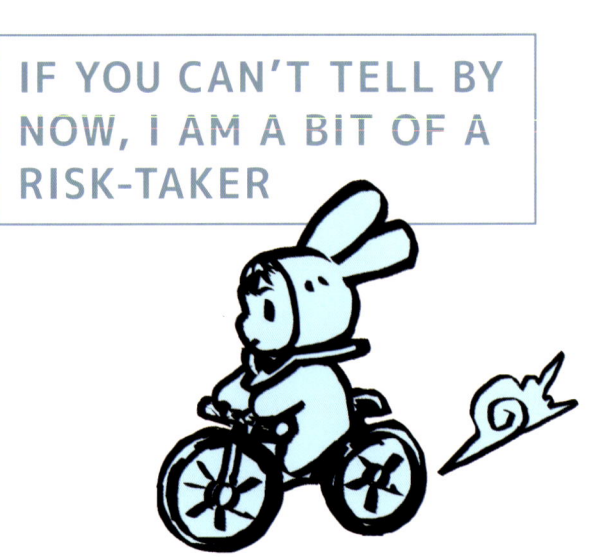

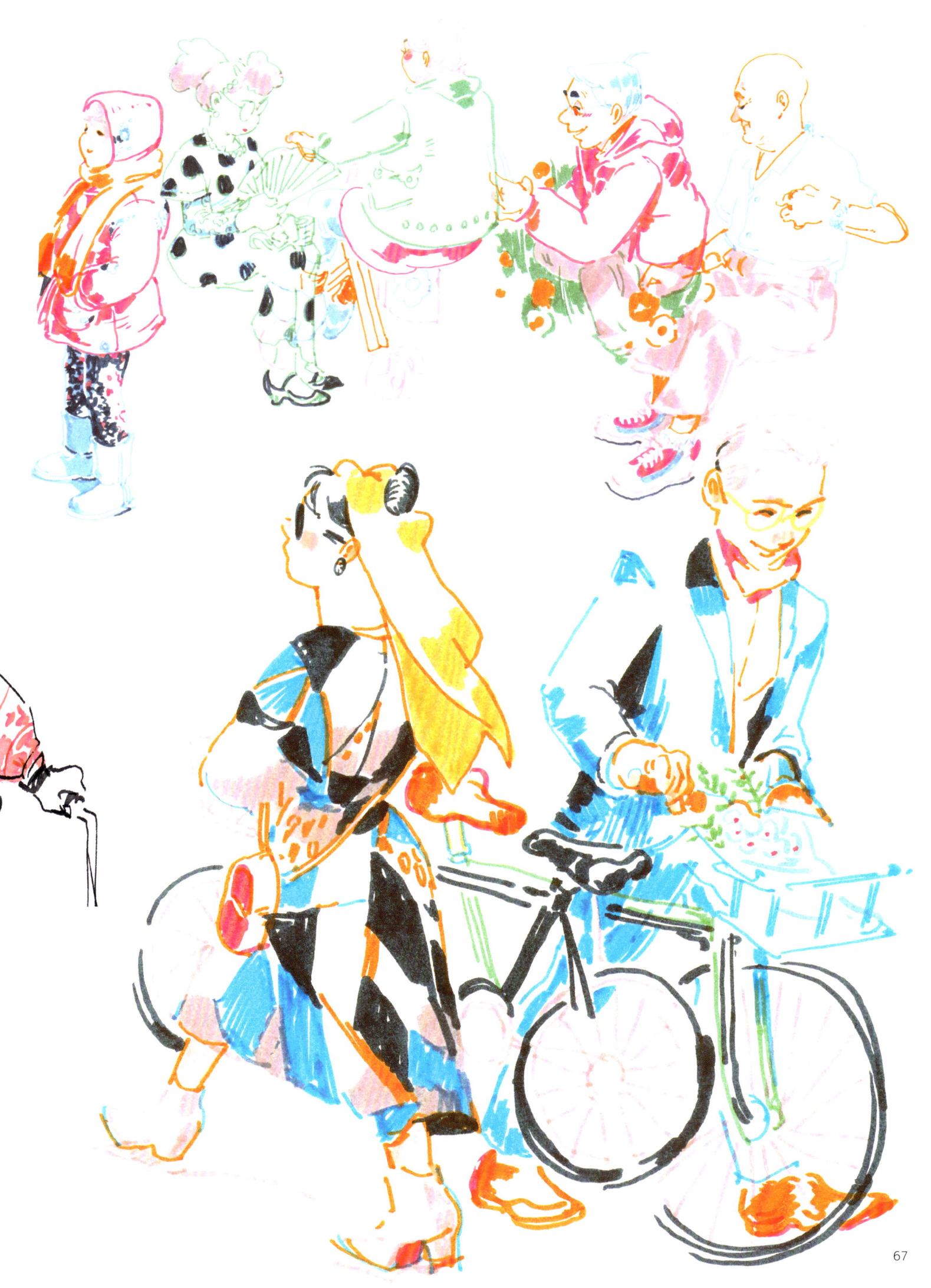

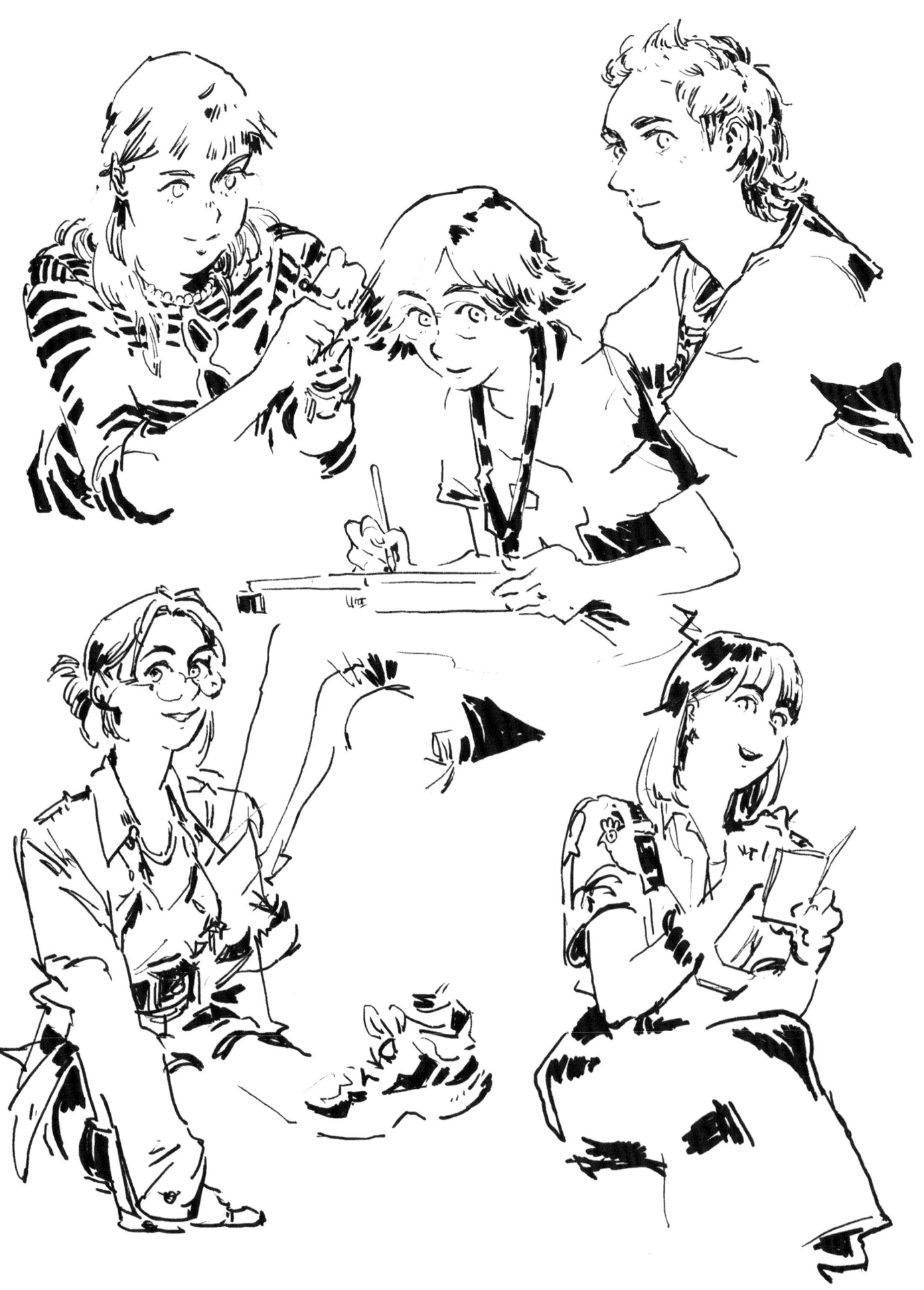

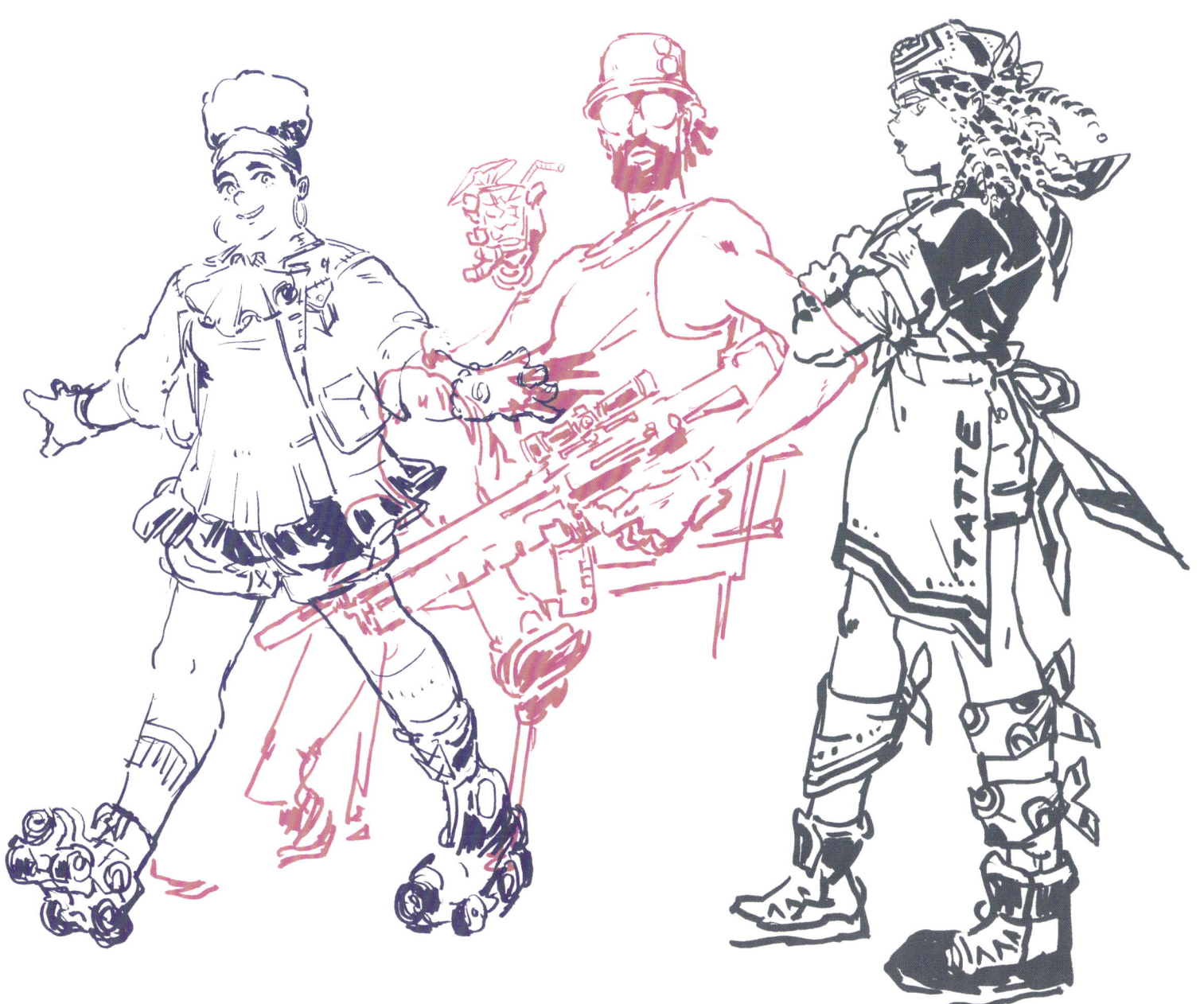

Doing conventions for the first time in 2021 was an eye-opening experience. Compared to films or games, where you work for many years before getting any feedback from a real audience, conventions were constant floods of live, relatively unfiltered reactions. It also helped that the fans were already super-biased.

Conventions were more gratifying than anything else I had ever done. I learned how much I thrived in an environment that utilized my entire being, not just my art skills. It was fun to talk to people, design a booth, create sales strategies, and travel and muscle my luggage around. I got to be a whole person, not just a cog in the machine. The first year we tried conventions, my wife and I mistakenly signed up for seven in a row, spanning from San Diego to Chicago to New York City to Boston. It was madness, but it was also the best time of my life.

I GOT TO BE A WHOLE PERSON, NOT JUST A COG IN THE MACHINE

STILL ROLLING

In my current life, I'm trying to juggle one too many dream jobs. My wife and I are new parents to our son, Conan, and I still work with Sabotage, still attend twenty or more conventions a year, and still want to work on returning to my original dream of making a manga. I've tried the latter several times in the past, only to fall short because I felt like I didn't have a story worth telling.

Knock on wood, I finally feel I have found that story within me. What you'll see in this book are definitely still works-in-progress and could change drastically, but as with everything I tackle in my life, I'm determined to not give up, to keep trying, and to give it my all.

When people ask me for advice on how to navigate the entertainment industry, I feel overwhelmed by how much I could share with them about my own experience. Much of my journey feels like it was either heartbreak or serendipity. It might sound silly or trivializing, but I wholeheartedly believe that life is like a giant gacha game.

> BUT LIFE ISN'T DETERMINED BY ONE ROLL

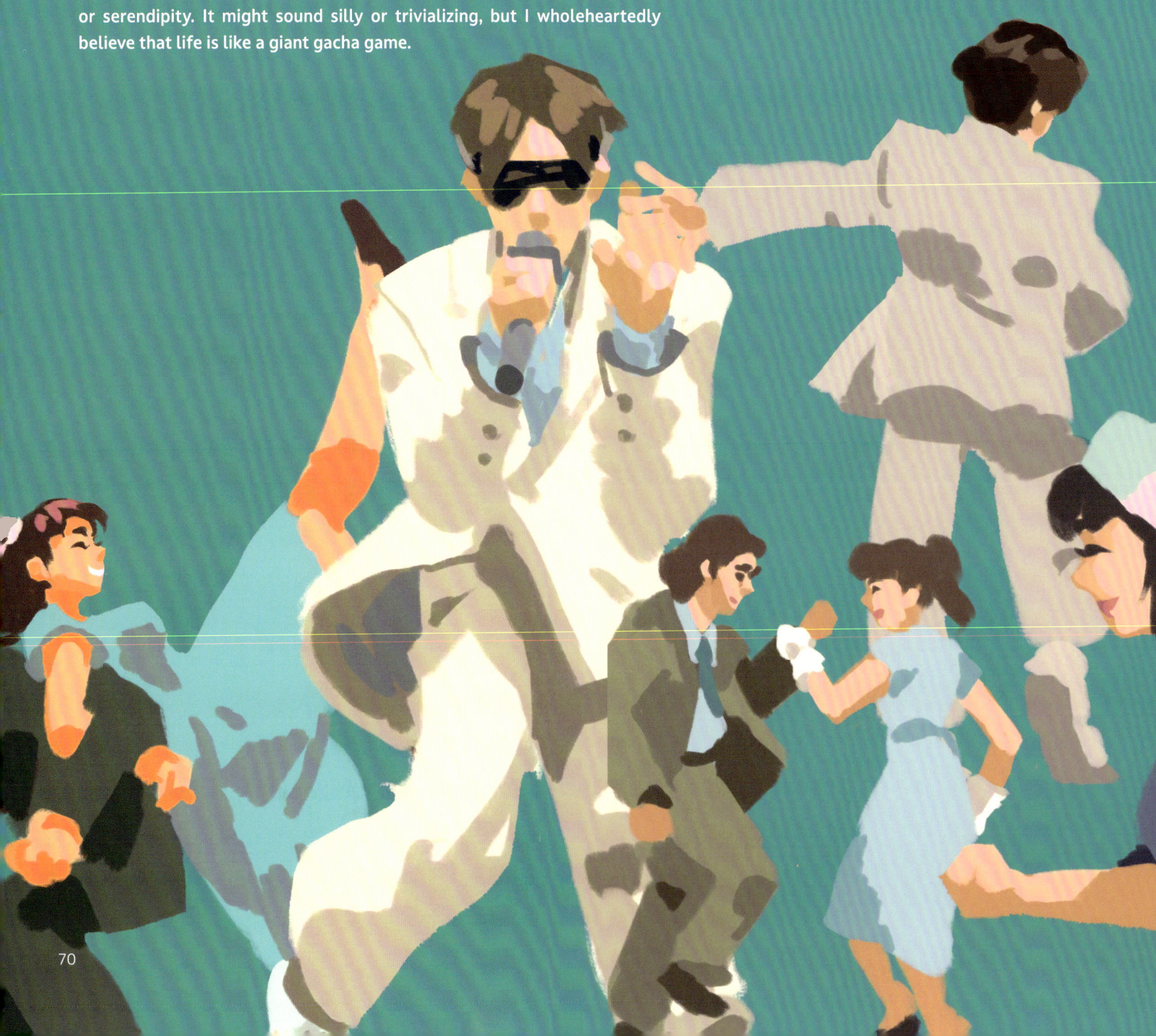

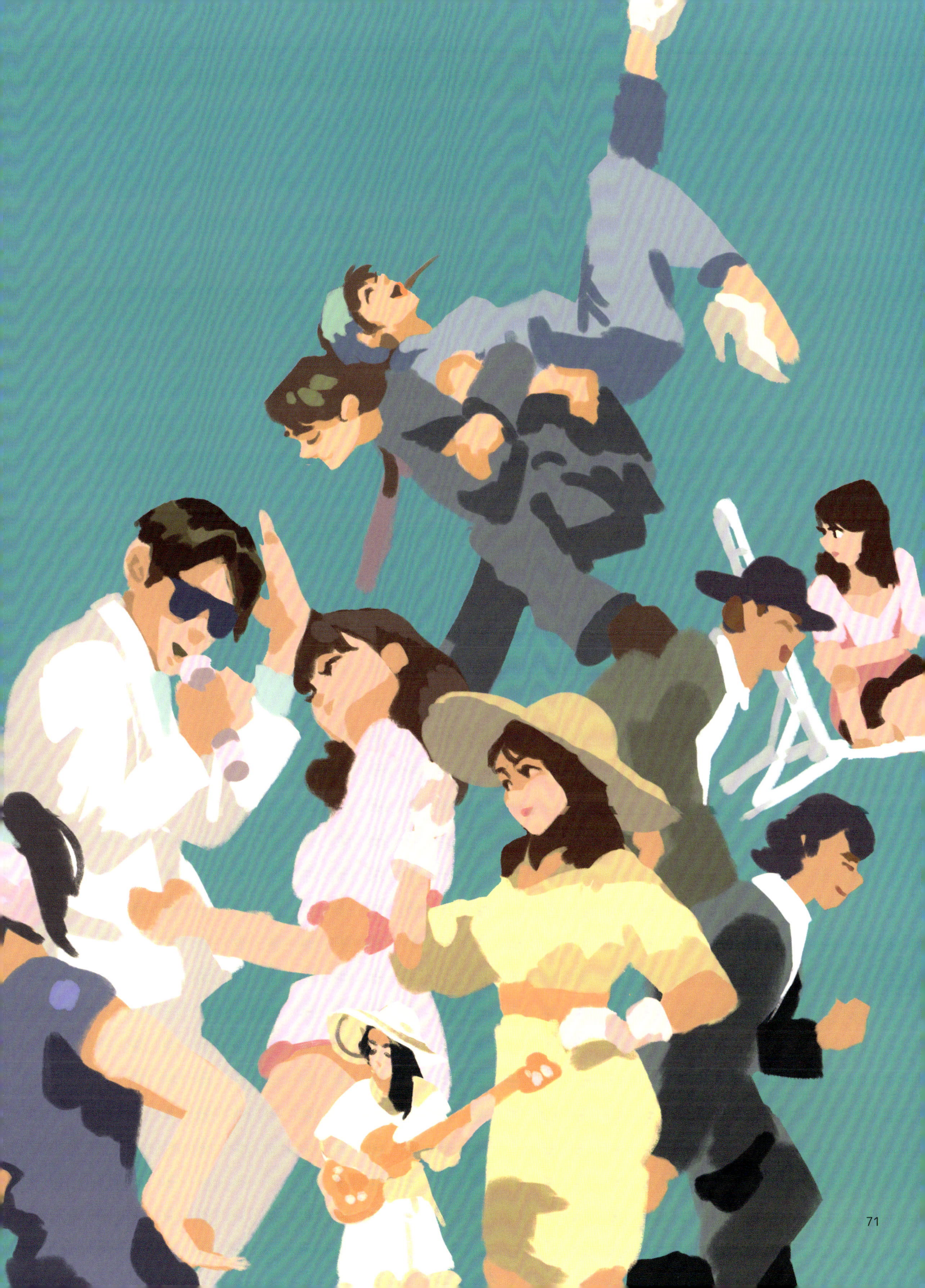

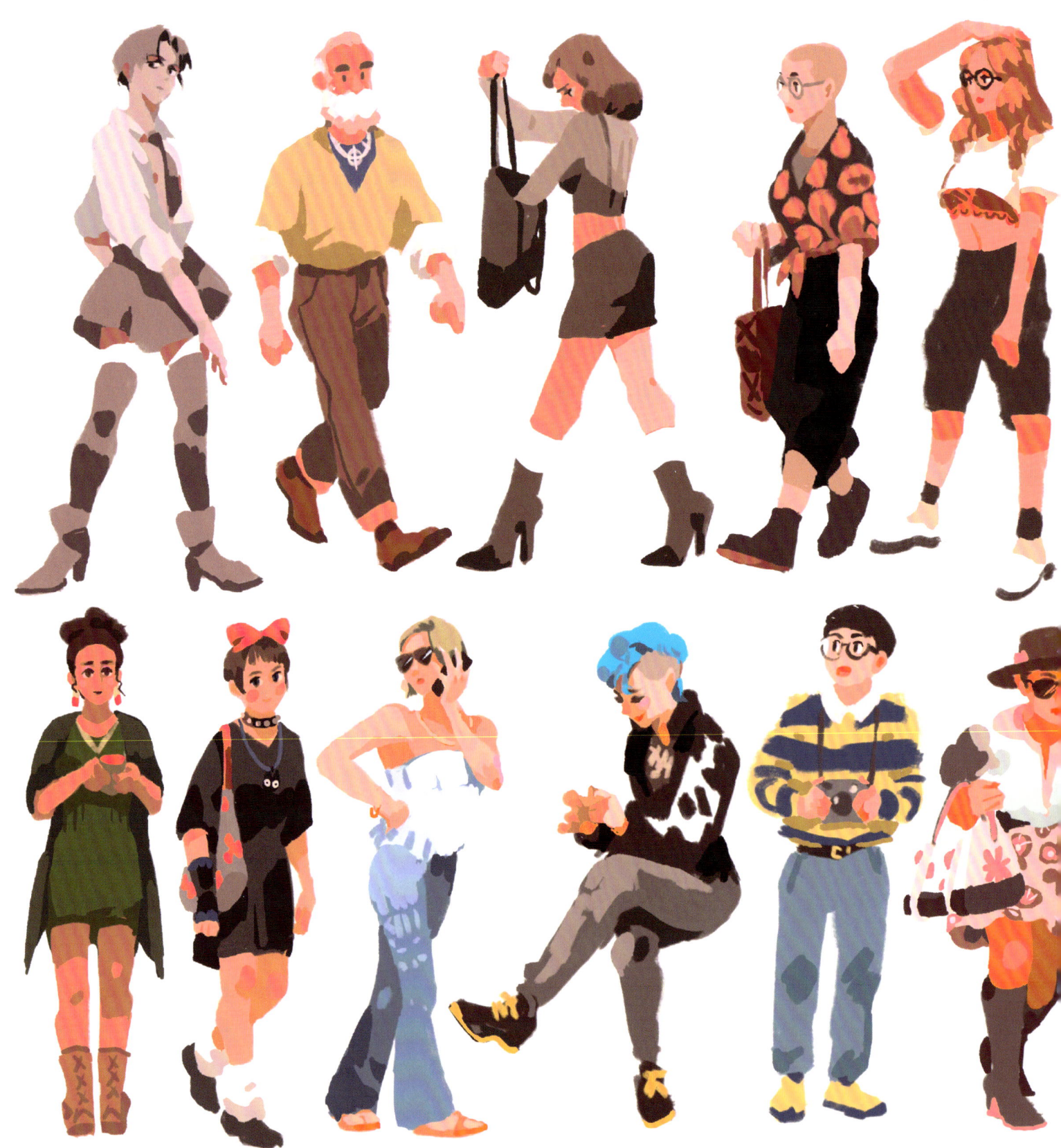

As much control as we think we have, there are enough random variables in life that it might as well be a dice game. Some people will get a five-star roll right off the bat and everyone else will jealously watch them pull ahead. Life may even seem to be going fine until you get stuck with a series of harsh one-star rolls. That's the sort of trauma that might scare someone into thinking they shouldn't try anymore. But life isn't determined by one roll. You might be born with phenomenal talent, but the amount of grit you have is another stat and requires a separate dice roll. Life is a series of unpredictable gambles like this, and I've come to realize that no single roll is make or break. Instead, it's about how often you can conjure enough strength to keep rolling and to keep giving it your all.

If the odds are 1/100 for success, then consider yourself lucky if you got it early, but be prepared to keep rolling at least a hundred more times. Don't be mad at yourself if it takes longer – those feelings won't help you. Just keep going, keep rolling. If you want to grow, if you want to chase your dreams, if you want to discover what you're capable of, you have to play the game.

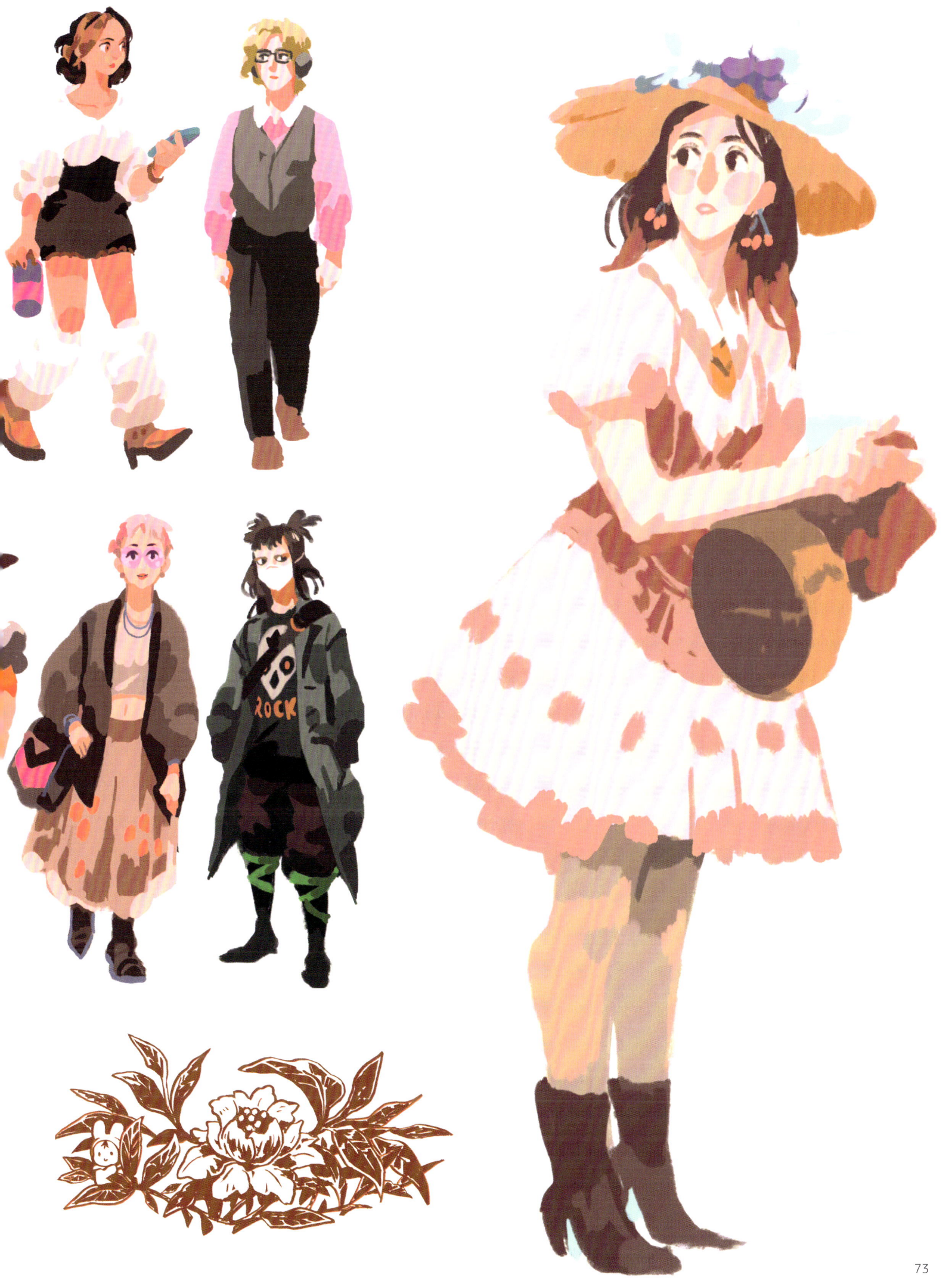

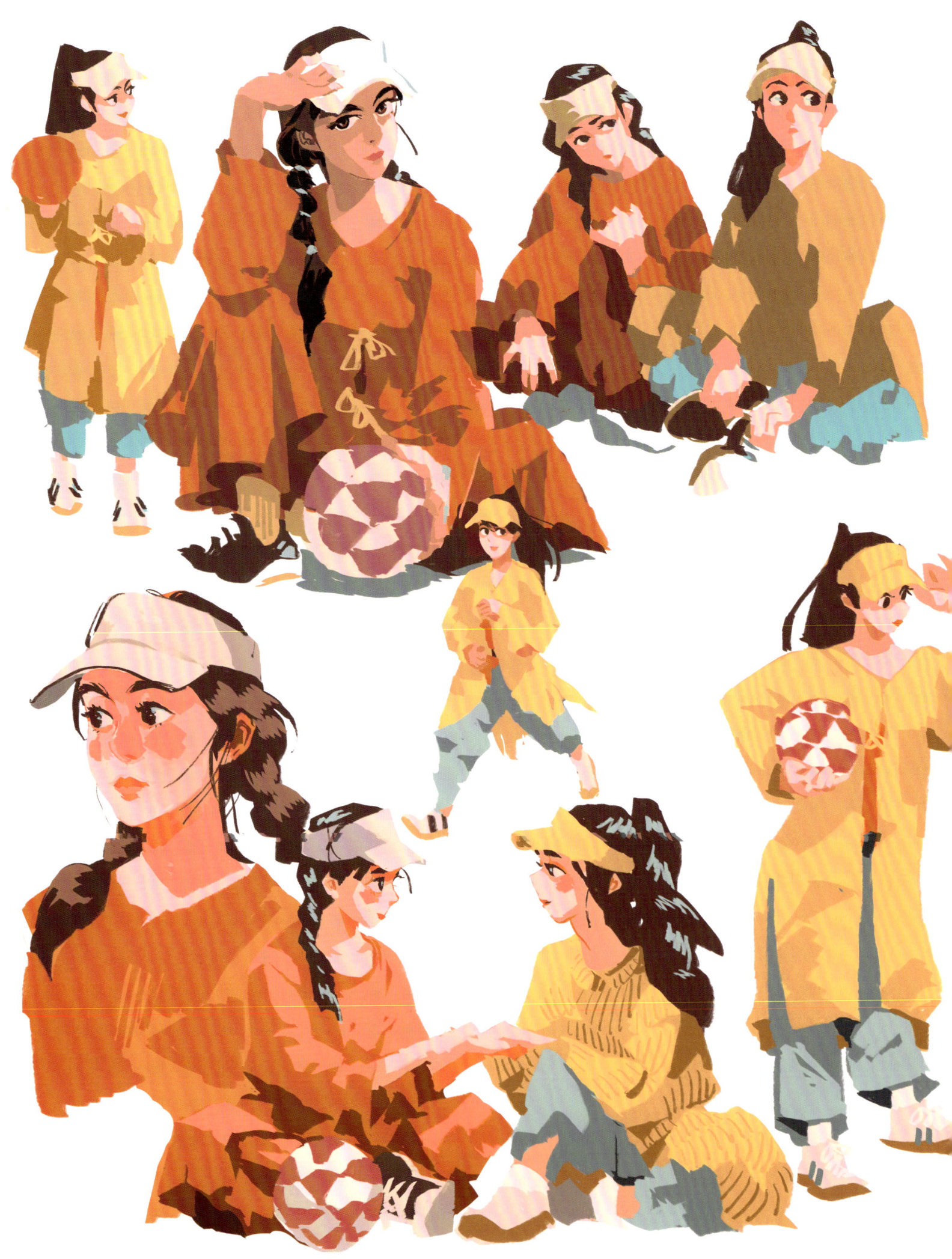

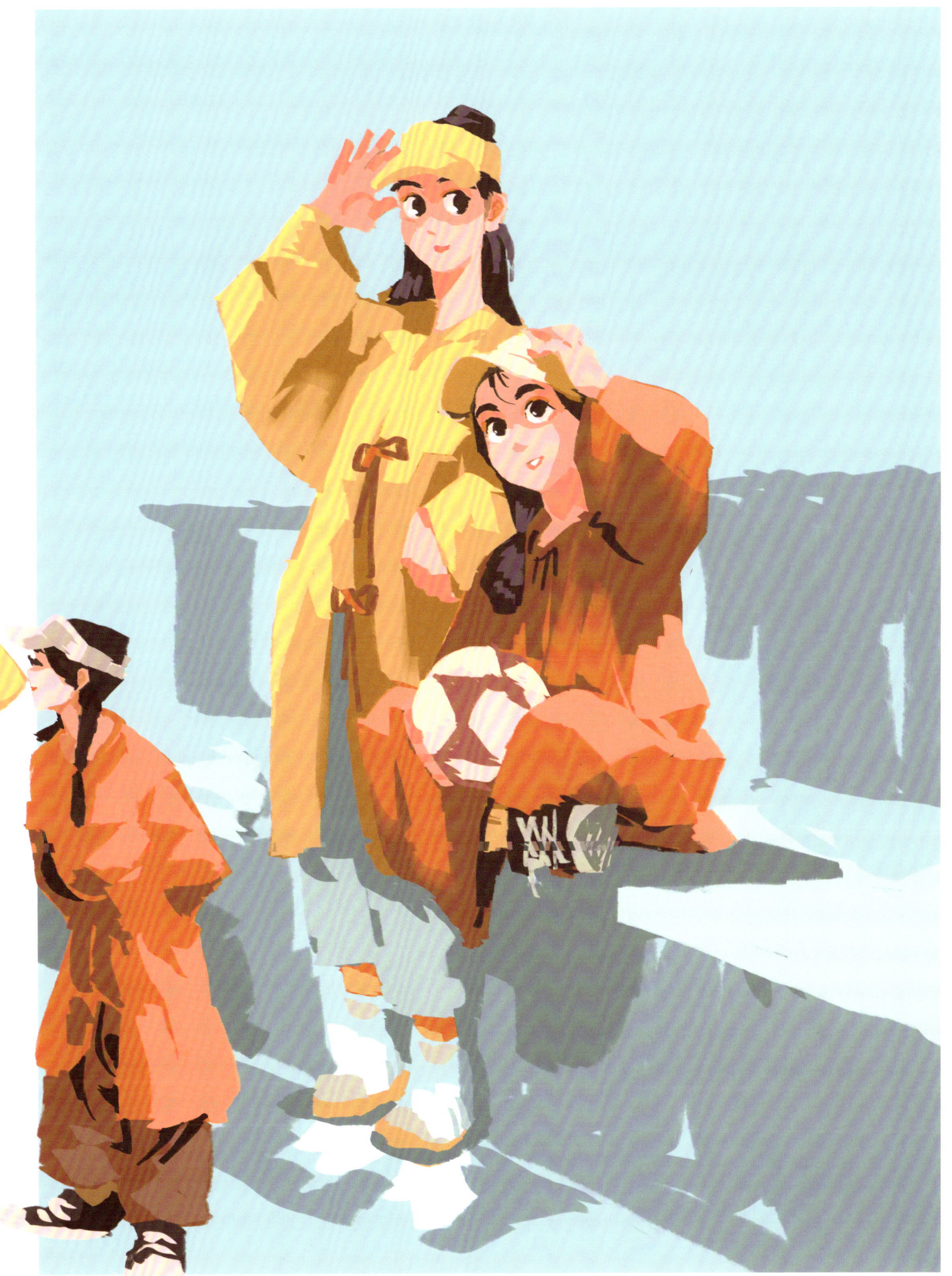

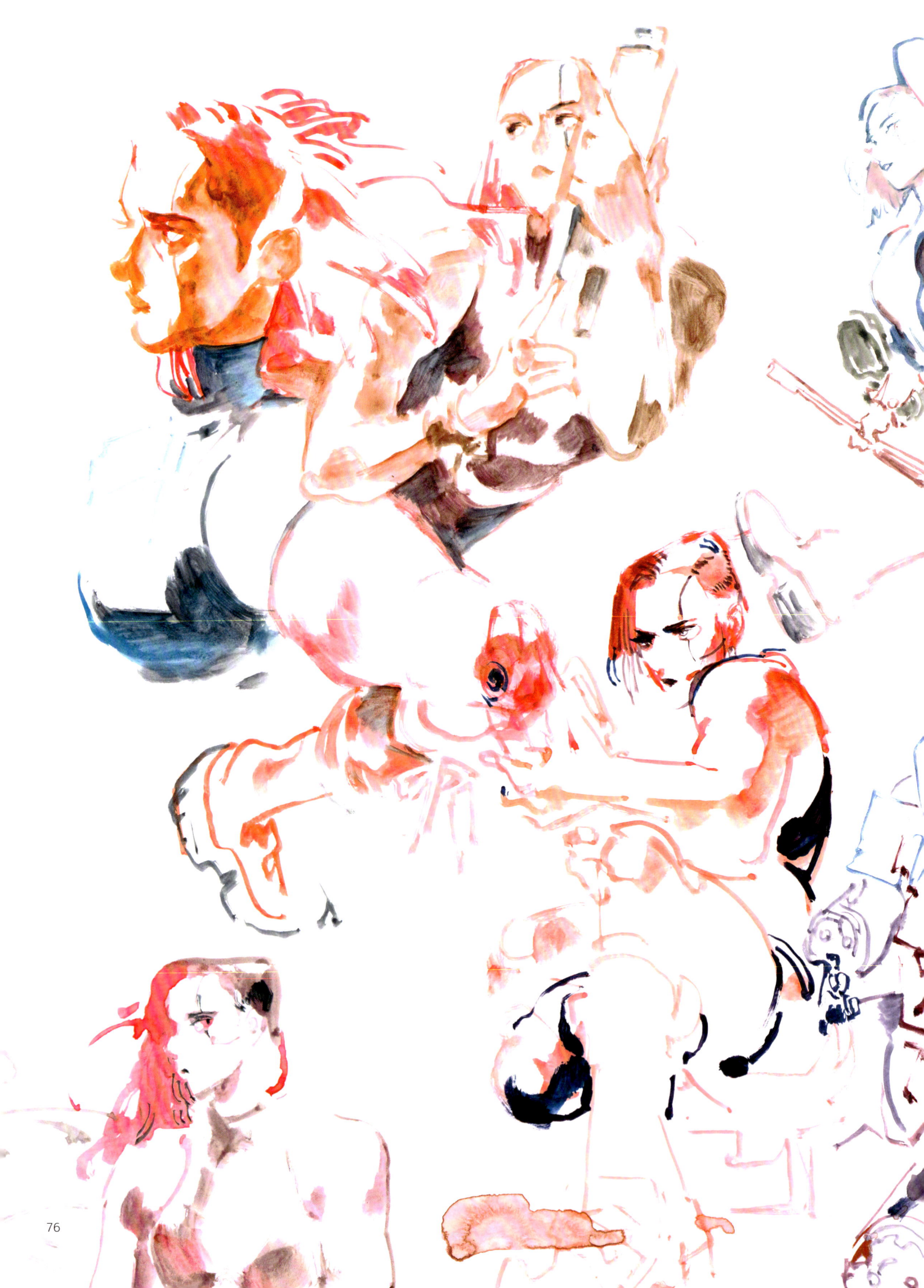

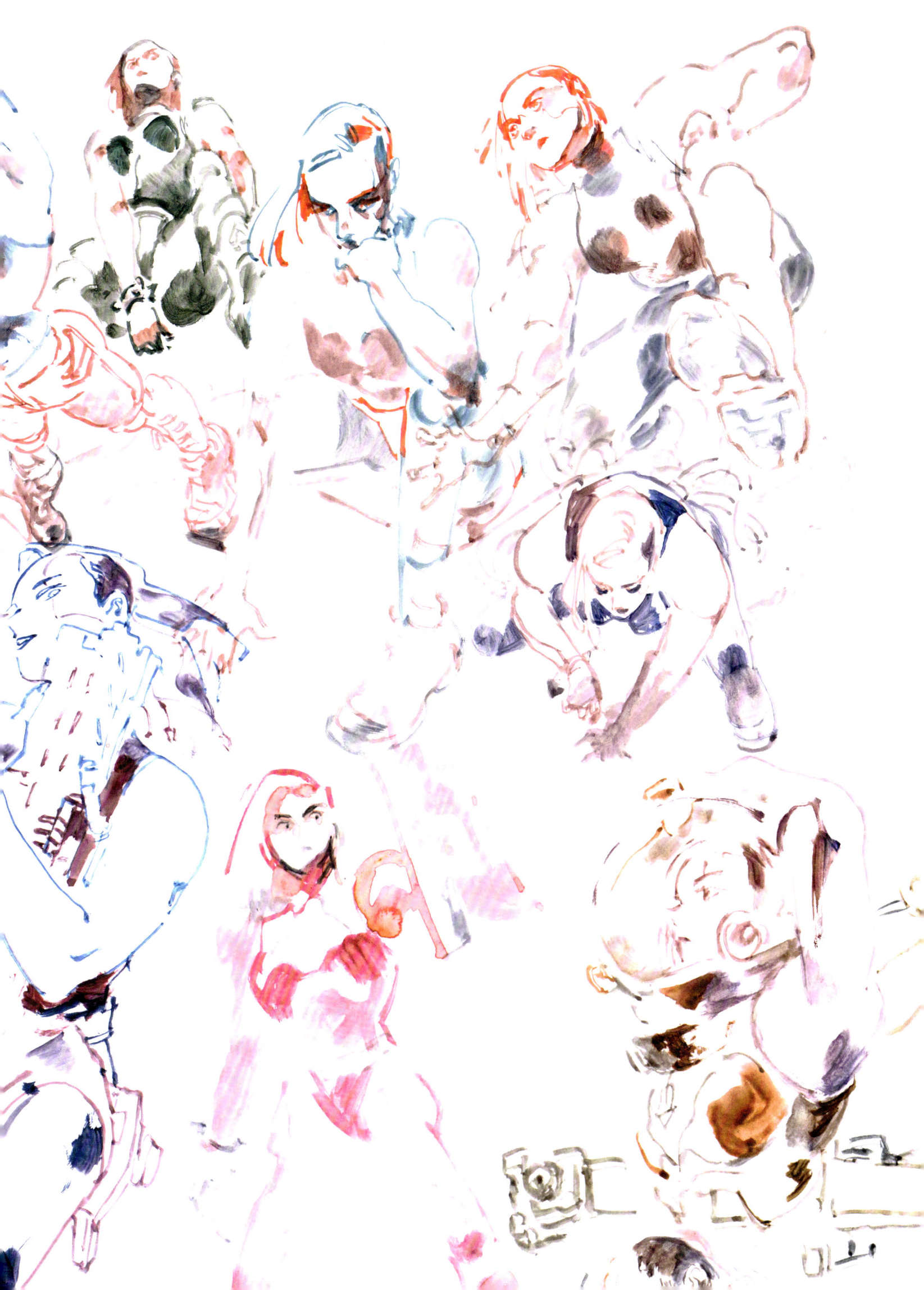

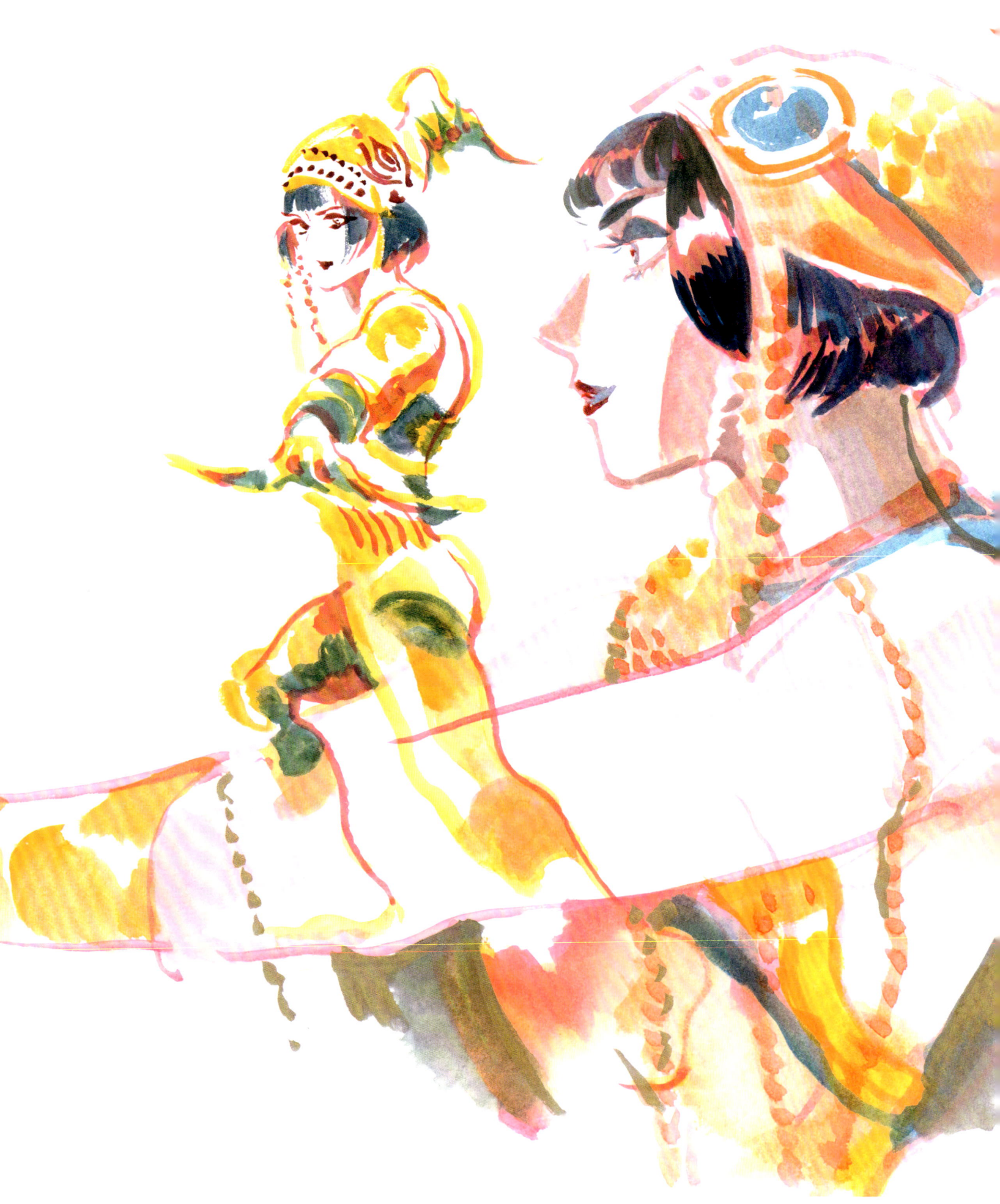

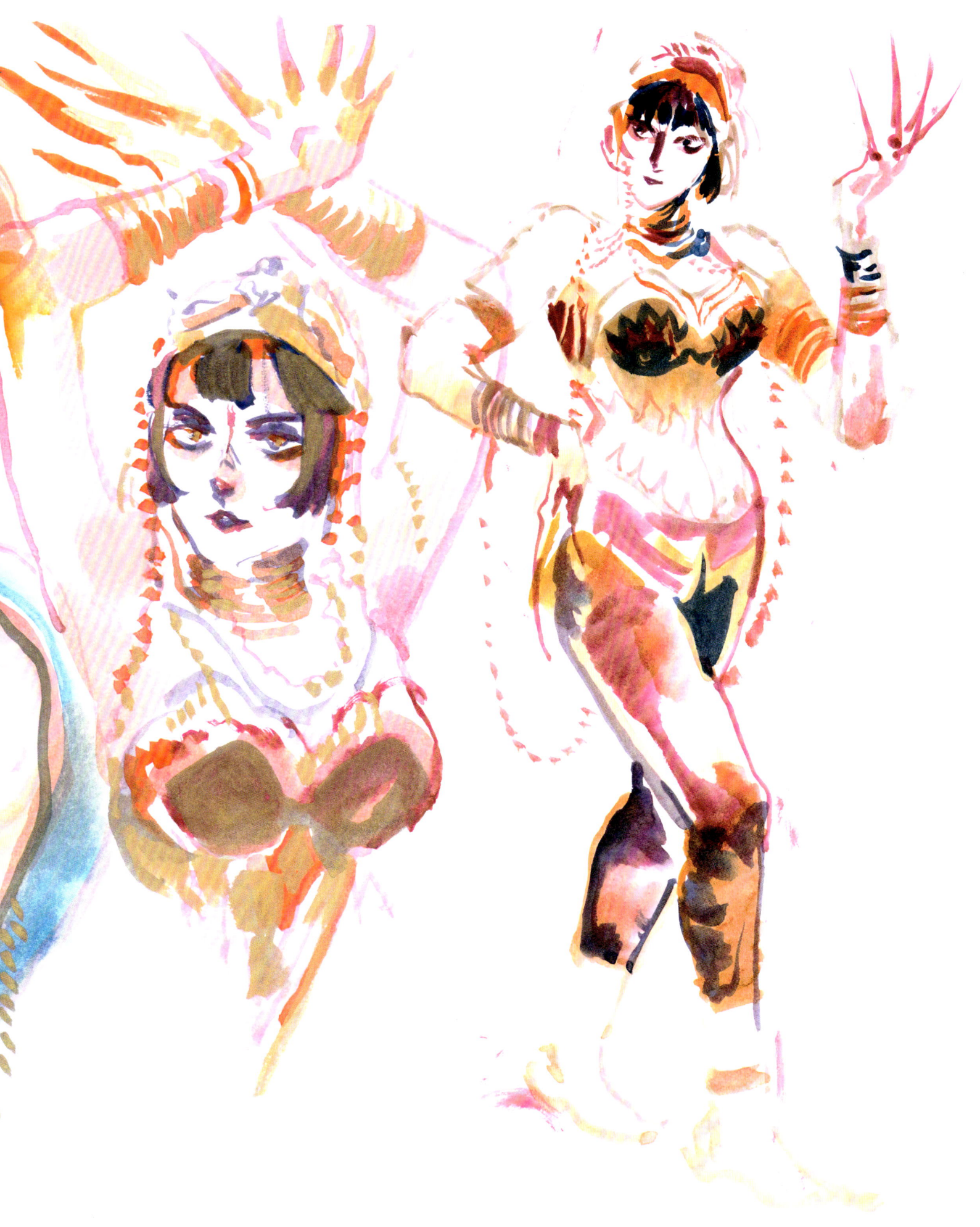

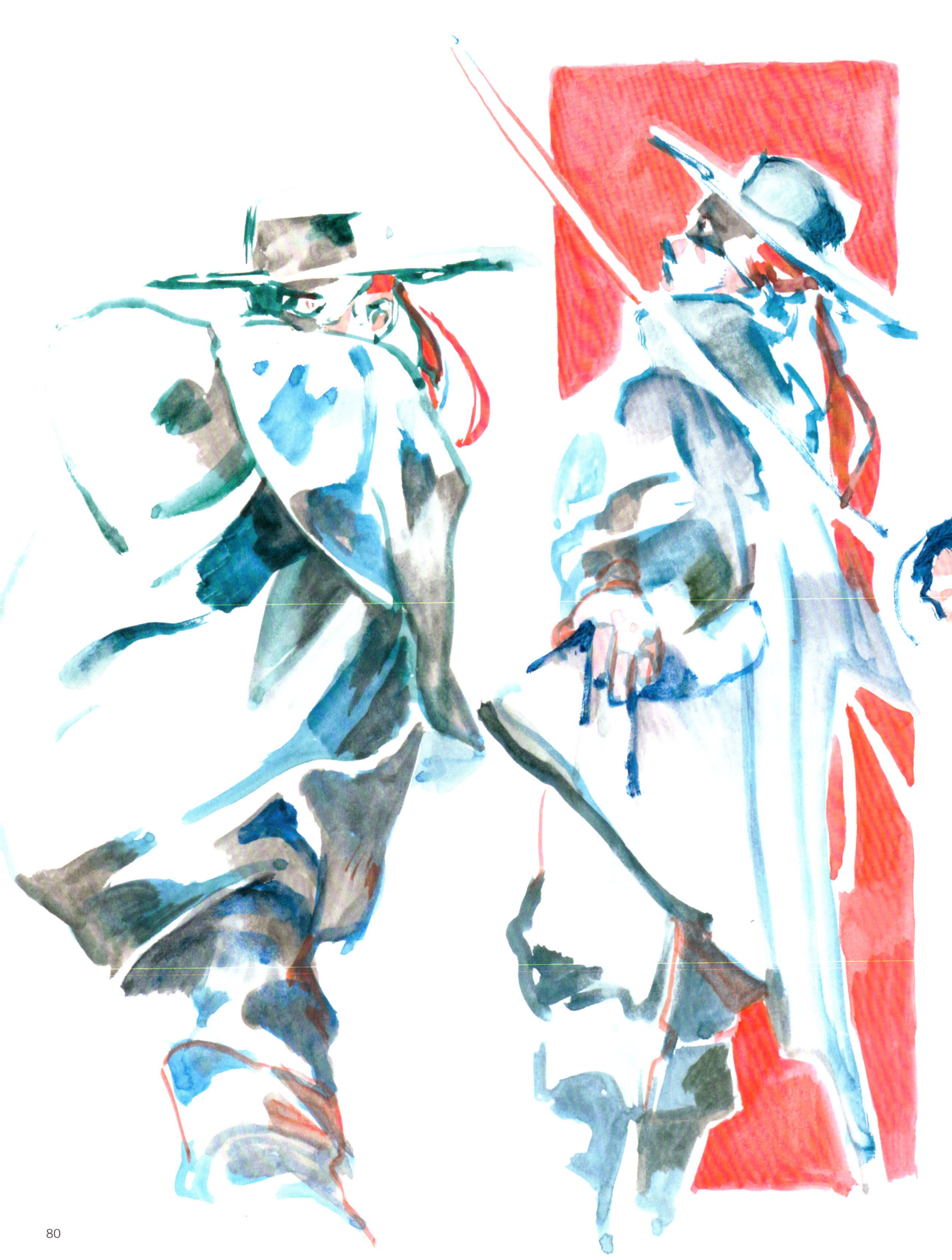

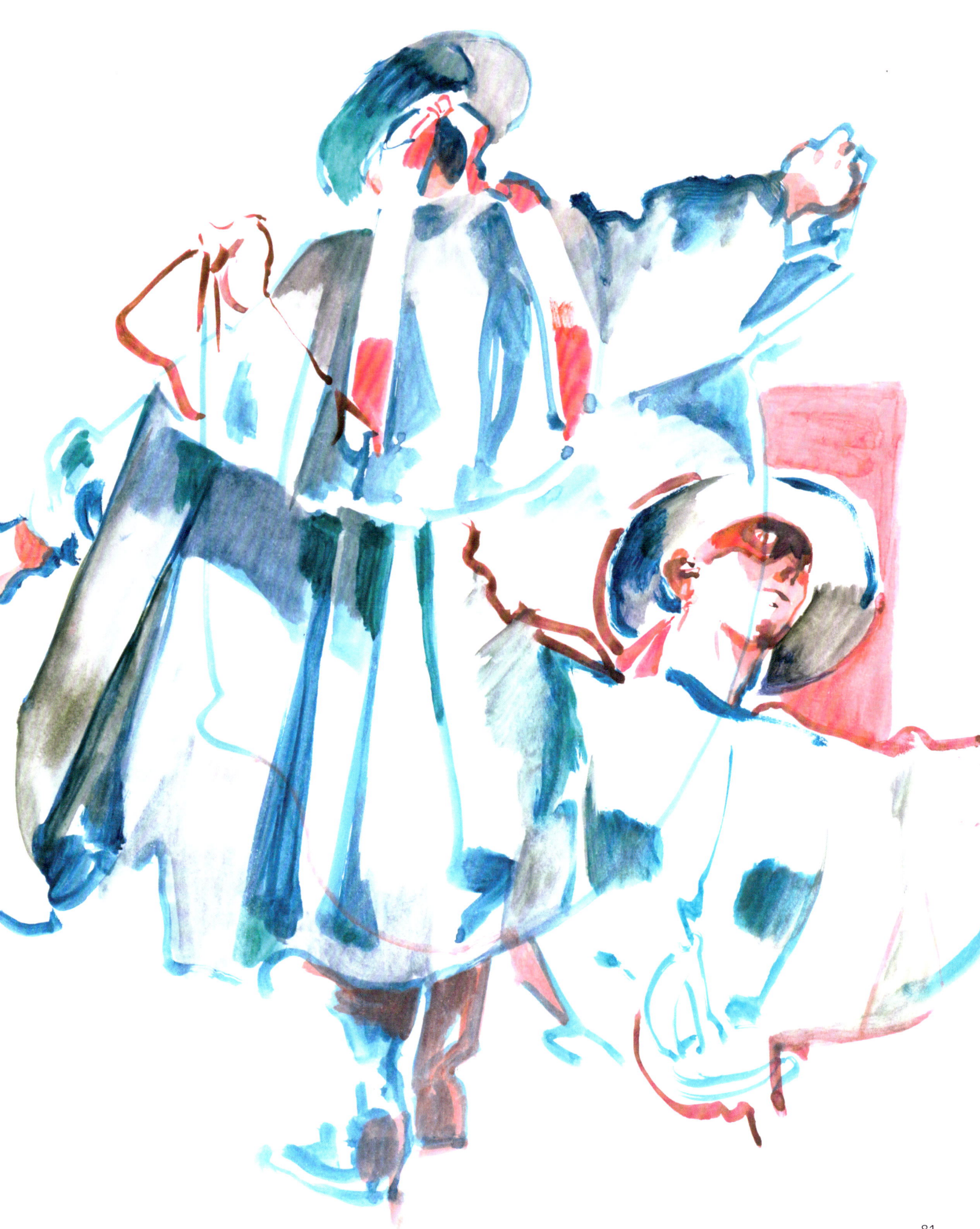

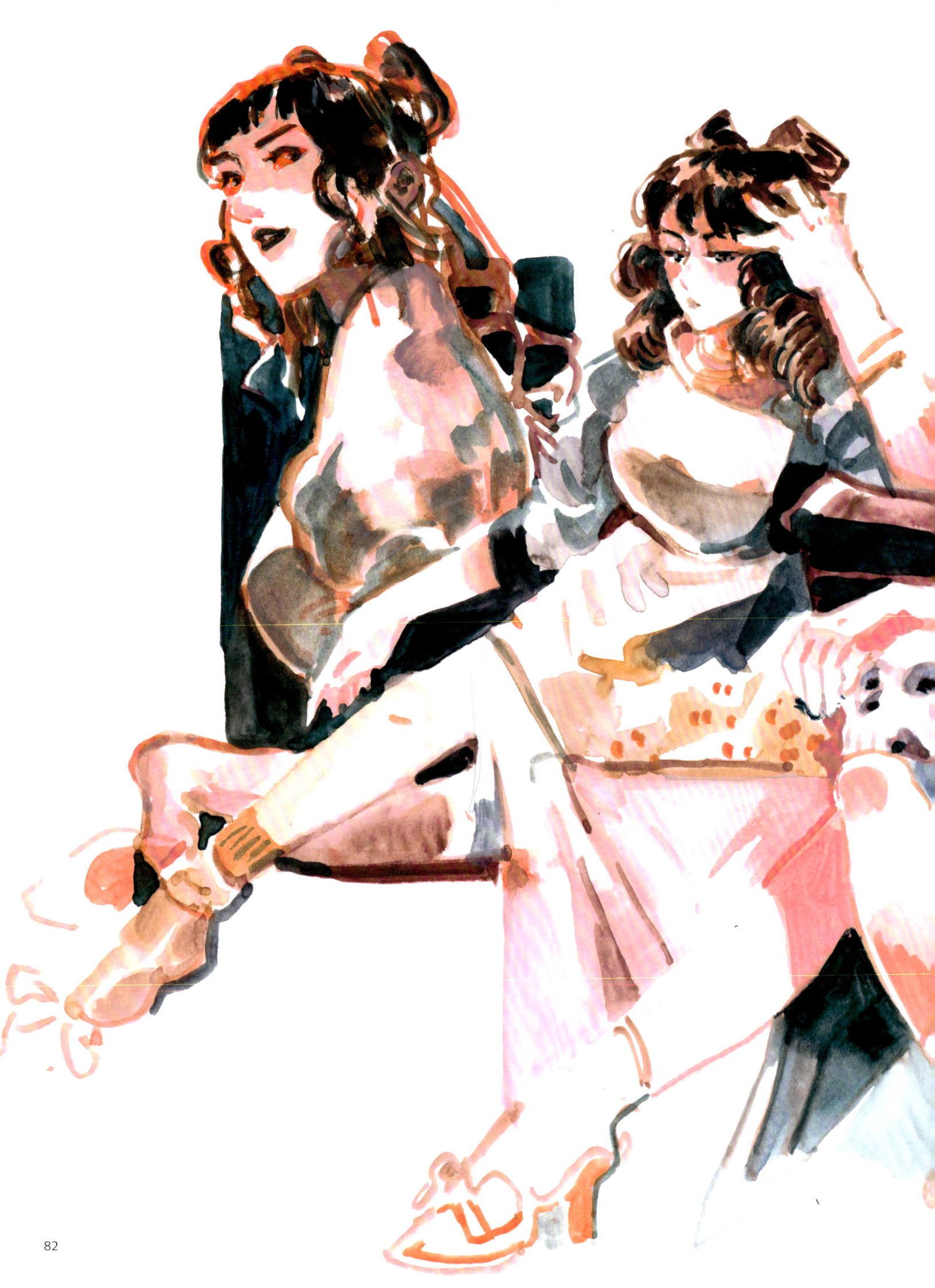

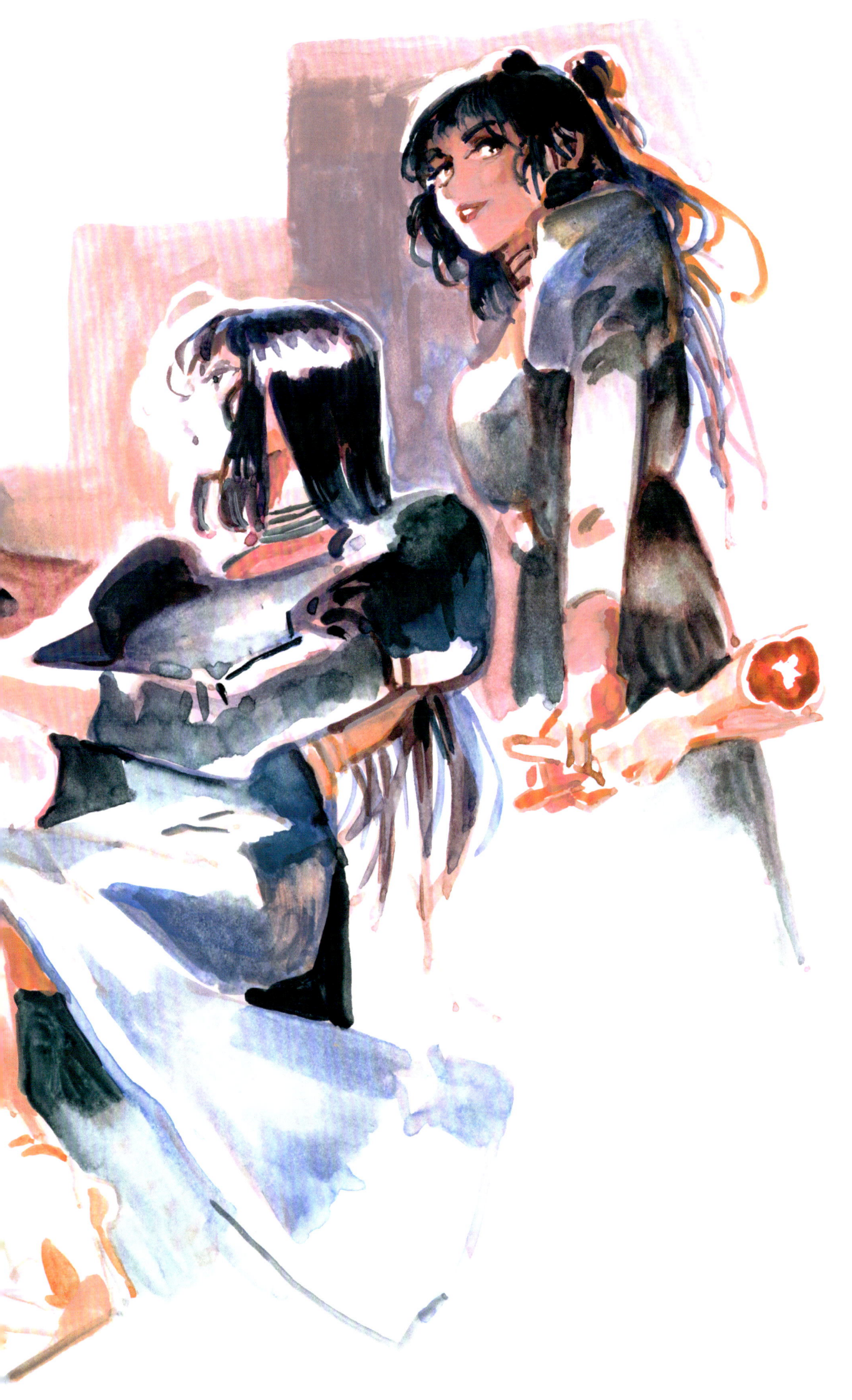

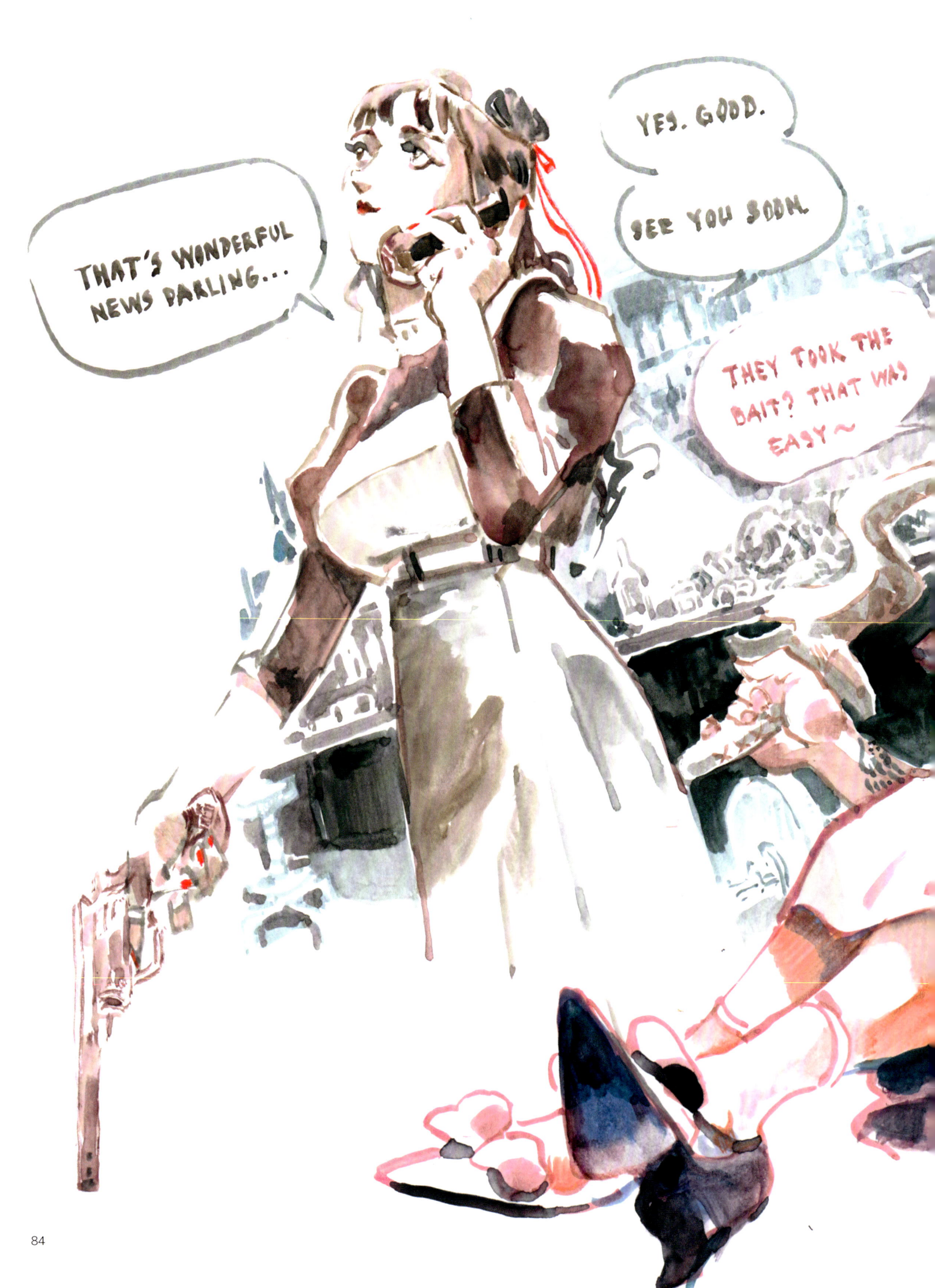

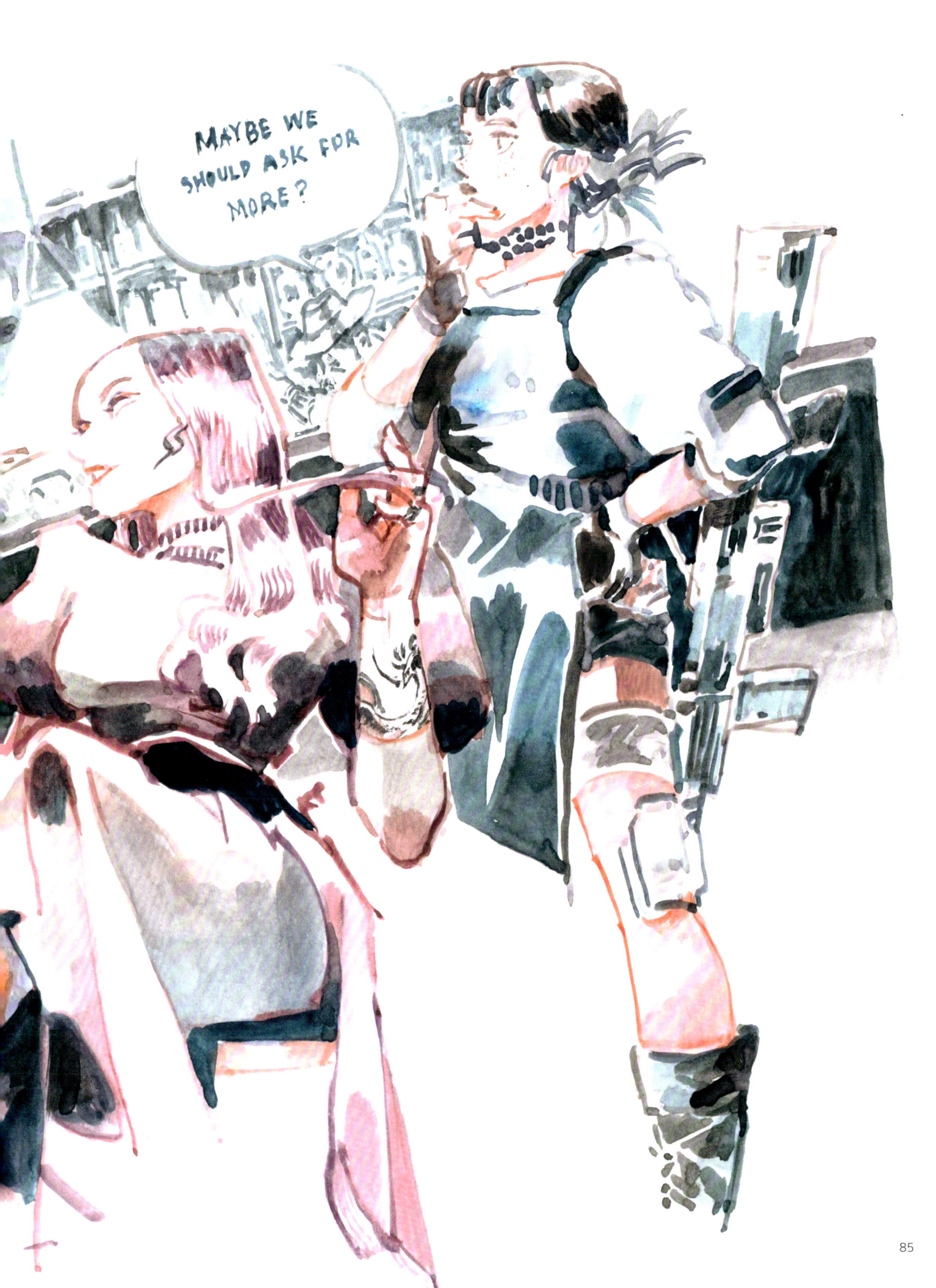

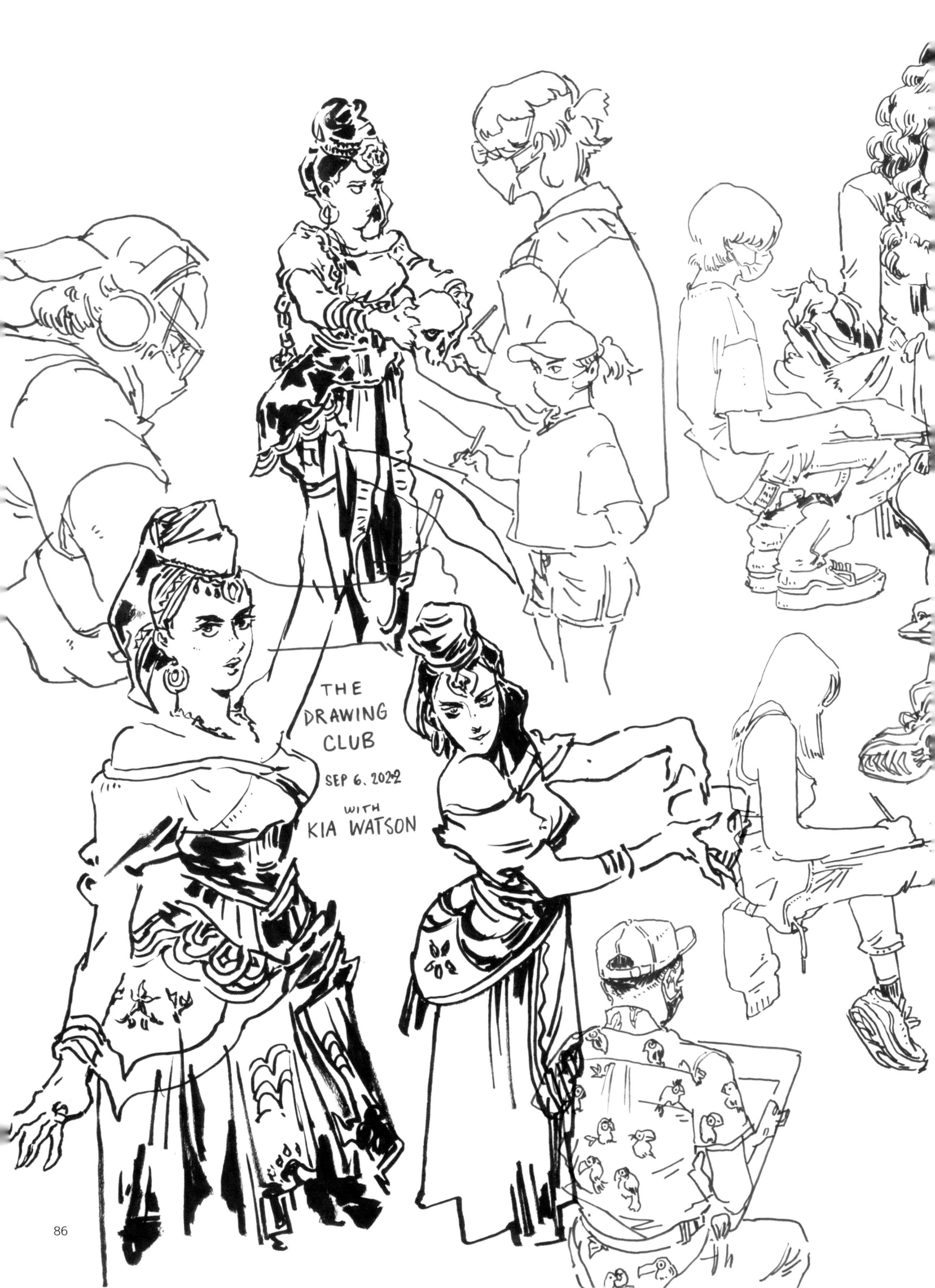

THE
DRAWING
CLUB

SEP 6, 2022

WITH
KIA WATSON

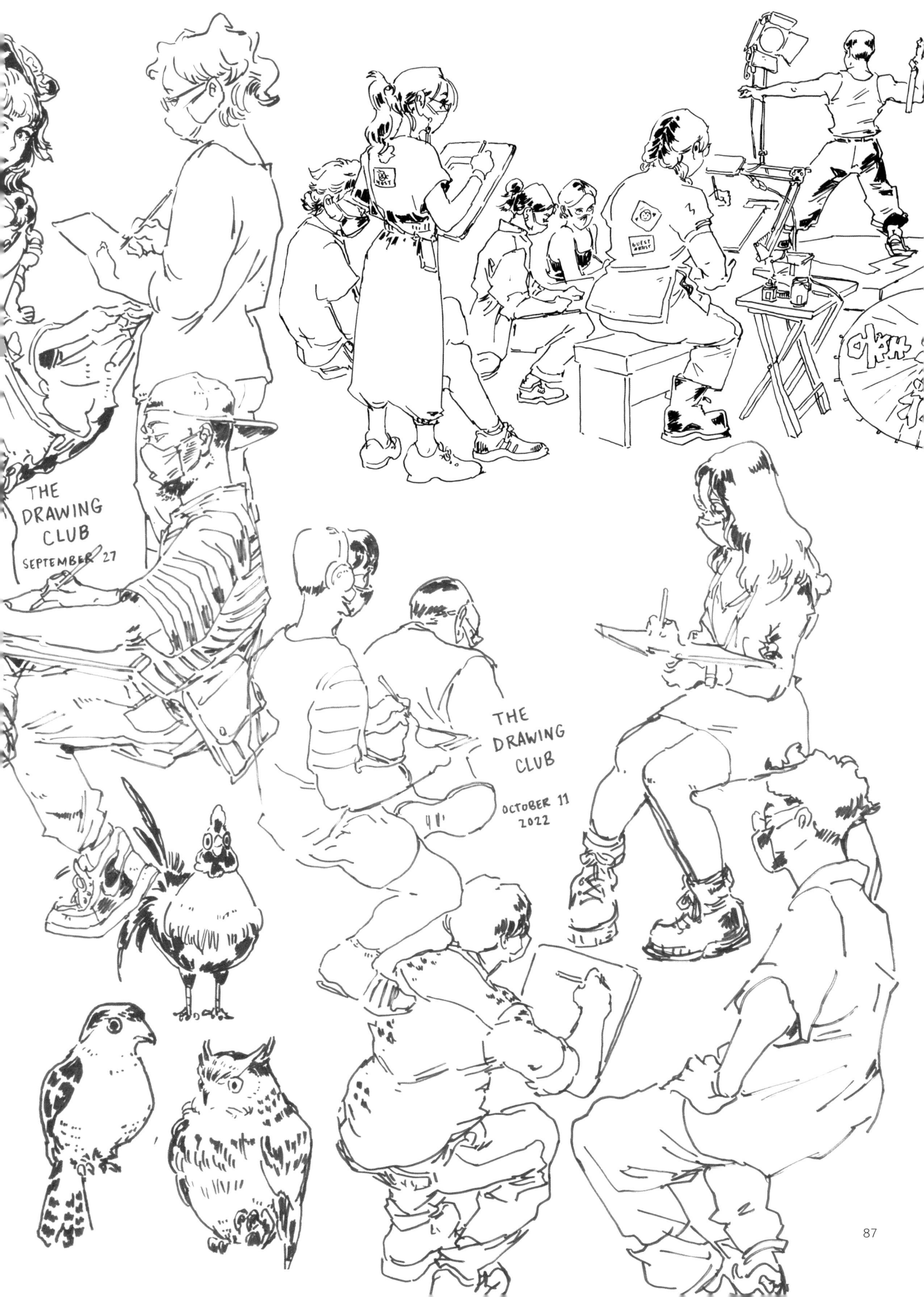

THE
DRAWING
CLUB
SEPTEMBER 27

THE
DRAWING
CLUB

OCTOBER 11
2022

CHARACTERS

捏人

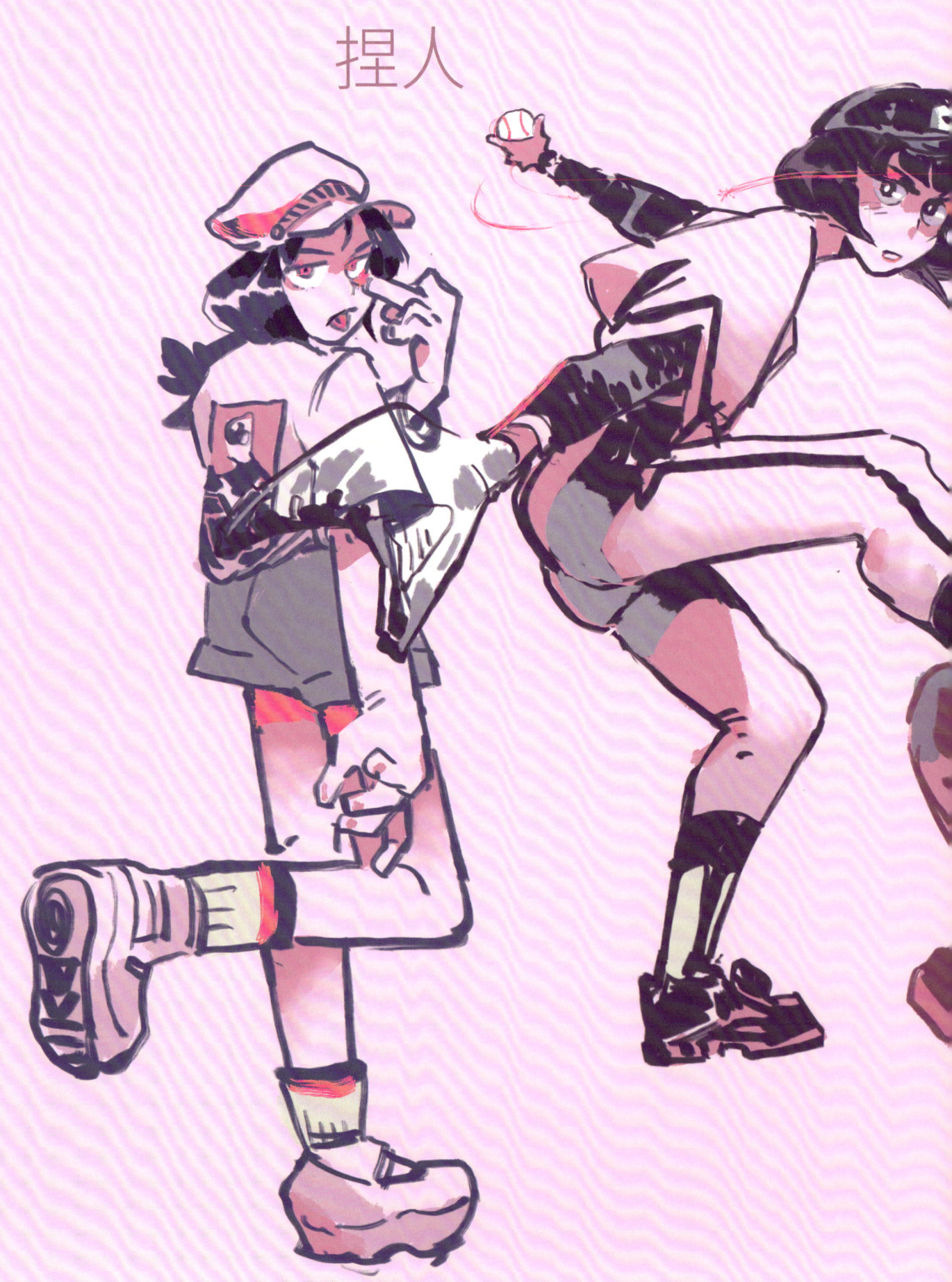

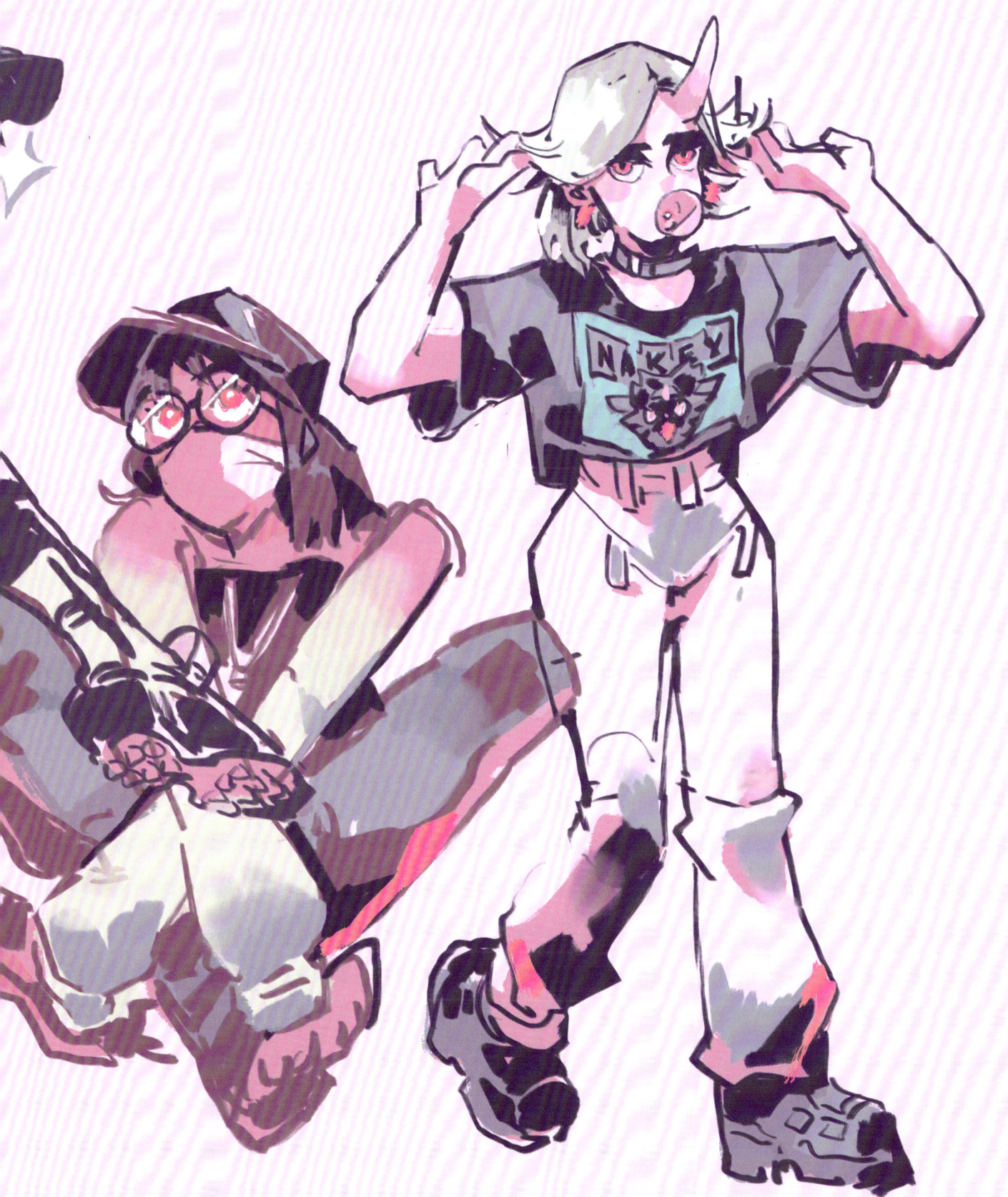

DEVELOPING ARTISTIC SKILLS & TECHNIQUES

A FILM-MAKER'S APPROACH TO DRAWING

Although I'm self-taught in the sense that I didn't go to art school, I'm a firm believer that each of the winding roads I've been down in my career has contributed a lot to my artistic abilities.

I took a long pause from art during my early twenties to focus on film, but doing so changed the way I thought about images at large. Actually, it may have had the biggest impact on how I approached (and still approach) my work compared to most artists. To put it simply, I construct a drawing in the same way that I would set up a shot for a film.

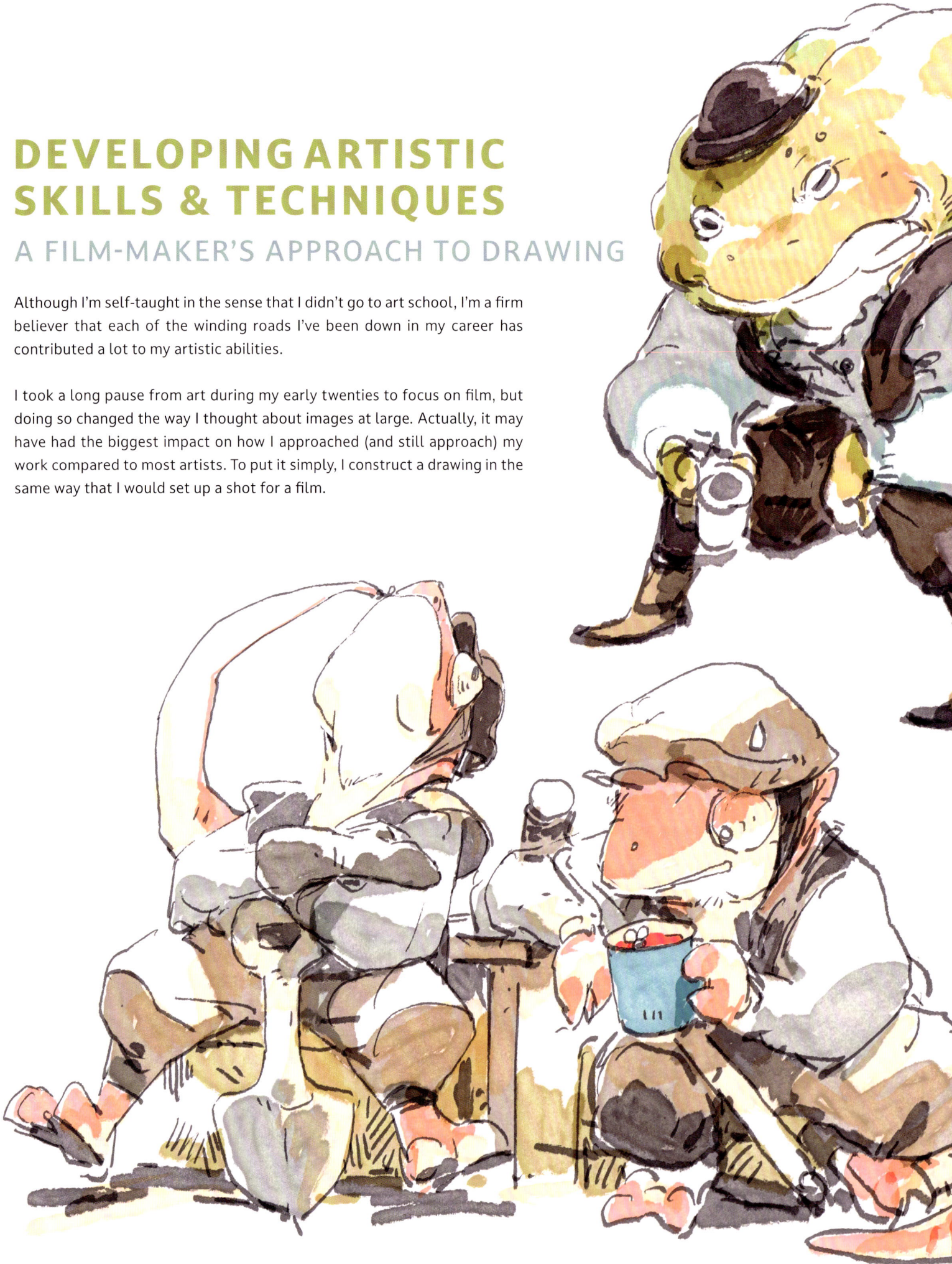

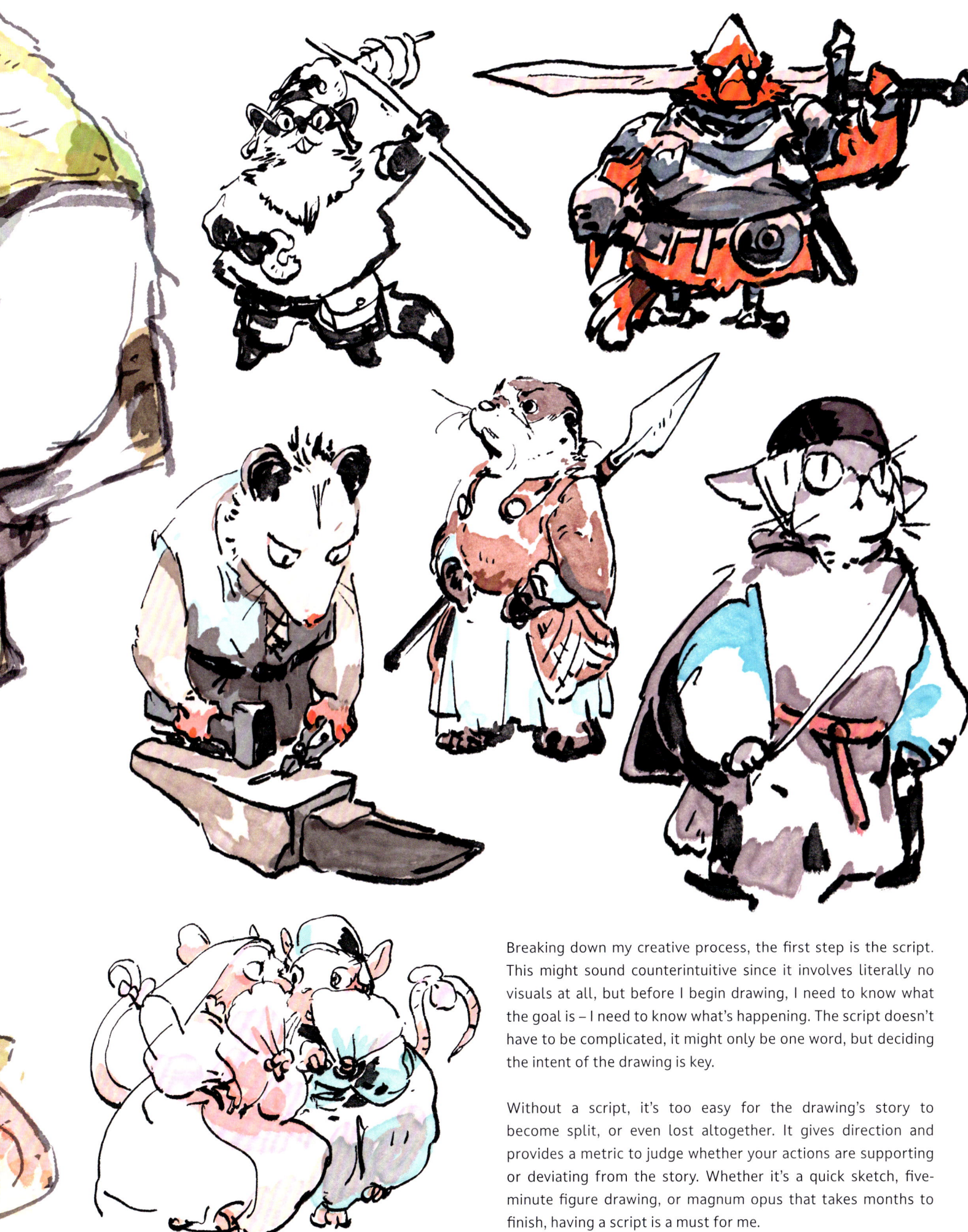

Breaking down my creative process, the first step is the script. This might sound counterintuitive since it involves literally no visuals at all, but before I begin drawing, I need to know what the goal is – I need to know what's happening. The script doesn't have to be complicated, it might only be one word, but deciding the intent of the drawing is key.

Without a script, it's too easy for the drawing's story to become split, or even lost altogether. It gives direction and provides a metric to judge whether your actions are supporting or deviating from the story. Whether it's a quick sketch, five-minute figure drawing, or magnum opus that takes months to finish, having a script is a must for me.

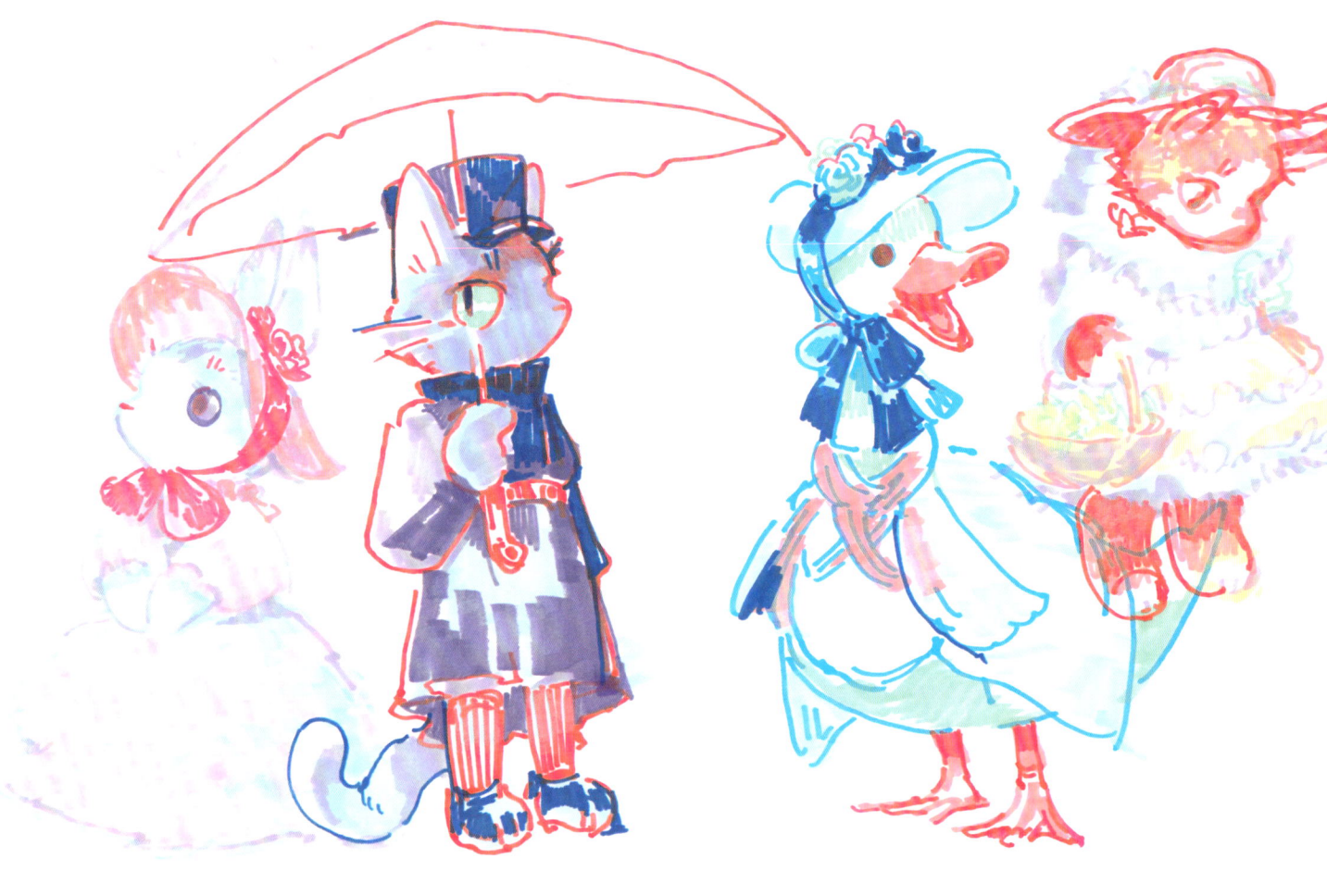

After the script is decided, the camera angle comes next. I get a ton of questions about how I choose my compositions, and the answer is that the 'script' tells me what's supposed to happen, and knowing that helps me decide the best viewing angle to see that action unfold.

My goal is to frame the action so that it's easy to understand. If the viewer doesn't know what's happening, then they've missed the whole point. In practical terms, this means I want a clear view of the main actor's face and any relevant body part that's involved in the key action. Basically, I want to see what my

character is doing and how they feel about it. Positioning them into the scene so that those things are obvious is what this step is all about.

When it comes to drawing the characters themselves – that's acting. The ability to draw the character with a convincing pose or emotive expression is dependent on how well you know the subject objectively, and if you can connect with their emotional state. This is a step that requires an intimate knowledge of the subject matter and takes years of study to master. I won't even try to touch on a subject that huge here, but I'll volunteer that

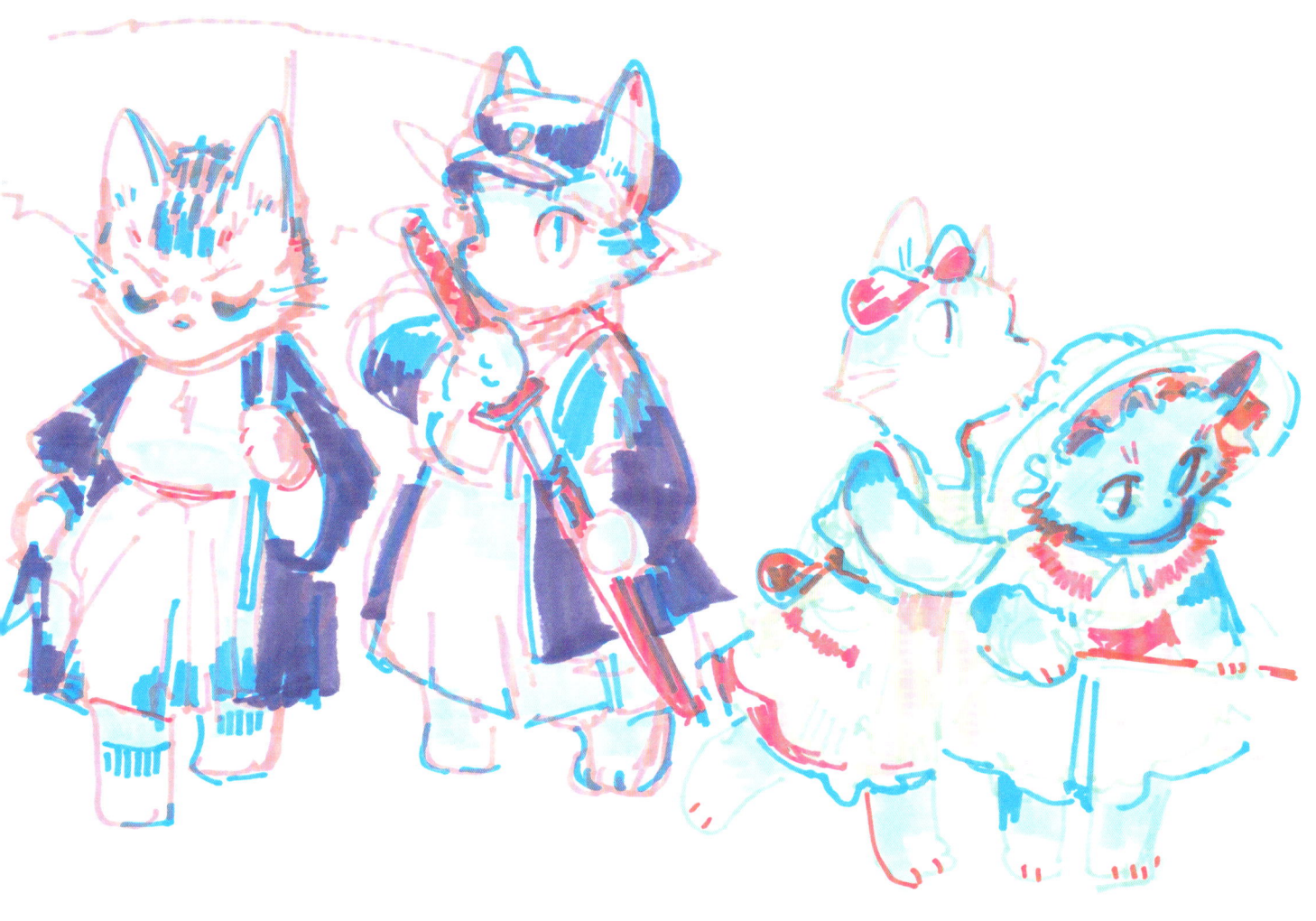

THE MOST BEAUTIFUL IMAGE MEANS NOTHING IF THE VIEWER CAN'T CONNECT WITH IT

in my experience, it's surprising how important the emotional component can be. The most technically accurate or beautiful image means nothing if the viewer can't connect with it.

Directing the viewer's eye is my next consideration, and I like to think of that as the role played by supporting actors, set design, special effects, or anything else that helps add specificity to the story. The actor might feel a certain way, but if their surroundings provide more information to help the viewer understand *why*, it can give the image a lot more impact.

For me, adding these components feels like piecing together a giant puzzle. I think about how the viewer's eye will be affected by the poses and emotion of the actors, and where it might go afterwards as a natural consequence of those factors. It almost feels like physics; the way the viewer's eye can be manipulated to move a certain way by the flow of line work.

I use my intuition to follow where the viewer might look next so that I can put something meaningful there; something that adds depth to support the main concept. It feels like I'm hiding a little easter egg for someone to discover.

GAME DEV ART SCHOOL

From a more technical perspective, the time I spent developing *Aegis Defenders* helped me a ton when it came to my foundations. Though I spent an equal amount of time balancing the roles of game director, designer, producer, and writer, I did also draw a lot. I was the only artist after all – a role that I viewed at the time as a lucky cost-saving measure for the game's budget. However, as a pixel-art game, the sort of artistic skills it utilized didn't concern things like draughtsmanship, proportion, anatomy, or anything like that.

Instead, pixel art is more about the readability of the silhouette through colour and posing. As was the case with film, this is a product meant to prioritize ease of communication. Art in games exists first and foremost to serve a practical purpose. Pixel art taught me the importance of readability.

In terms of the characters, it taught me the importance of key frames; how I could communicate a frame of action clearly to a viewer with one piece of artwork.

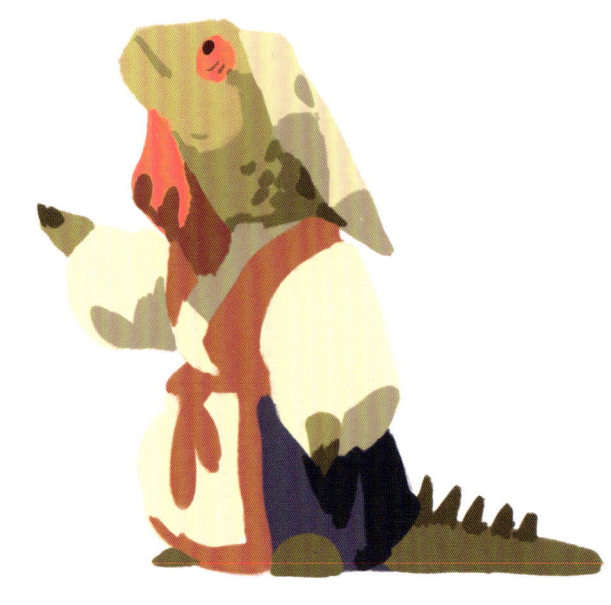

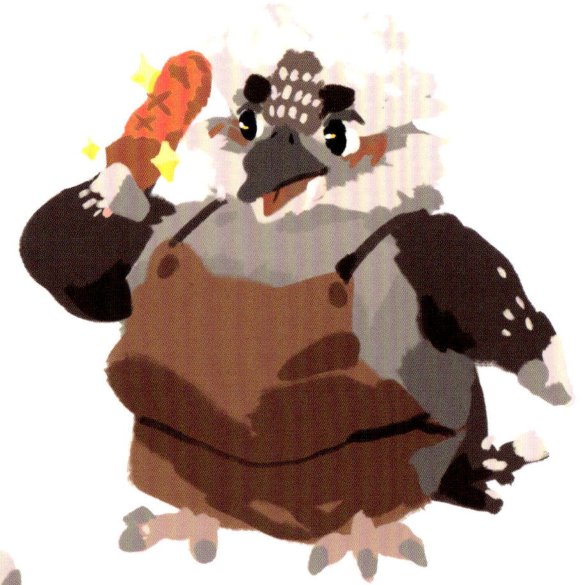

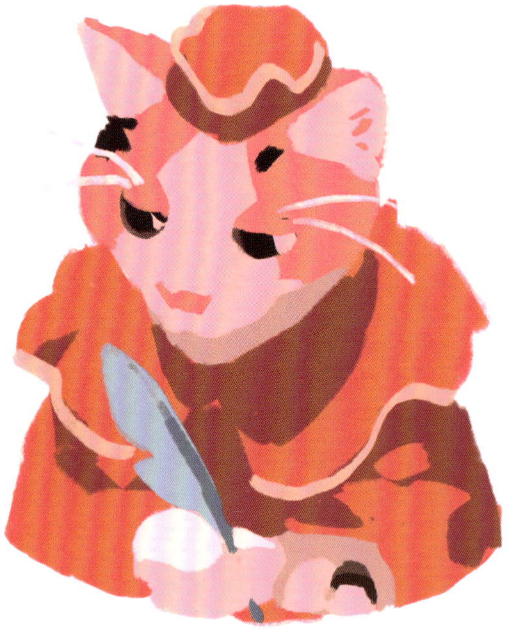

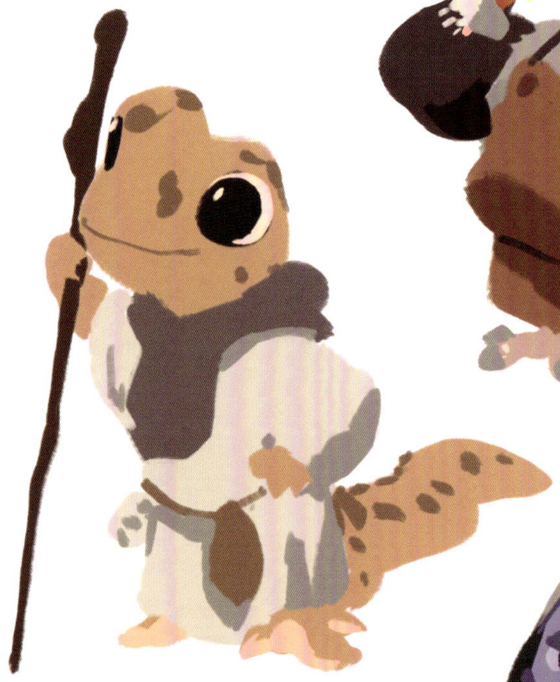

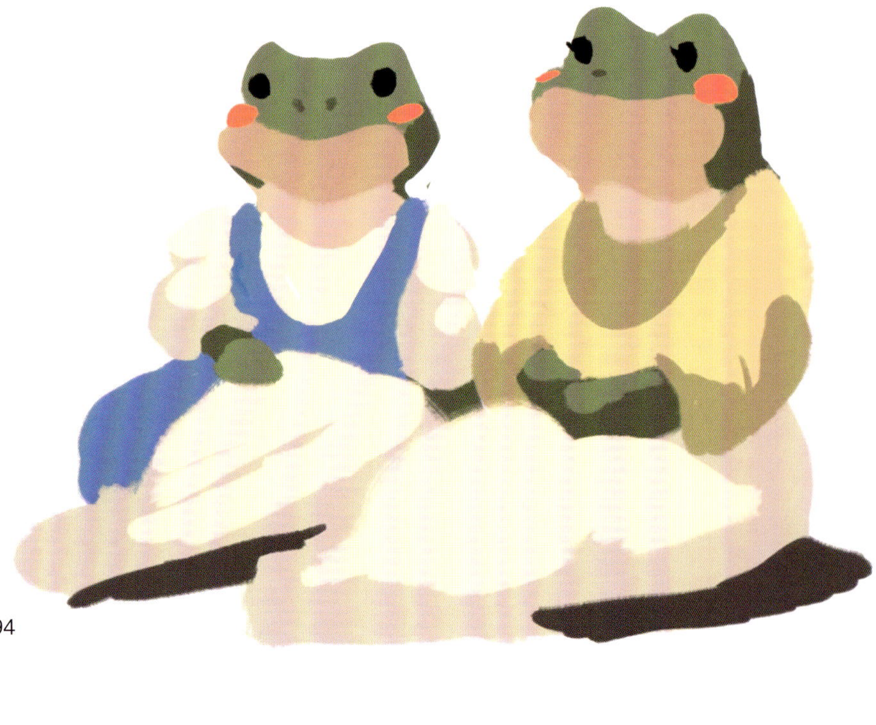

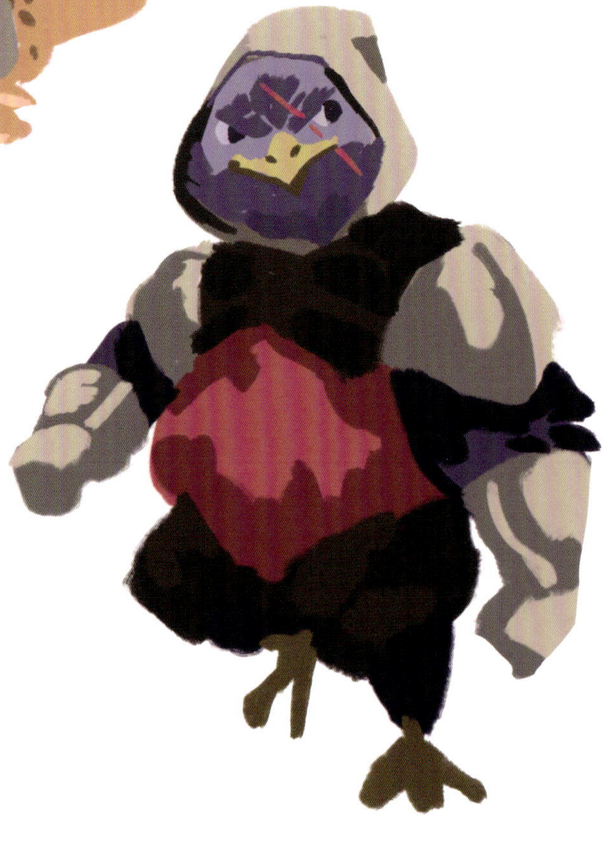

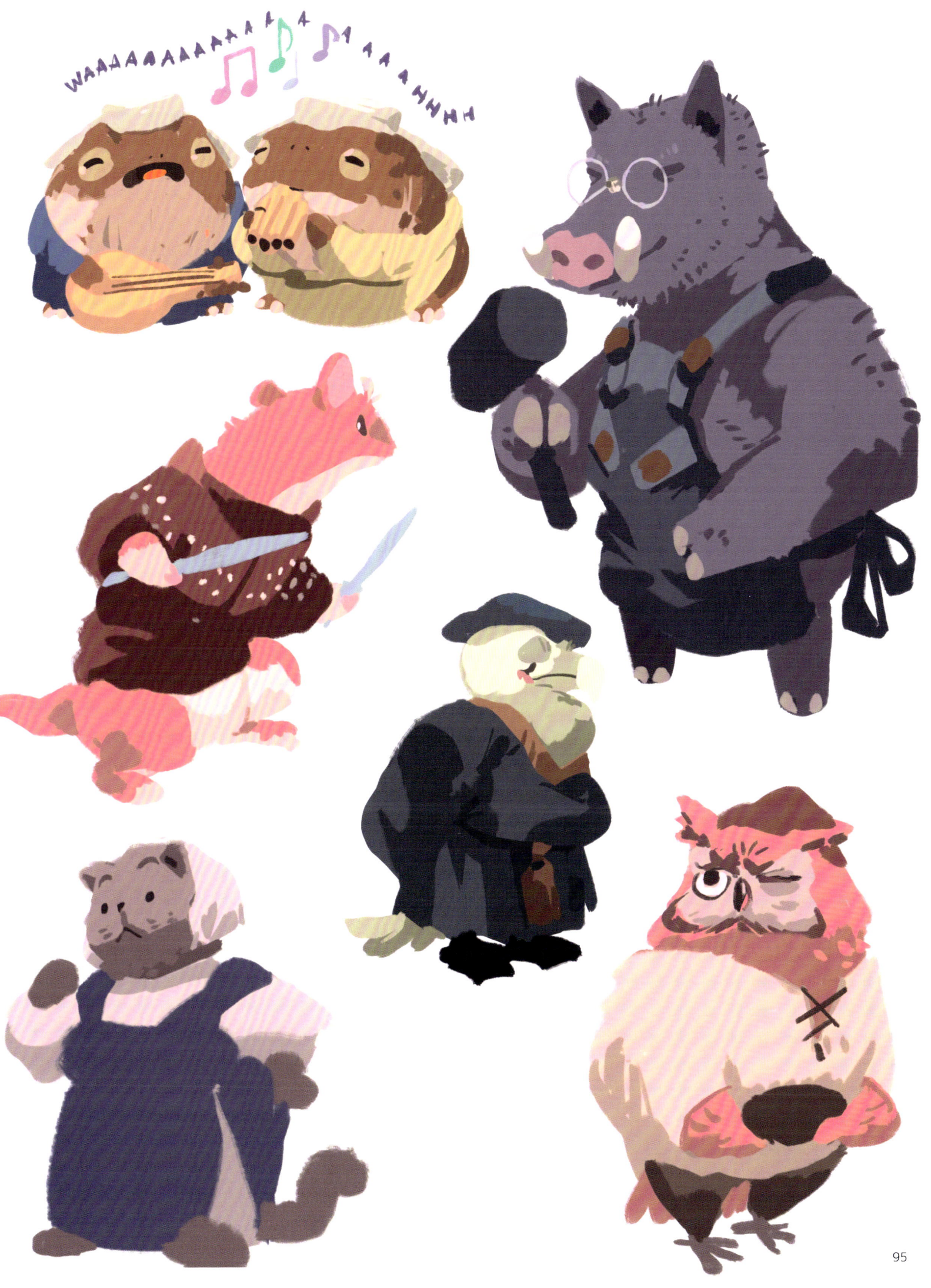

WAAAAAAAAAAAAAA ♪ ♫ AAAAHHHH

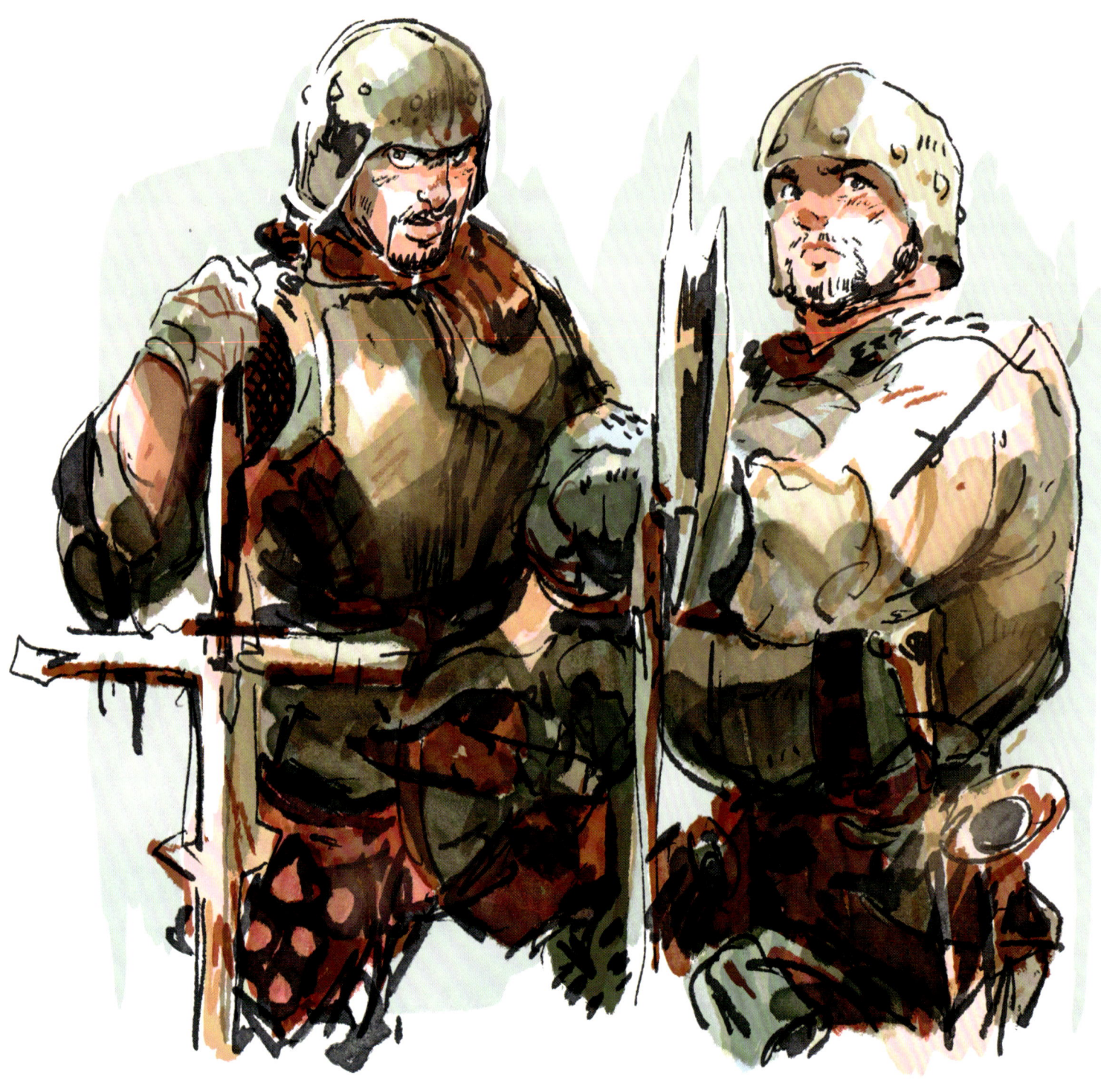

Working on an action game taught me that simple things, like getting the exact pixel distance between objects right, could make a big difference to players – whether they felt rewarded by their choices or frustrated.

I learned how to control a viewer's attention. Sometimes this meant I would use loud colours and a variance in scale to guide their eyes to a smaller prop. Other times it meant using more muted, repetitive, textural art to add atmosphere without ever stealing attention away from the action at hand.

By necessity, pixel art showed me how colour, scale, and texture can push or pull a viewer's interest around, with the goal of guiding them to the most important information. This was a pivotal skill I would later use all the time in my illustrations.

I LEARNED HOW TO CONTROL A VIEWER'S ATTENTION

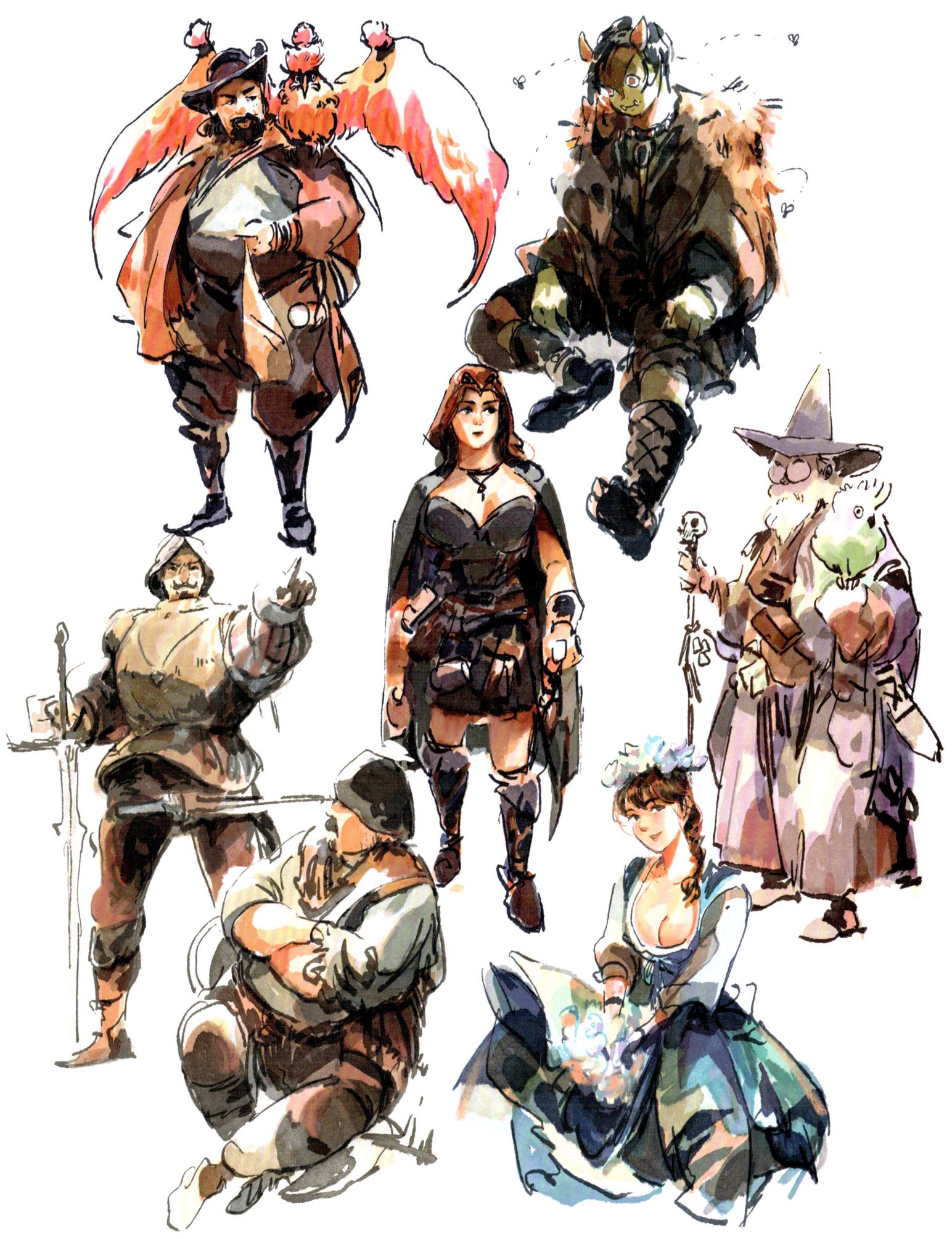

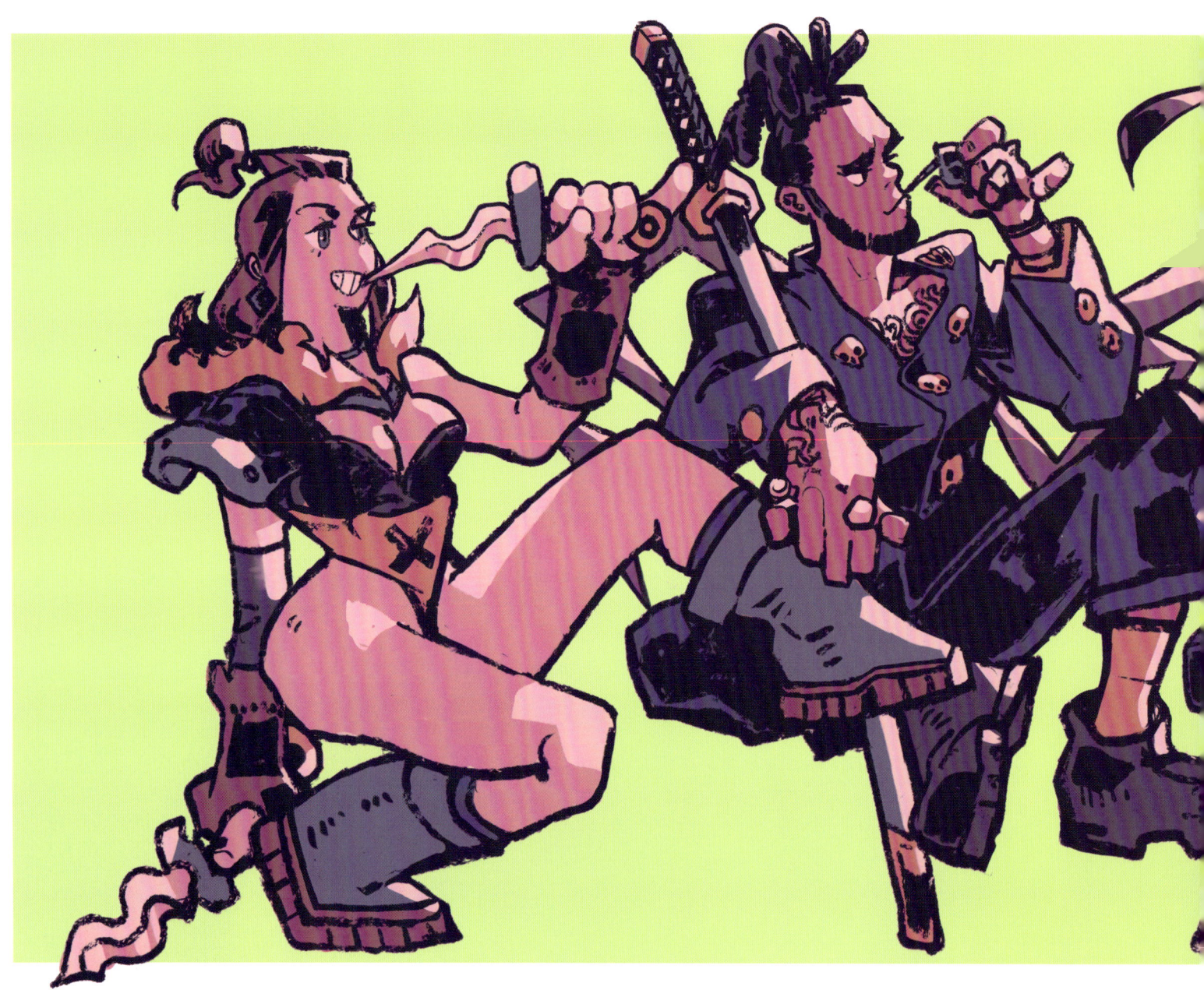

5–10 MINUTE COLOUR THEORY

During the time that I was working my butt off on *Aegis*, there were two things I did to blow off steam. First was cooking dinner for my wife, who often came home too late and tired from her teaching job to do anything but rest, and the second was a free weekly figure-drawing workshop near where we lived. For those who are less familiar, live figure drawing is when a bunch of artists gather around a model and draw them as the model occasionally changes pose.

In the four years of development on *Aegis*, I went to figure-drawing class almost every week. Not because I thought I was training to become an artist, but

just to relax. The class was a time when I could unwind and turn off my brain. It was just a break. In fact, for the longest time, it was hard for me to even fathom that figure drawing might be useful in my professional work.

My approach to figure drawing at the time was impacted by a conversation I had with a friend in high school. She had asked, 'How can you draw what's in your head if you can't draw what's in front of you?' The idea that you needed to be able to replicate what was in front of you before you'd be able to replicate what you were seeing in your imagination made a sort of intuitive sense. With that goal in

mind, I really just wanted to practise that skill of transferring what I was seeing in front of me onto the page. Initially, it was an exercise in observation and dexterity more than anything else. However, to my surprise, it would eventually help me have two huge breakthroughs.

The first thing figure drawing helped me learn was colour theory. Figure drawing is so fast paced, and I quickly became impatient with using pencils and even pens after a while. Brush pens, with their ability to have really big and small strokes based on pressure, were an improvement, but eventually, that became boring, too.

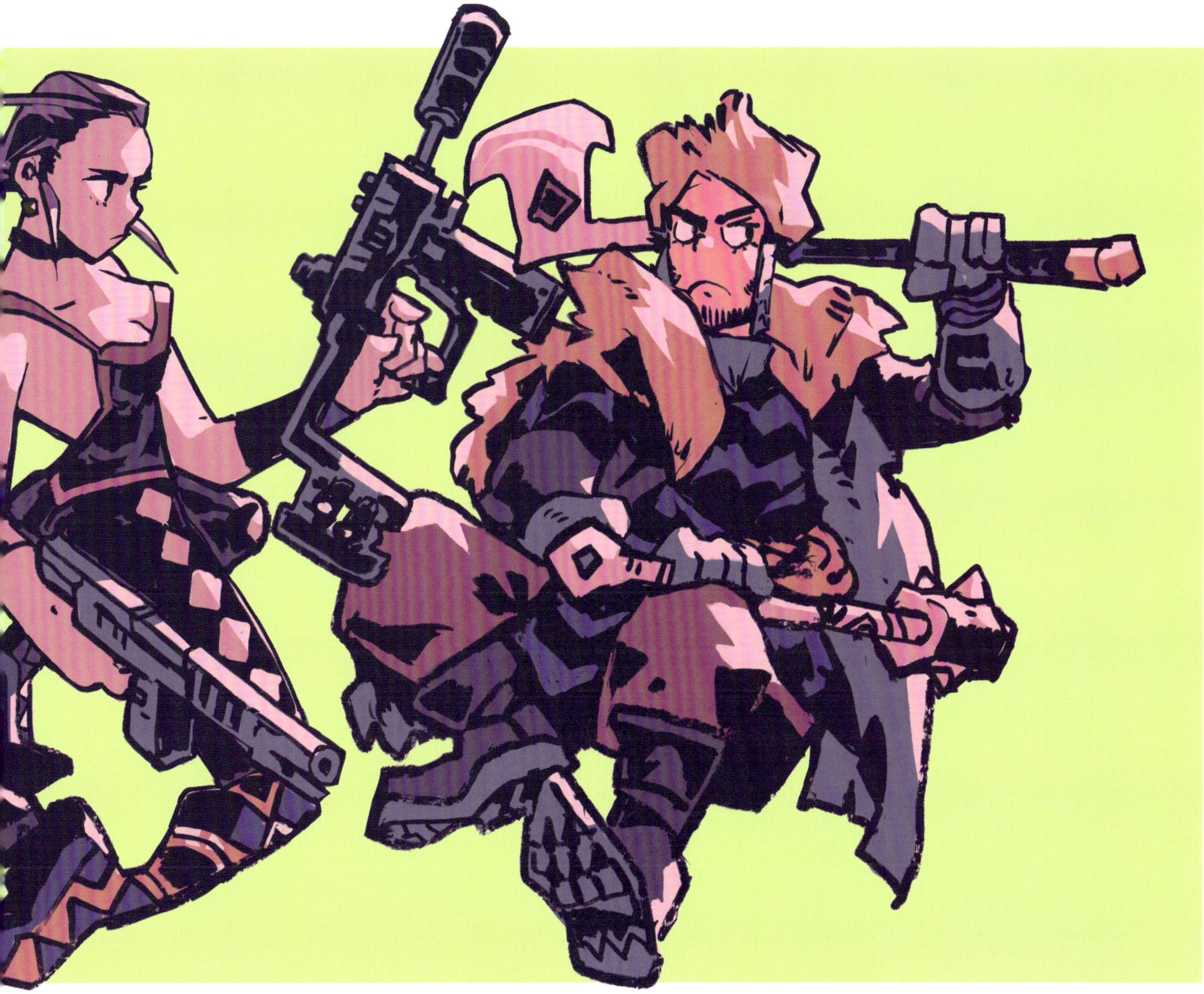

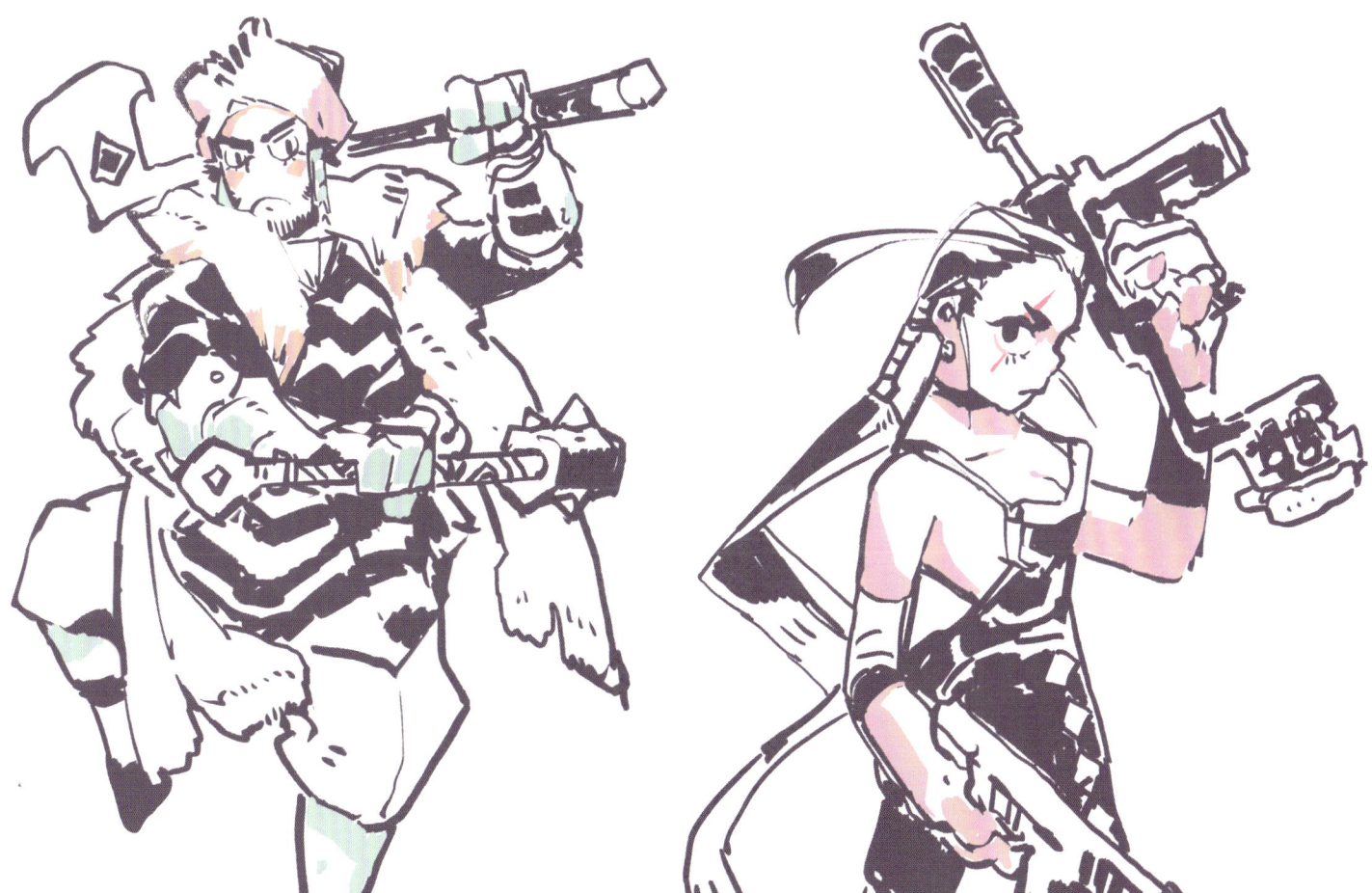

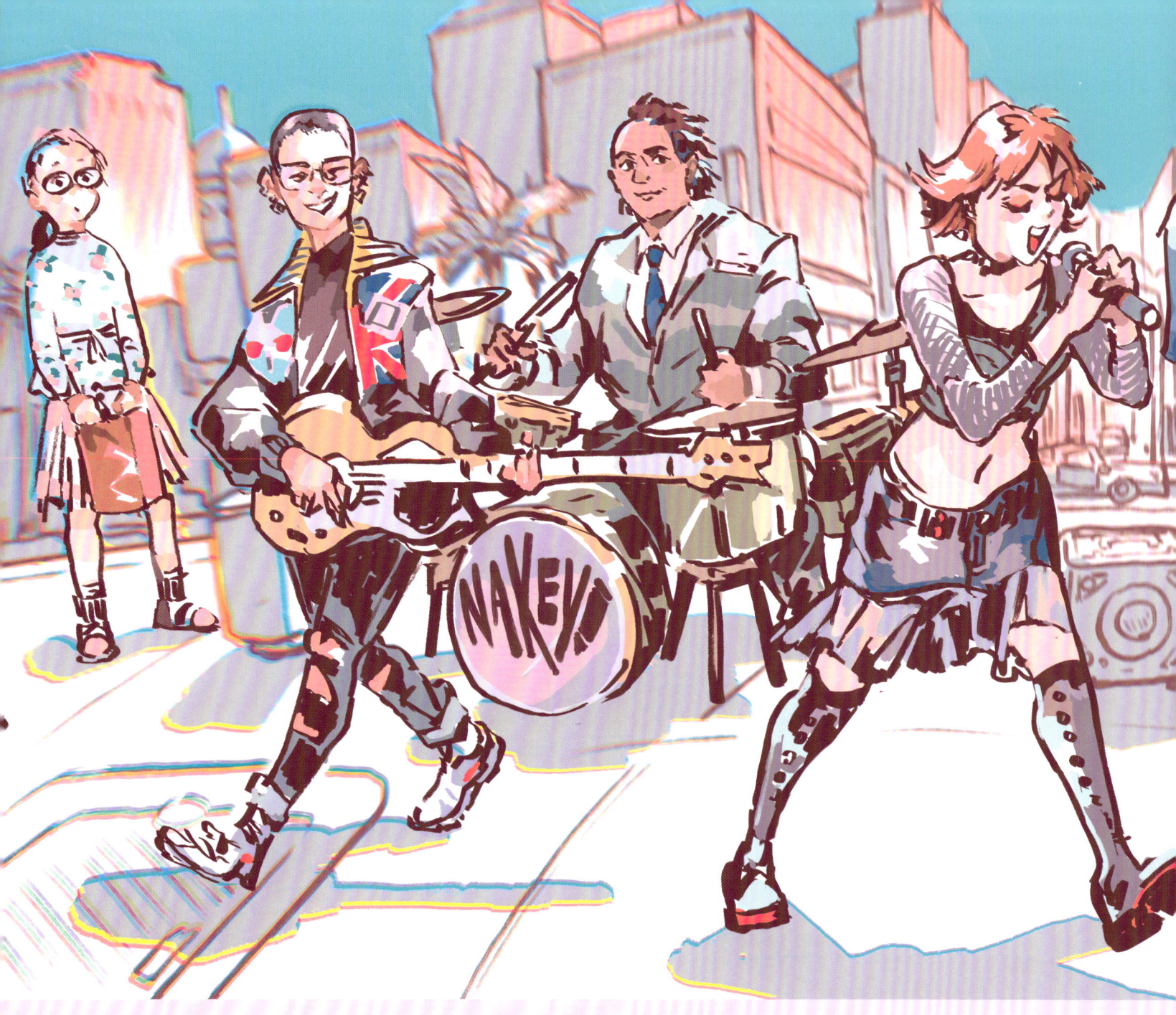

When I discovered that watercolour was actually the fastest way to get pigment on the page, I began my journey of understanding colour.

There was no time to pick accurate colours, so I just started picking randomly. That was how I discovered that the hue of a colour didn't really matter, so long as I could control its value – its lightness and darkness. Still, through trial and error, I learned which colour combinations were most pleasing, how colours could all affect each other, and the properties of each colour as it blended.

Figure drawing also taught me how to trust my own eyes. To give some background to what I mean, the way we draw something is often a combination of our idea of it and the objective reality of what it really is. For instance, the symbol of an eyeball versus a literal eyeball. This is why it can be difficult to improve at

drawing, because our brain starts combining these concepts (for example, stamping in an anime eyeball that's facing forward, when the head is actually slightly in profile).

It's typical for artists who like comics of any kind to do this, me included, because when we're growing up and still learning, the result is often better and easier with the symbolic, stamping approach. That's why it took a lot for me to make this leap.

So back to when I was figure drawing, I had to make a choice to unlearn some of my habits and try something new. Thankfully, because of the speed at which figure drawing goes, my drawings felt less precious, and so I decided to be more daring. After all, it would only be a few minutes until the next pose began anyway.

The particular set-up that night was an intense-lighting scenario, where a big shadow was cast across the model's face.

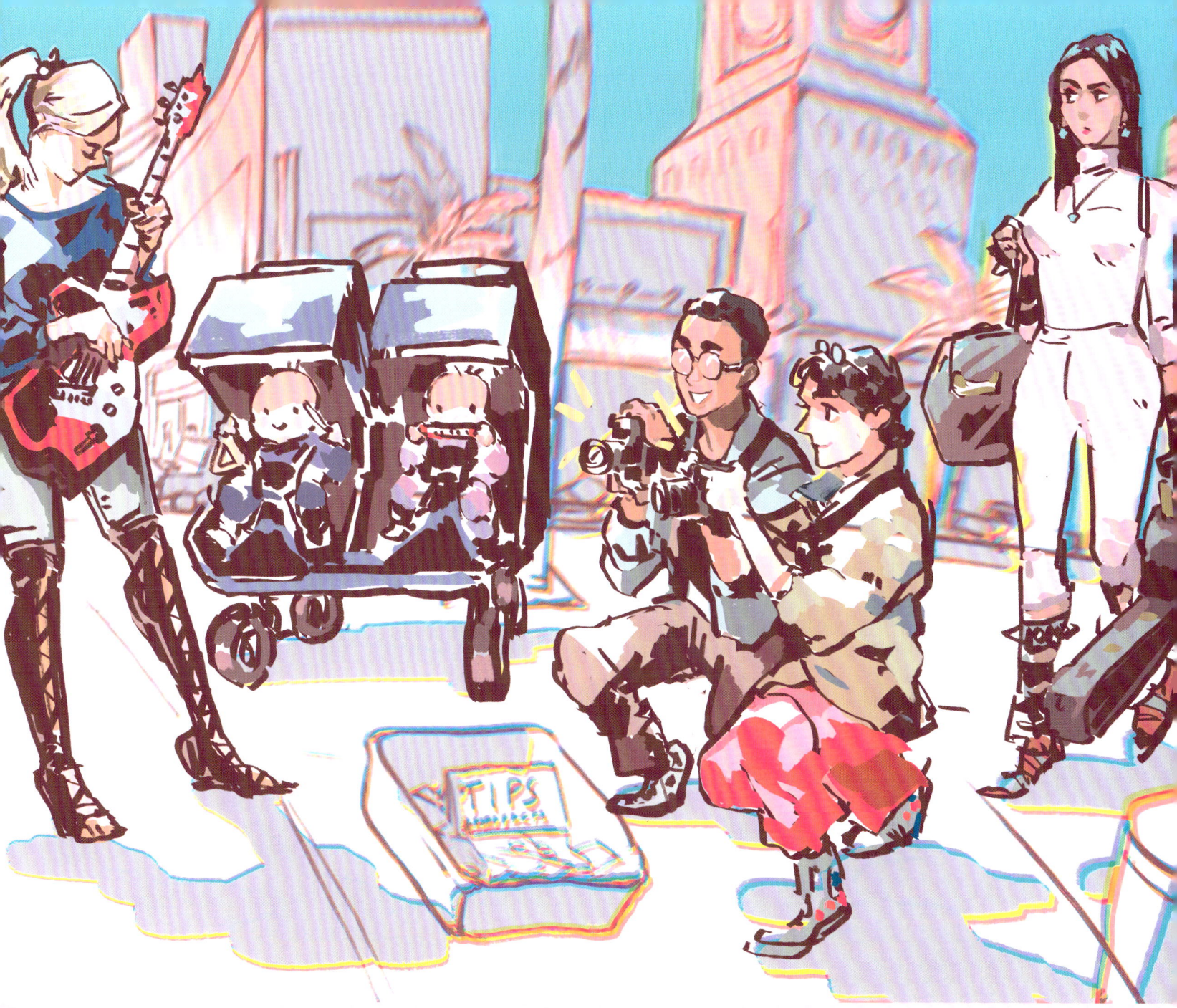

Shadows like that can be really intimidating because the shadow shape can go through the entire face – to draw it feels almost like you're interrupting the face. You might have drawn a really beautiful mouth, or nose, or eyes, but then all of a sudden, you're drawing all over it.

That night I decided to take a risk and just go for it, venturing into the parts of the model's face that I had always avoided, for fear of making her look really unflattering. It was the first time I fully trusted myself to just copy what I was seeing in such an objective way, and the result looked more realistic than anything I had tried so far. Letting go of those constraints was an eye-opening moment for me. It felt as if I was finally able to get past a wall that had been holding back my learning for a long time, and it made me even more curious to see what else I could learn because of it.

> LETTING GO OF THOSE CONSTRAINTS WAS AN EYE-OPENING MOMENT FOR ME

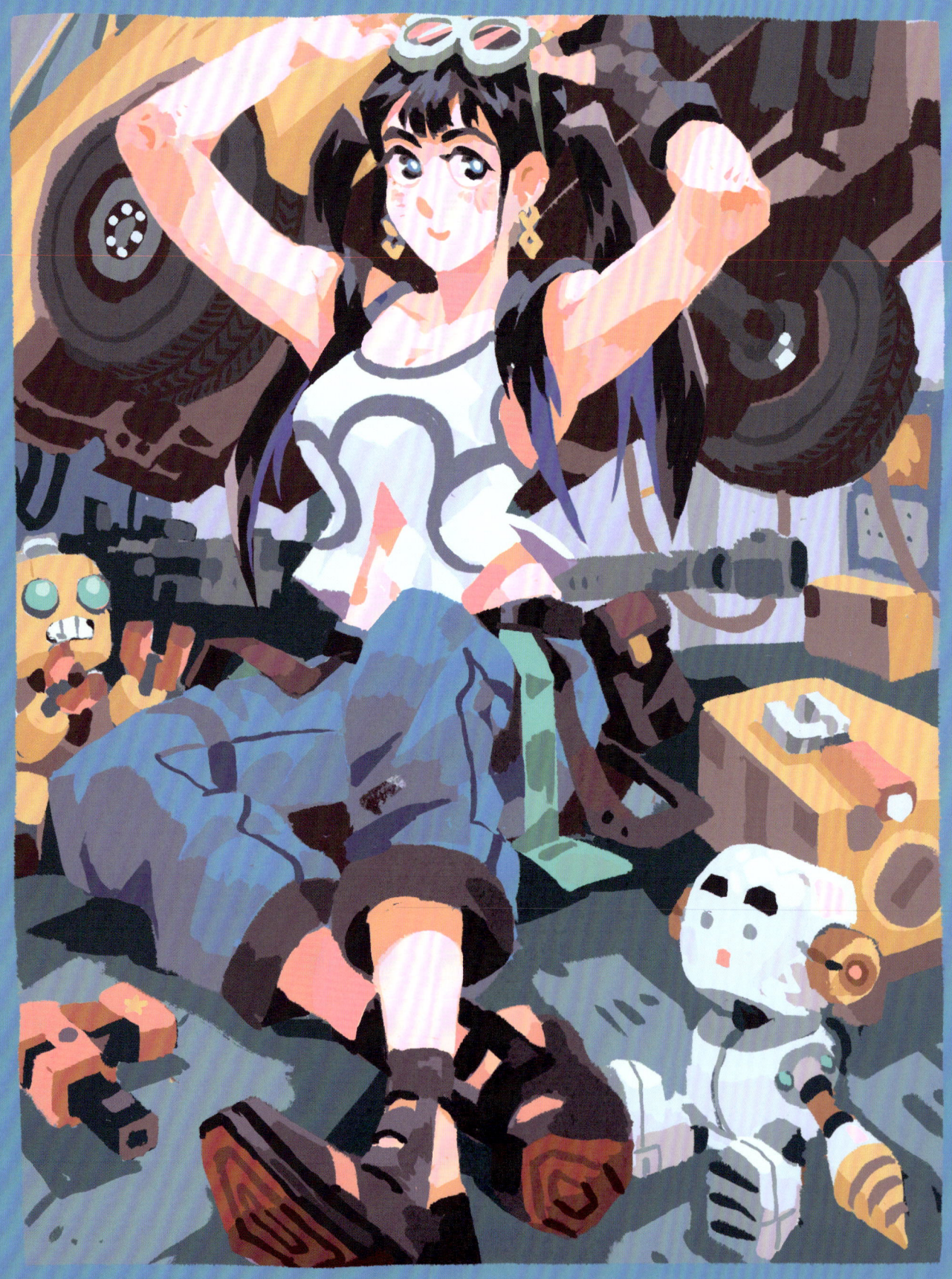

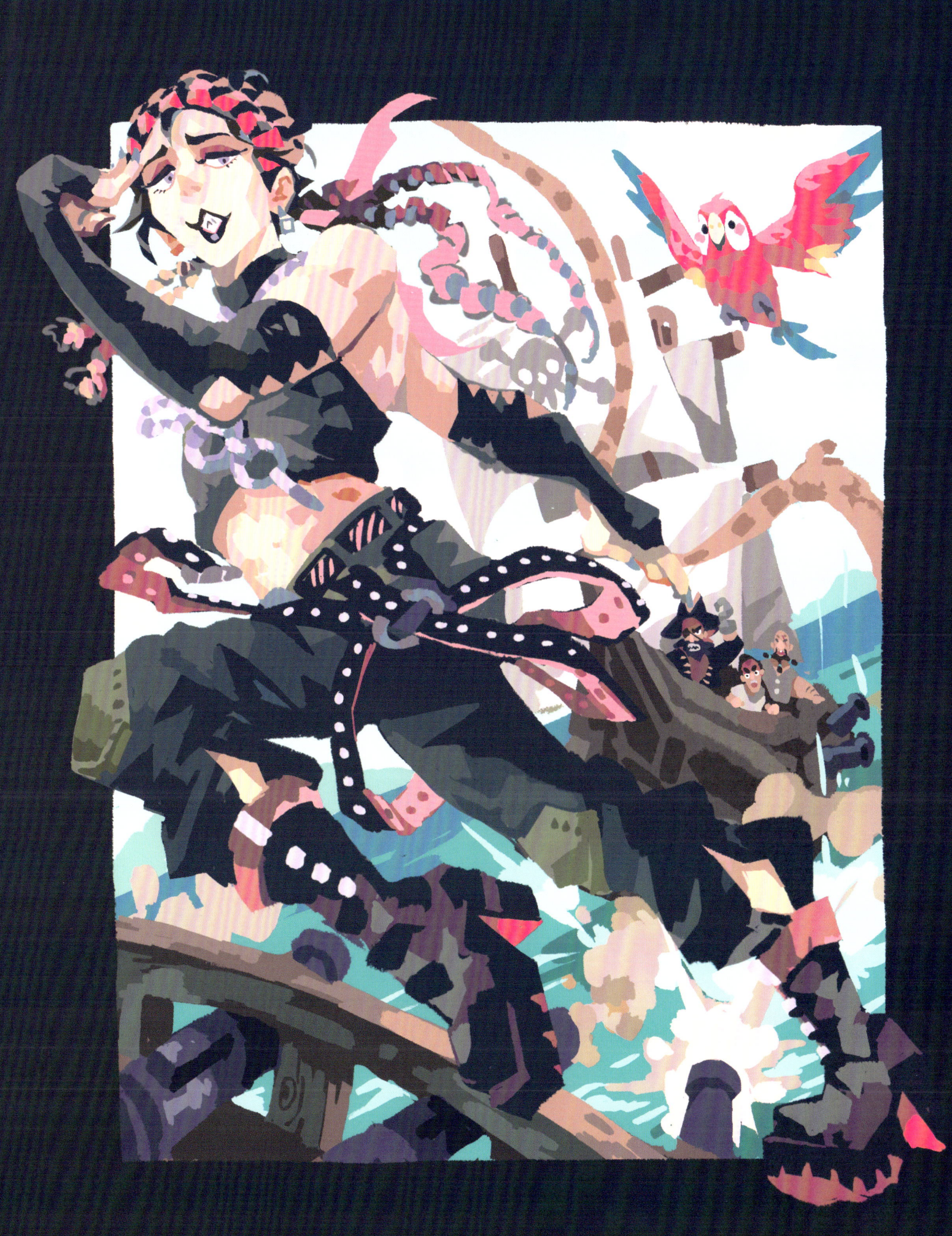

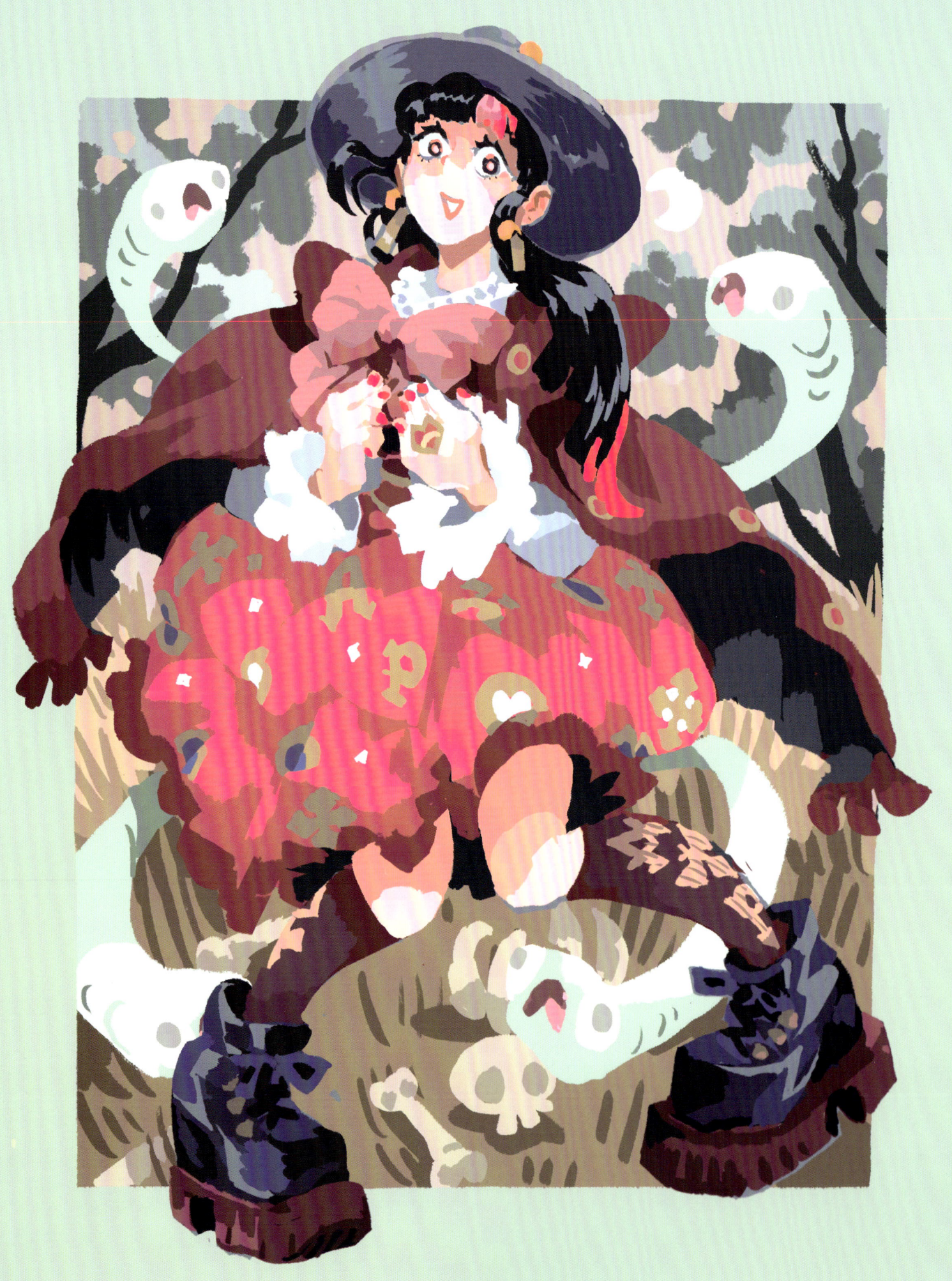

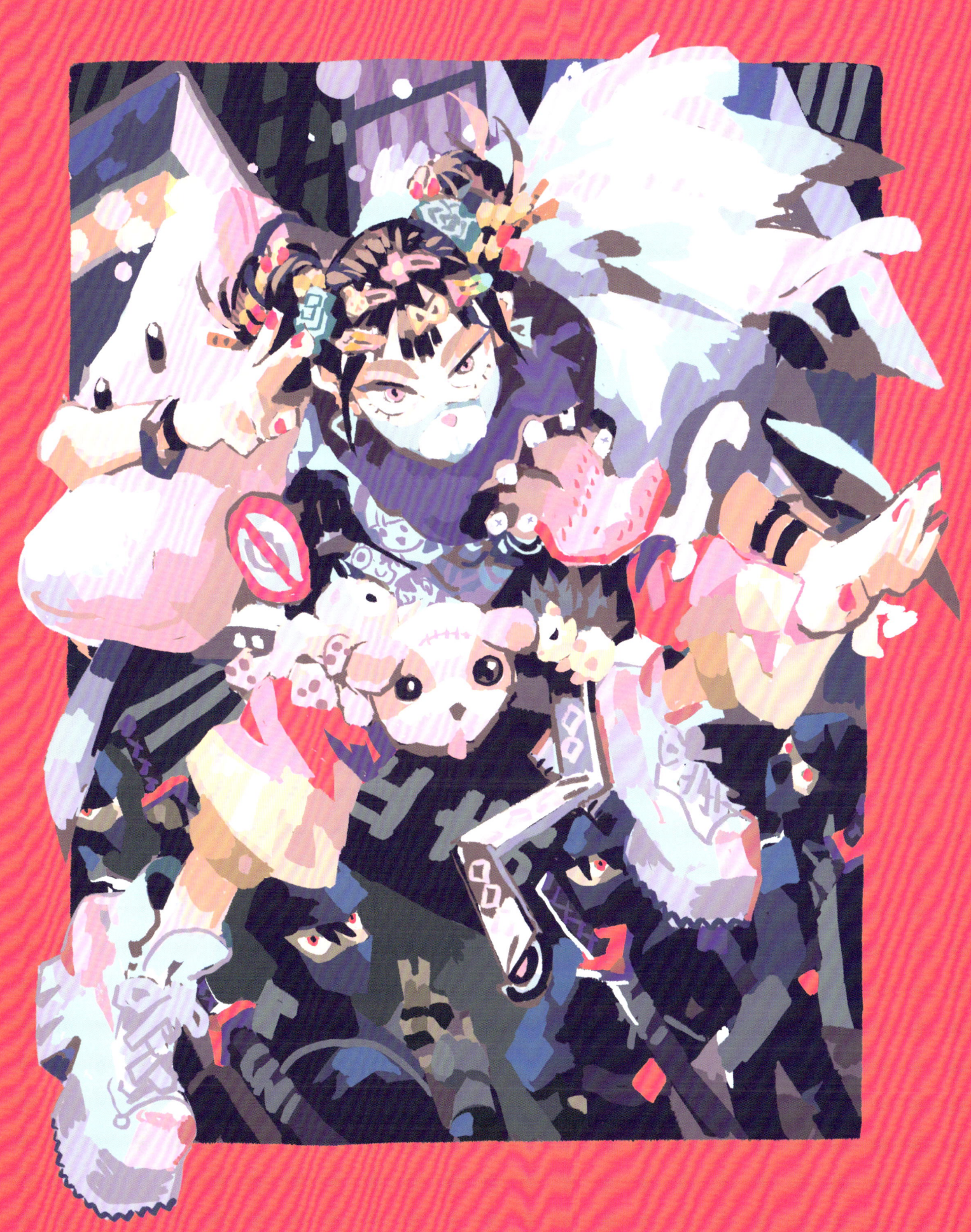

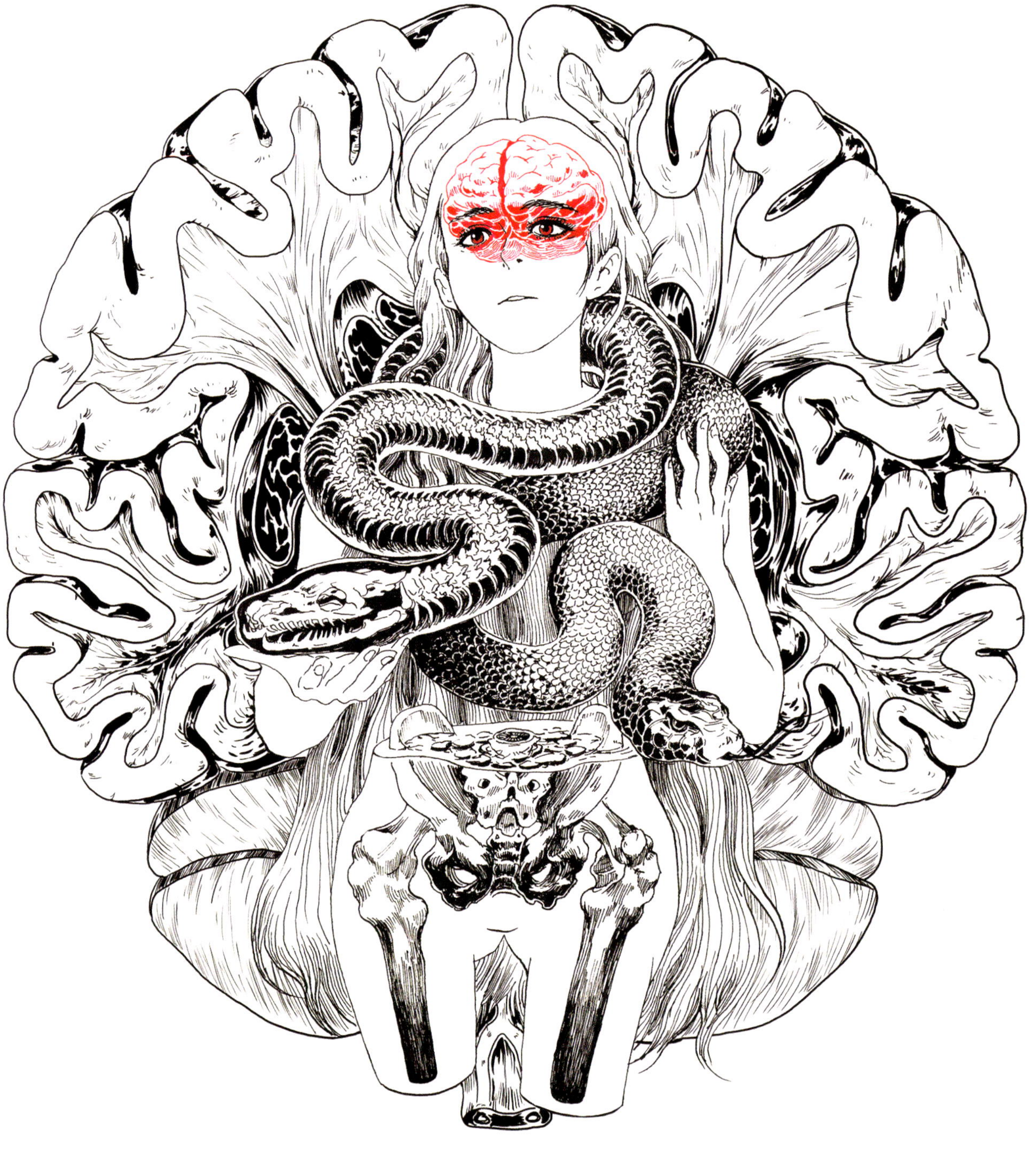

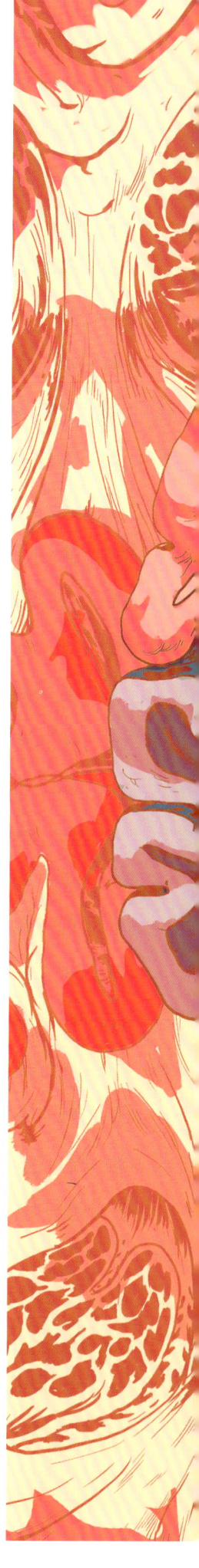

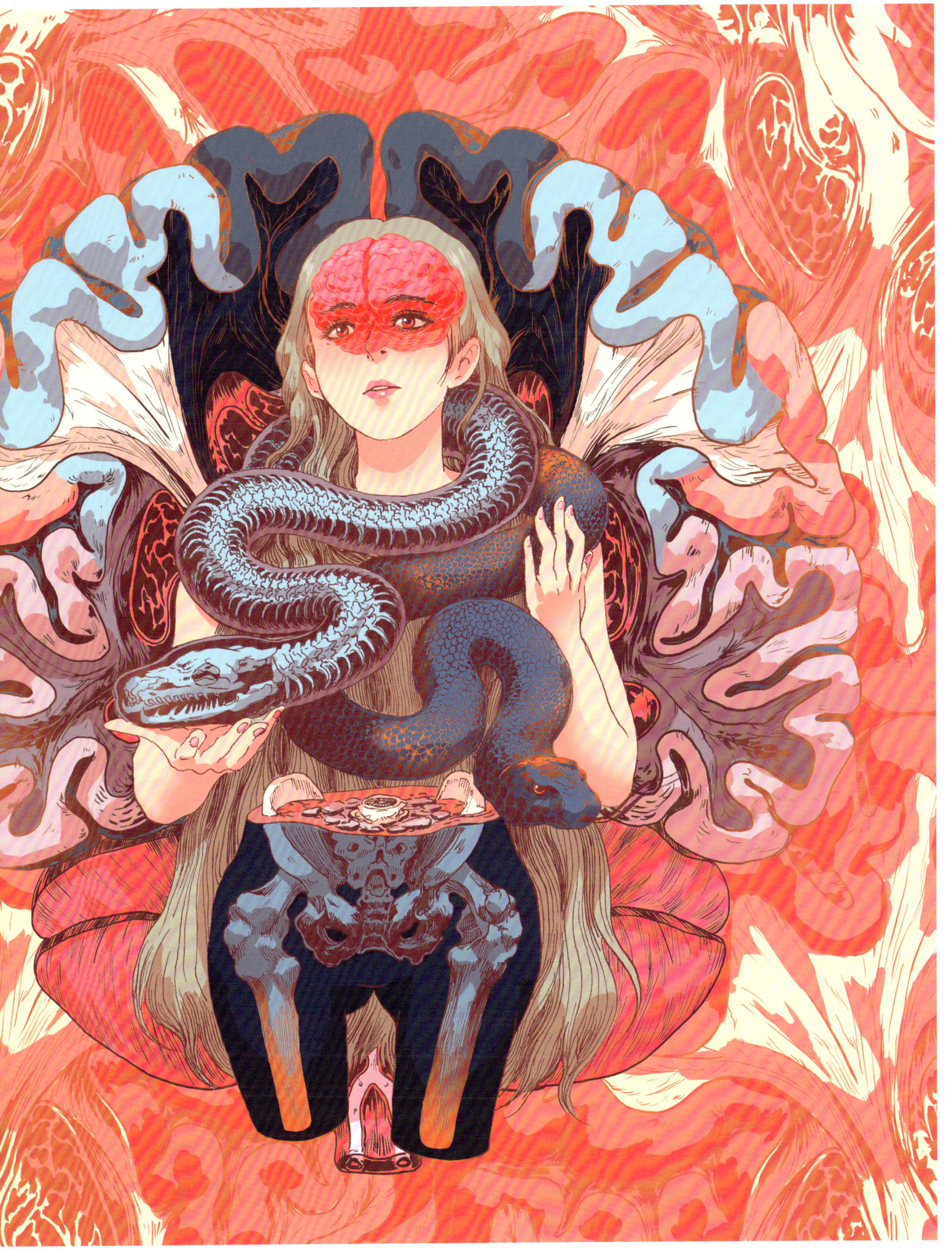

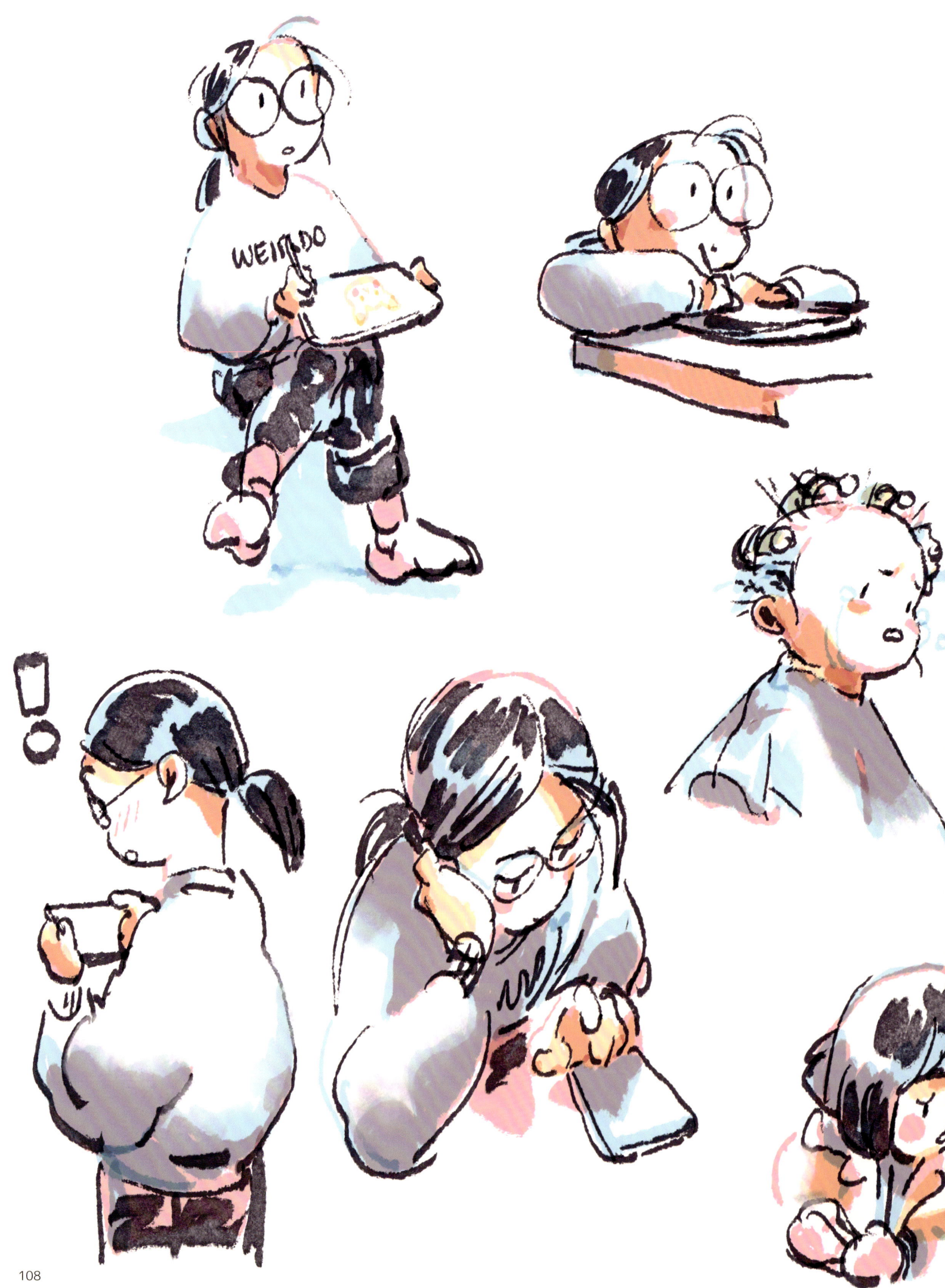

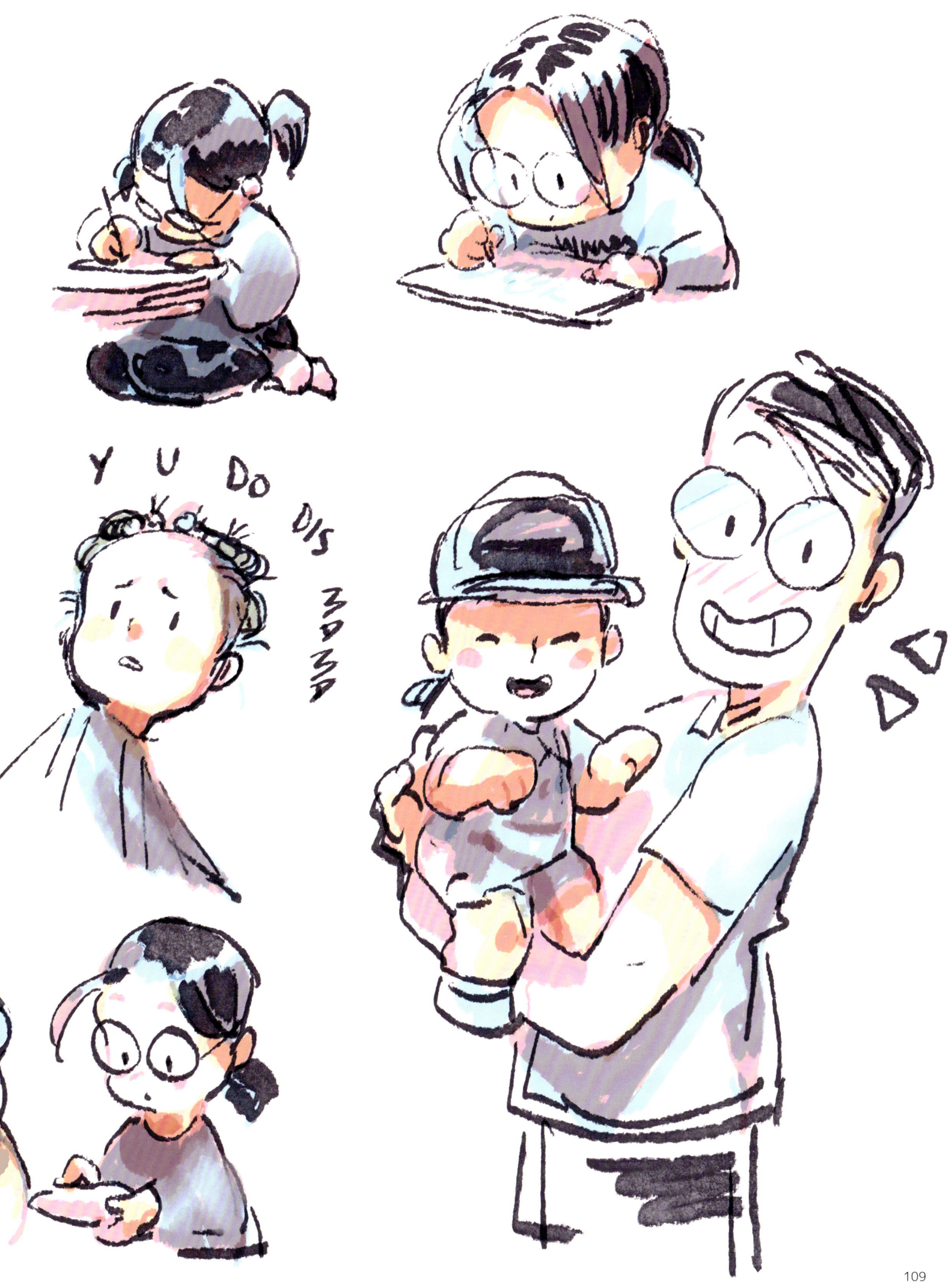

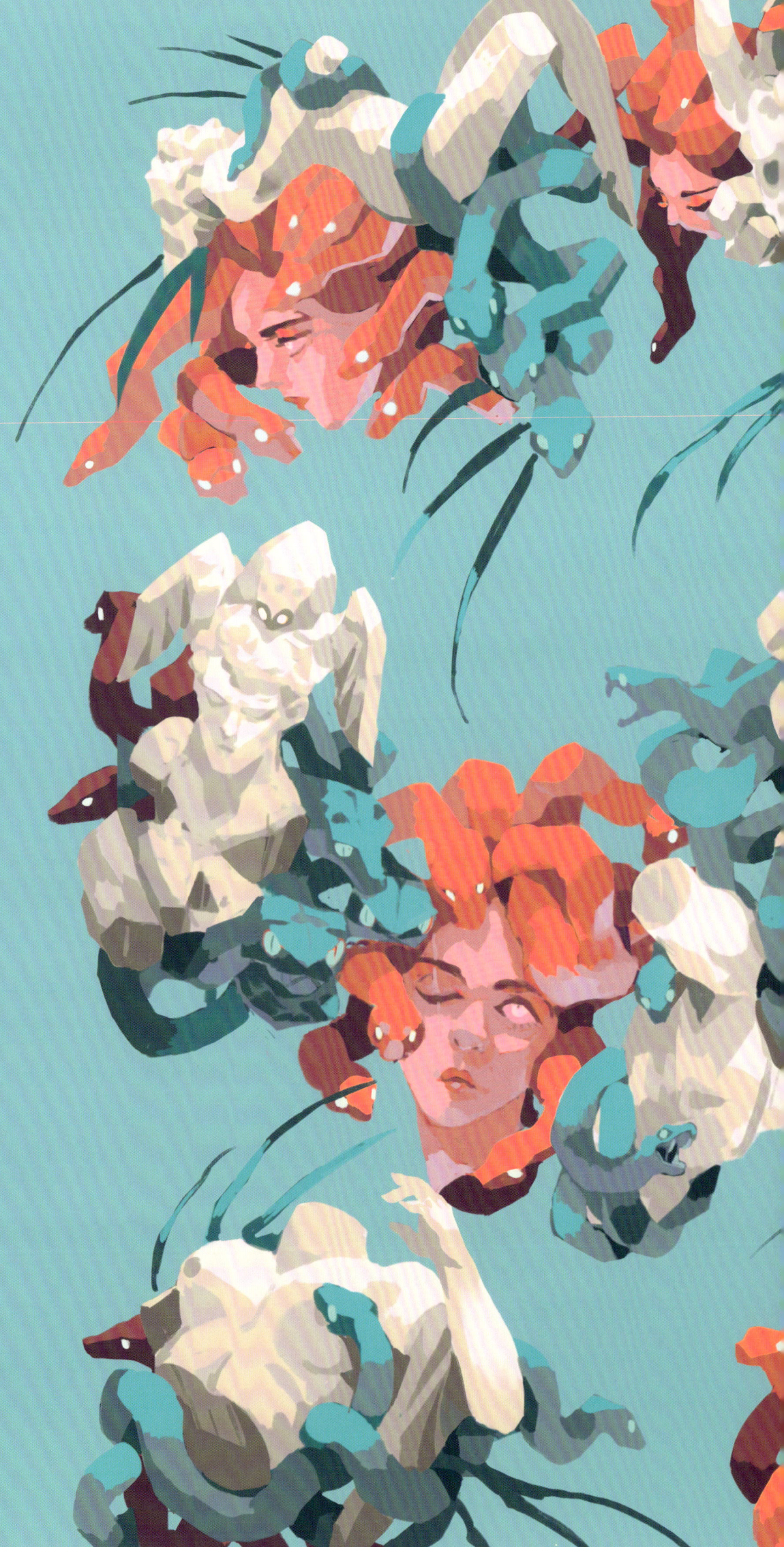

MEDUSA

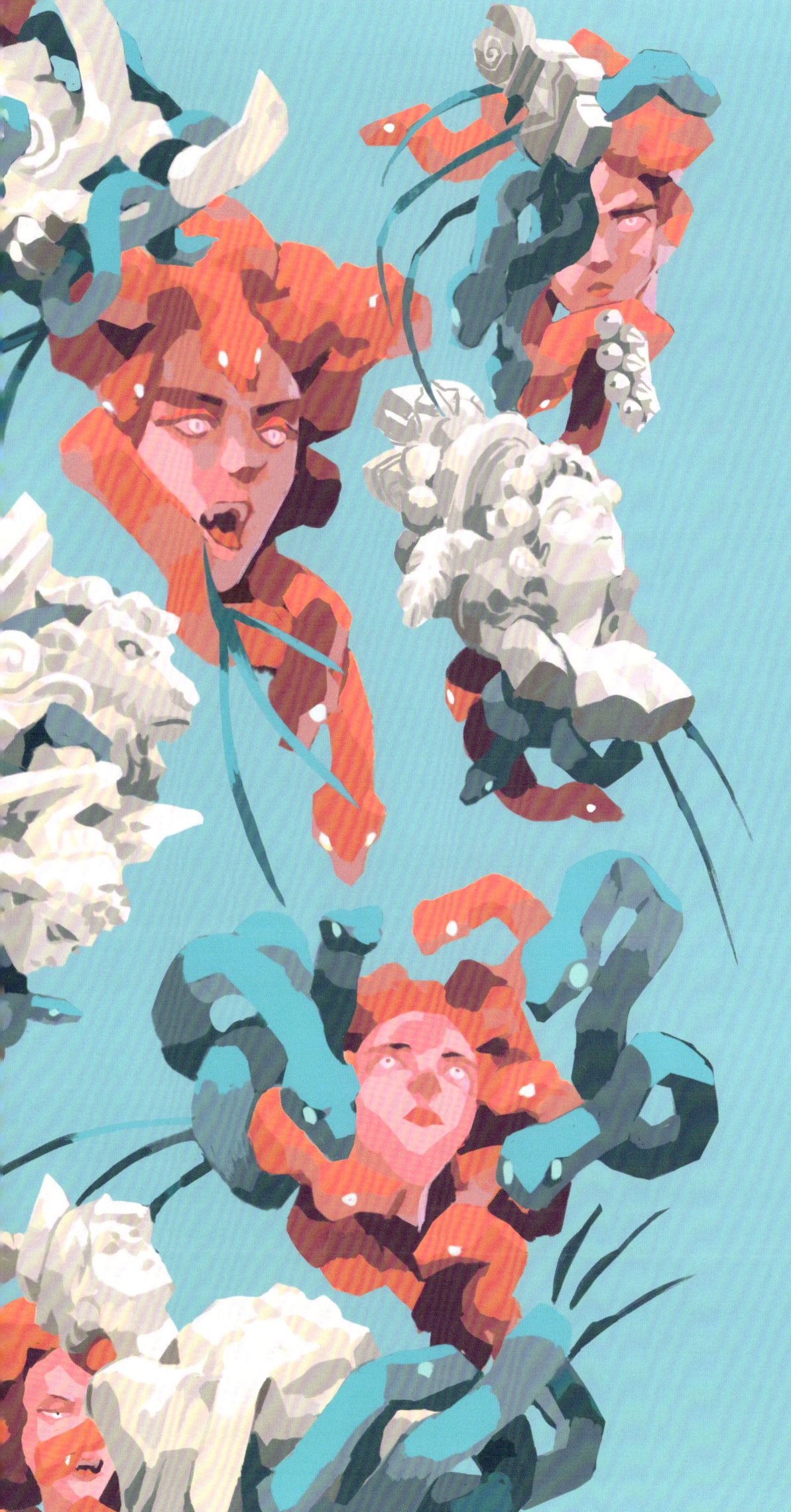

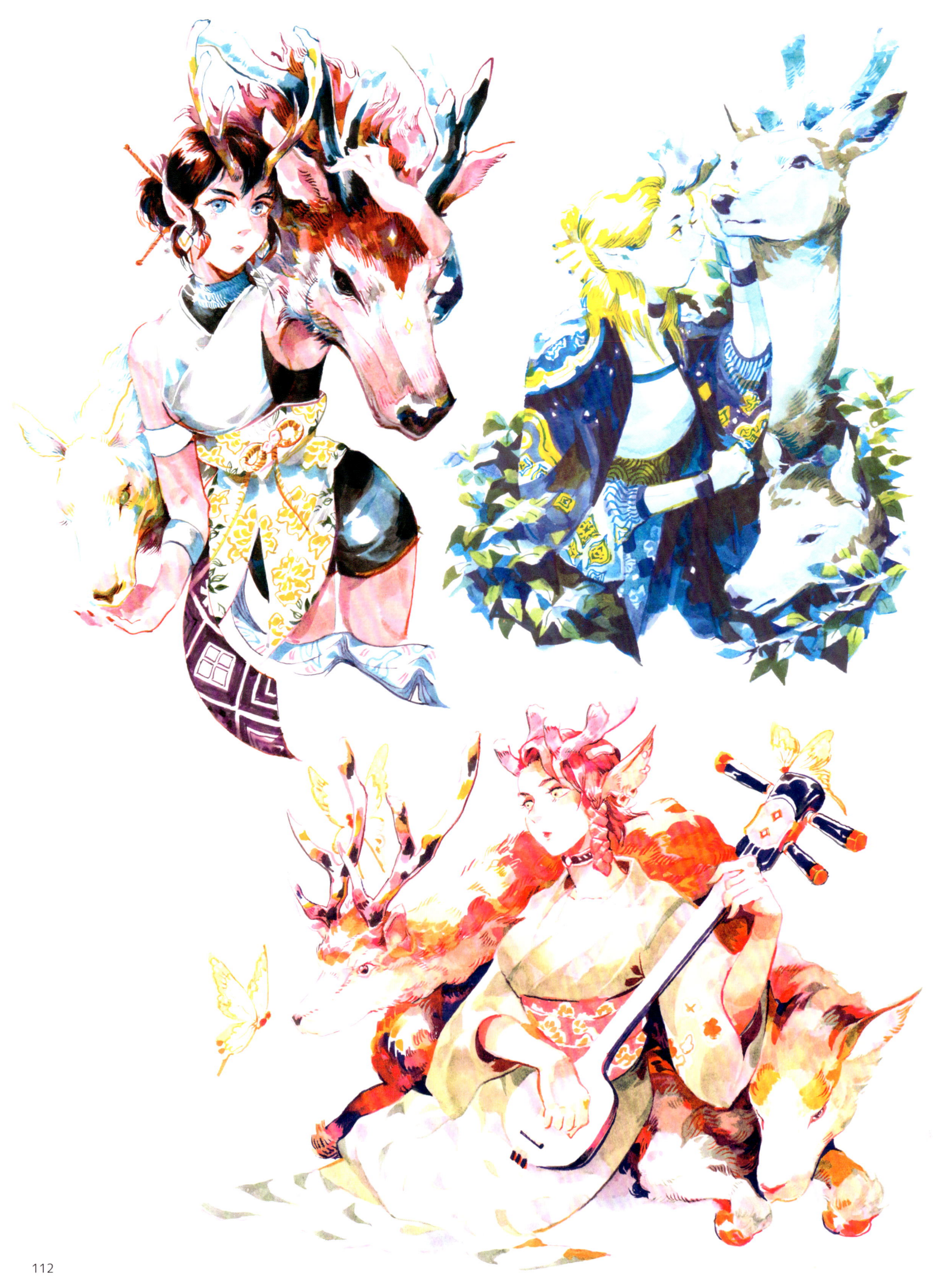

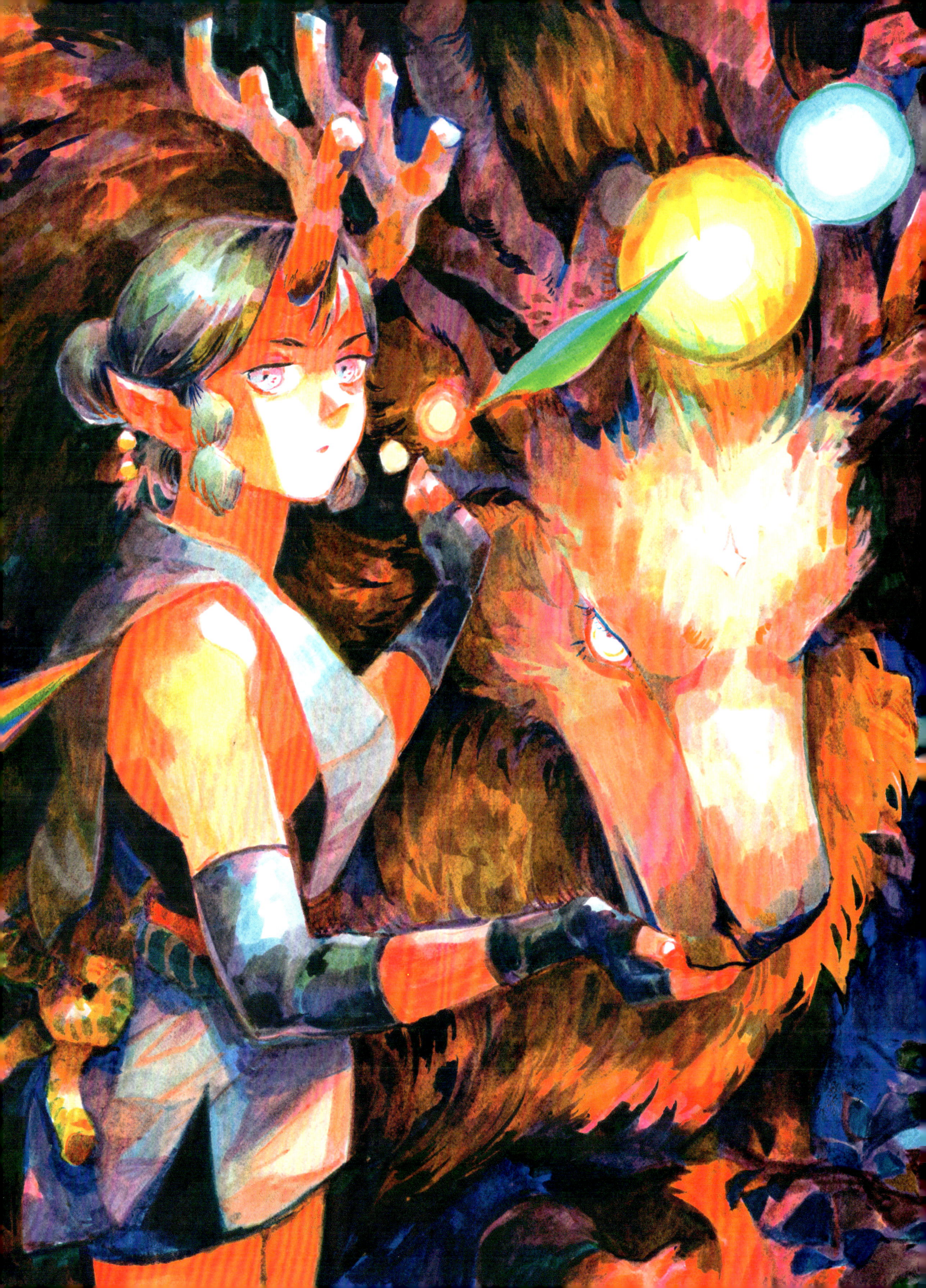

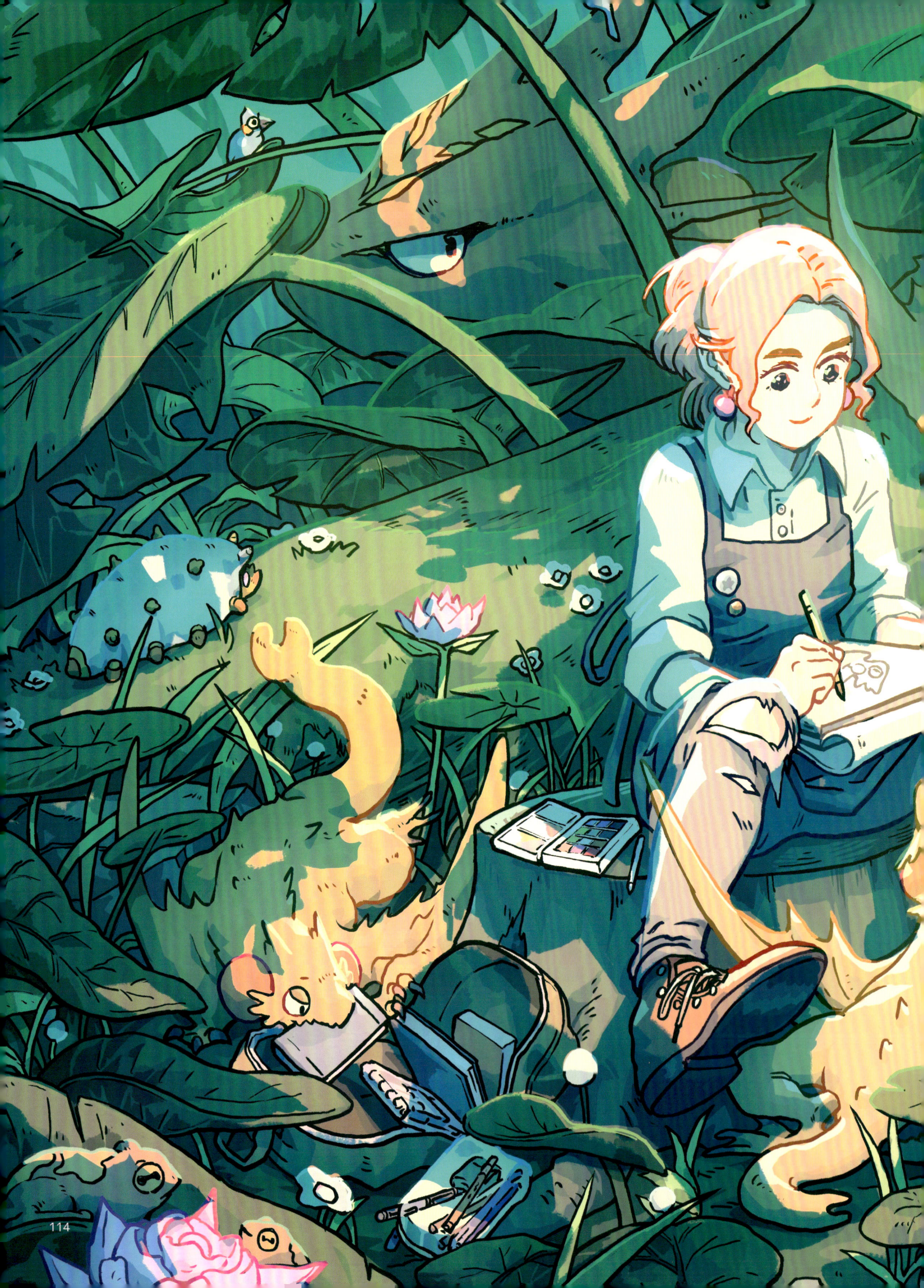

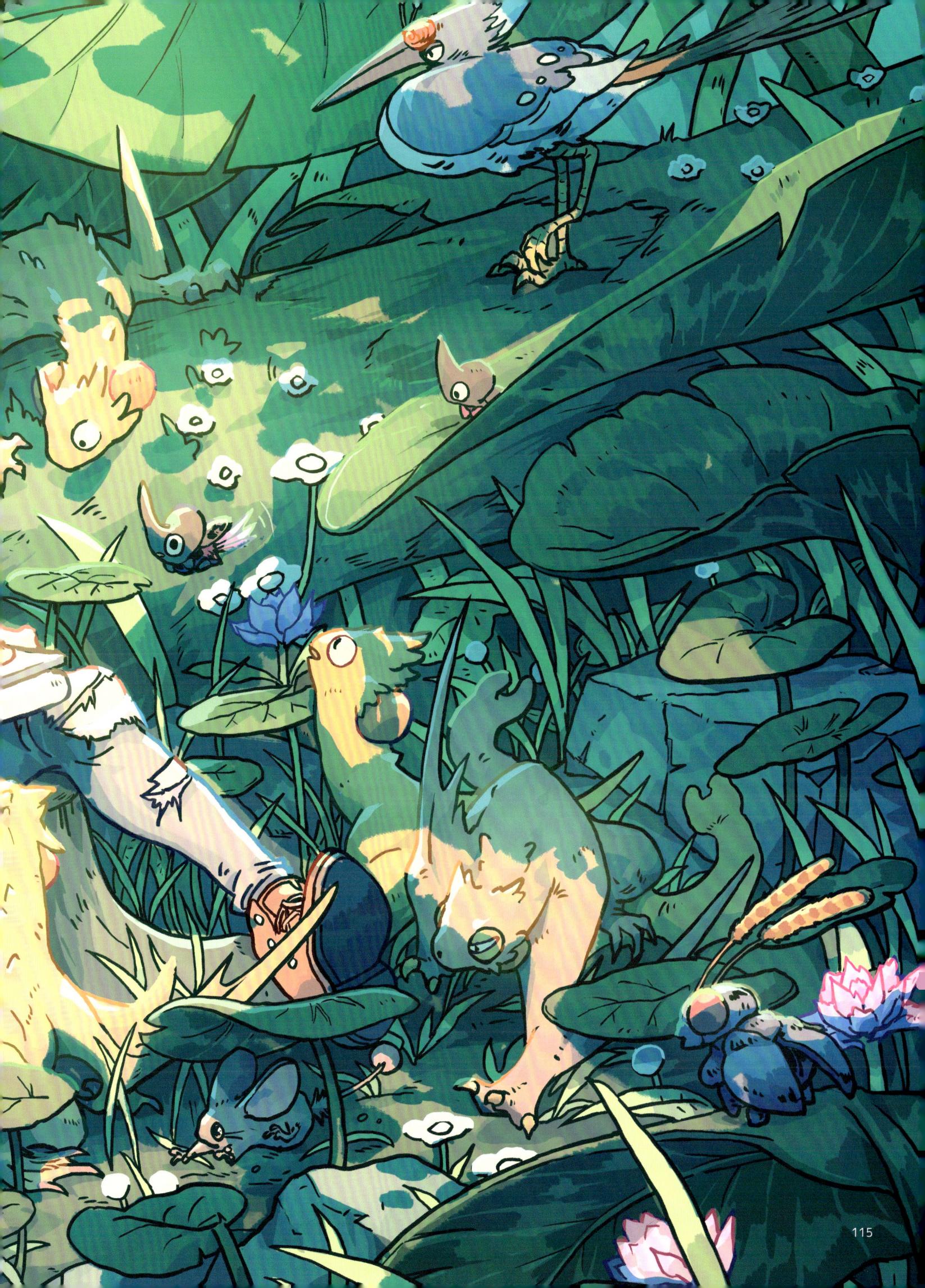

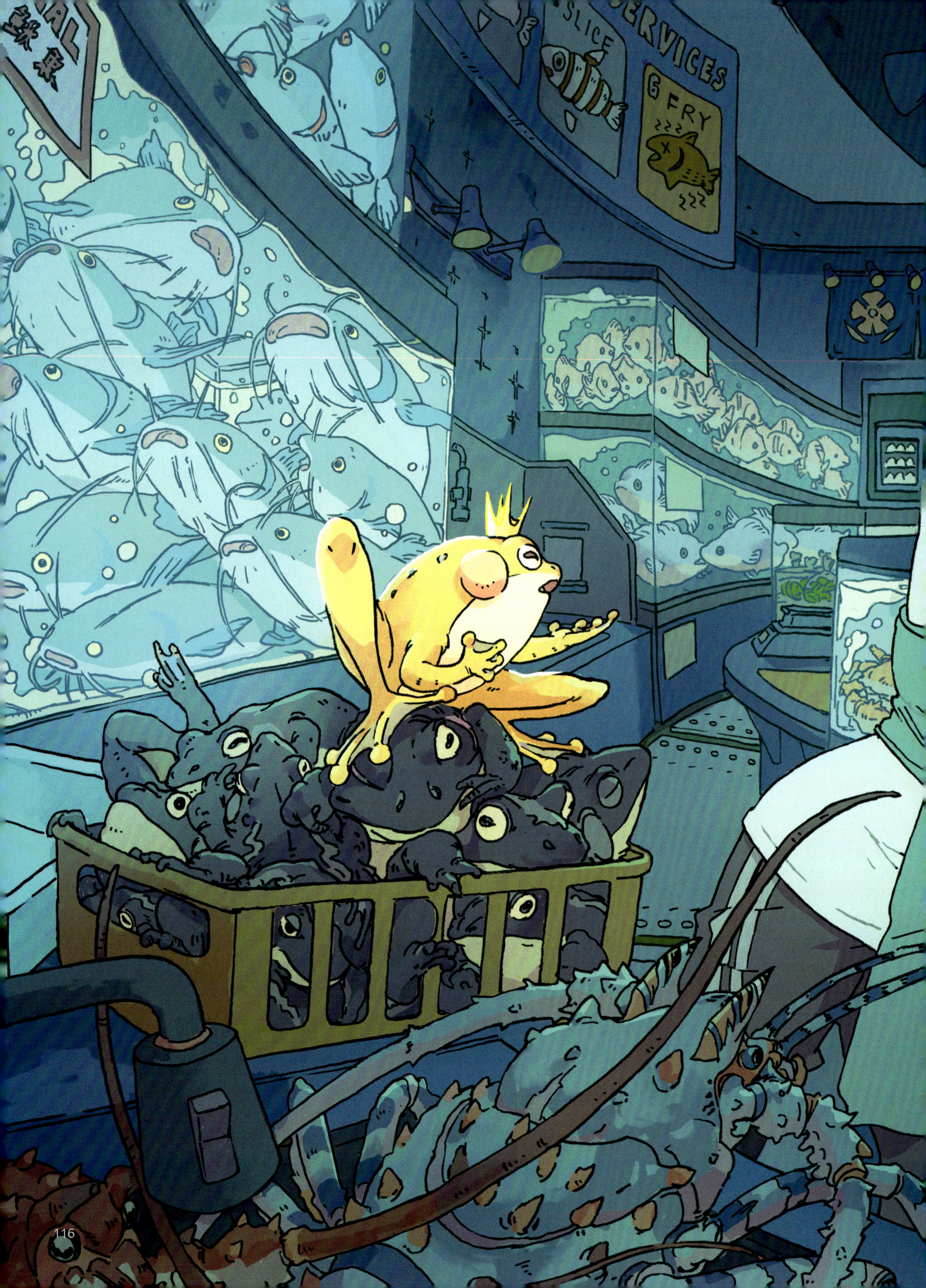

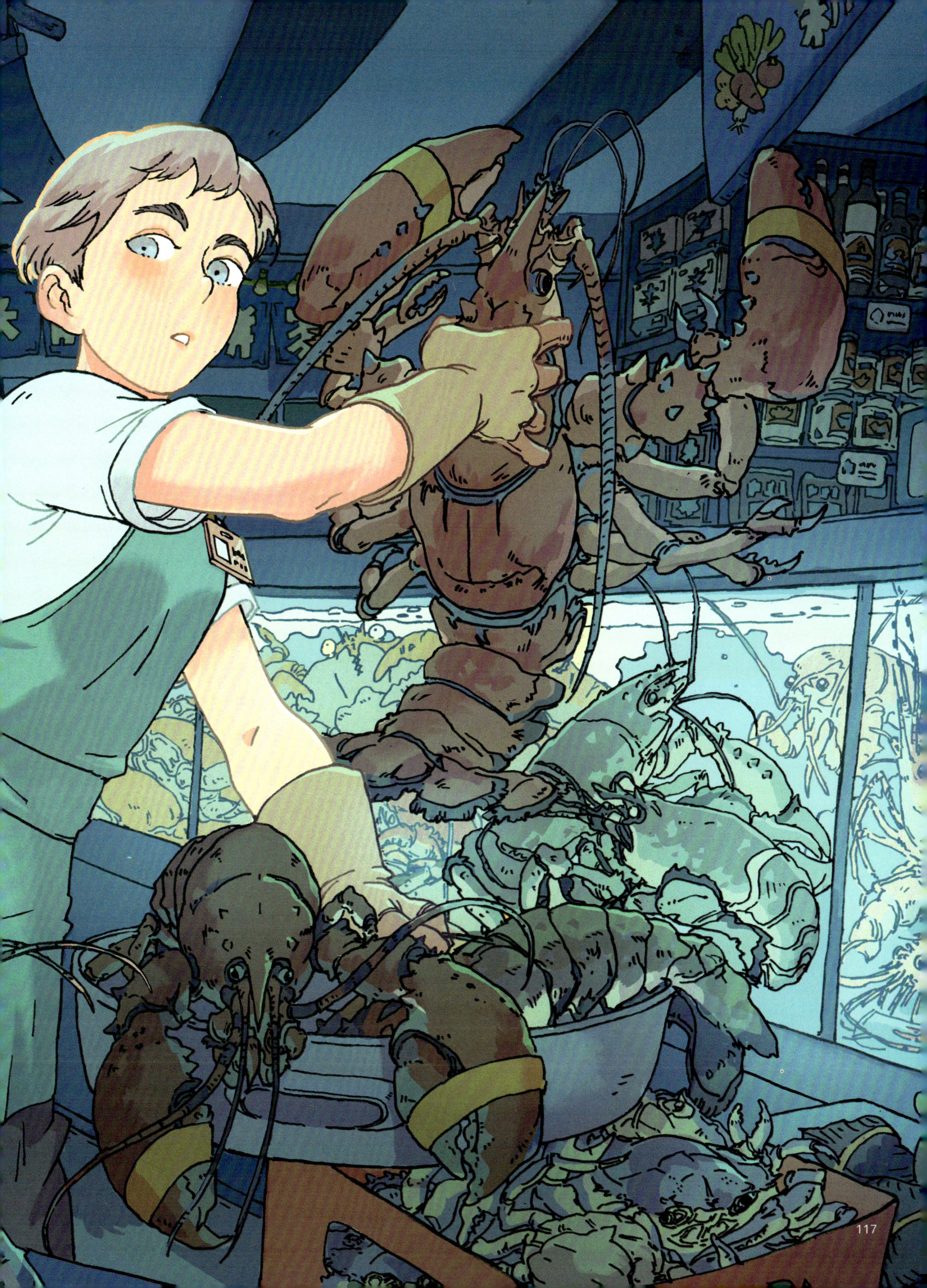

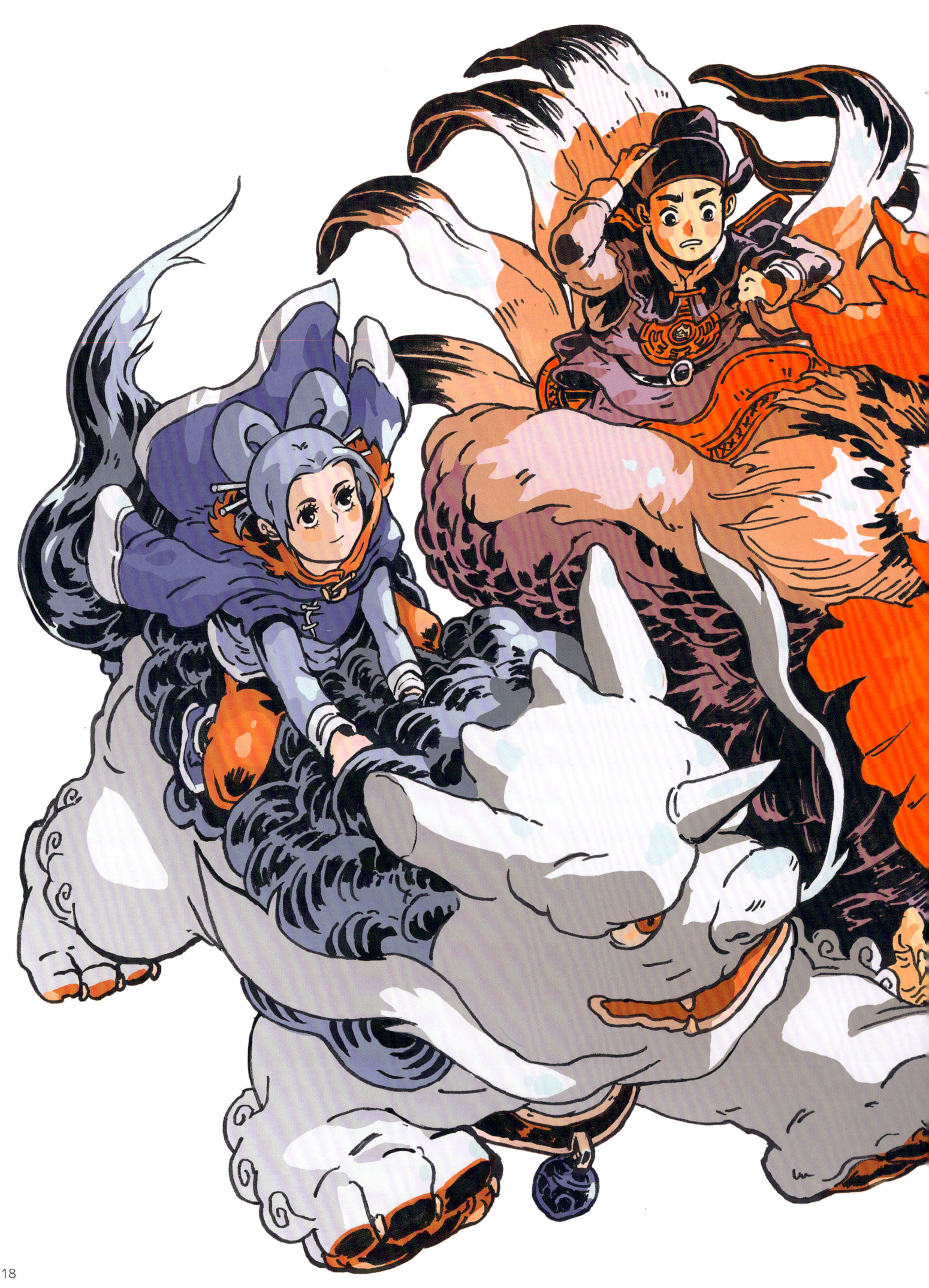

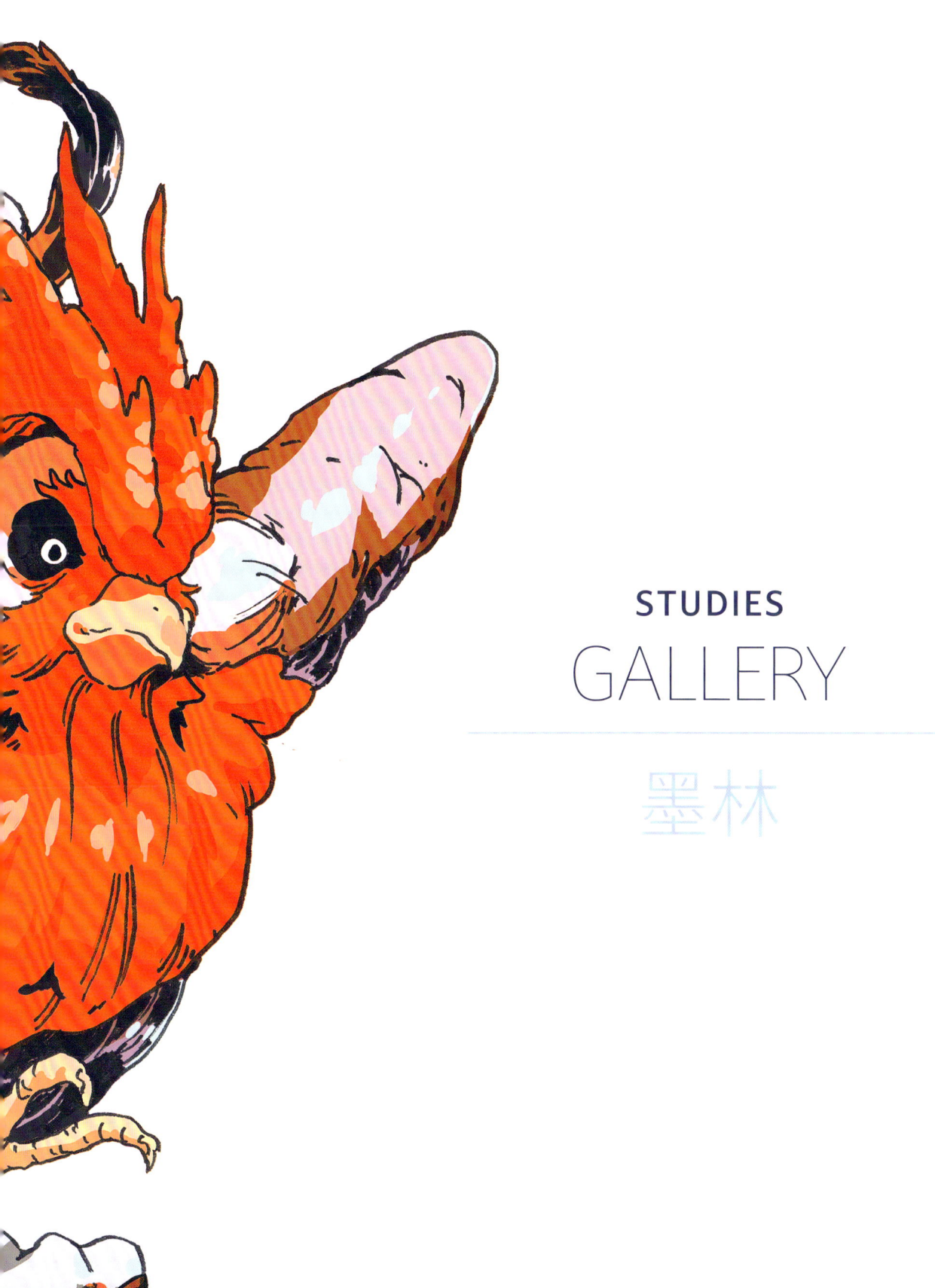

STUDIES
GALLERY

墨林

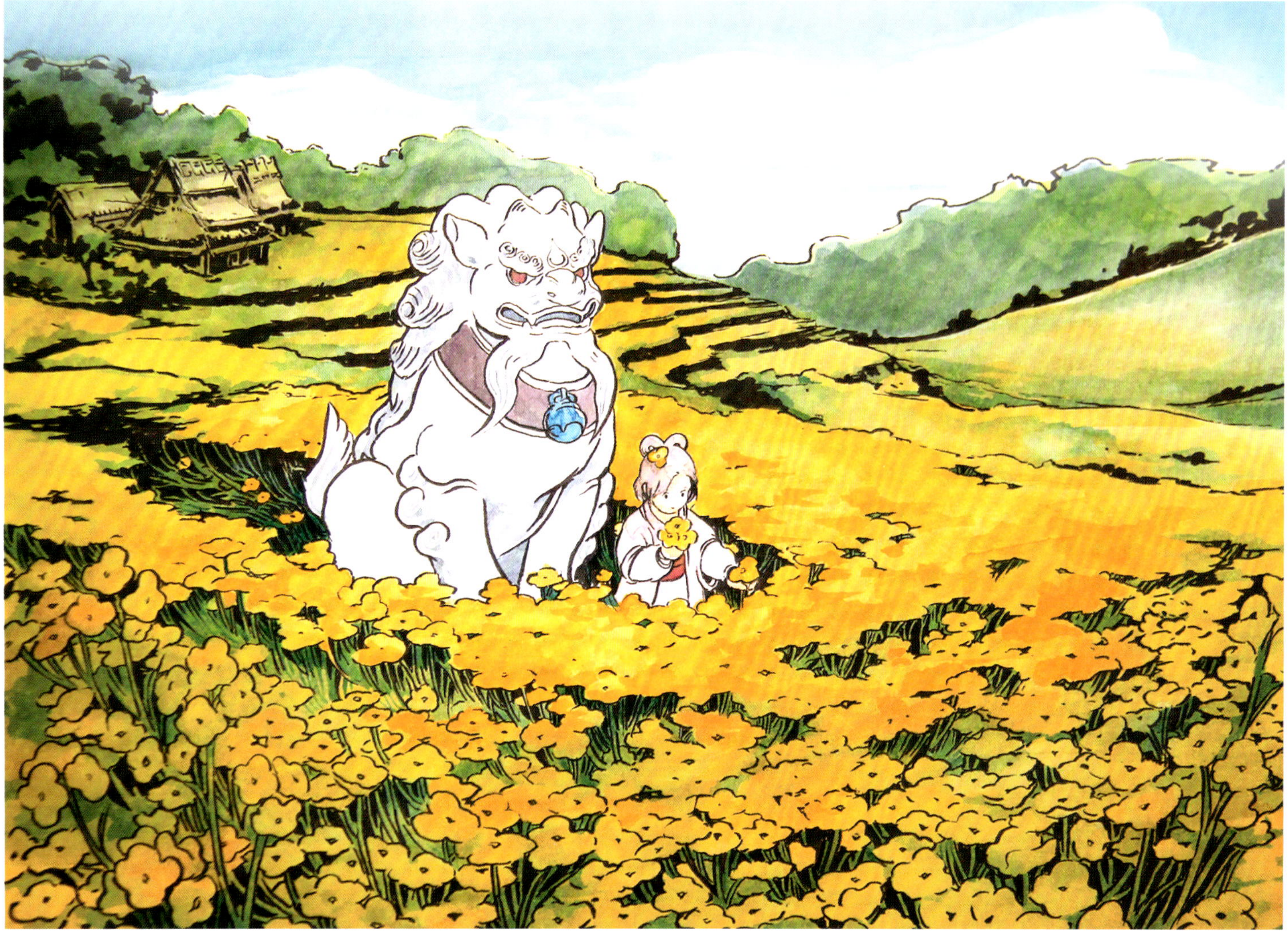

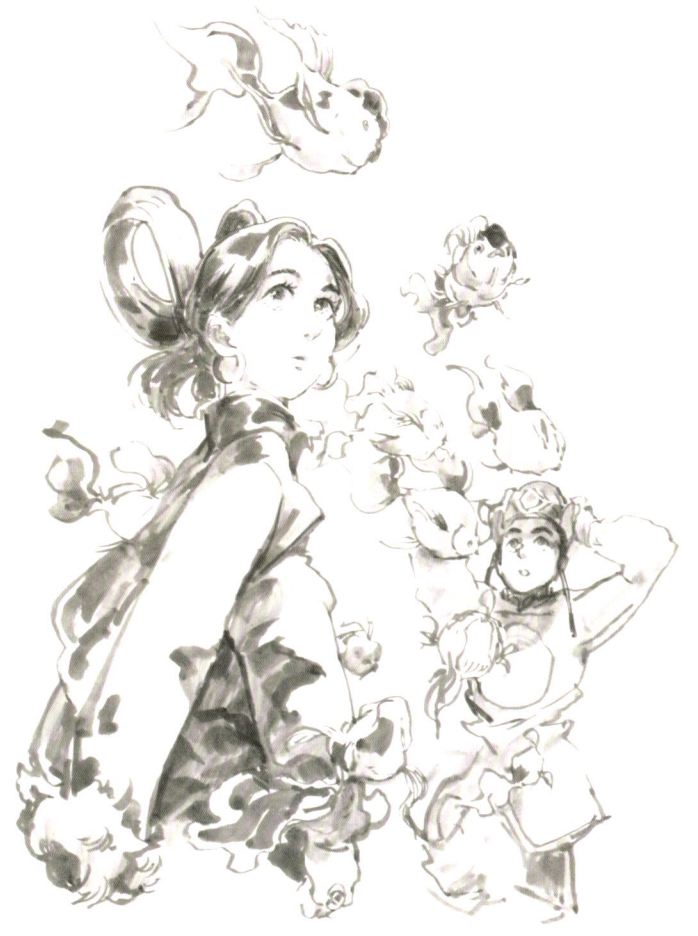

BING BING

Bing Bing is a character I created during my first year of Inktober. She is a typical magical girl, but of Asian descent. The original prompt was 'flower', and so I drew a girl accompanied by a Chinese lion in a field of flowers.

In my head, I wrote the story of a girl whose grandmother was transformed into a lion, yet continued to watch over her. Drawing and thinking of stories at the same time is one of my most cherished pastimes. It's also one of the more natural ways my ideas come to me because I visually get to see whether something evokes the feelings I want, rather than just hoping they might through writing.

As I've drawn Bing Bing over the years, the story has evolved. Now, her mission has become to save her grandmother and uncover the mystery that led to this transformation. I imagine that she must go on many adventures, travelling far and wide to look for the cure, helping strangers along the way. It's a light-hearted story about how we must learn to care for each other in different ways as we grow older.

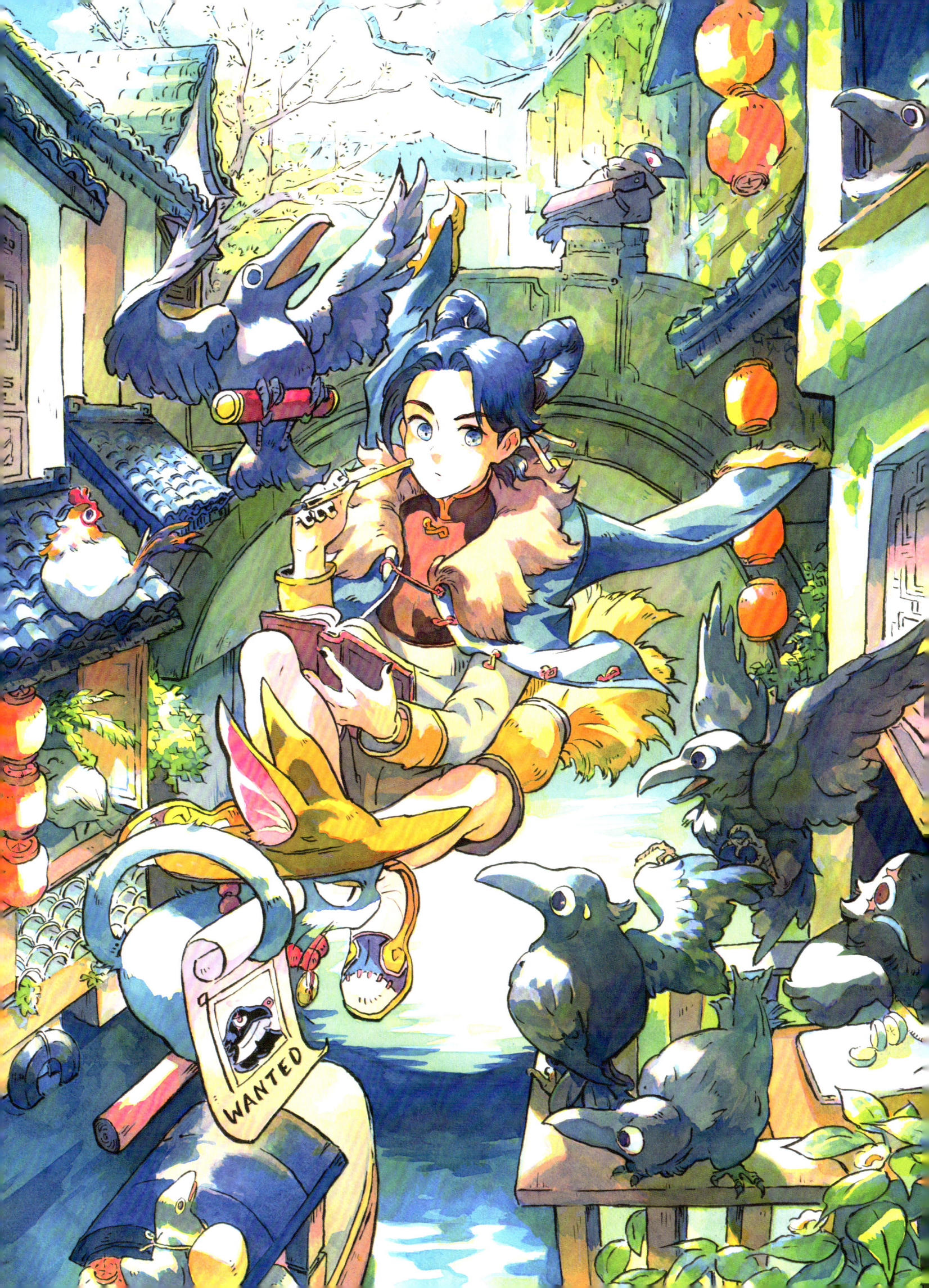

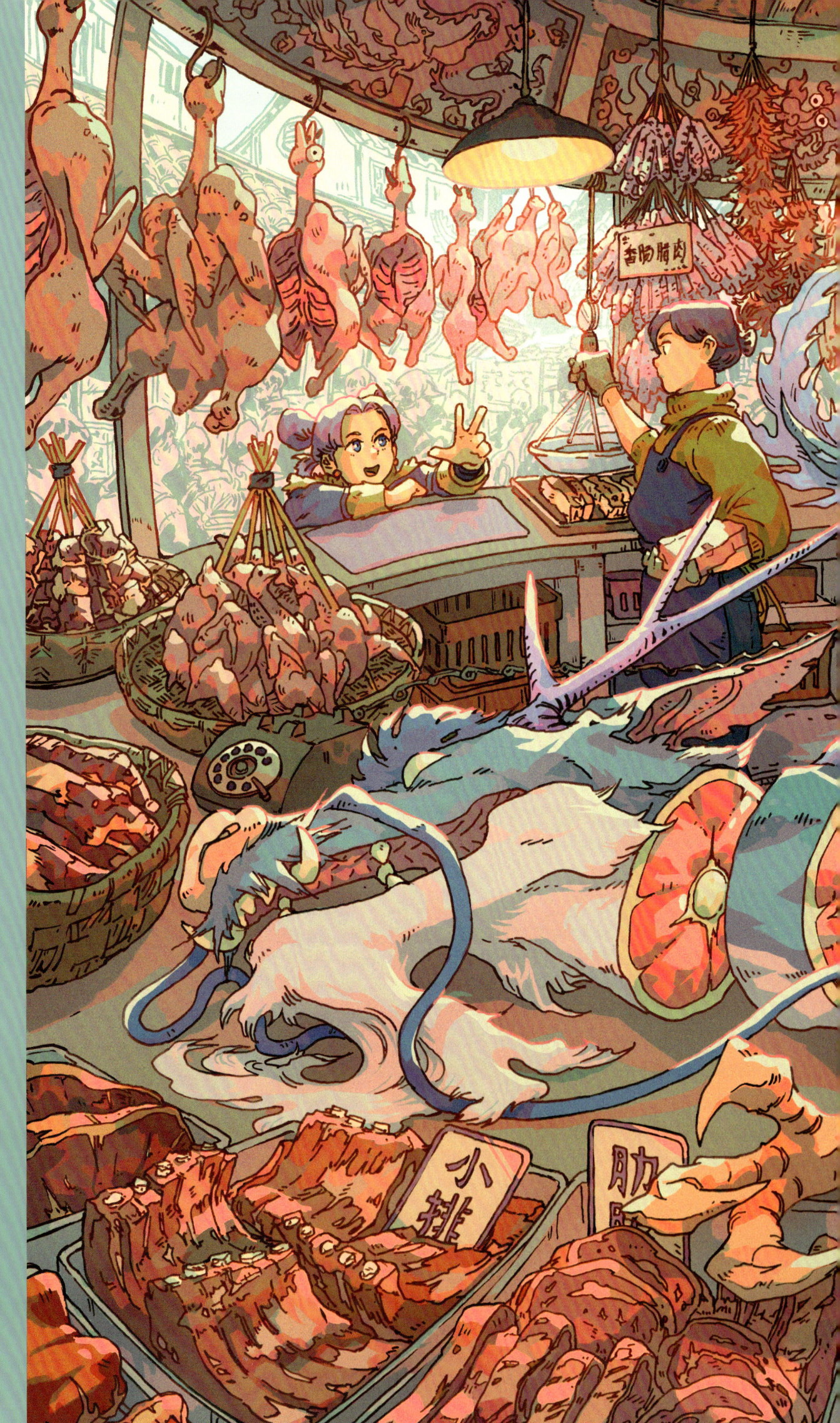

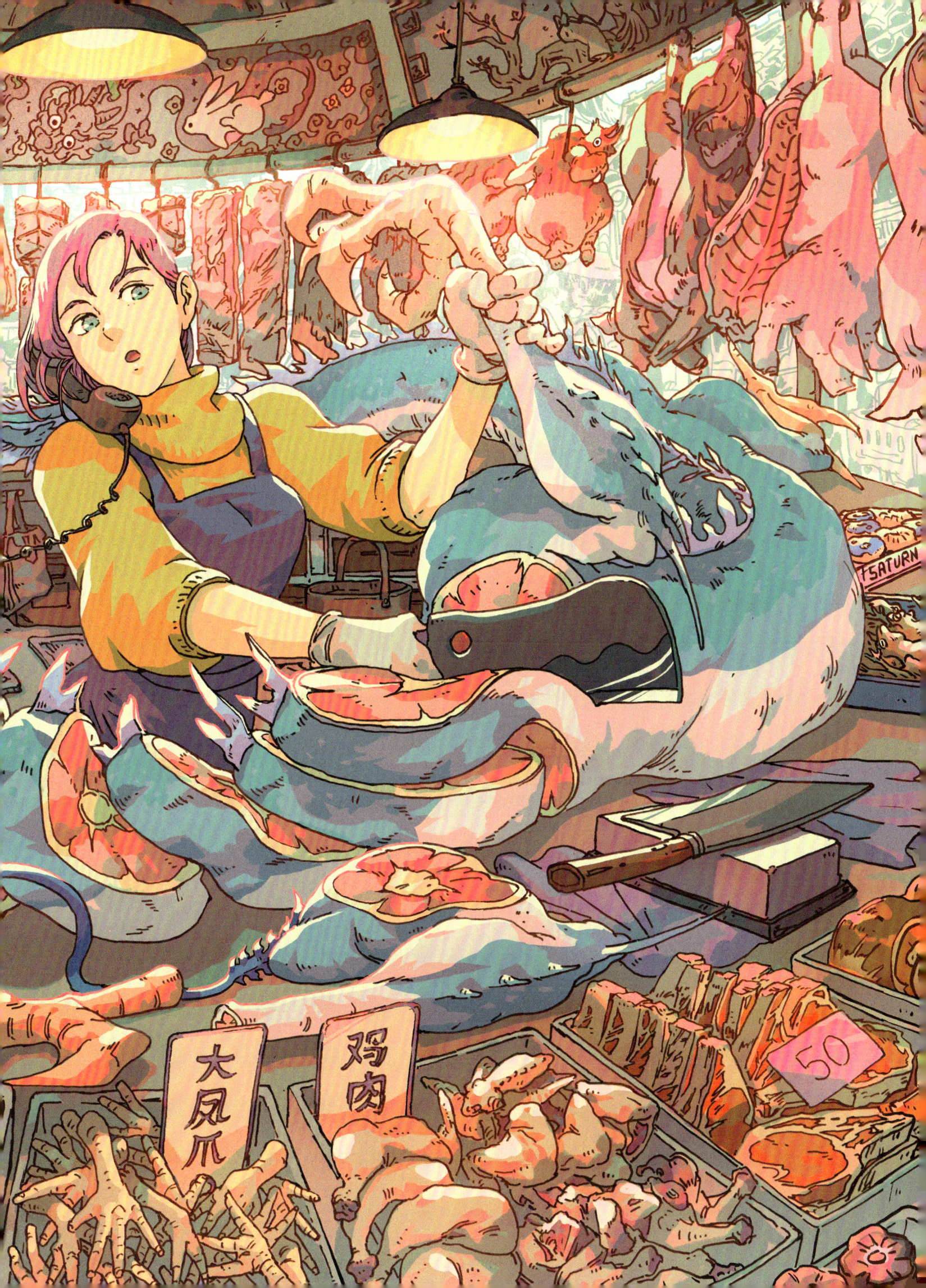

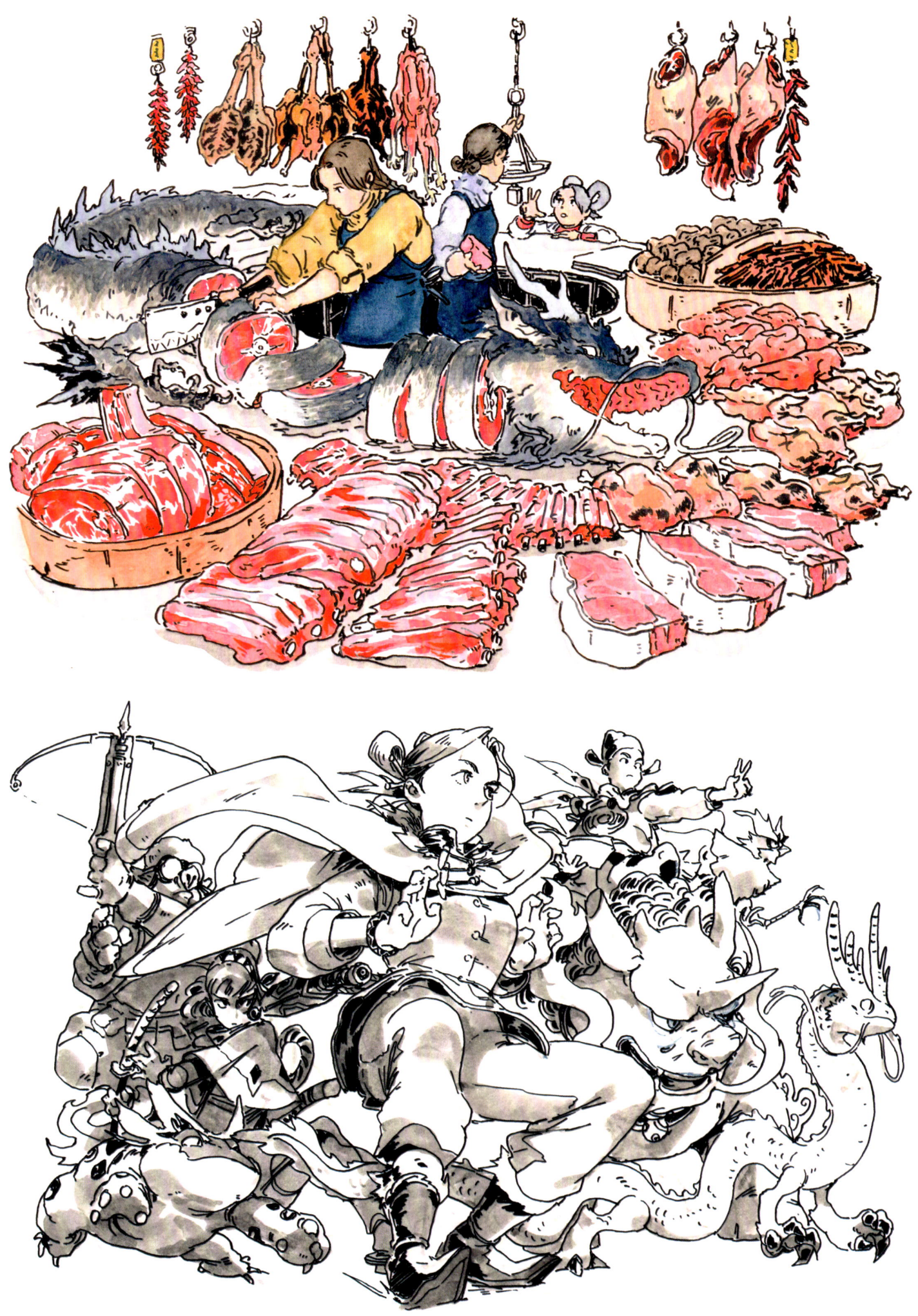

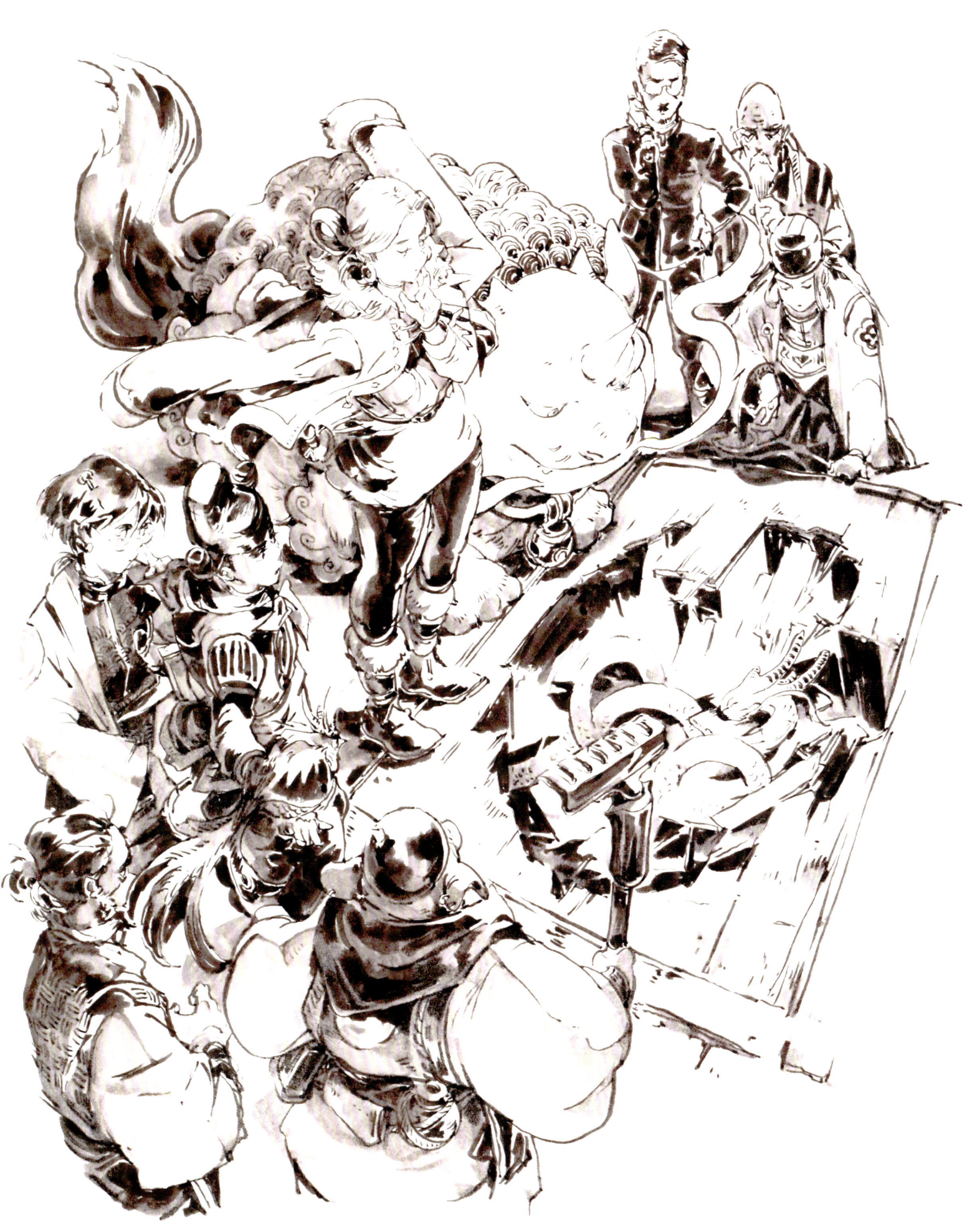

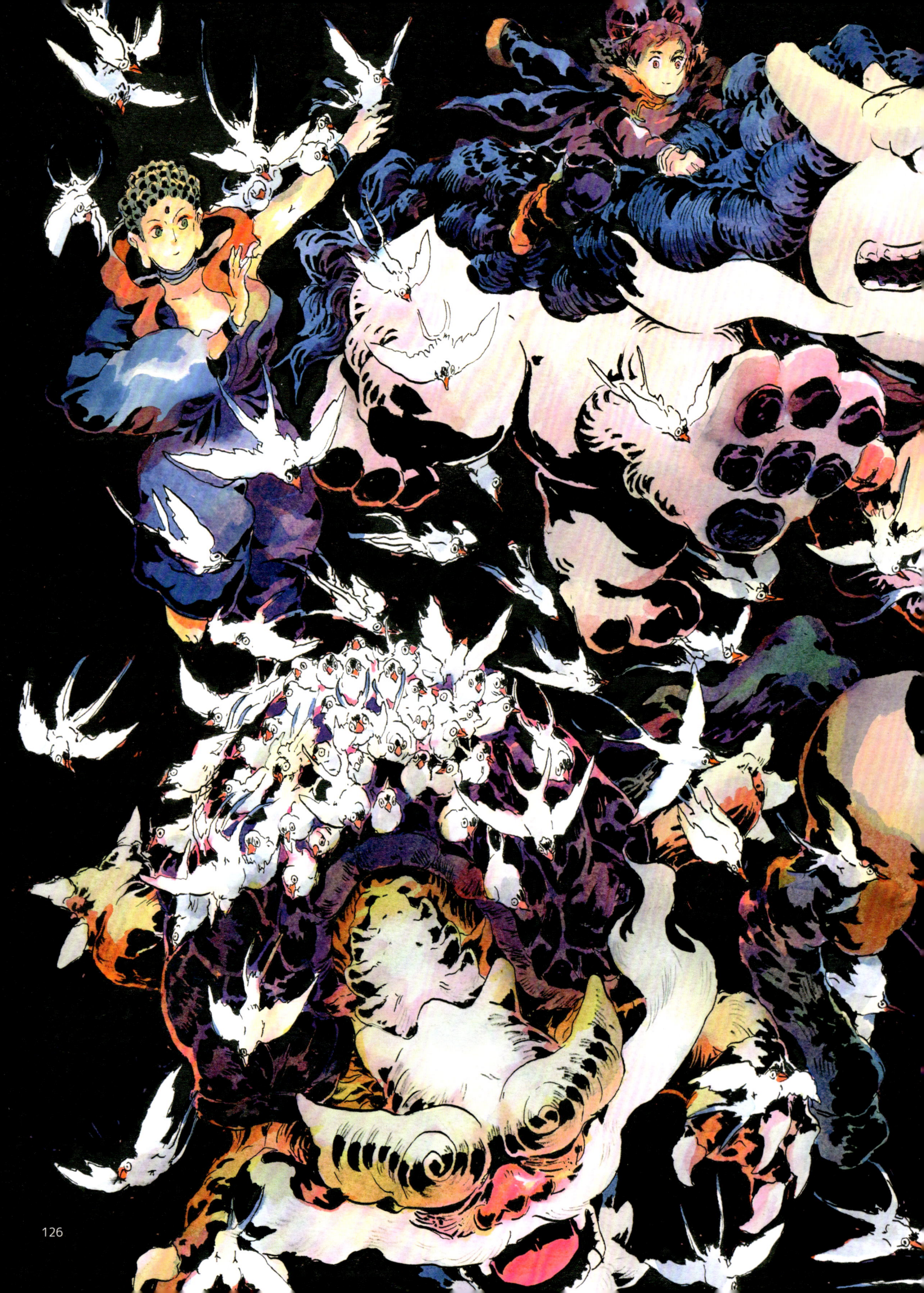

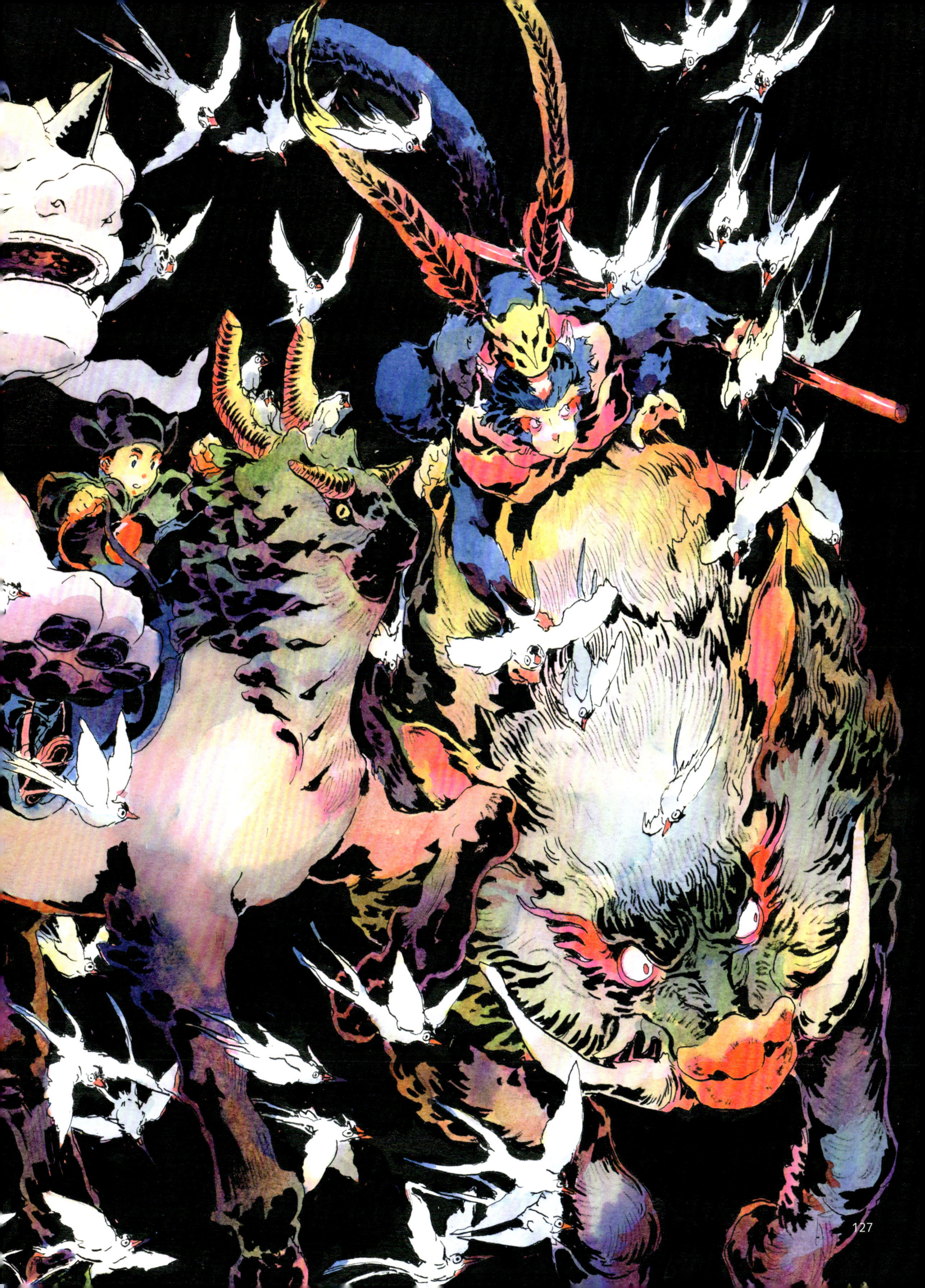

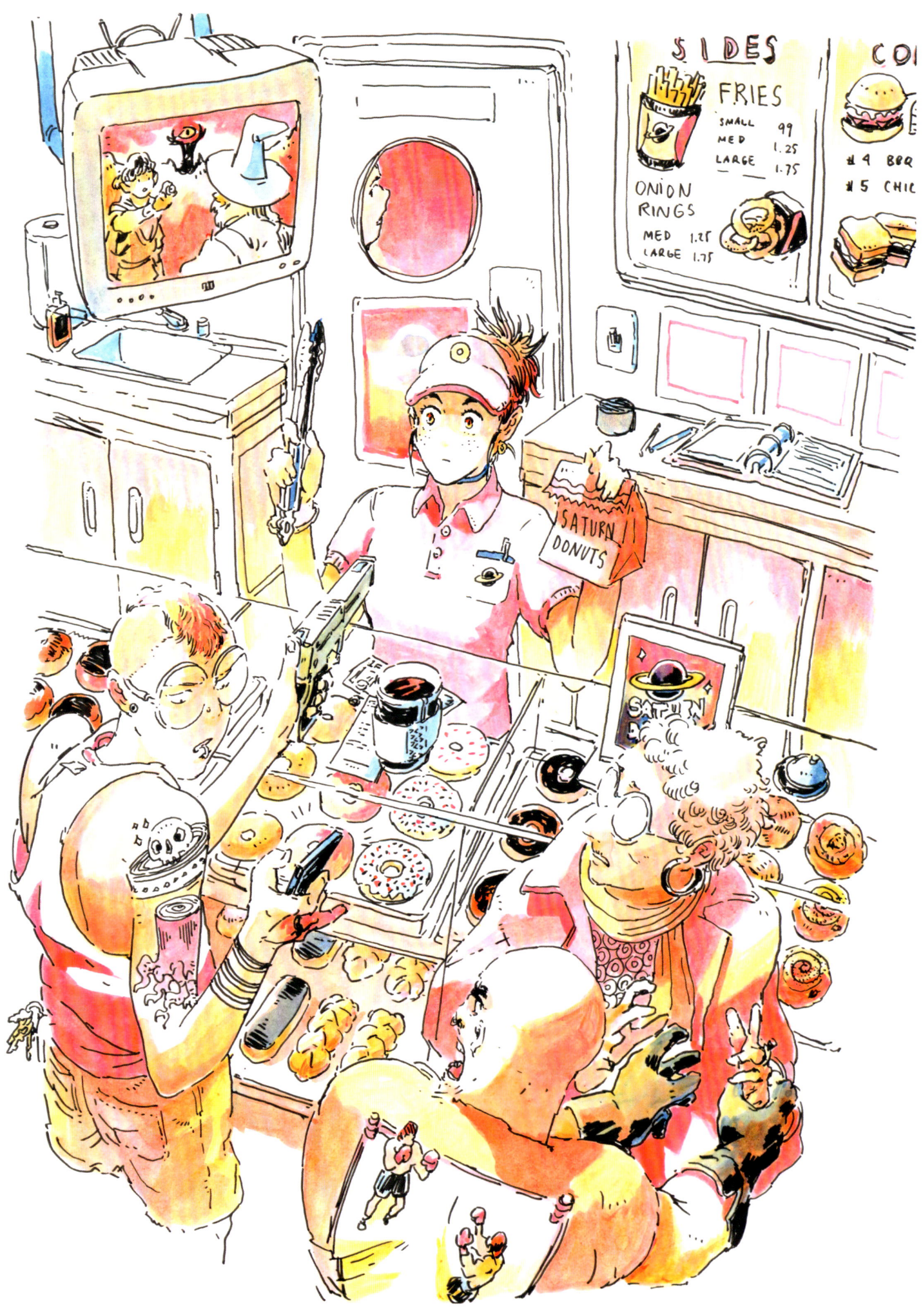

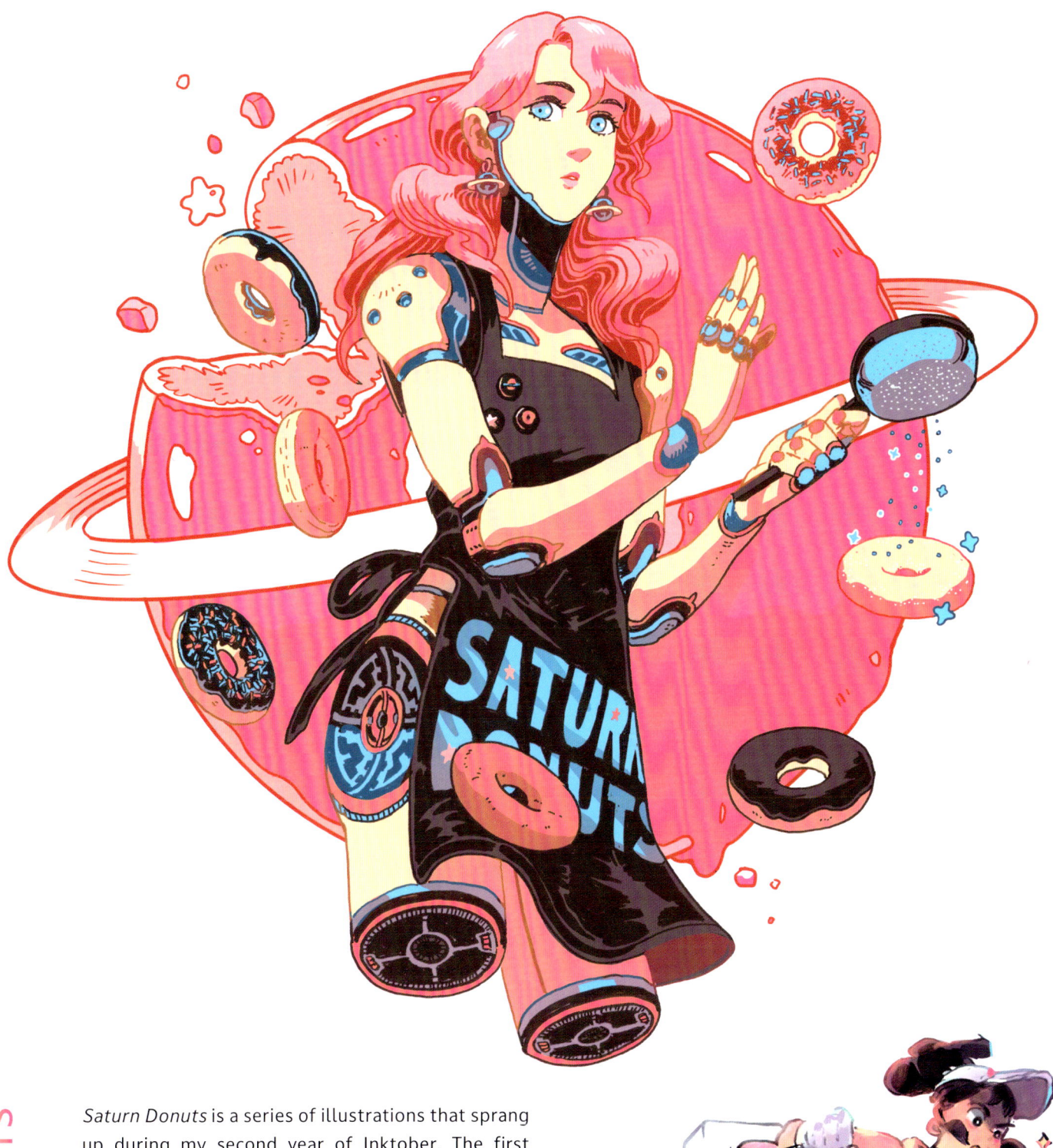

SATURN DONUTS

Saturn Donuts is a series of illustrations that sprang up during my second year of Inktober. The first day's theme was 'ring', so I made an illustration of a robbery occuring in a donut shop, featuring as many interpretations of a ring as I could think of.

Of course, this includes the rings of Saturn and the ring of a donut, but some of my other favourites were boxing ring, towel ring, and the 'one ring to rule them all'. After a successful first drawing, the rest of my Inktober series that year featured the girl from the donut-shop scene delivering donuts to whatever the theme was each day. What started as a running joke became an expression of my journey to find balance in my own work life.

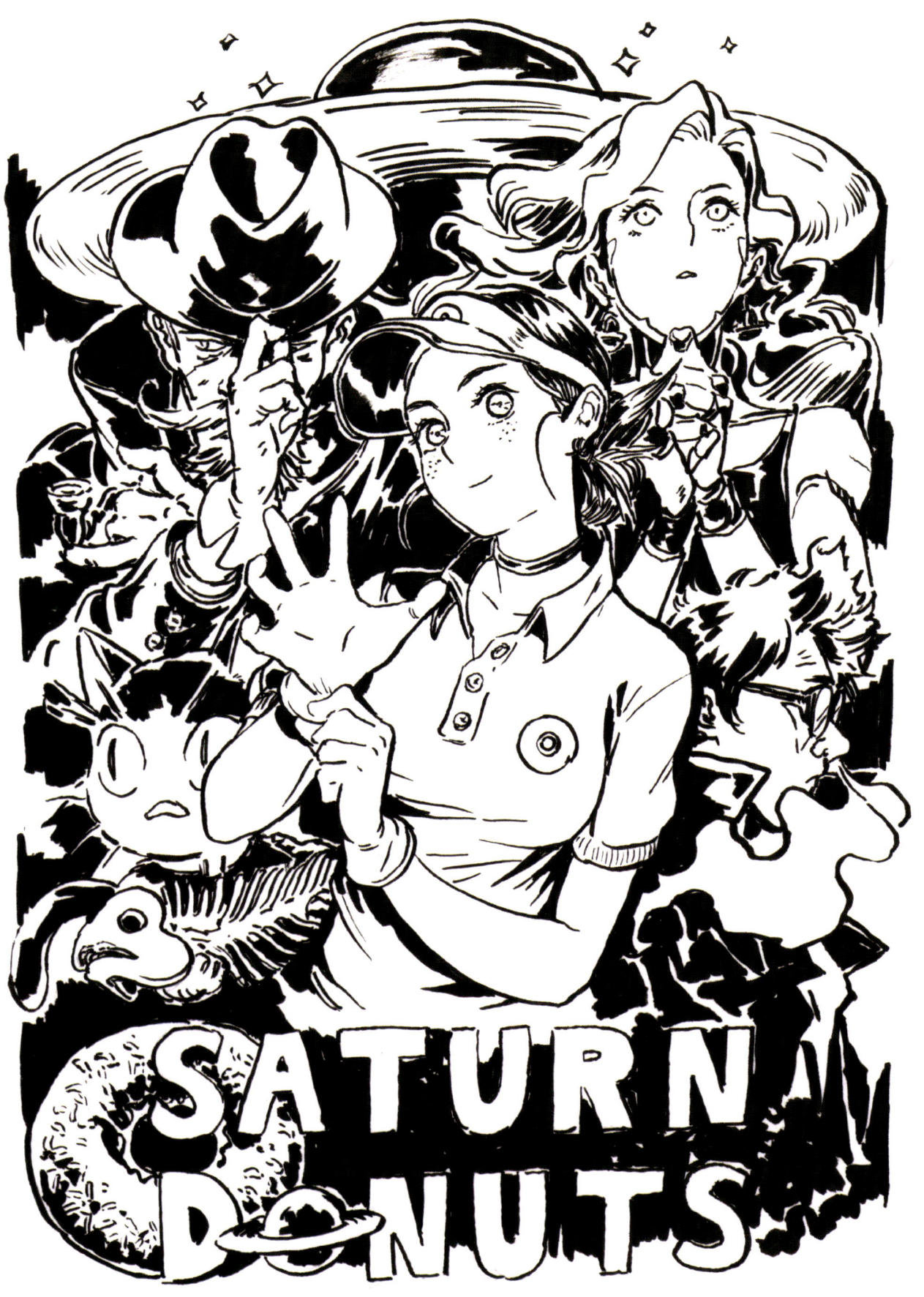

The illustrations of the *Saturn Donuts* girl generally feature her going above and beyond to deliver donuts to far-flung alternative universes, but when that began to feel predictable, I introduced her to other characters. These included her mad-scientist grandma, who invented the technology that allowed travel between dimensions, and a female mech who was created by grandma to help run the business.

Outside of the *Saturn Donuts* employees, I also created rival businesses, namely the evil, pipe-smoking Bagel Baron and the Cronut Gang, who deliver cronuts instead of donuts and are far more irresponsible and reckless than the protagonist.

I have no idea what these three businesses are so competitive about, but the silliness of the world is something I enjoy a lot.

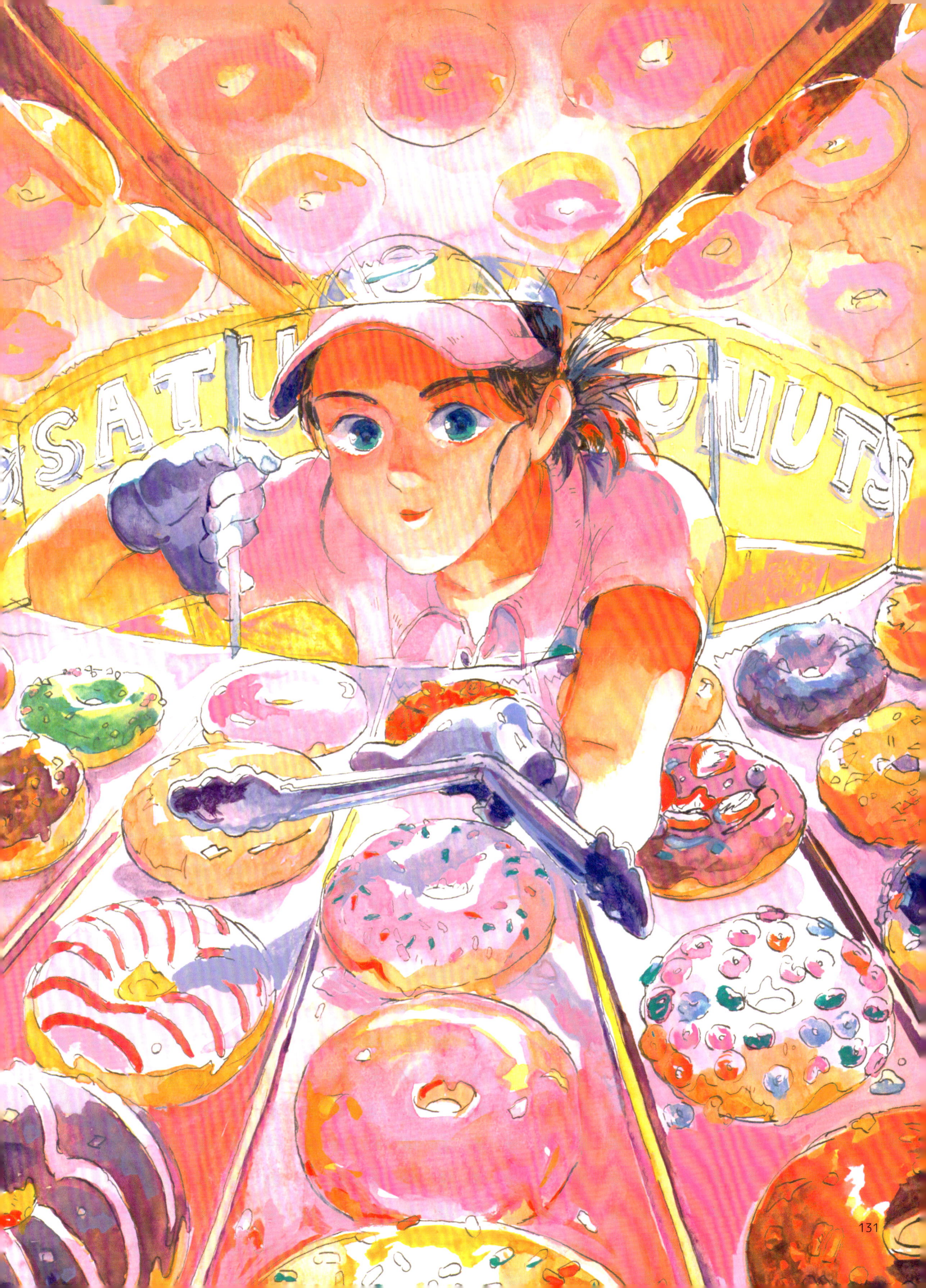

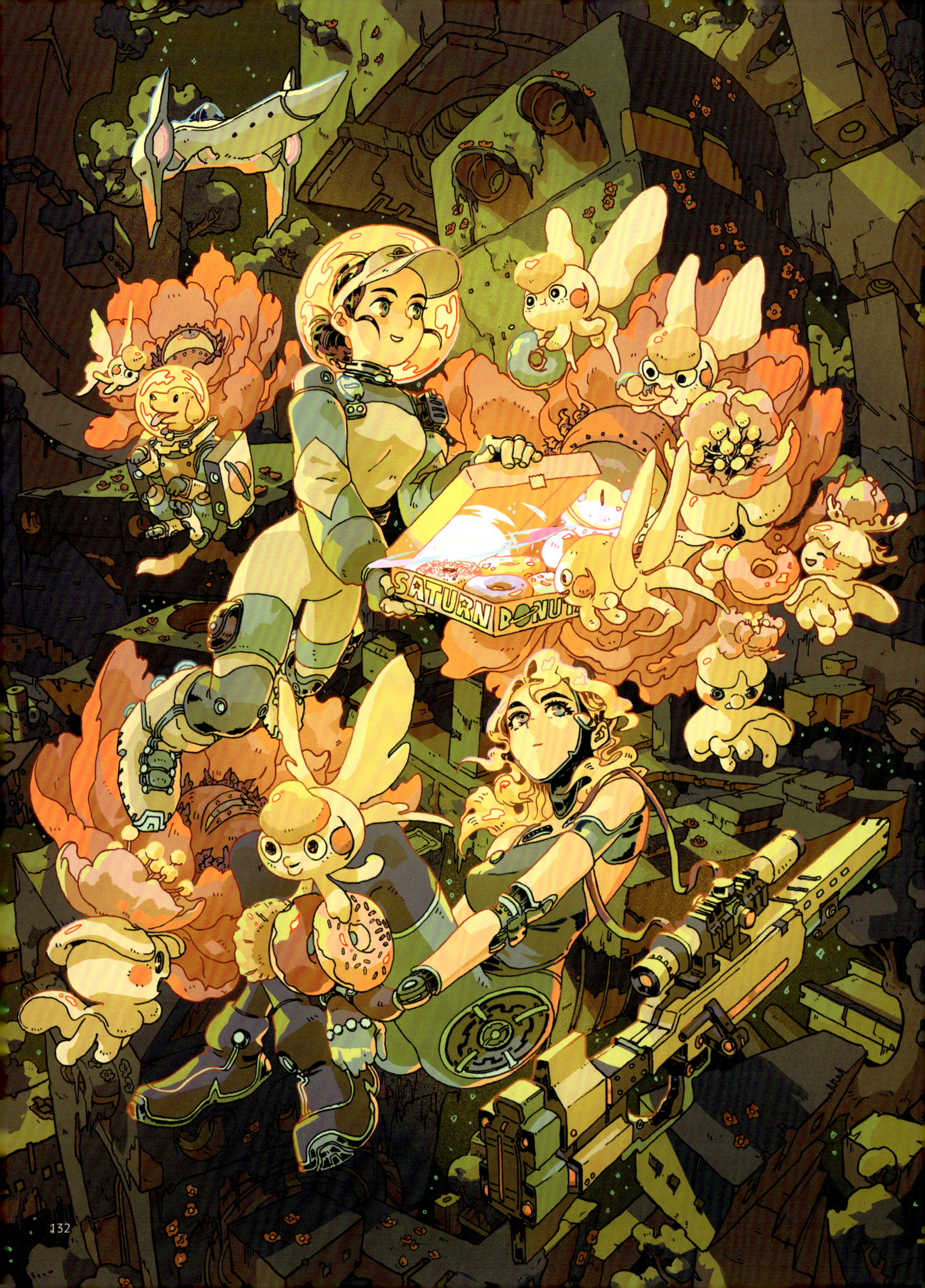

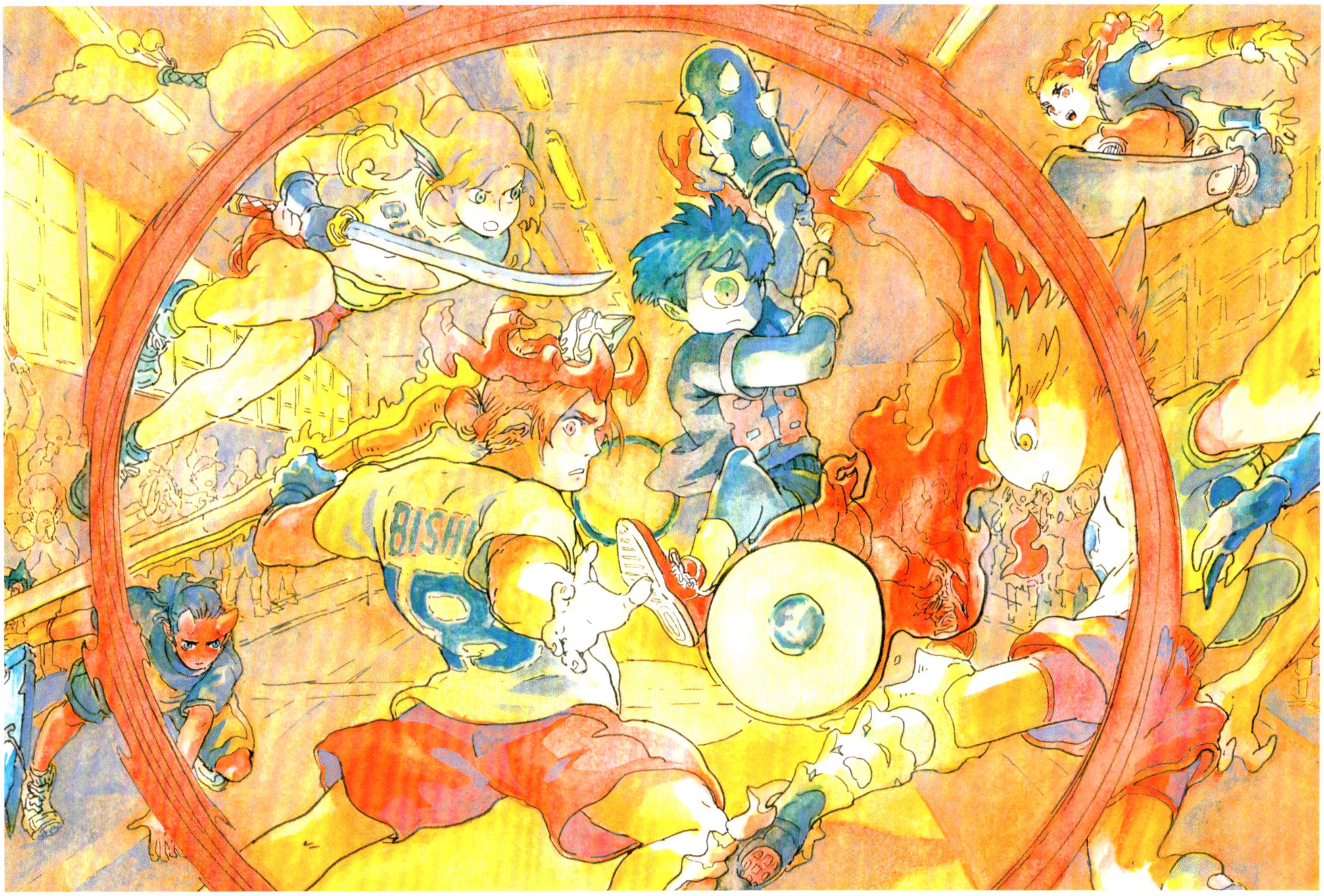
BISH
8

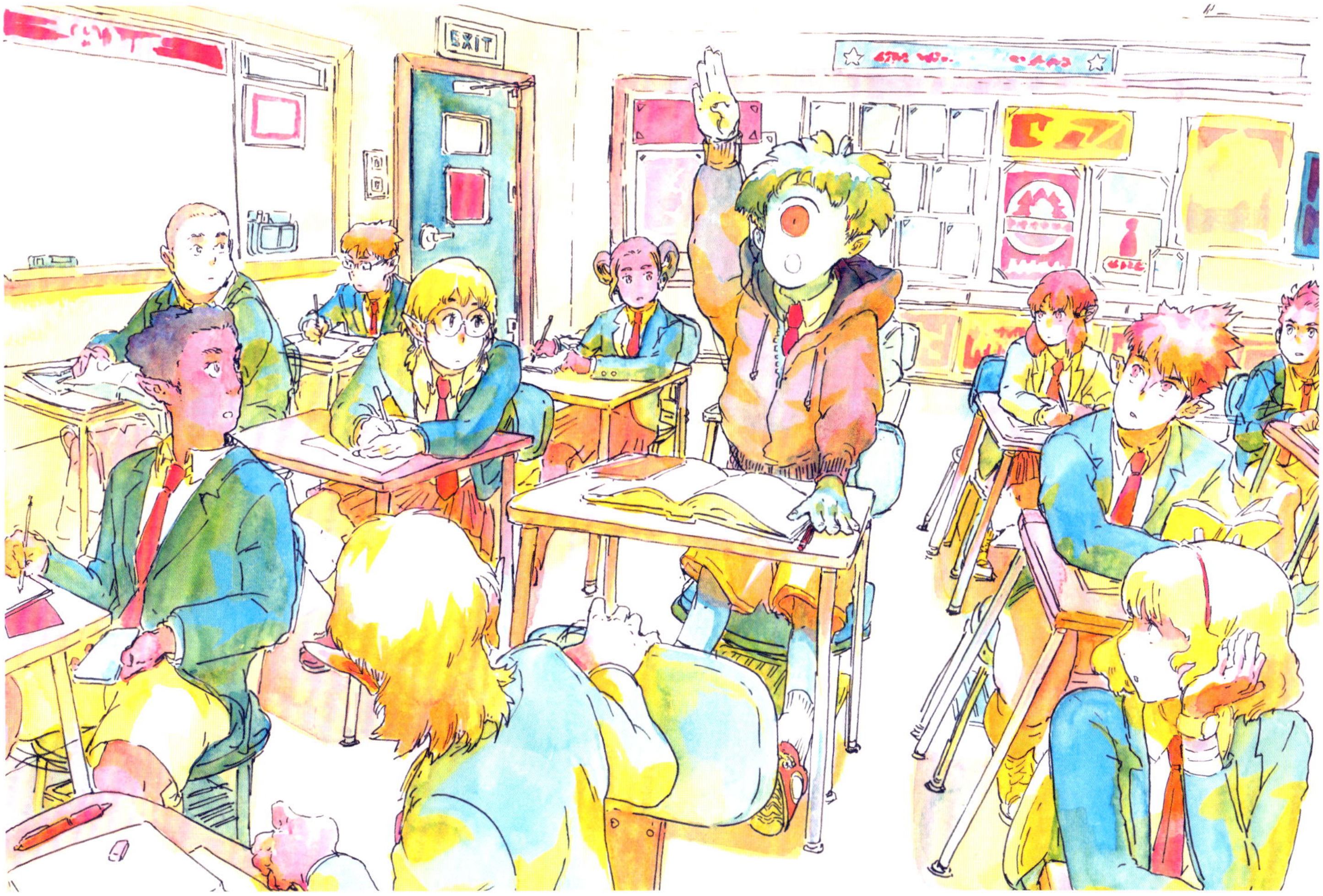
EXIT

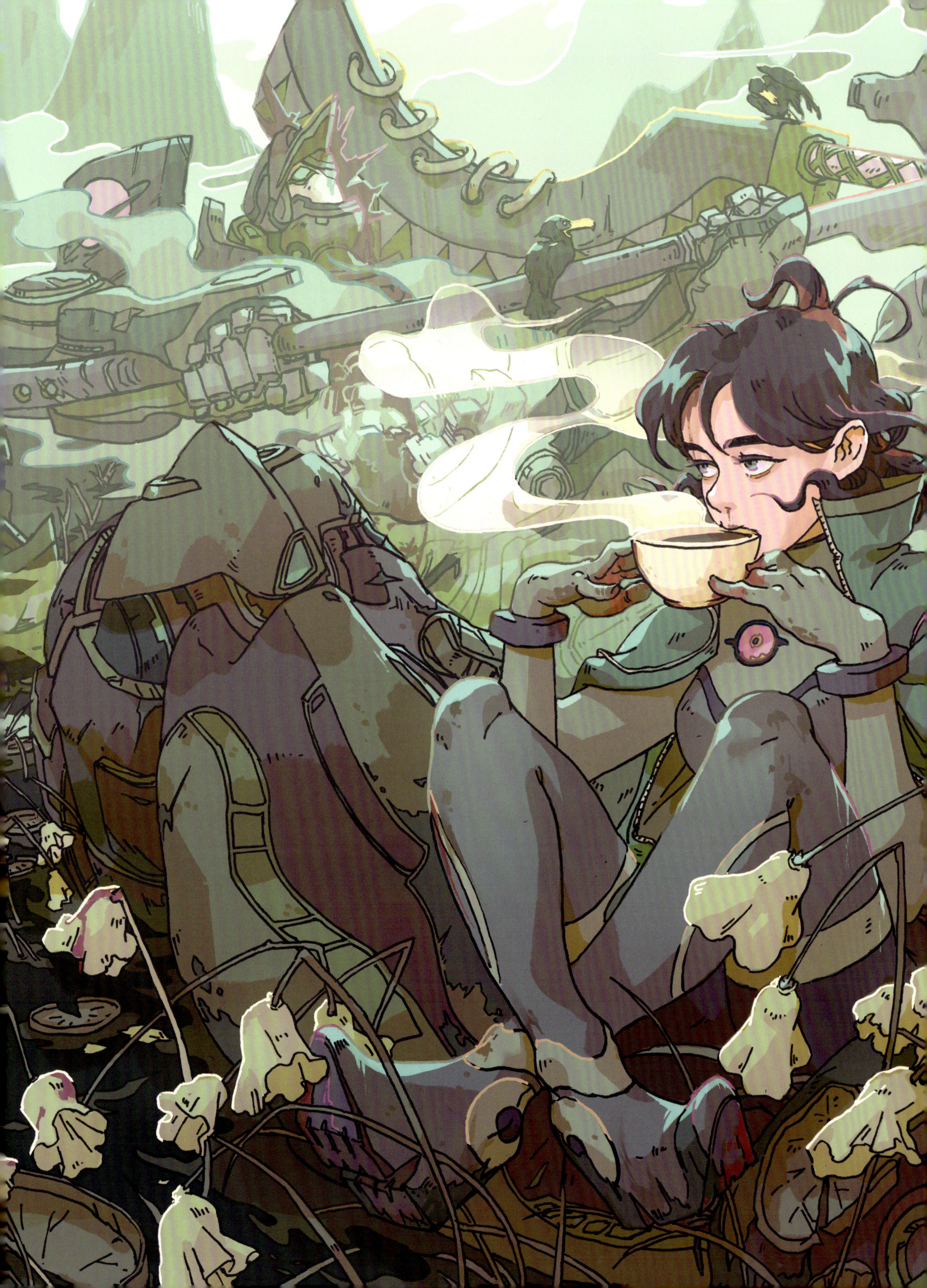

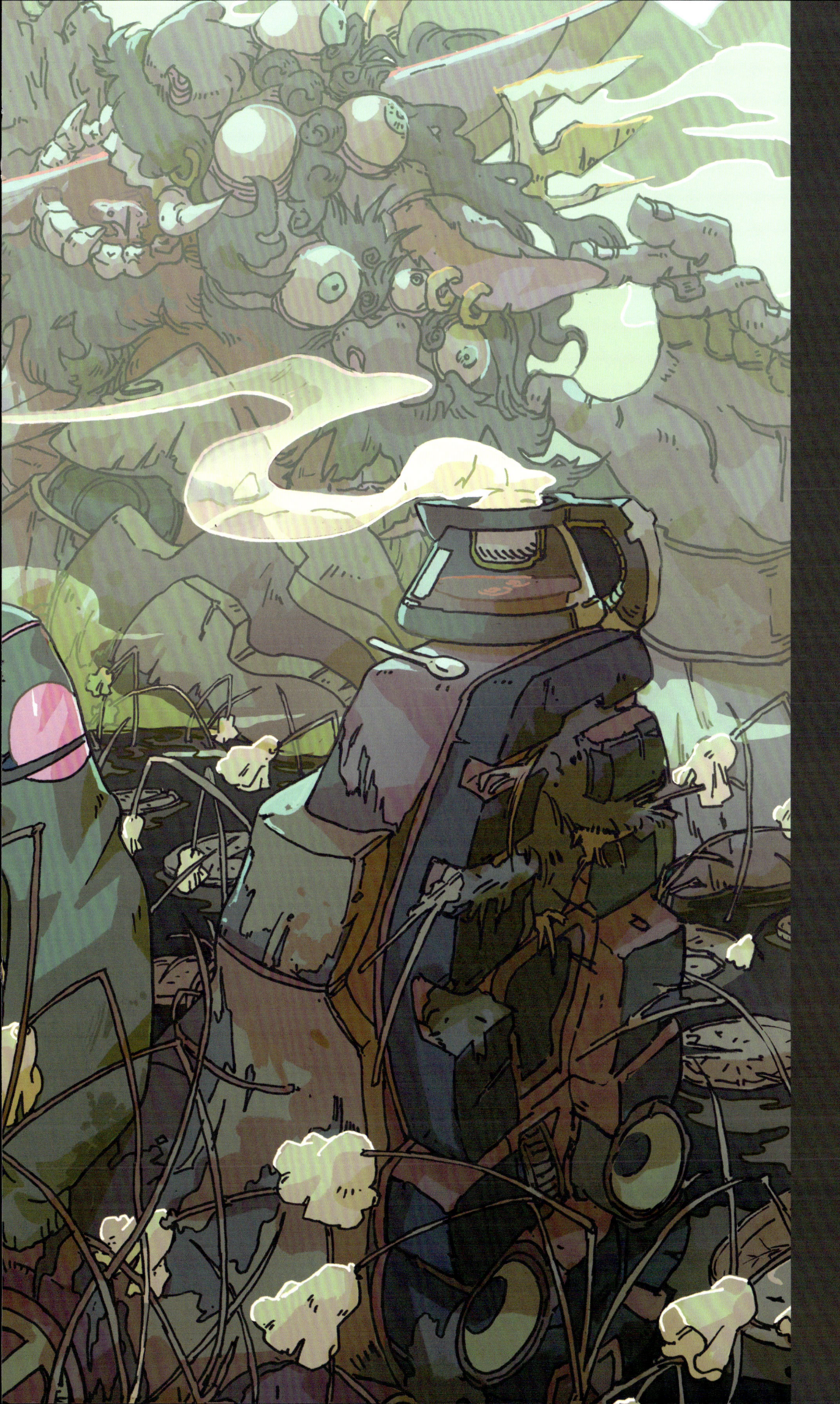

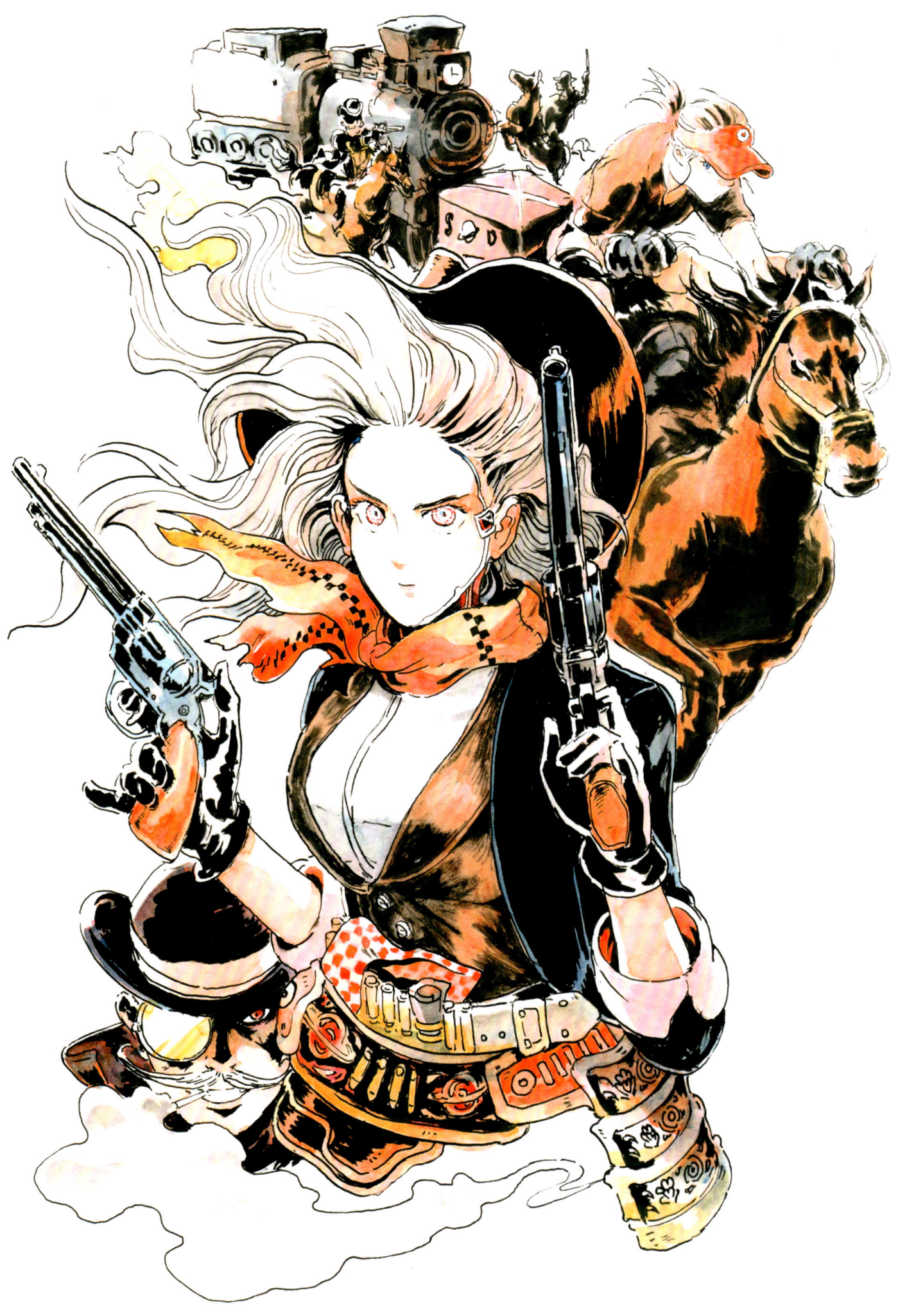

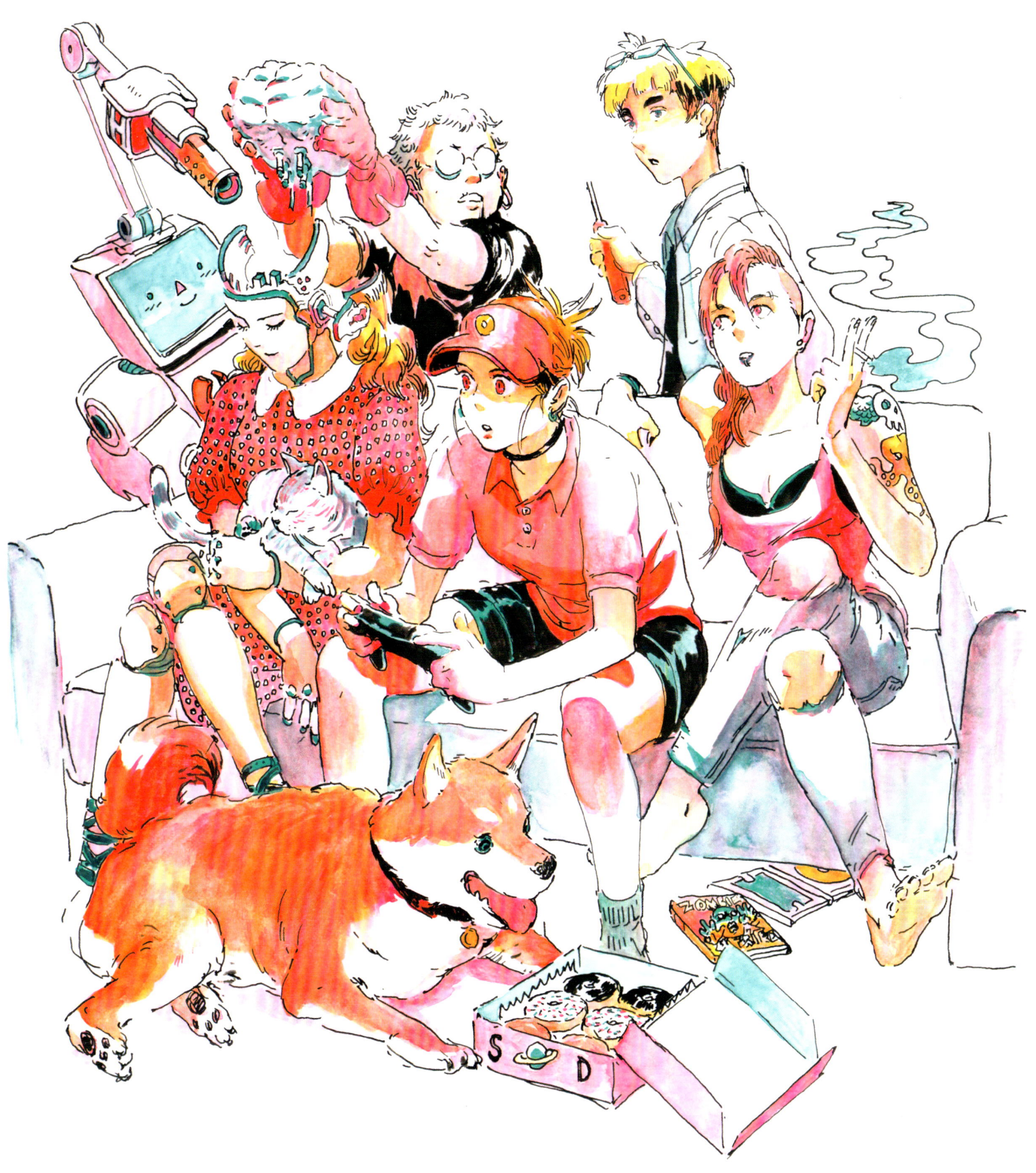

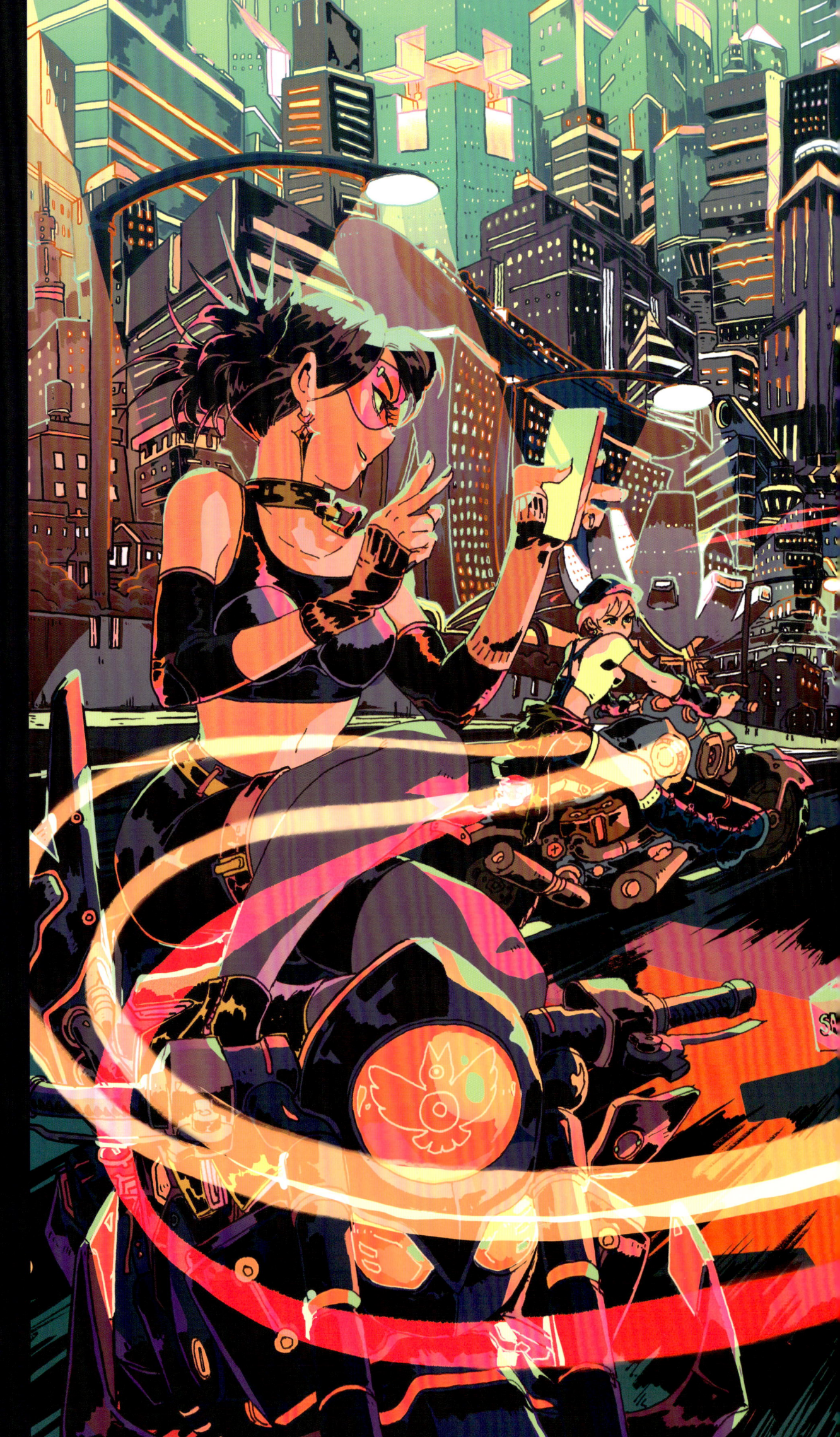

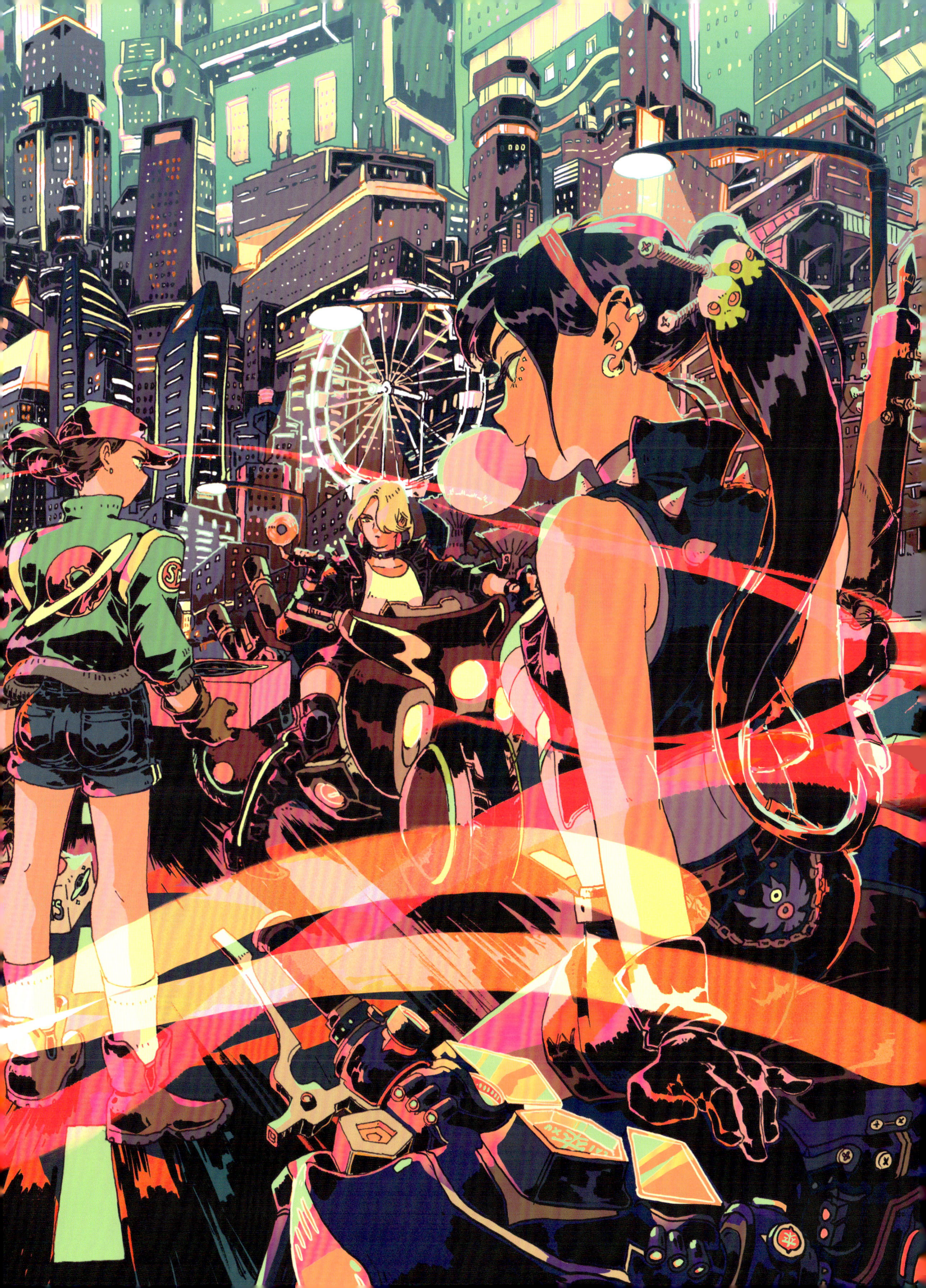

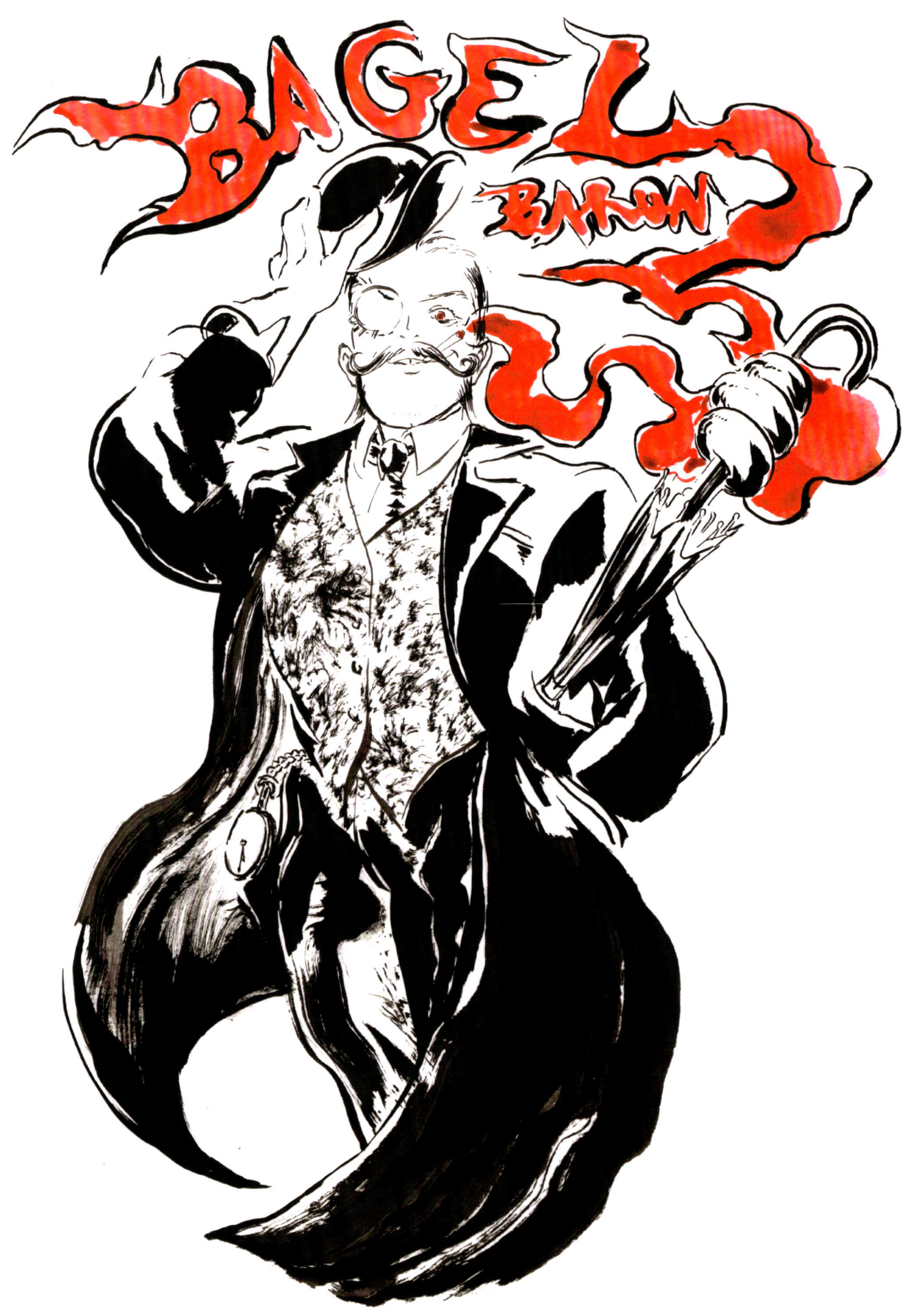

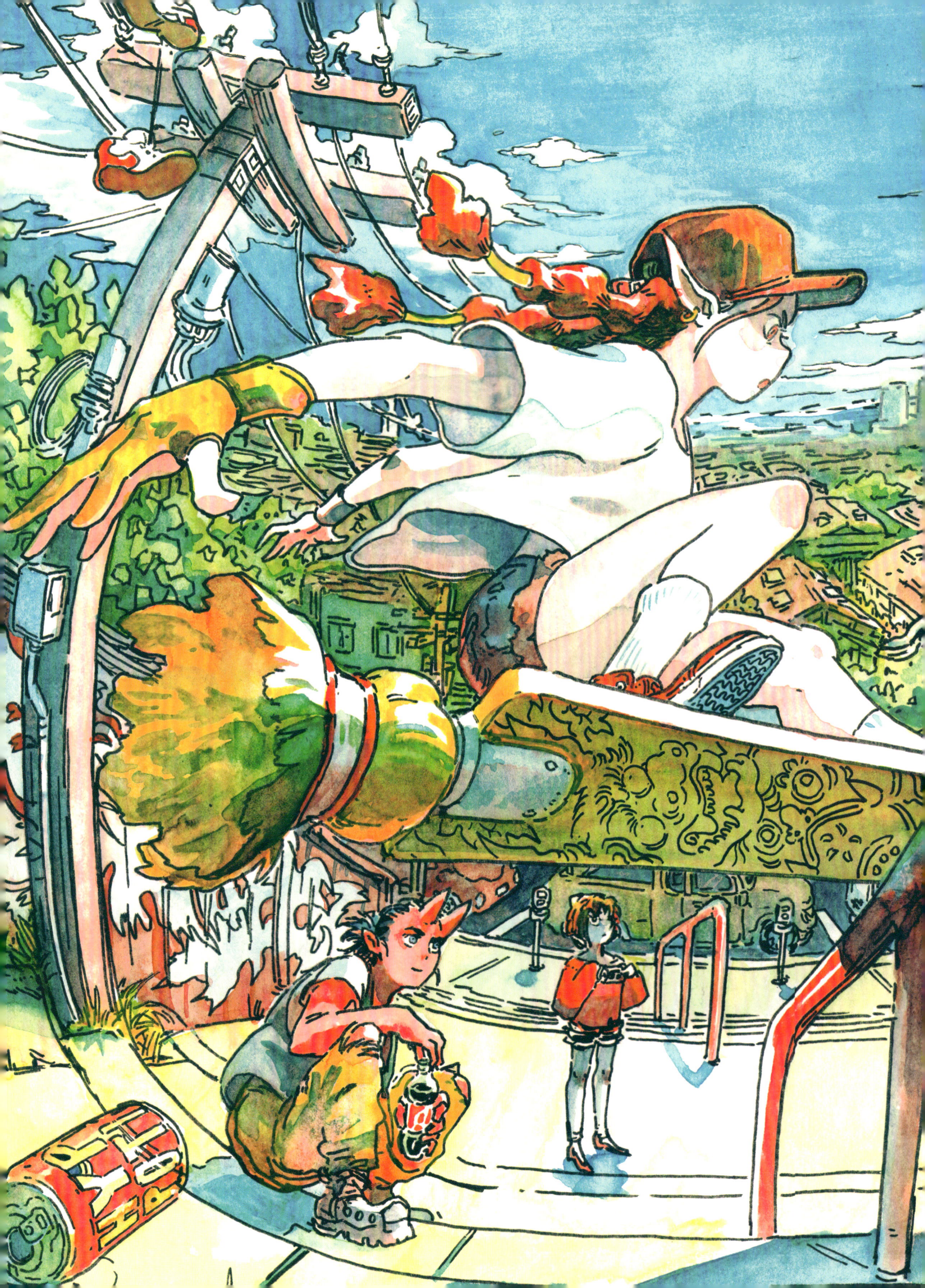

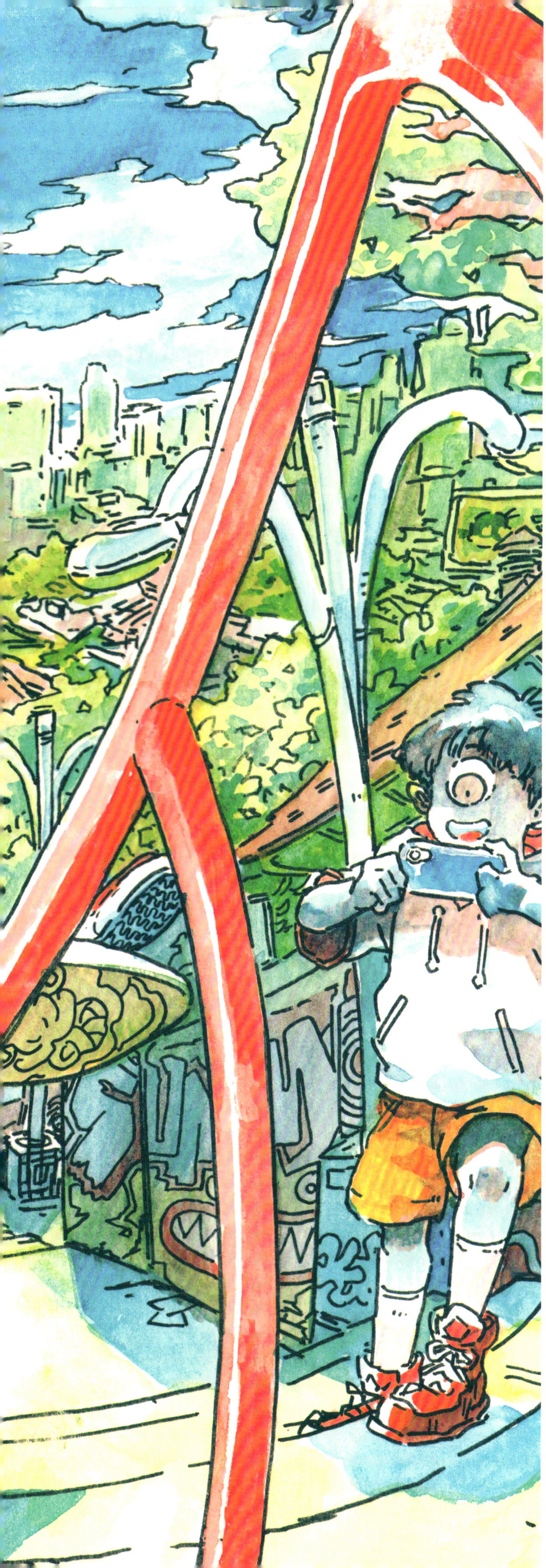

Summoners Club is a project I created to pitch to Netflix, and the original logline went a little something like this:

'Magical-sports anime about a trio of underdog, monster kids from a low-income magic school aiming for the Summonball Championships. Harry Potter minus the white privilege.'

It was mostly inspired by my wife's time as a teacher at a low-income, inner-city school, alongside my own experience of feeling like an outsider growing up. Its main character, Milo, is a cyclops who has pure passion for the sport, but who also has to navigate being a monster kid in a society that doesn't understand or care about him.

I spent a lot of time developing the Summonball sport and mechanics of how battles would play out – something akin to hitting a magical ball through a hoop using magic. Visually, I like the world of *Summoners Club* the most, but unfortunately, the reality behind the racial themes became too dark for me, given the playful character designs and upbeat tone I was originally aiming for.

I don't think it's impossible for me to eventually crack the code on this one, since it always felt like this story was only a few tweaks away from hitting home. But, as it stands, I think this is one where I'll have to wait until something clicks.

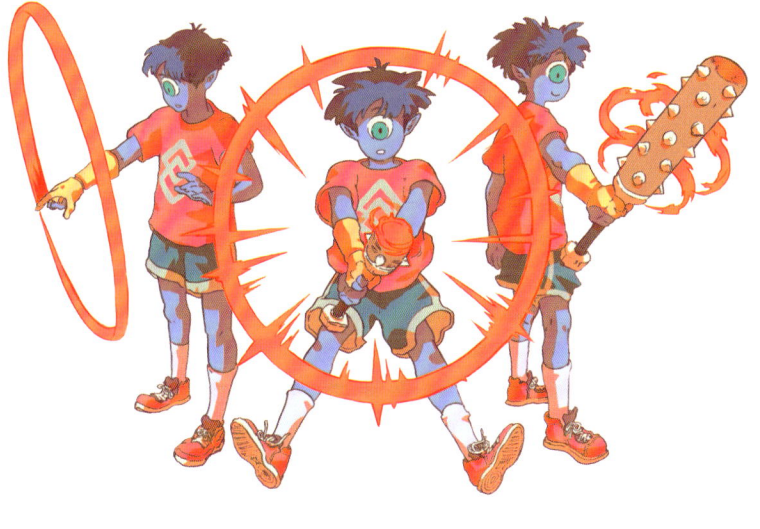

143

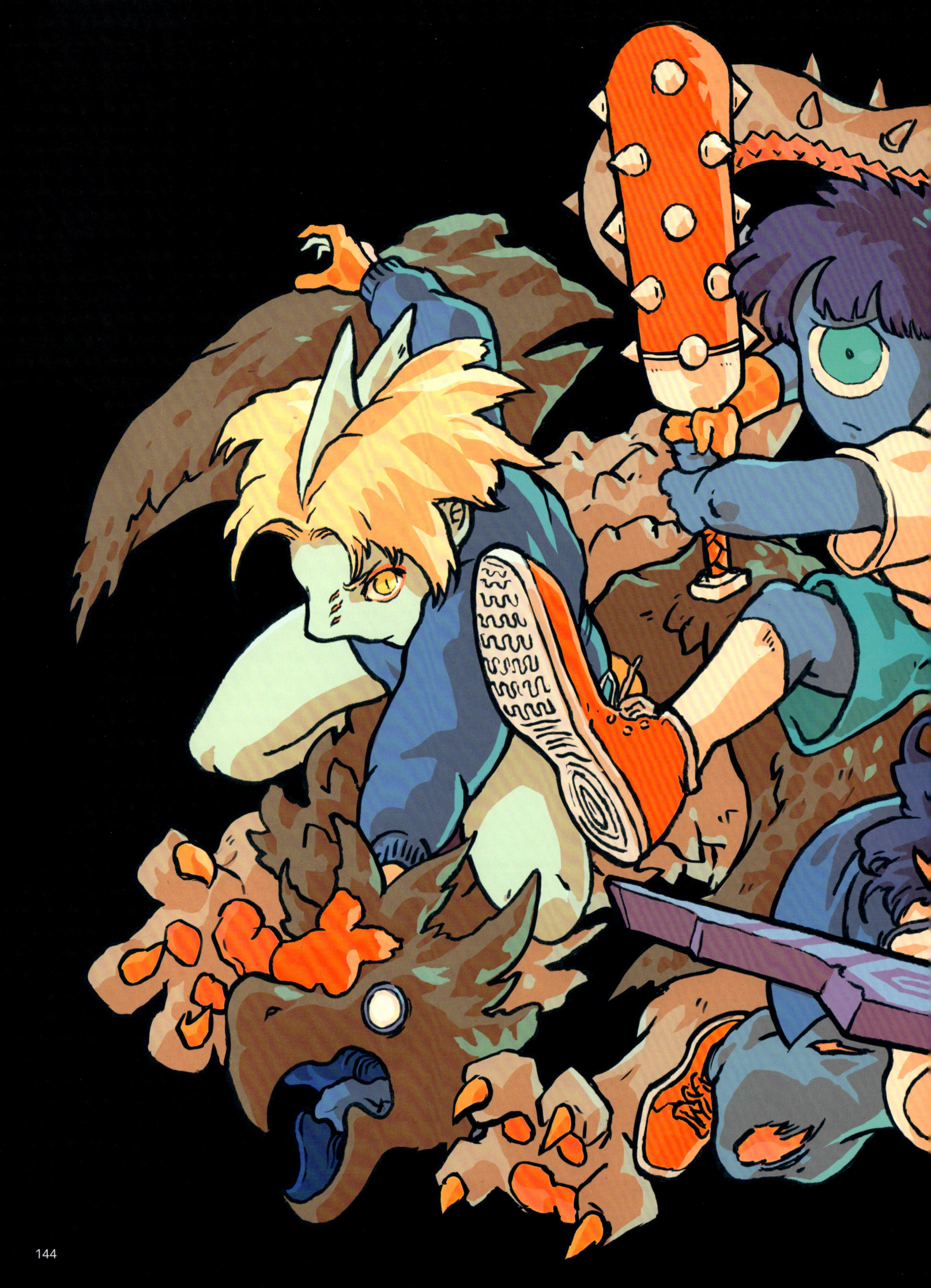

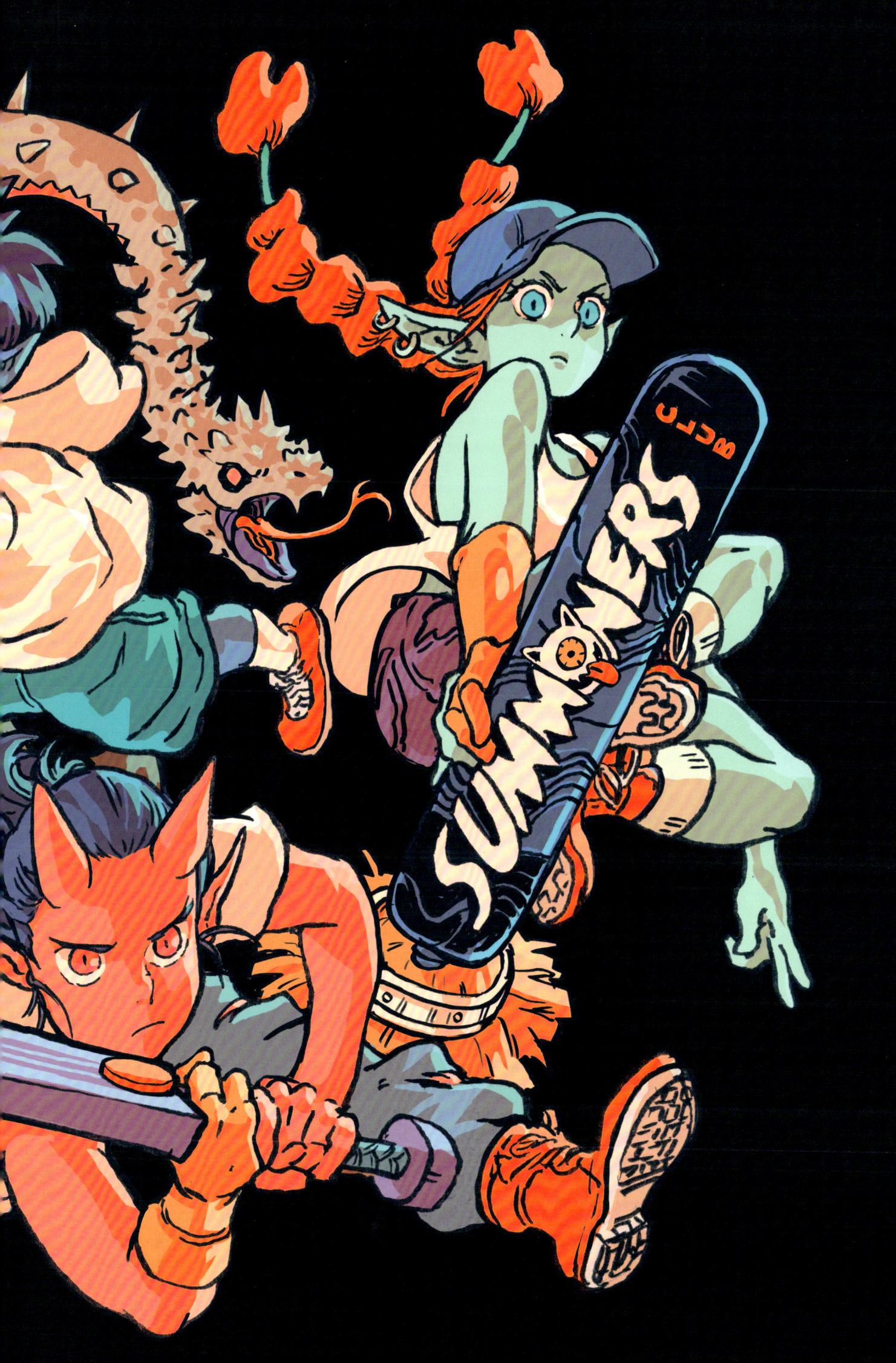

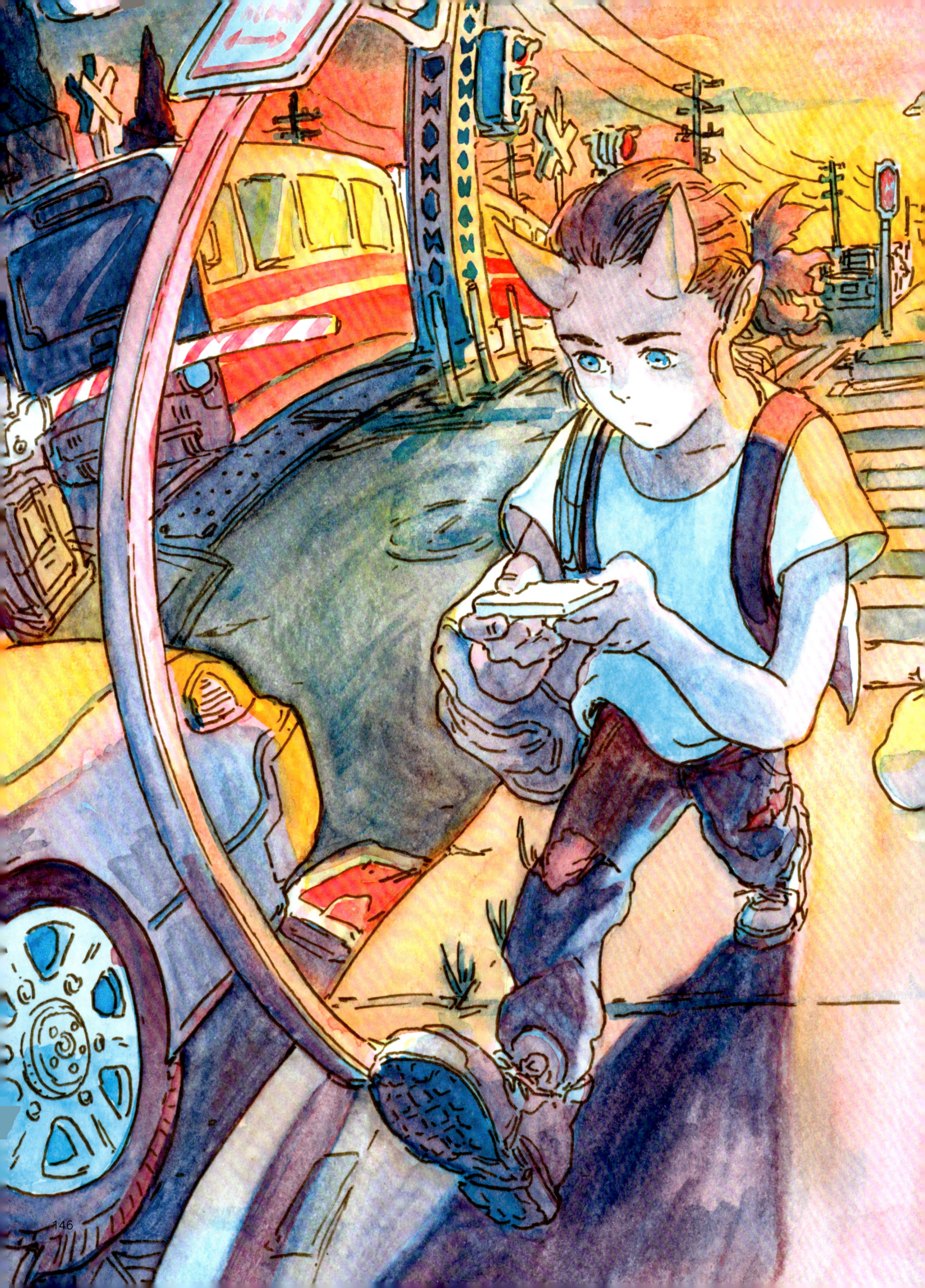

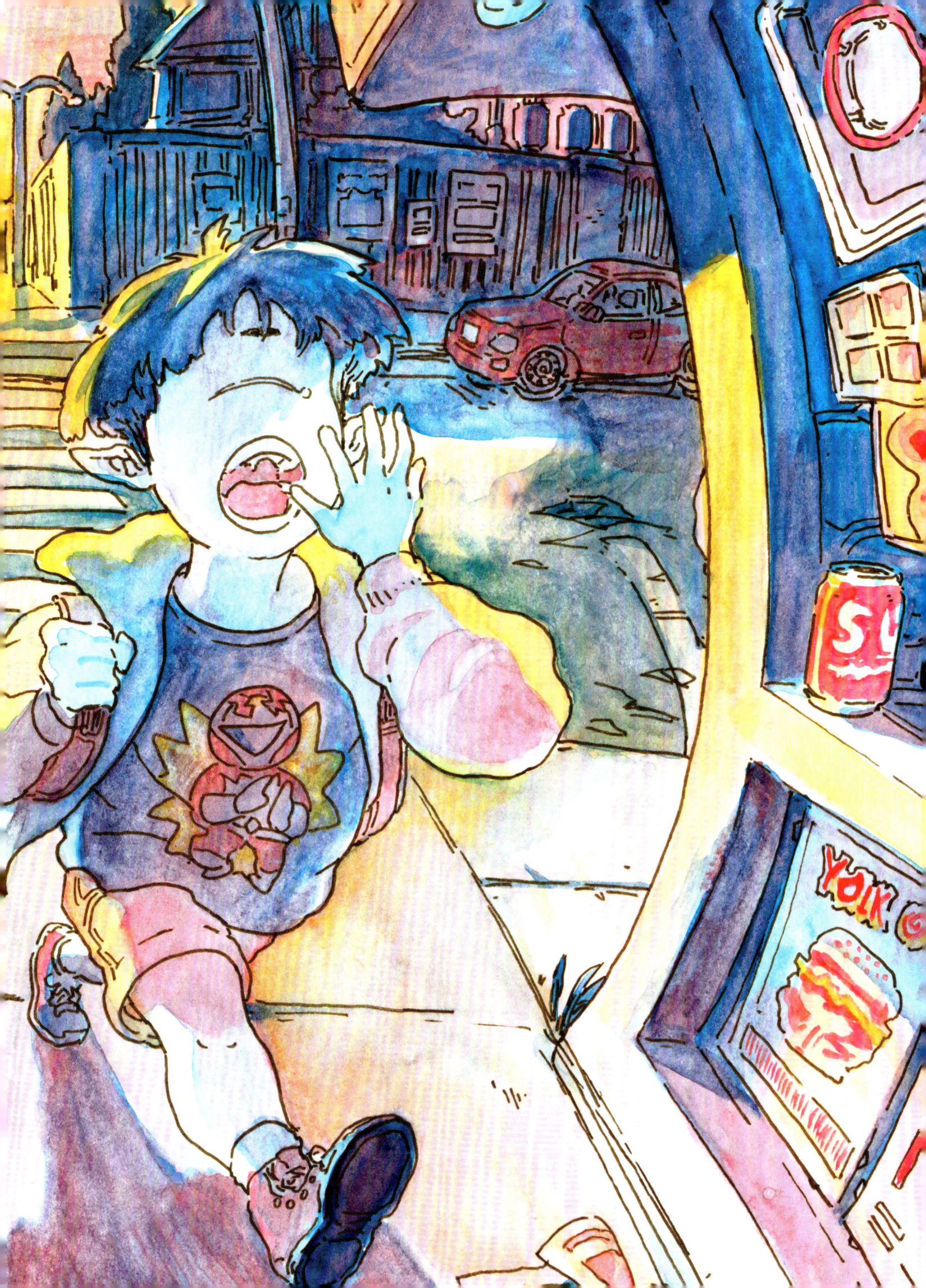

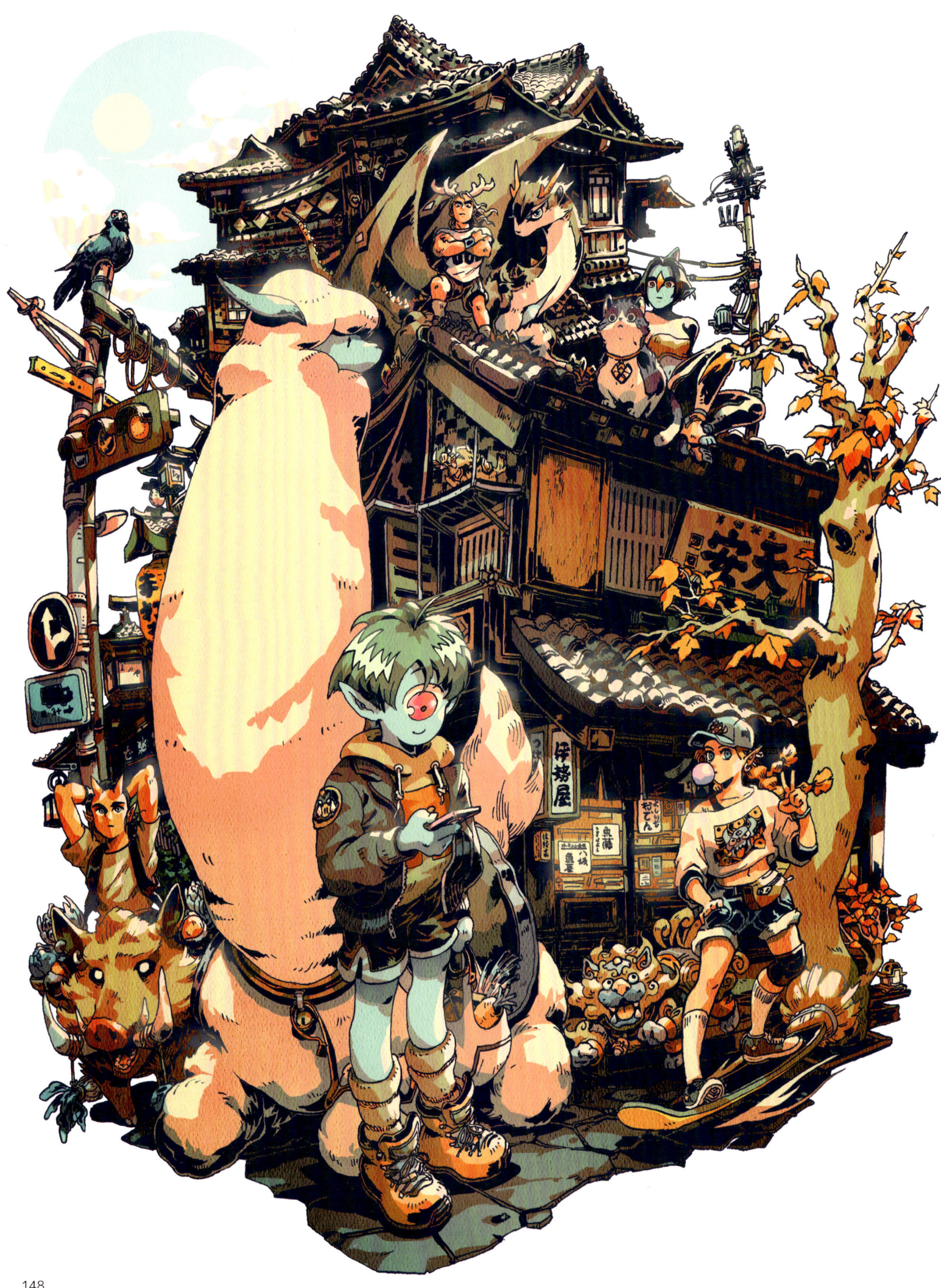

148

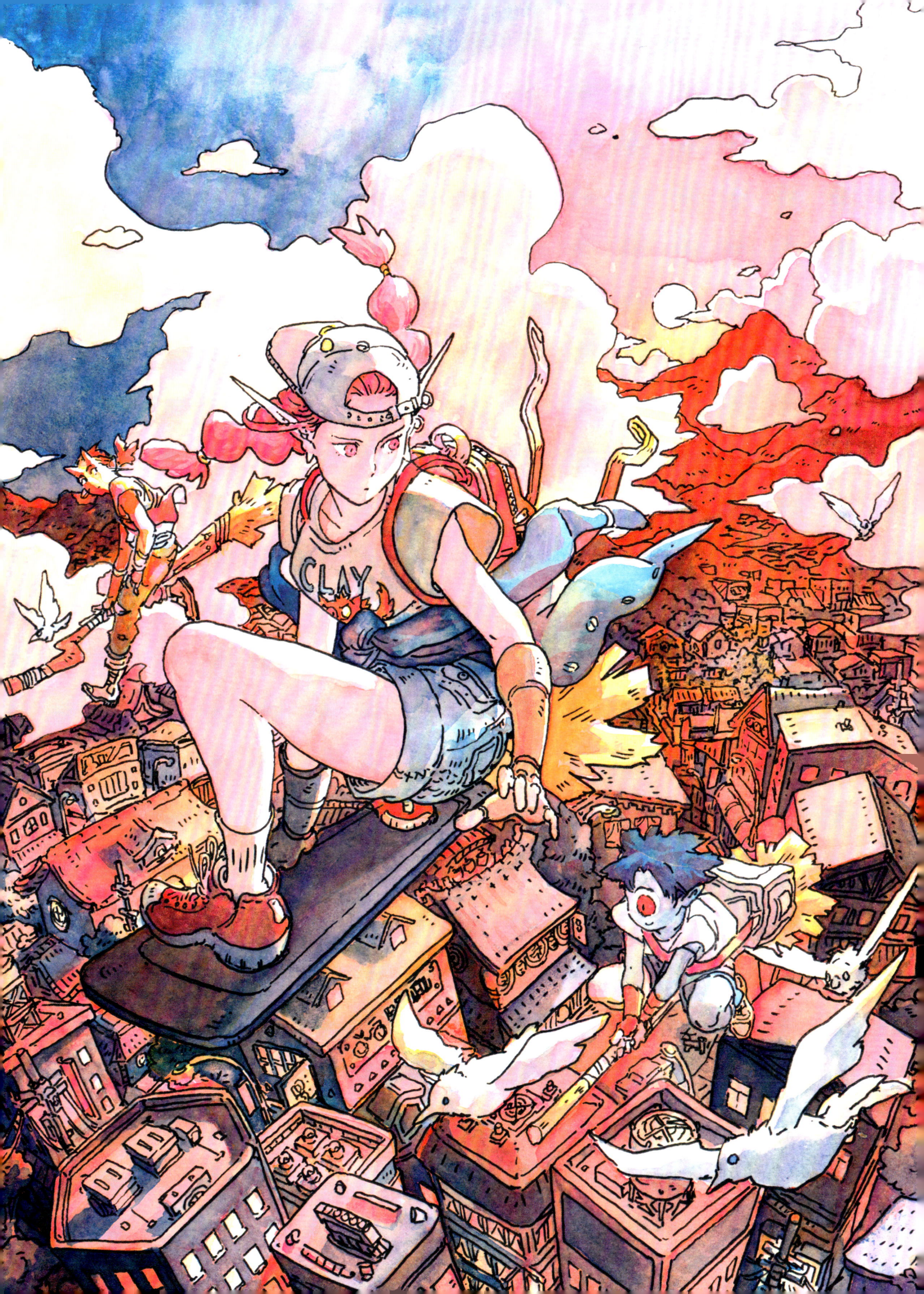

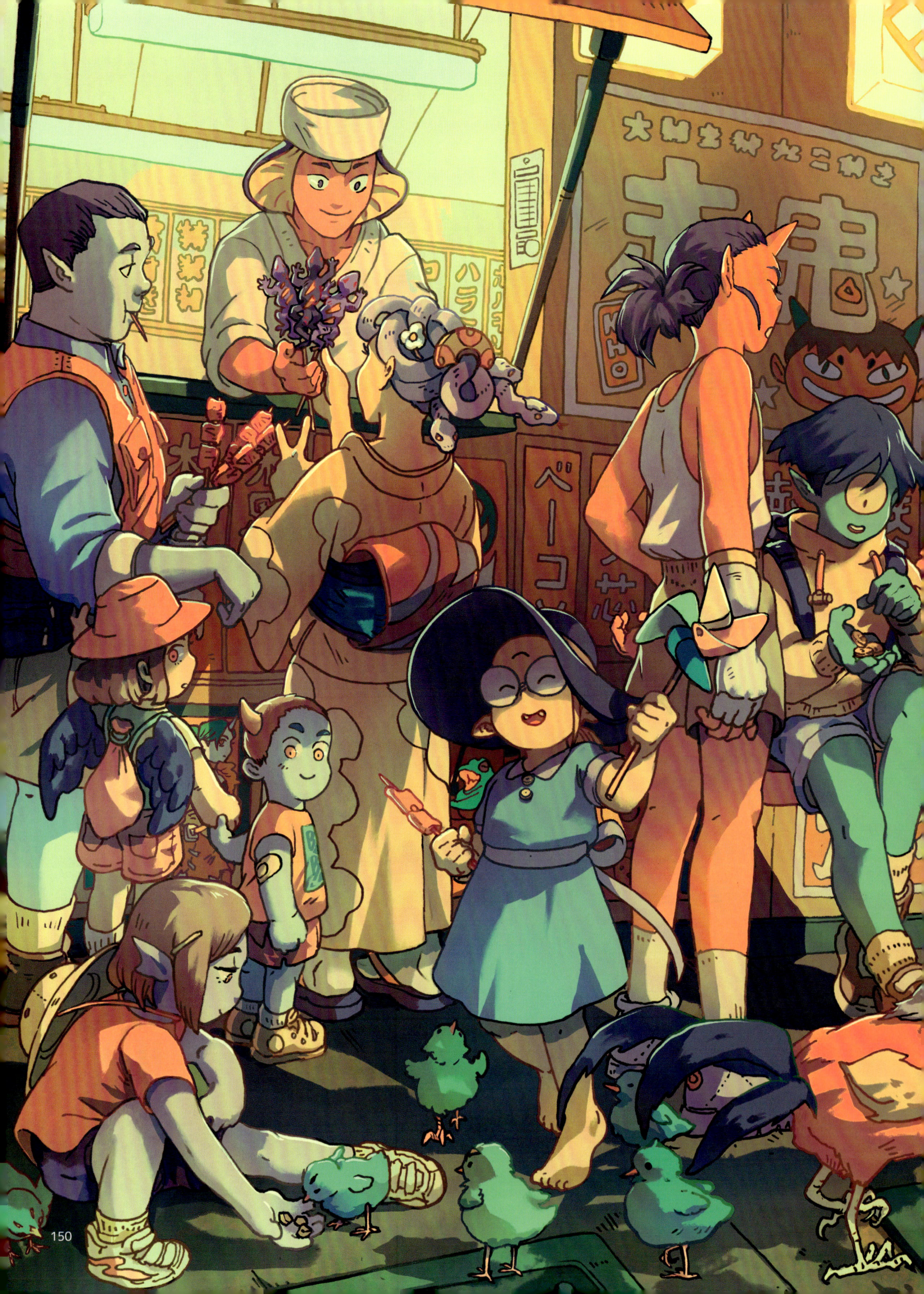

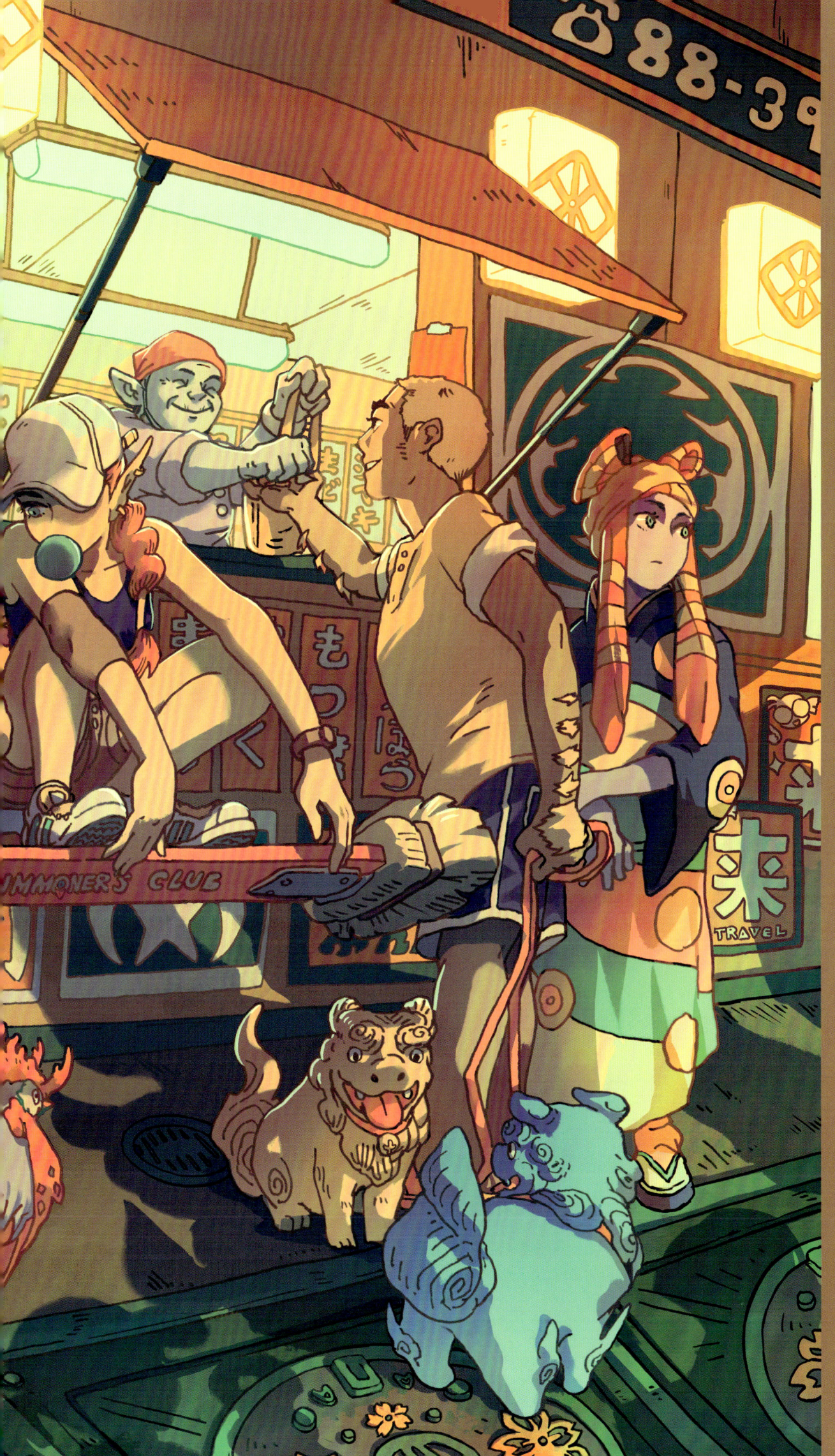

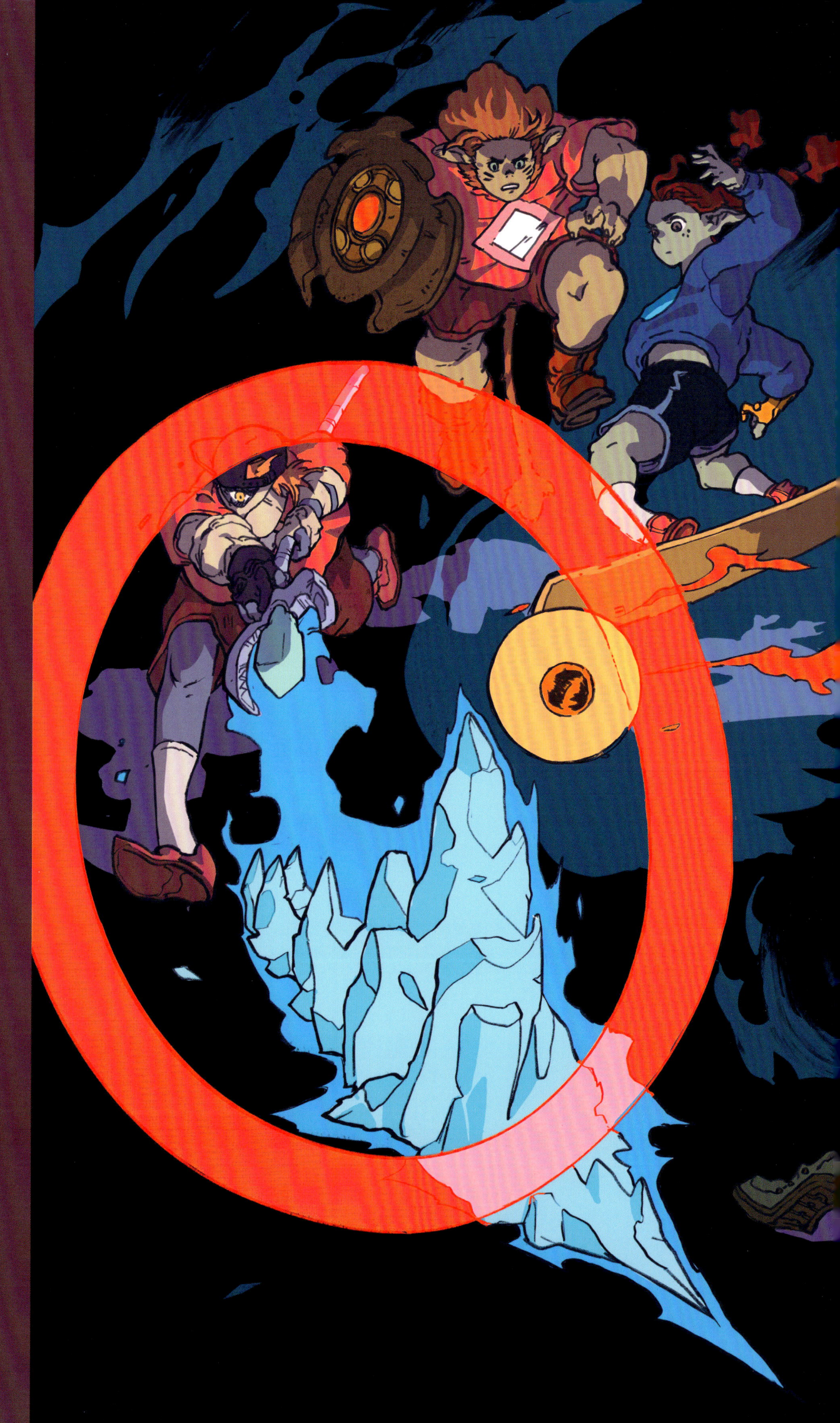

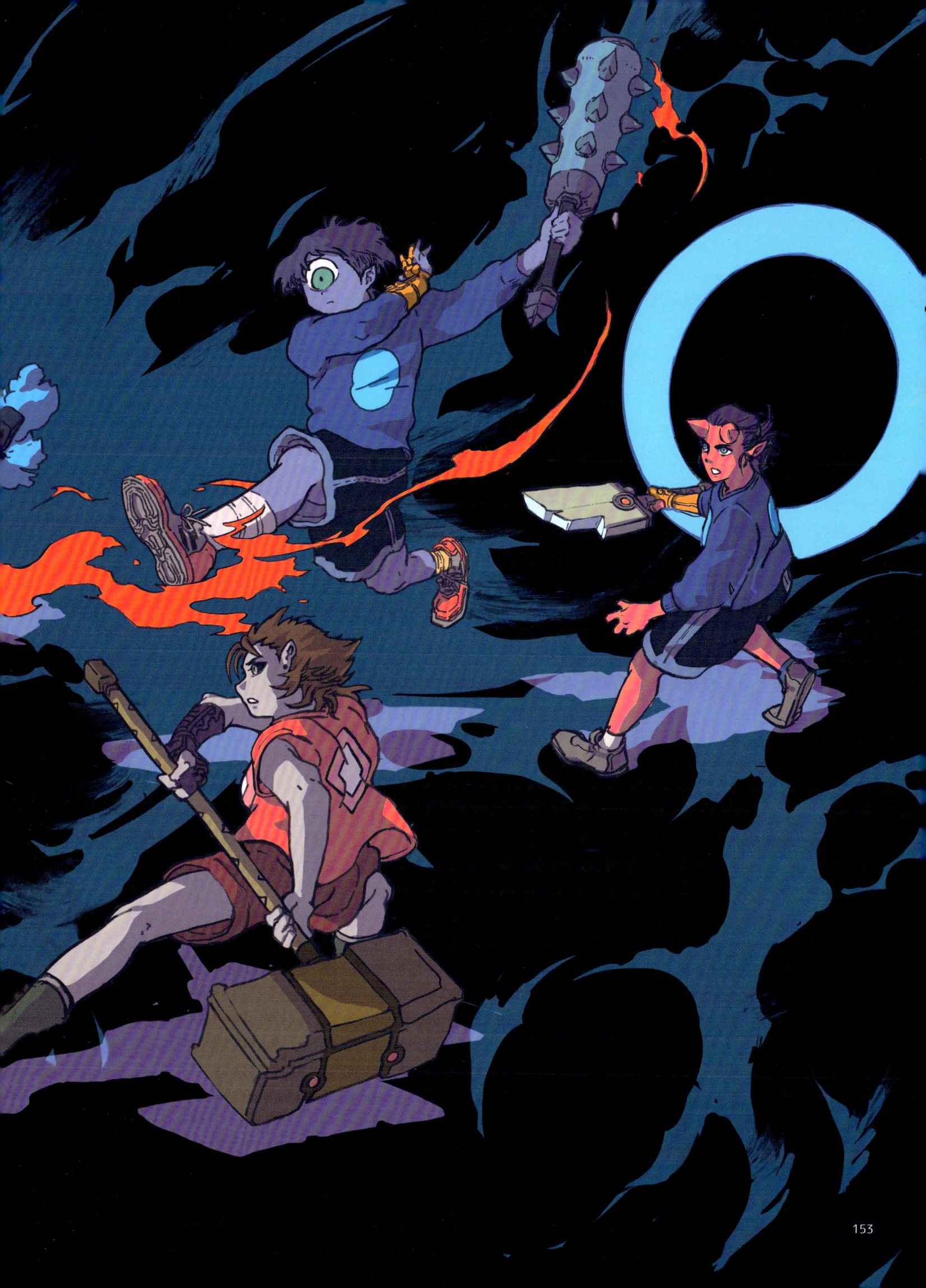

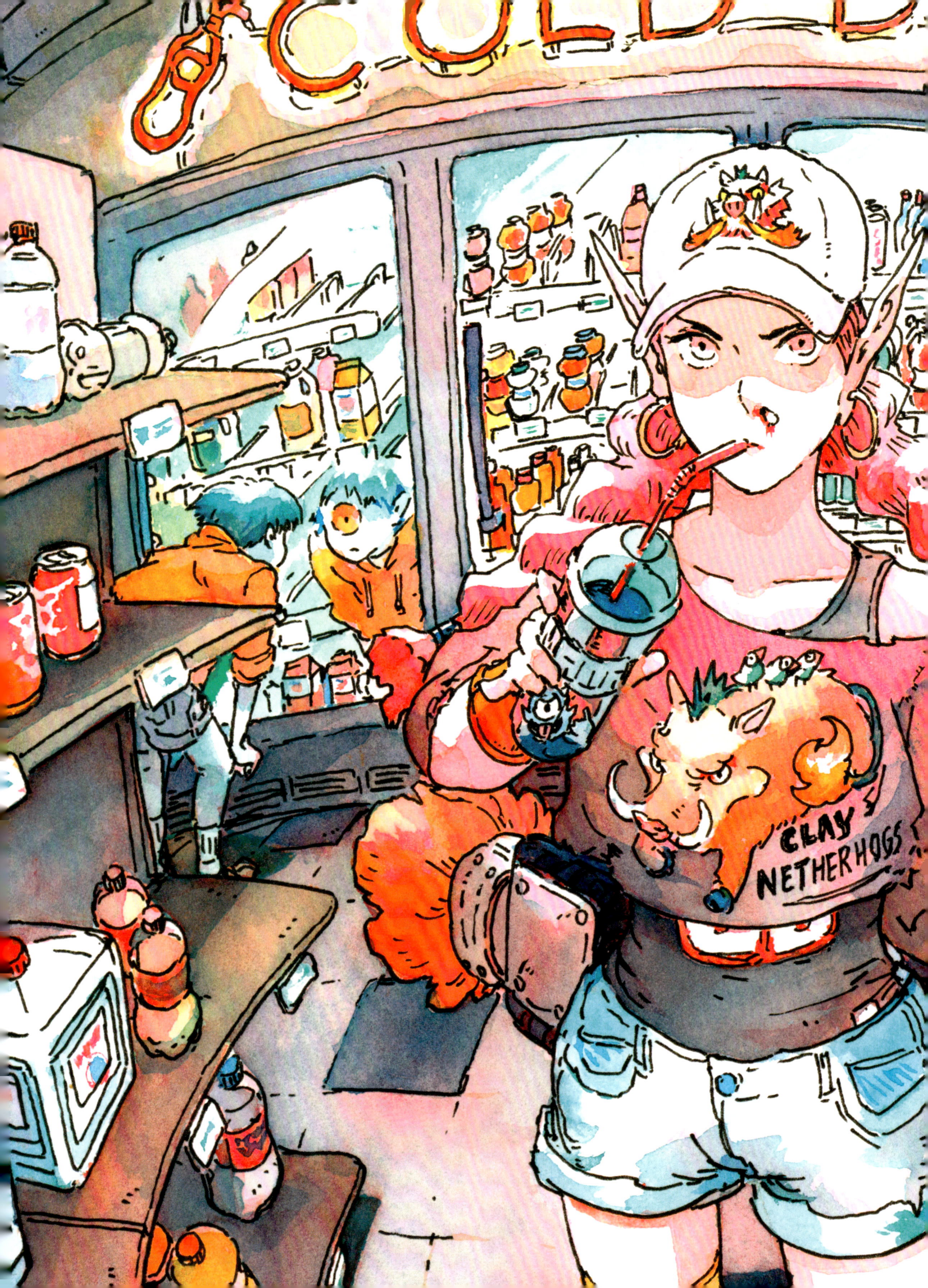

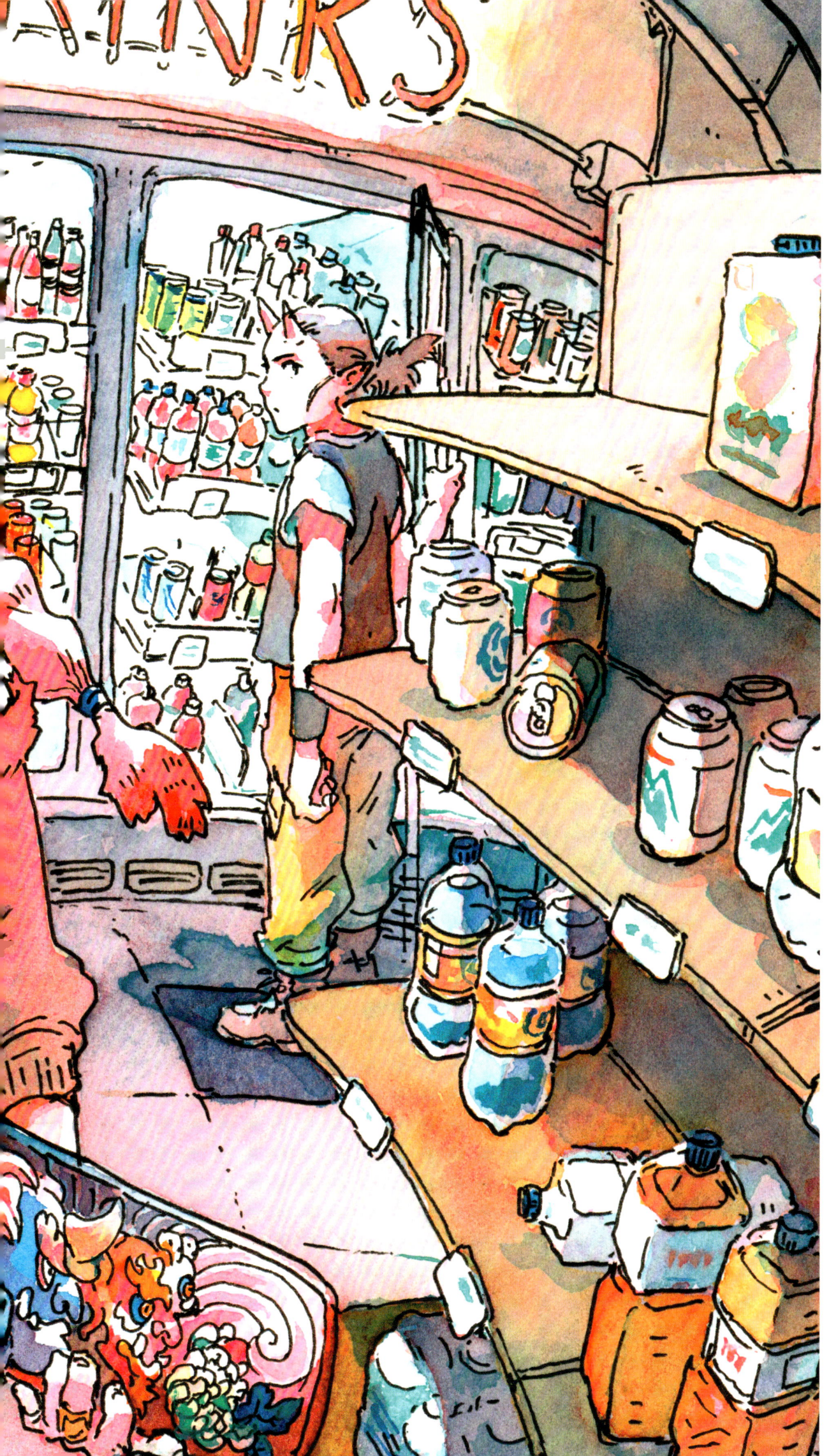

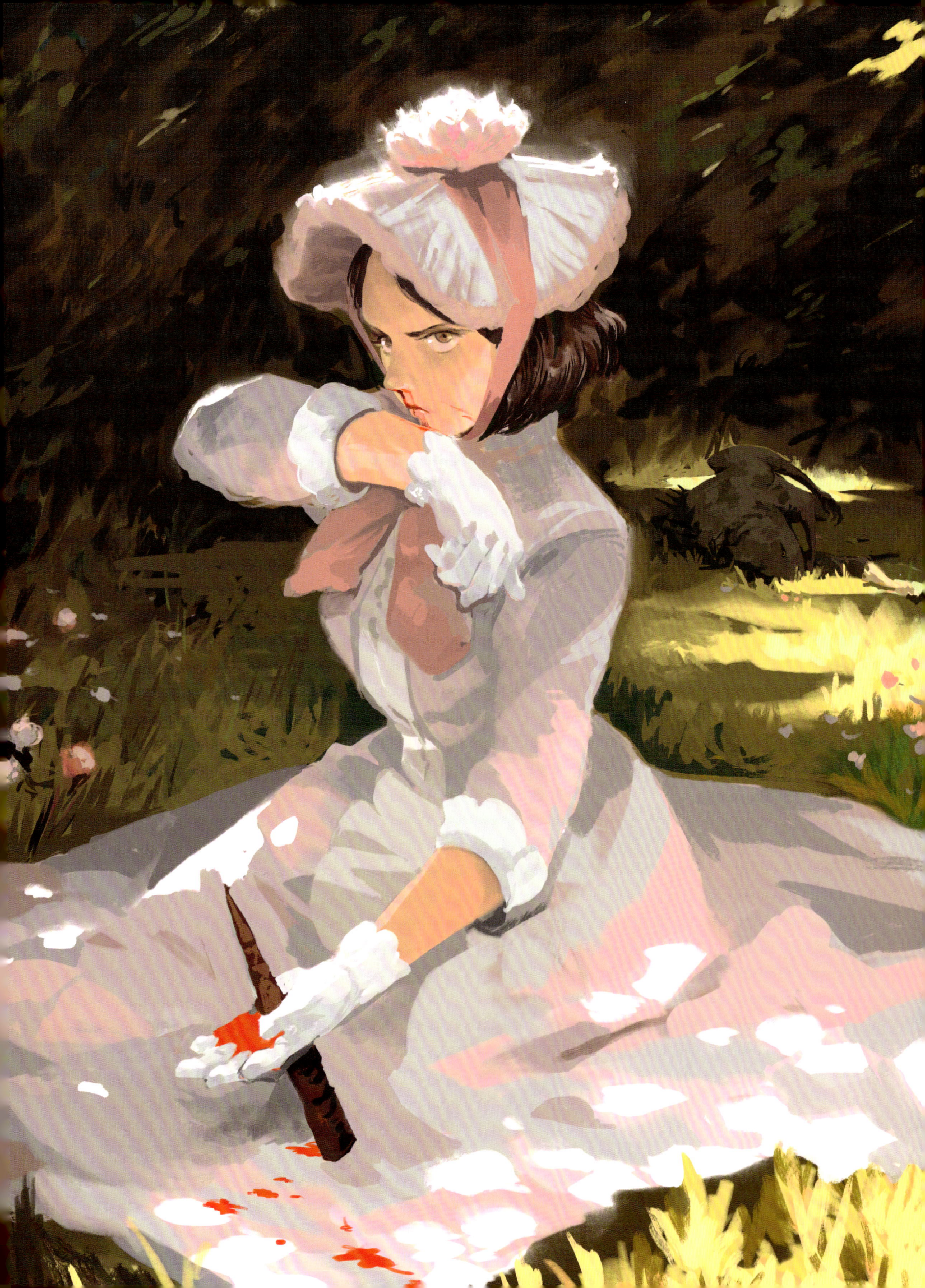

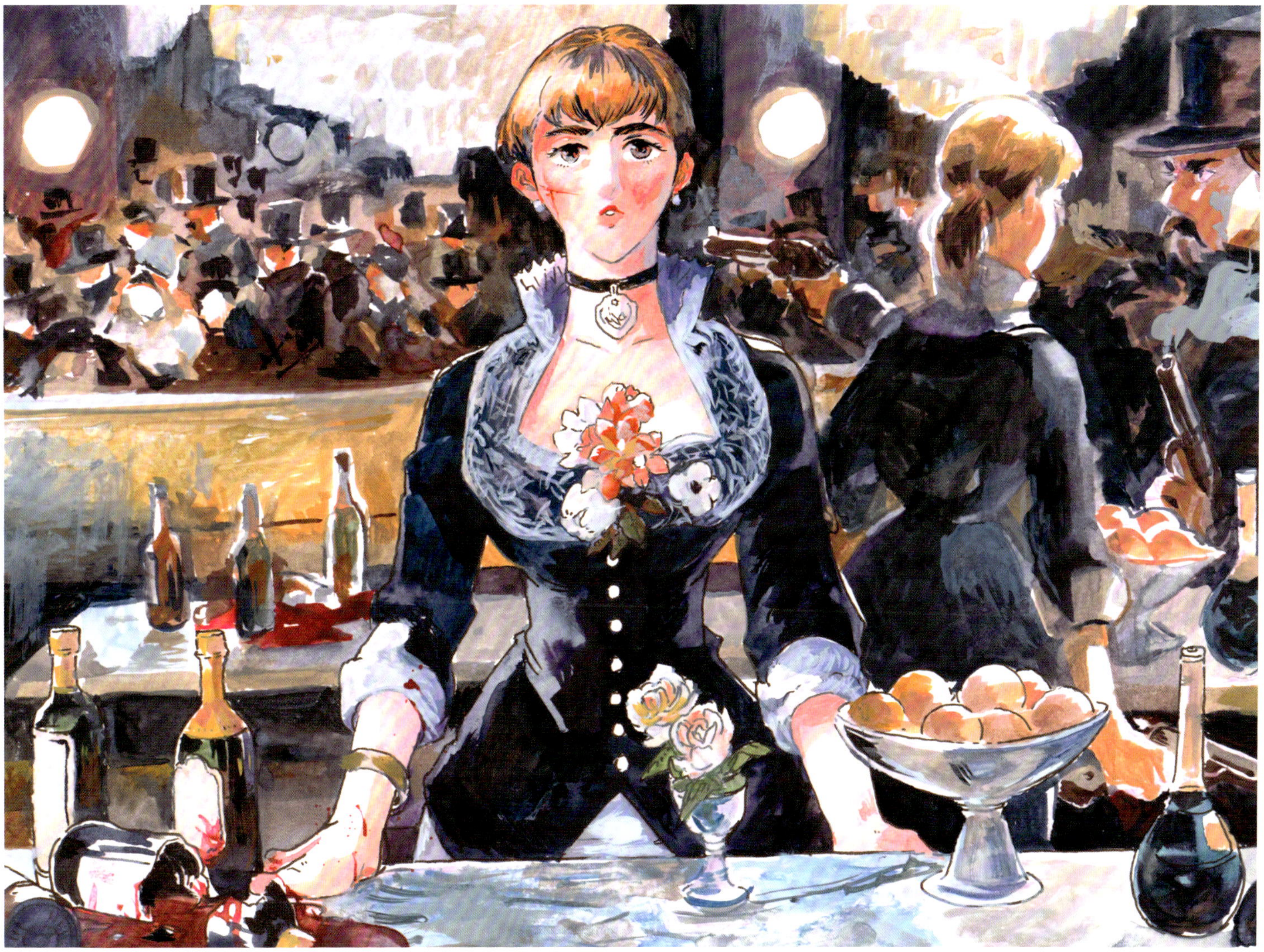

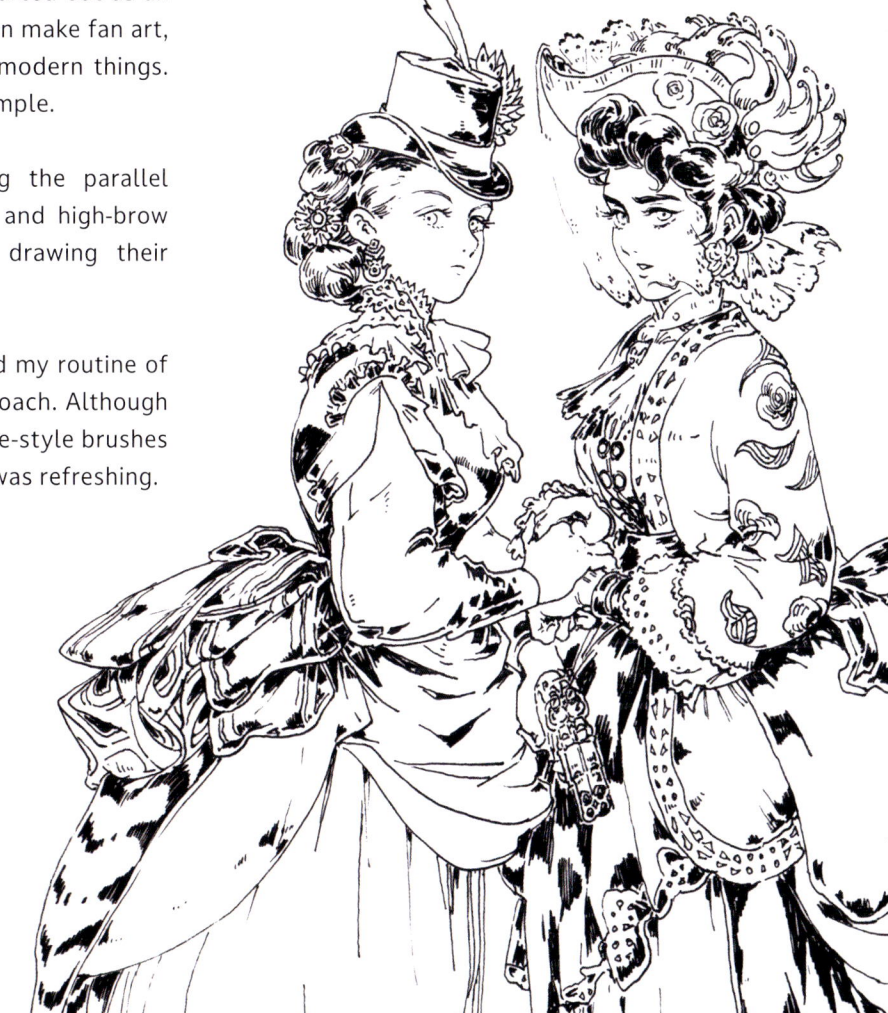

ANIME FRENCH IMPRESSIONISM

Anime French Impressionism is a series that started out as an inside joke with my wife about how, since I often make fan art, it would be fun to do this for less trendy or modern things. French Impressionist artists like Manet, for example.

There's something really fun about drawing the parallel between a contemporary anime-girl artwork, and high-brow portraits that were functionally also men drawing their dream waifu.

It was also a more serious excuse to go beyond my routine of line-art focused artwork to try a painterly approach. Although I still did most of these works digitally, gouache-style brushes felt separate from my normal practice, so that was refreshing.

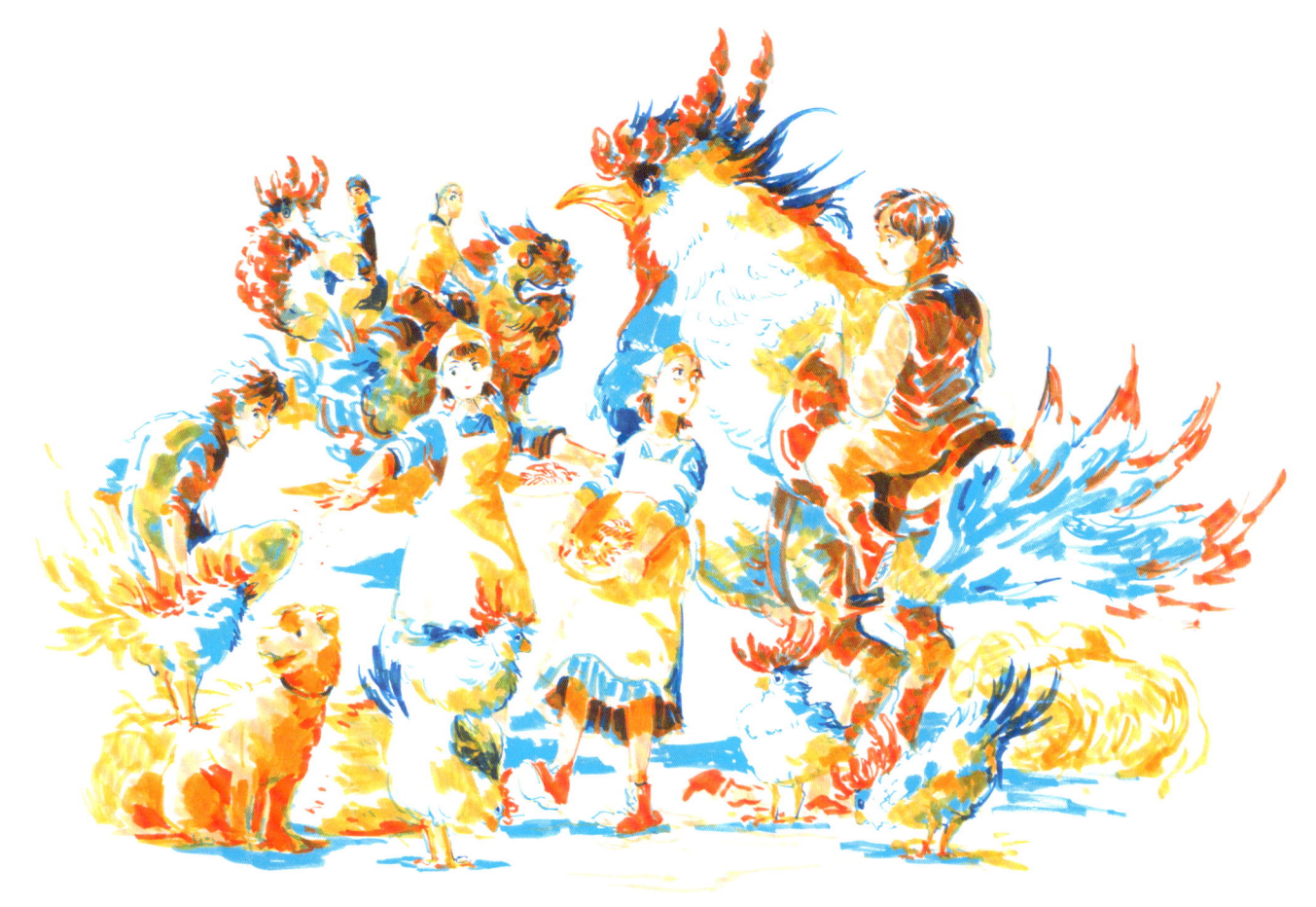

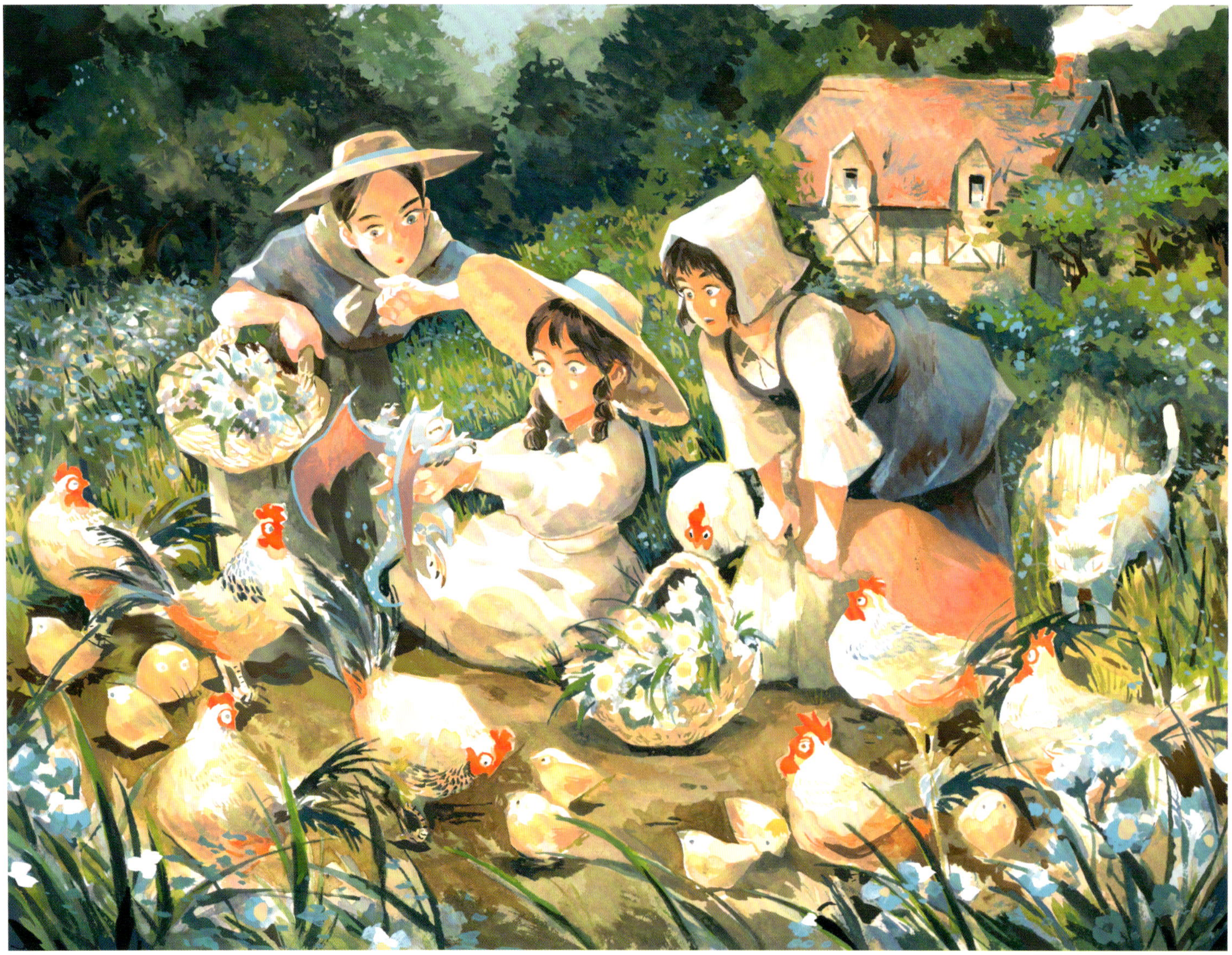

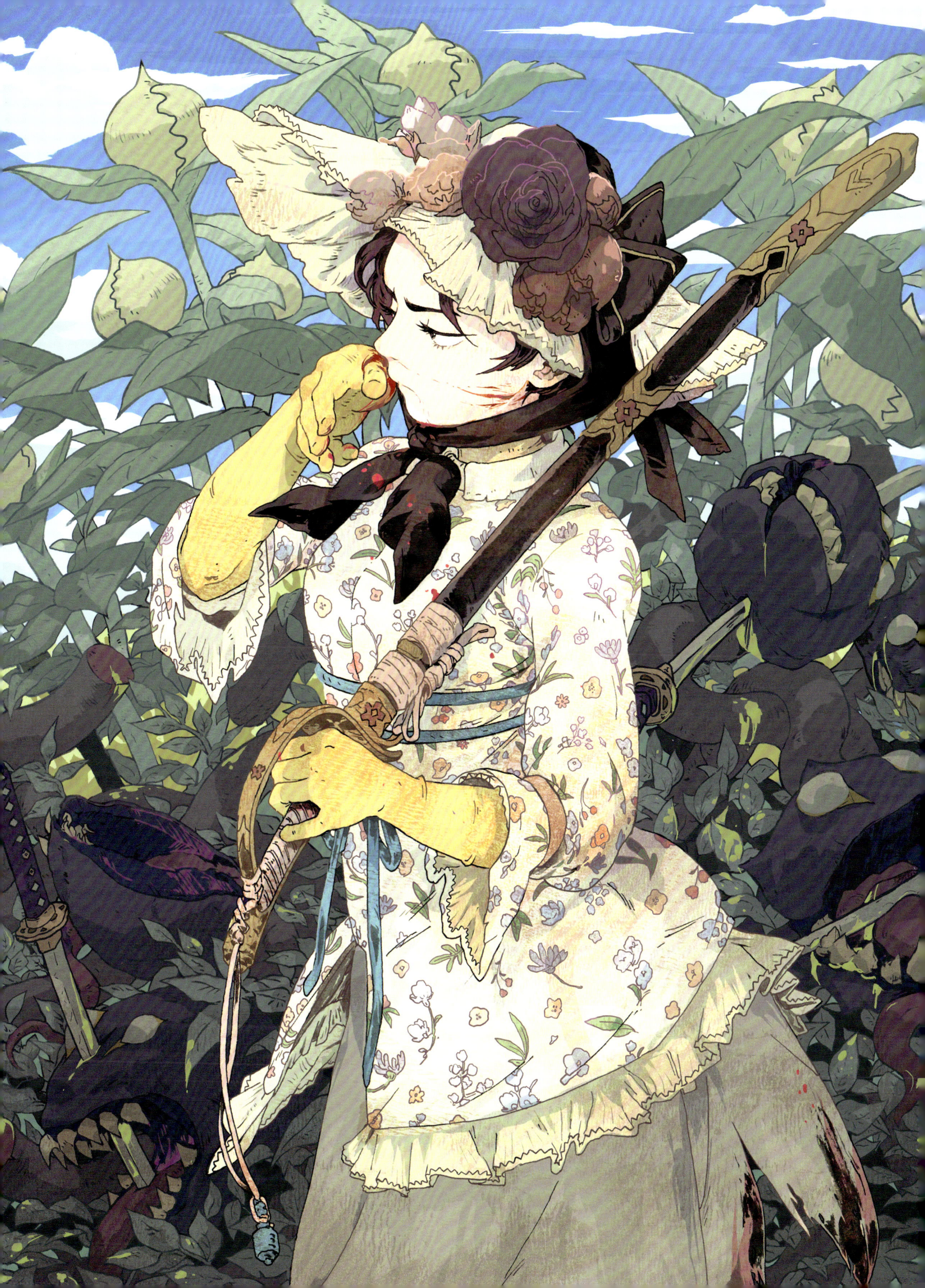

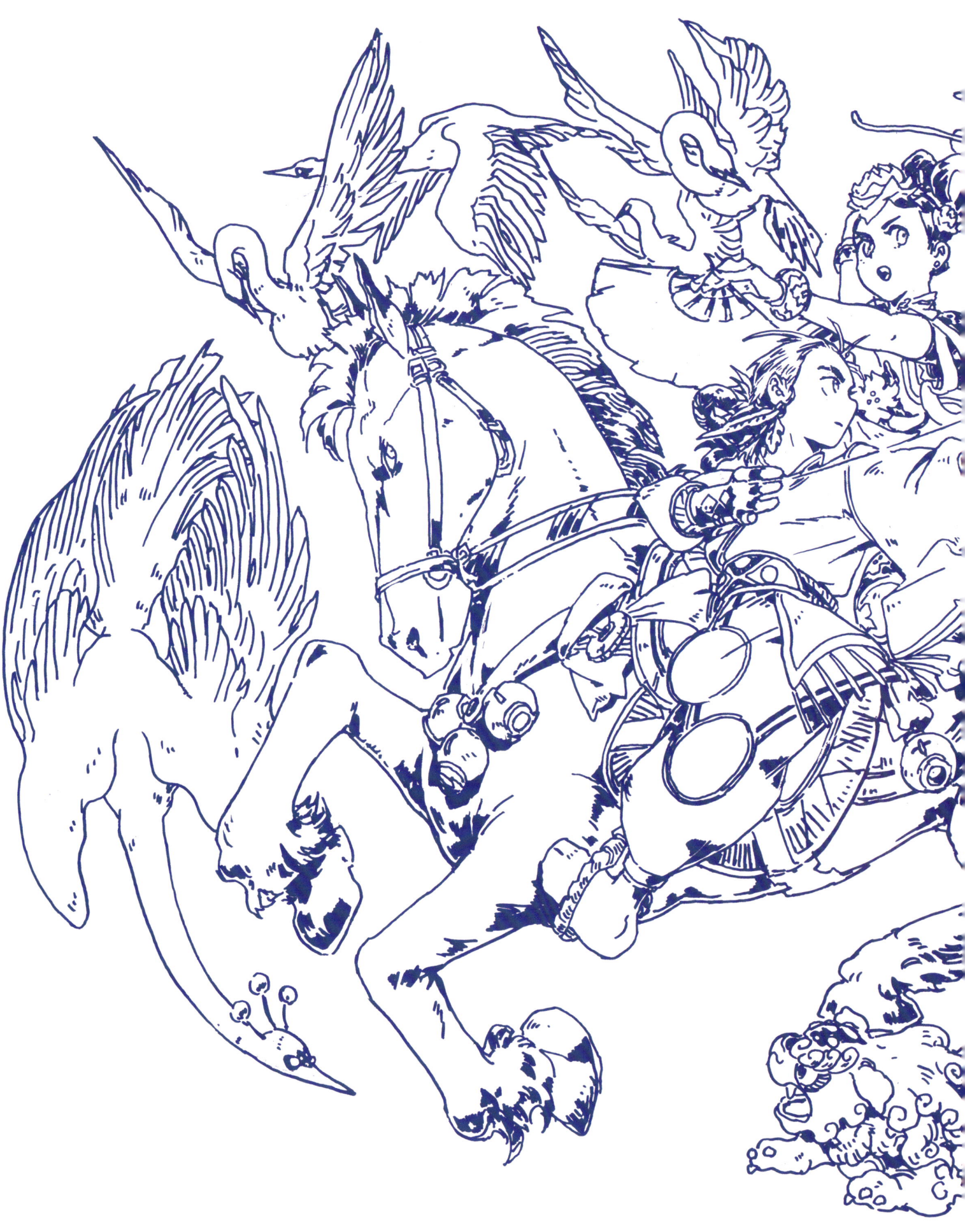

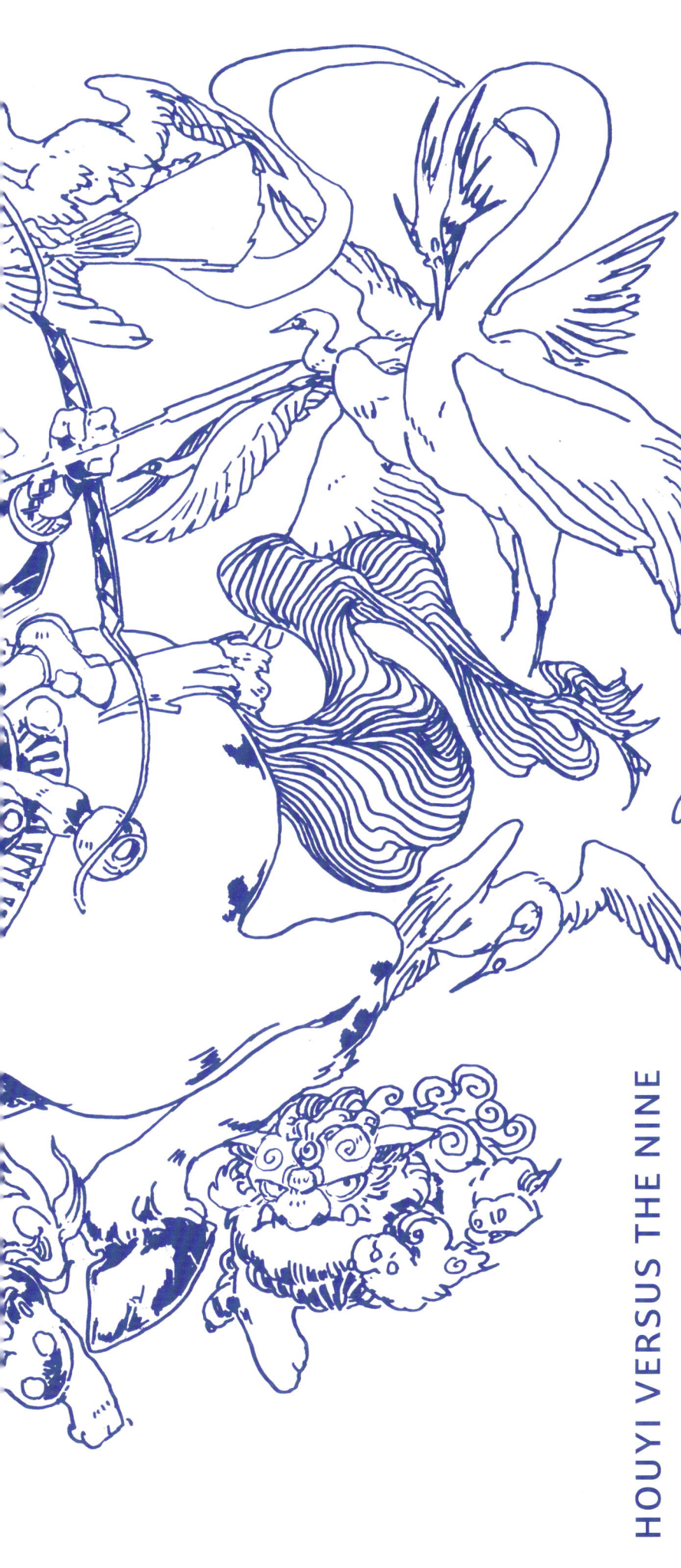

HOUYI VERSUS THE NINE

Houyi Versus the Nine is based on the Chinese mythology where a warrior must take down nine sun birds that are causing chaos on Earth. Alongside moon-goddess Chang-E from the source story, my version originally casts Houyi as a brave outcast-warrior whose blindness makes him uniquely suited to taking down the bright birds. Relying on goddess Chang-E to guide him, they fight their foes together.

The reason I didn't move forward with this story, though I got as far as storyboarding the first chapter, was that I never found an angle on Houyi I was excited about. He was more of a blank slate, like Link from *Zelda*, rather than someone whom I felt had a story worth telling. He could function as a decent video-game protagonist, but for a graphic novel, I still needed to figure out his character arc.

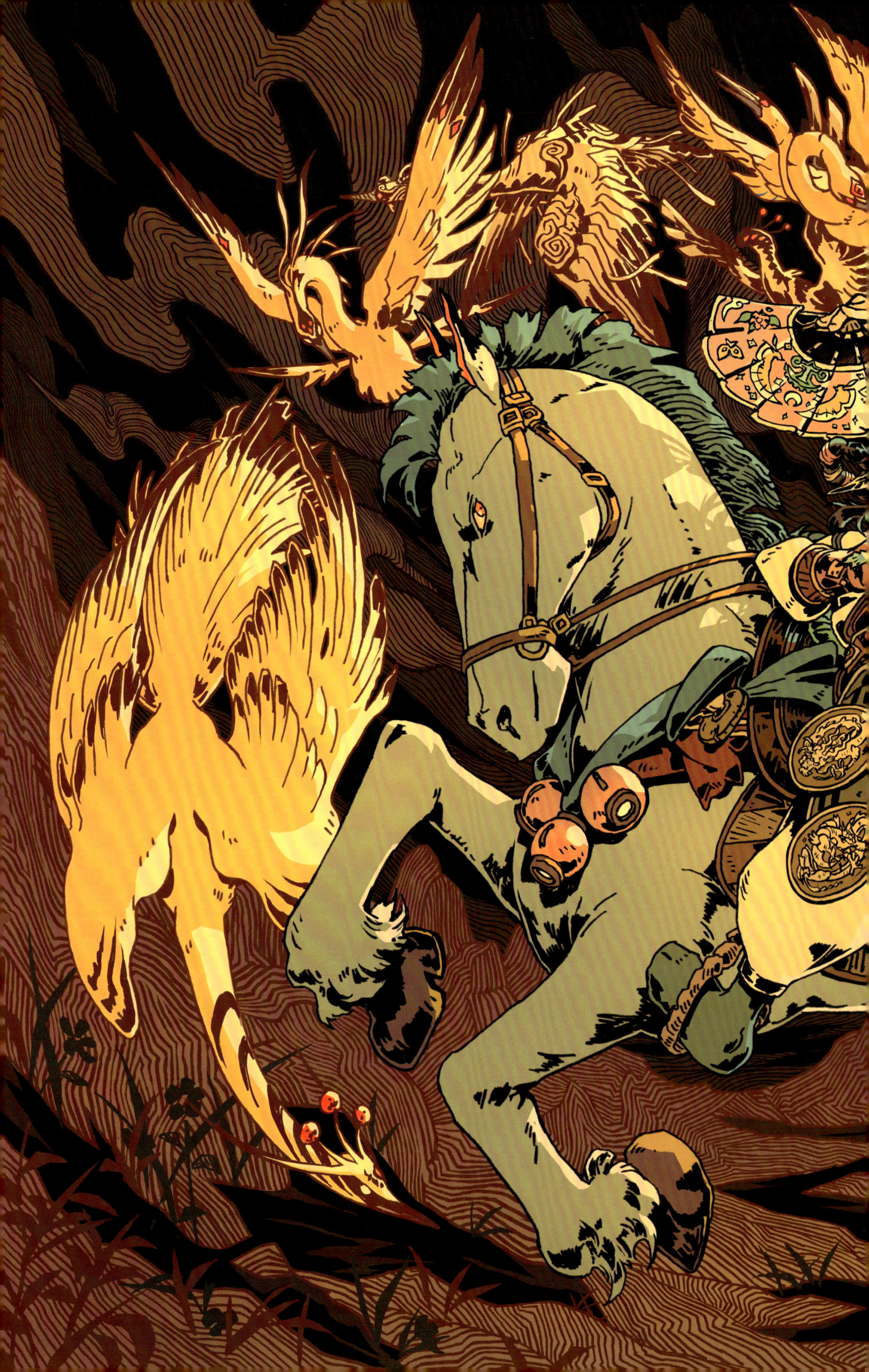

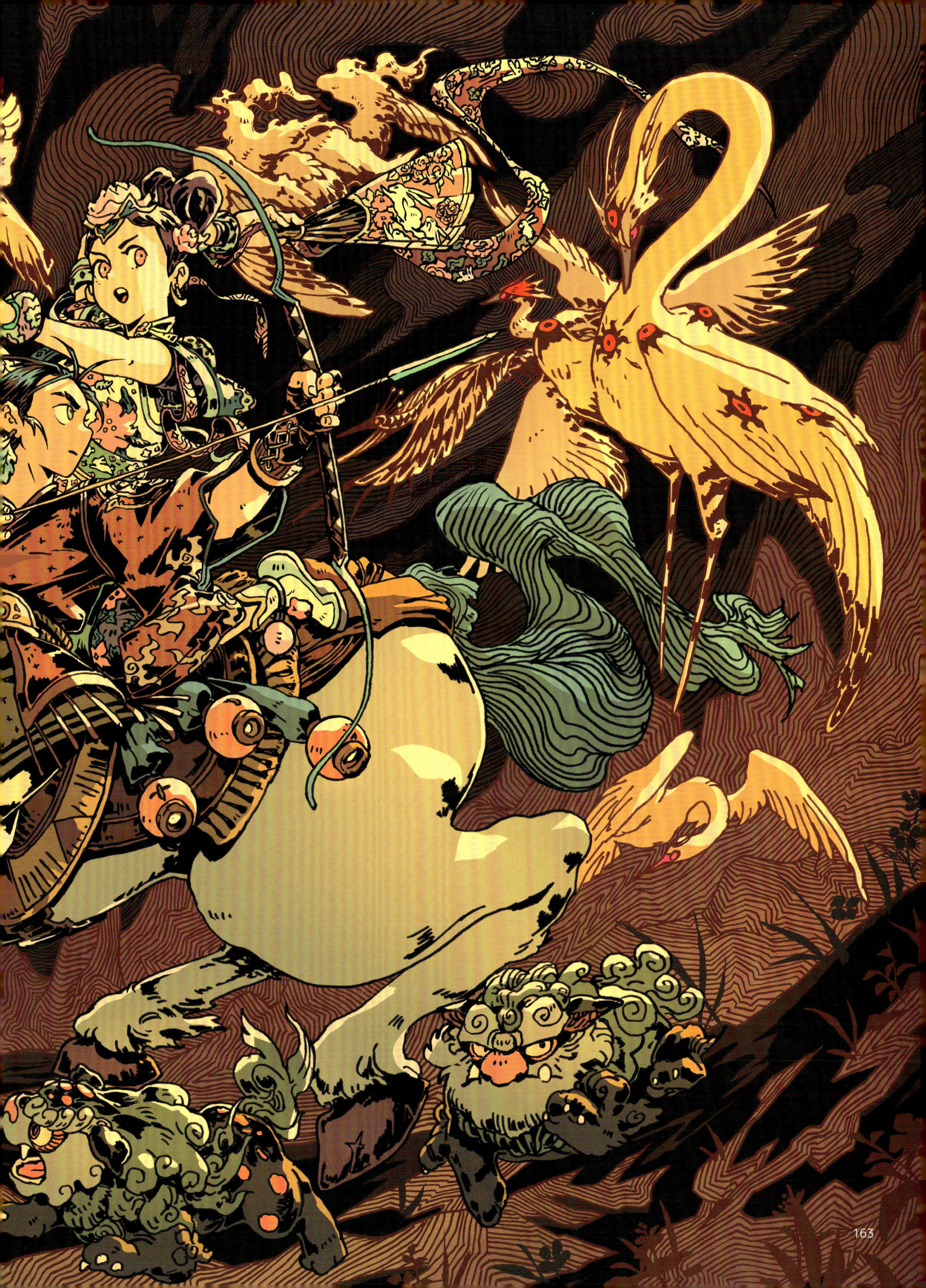

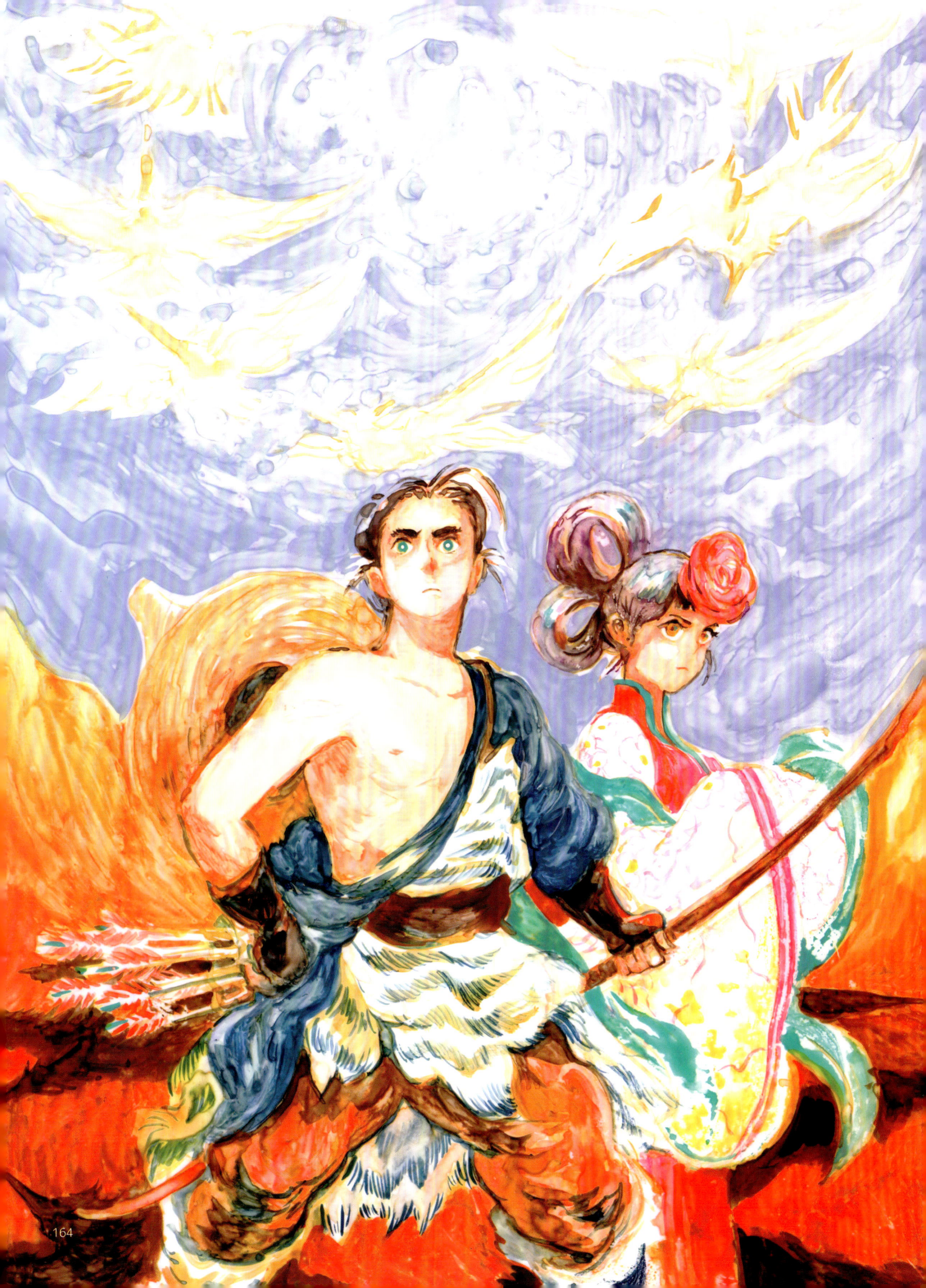

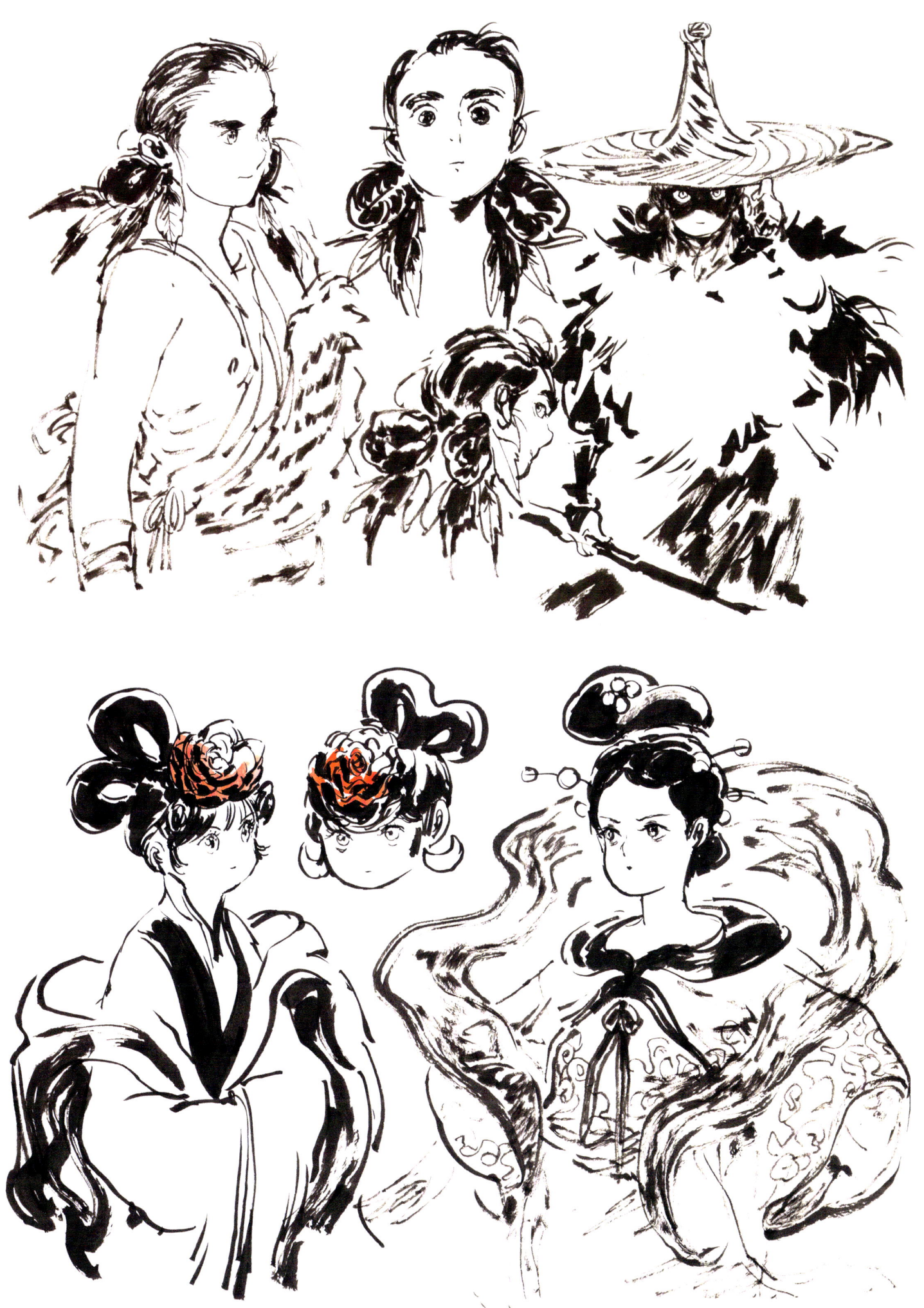

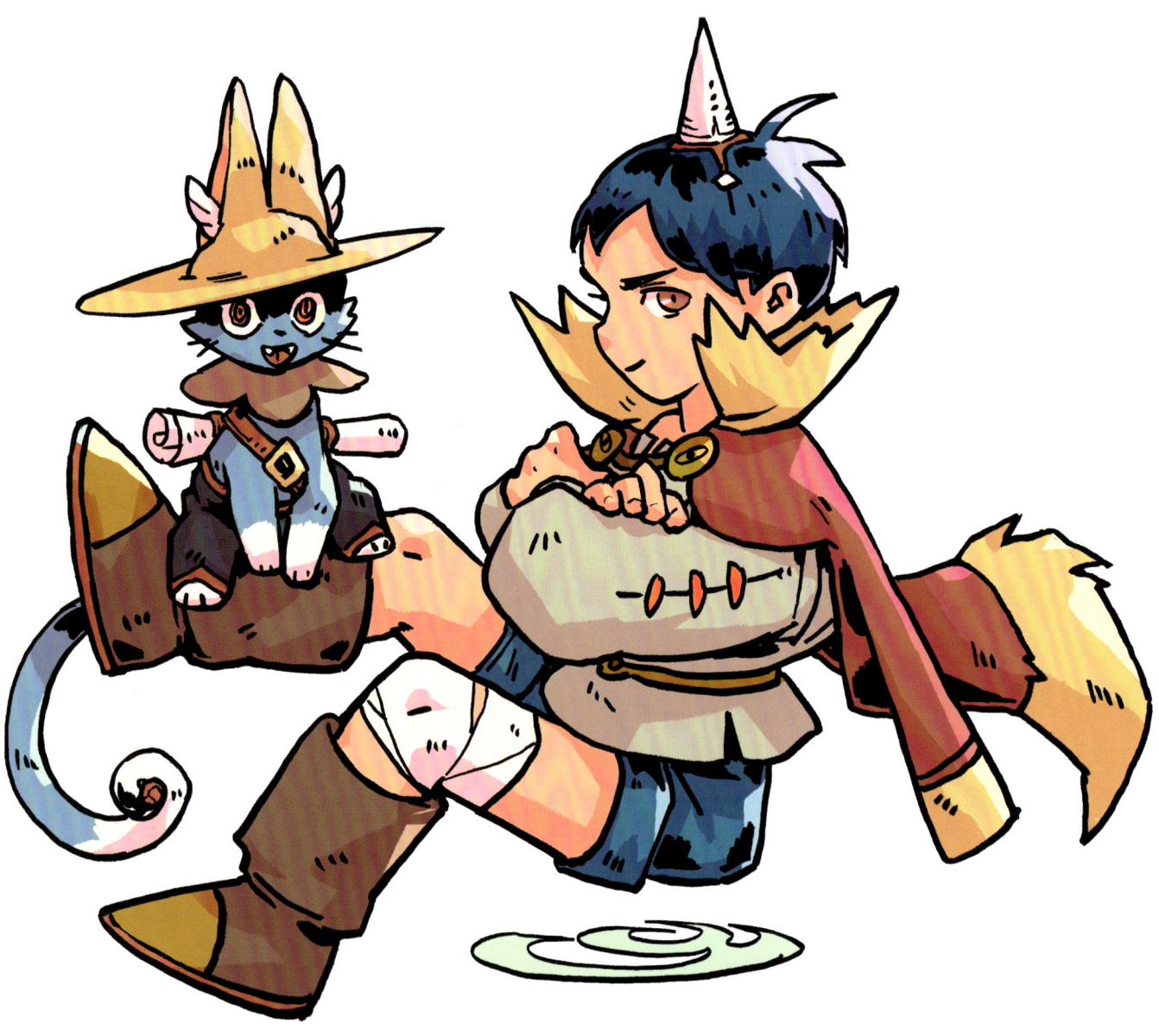

Bad Boy Juju is a satirical shounen in which the main protagonist wants to be the King of Demons; an objectively evil ambition.

Juju's origin story is that he was actually killed by a demon, but his mad-scientist father was able to use demon blood to revive him.

However, as a half-demon, half-human who has brain damage from being dead for too long, Juju's concept of evil is somewhat fluid, allowing him to believe things like, *I want an army of slaves but simultaneously, slaves deserve dignity, respect, and should be treated like friends.*

The more shounen component to the story is that Juju also possesses some of the qualities and powers from the demon's blood; a demon who happens to be the reigning Demon King. Juju's father tries to rein in his son and teach him how to be a proper heir to his thriving family business, but all Juju wants is to chase his own dream. This will inevitably lead towards a face-off with Juju's blood 'father' to become the King of Demons.

I'm not quite sure how just yet, but as I can relate so much better to Juju's human father now, I'm excited to give him a complicated emotional arc – one that is antagonistic yet comes from a place of undying love.

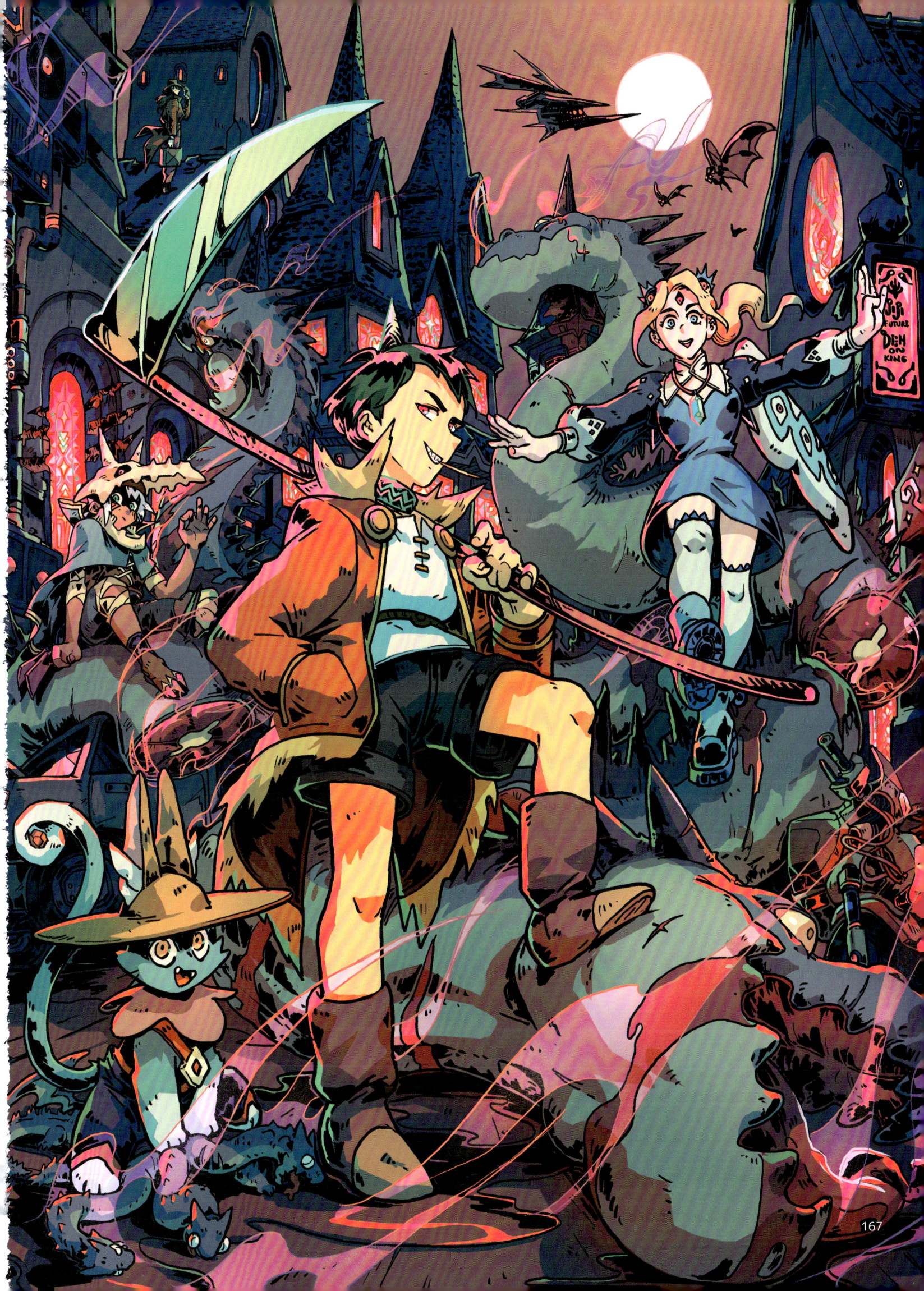

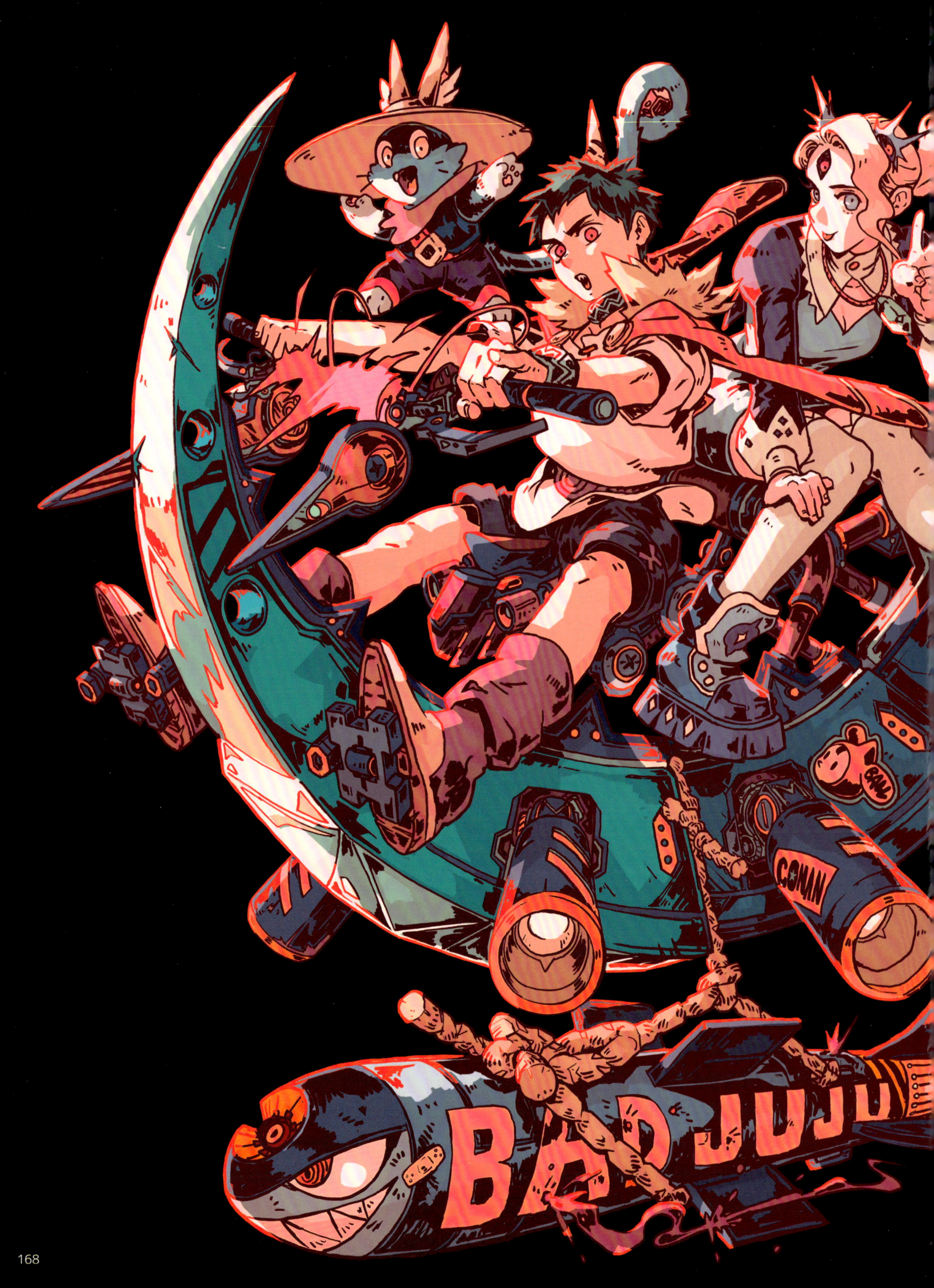

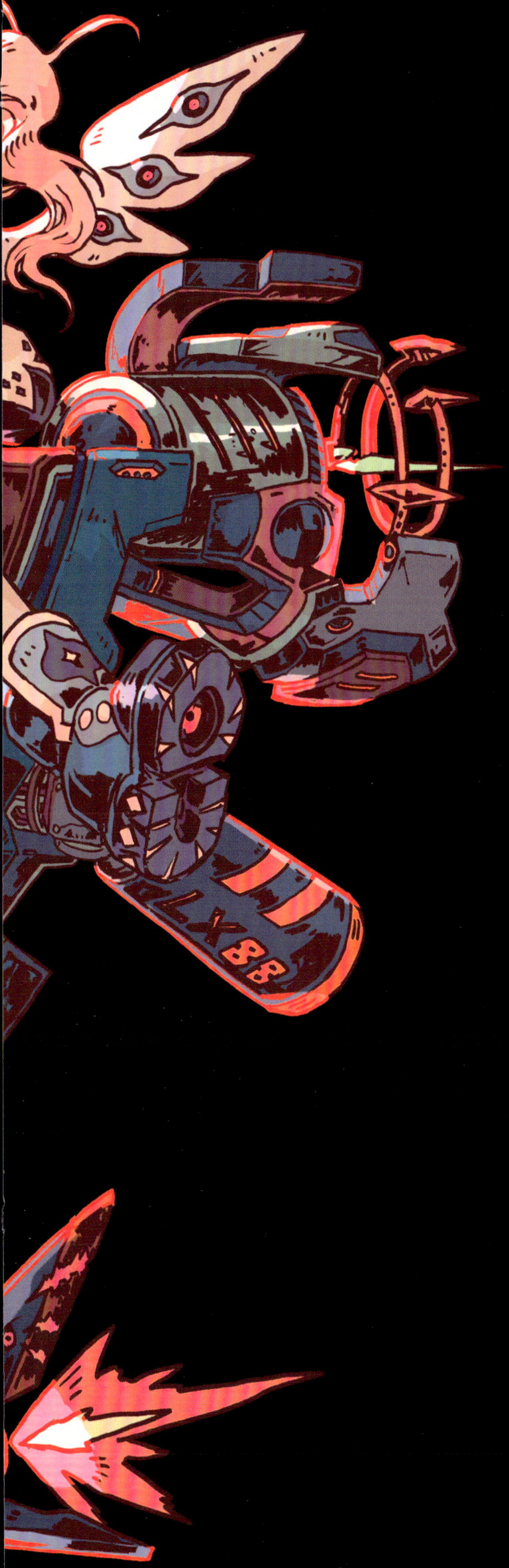

I wanted to use this book as a chance to flesh out Bad Boy Juju's story. As a busy new father, however, I've probably only done about twenty per cent as much as I'd hoped. But I'm not too mad about it for a couple of reasons!

For the longest time, I've tended to abandon story ideas, feeling that the projects lack the core emotional connection I need to put my all into them. With this story, my relationship with my son has given me that core connection.

MY RELATIONSHIP WITH MY SON HAS GIVEN ME THAT CORE CONNECTION

The origin of this discovery was a moment that happened at San Diego Comic-Con 2023. We had an amazing and busy year, which made me feel both proud (contemplating that my parents might be proud), and too exhausted to have any emotional defences up. So, in a conversation about how to improve work efficiency, I tried to give advice about how I think I'm more productive because I'm less precious about my work.

When pressed on how I came to feel this way, I dug deeper than I ever had before, vocalizing some inner beliefs given to me by my father – such as the idea that artwork has no value to begin with – and admitting that multiple heartbreaks had taught me that no matter what I did, it wouldn't matter either way. As I relayed this story to my friend, emotionless and matter-of-fact, it actually made her cry and that shocked me, since I had wholeheartedly become used to these realities.

After realizing I still had baggage to process, I began to think about my own role as a parent to my Conan. I thought about what sort of relationship I wanted with him, but was also able to relate to my father's concerns and fears for my younger self. To be clear, I have no resentment about my childhood – if anything, it was merely my fear about unpacking my own feelings that was holding me back.

I always belittled the child inside me, not letting him feel his feelings, but now that I spend my days trying to relate to my son, things are different. I treat all my son's feelings as valid, and I've learned to grant myself that same courtesy.

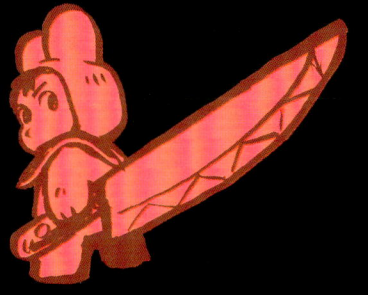

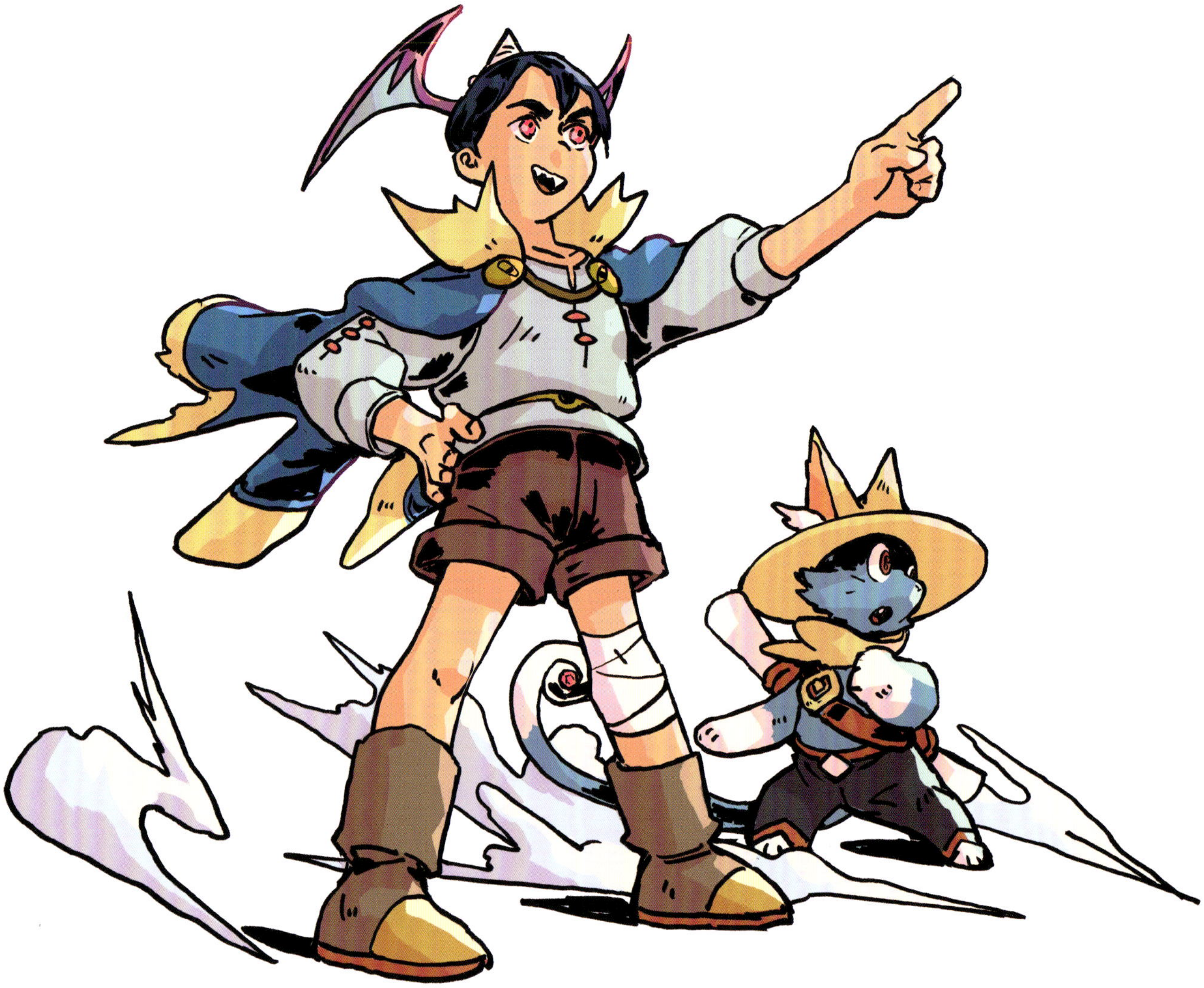

My process for developing *Bad Boy Juju* has been quite different from my previous efforts. Where I'd spent endless hours writing scripts for *Summoners Club*, storyboards for *Houyi*, and completely off-the-cuff improvization for *Saturn Donuts*, *Bad Boy Juju* has been a mixture of all three. I suppose I could say I've spent the last five years trying to figure out how I work on a story.

Too much planning can destroy the playfulness, but not enough planning can leave the story too unpredictable, making it harder for me to make sure it hits themes that I resonate with.

On the more fun side of this, drawing the *Dragon Motorcycle* piece and some of the others has really forced me to think about who else Juju needs to meet on his journey, what sort of impressive set pieces would make sense, and, most importantly of all, what sort of artwork and tone it would need to have to keep me interested.

You can tell from the original designs that *Juju* had to be aged up a lot, mostly because I just like to draw older characters. Also, including more mecha felt necessary to add some uniqueness to the Neo-Goth look I wanted to explore.

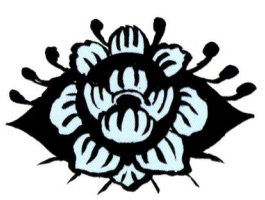

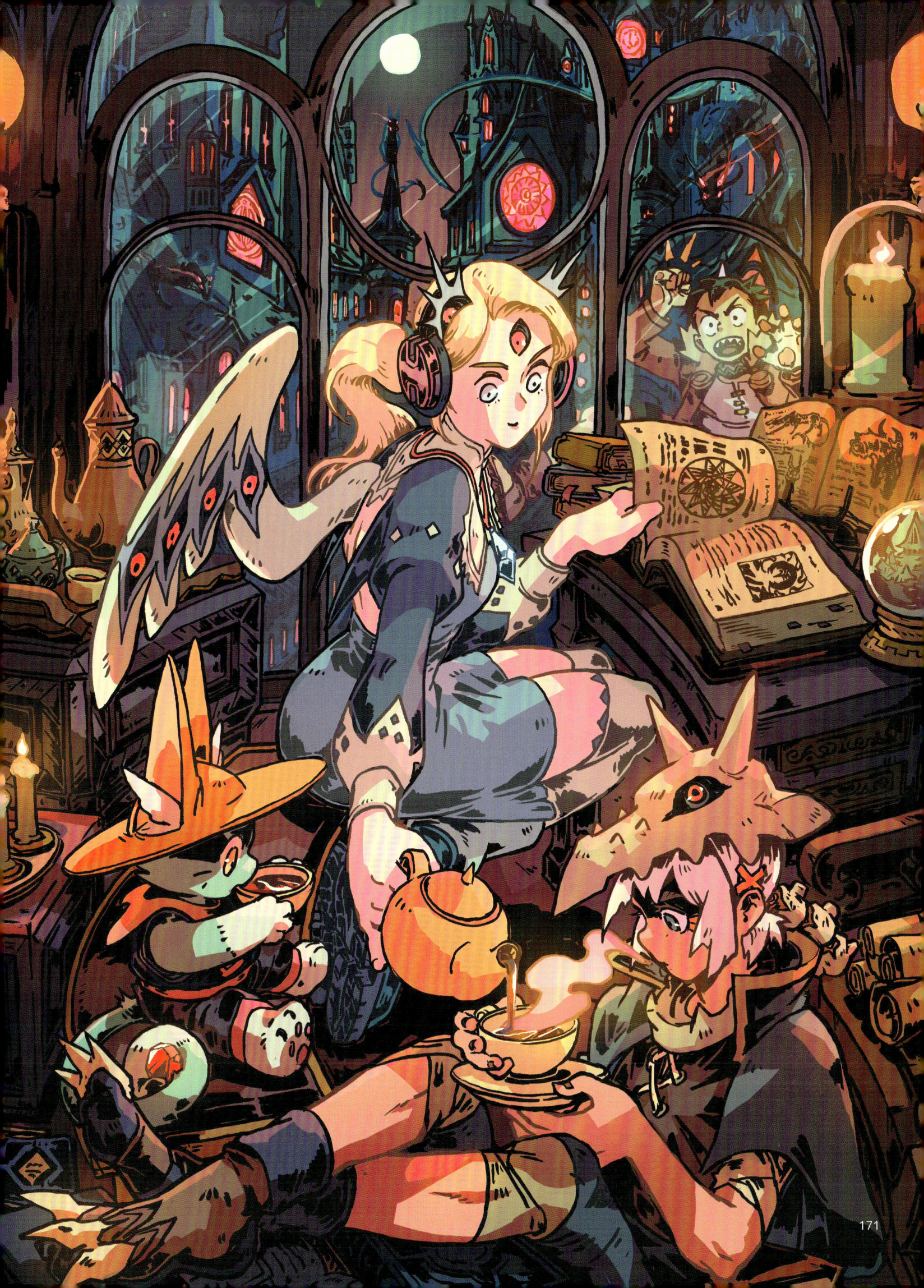

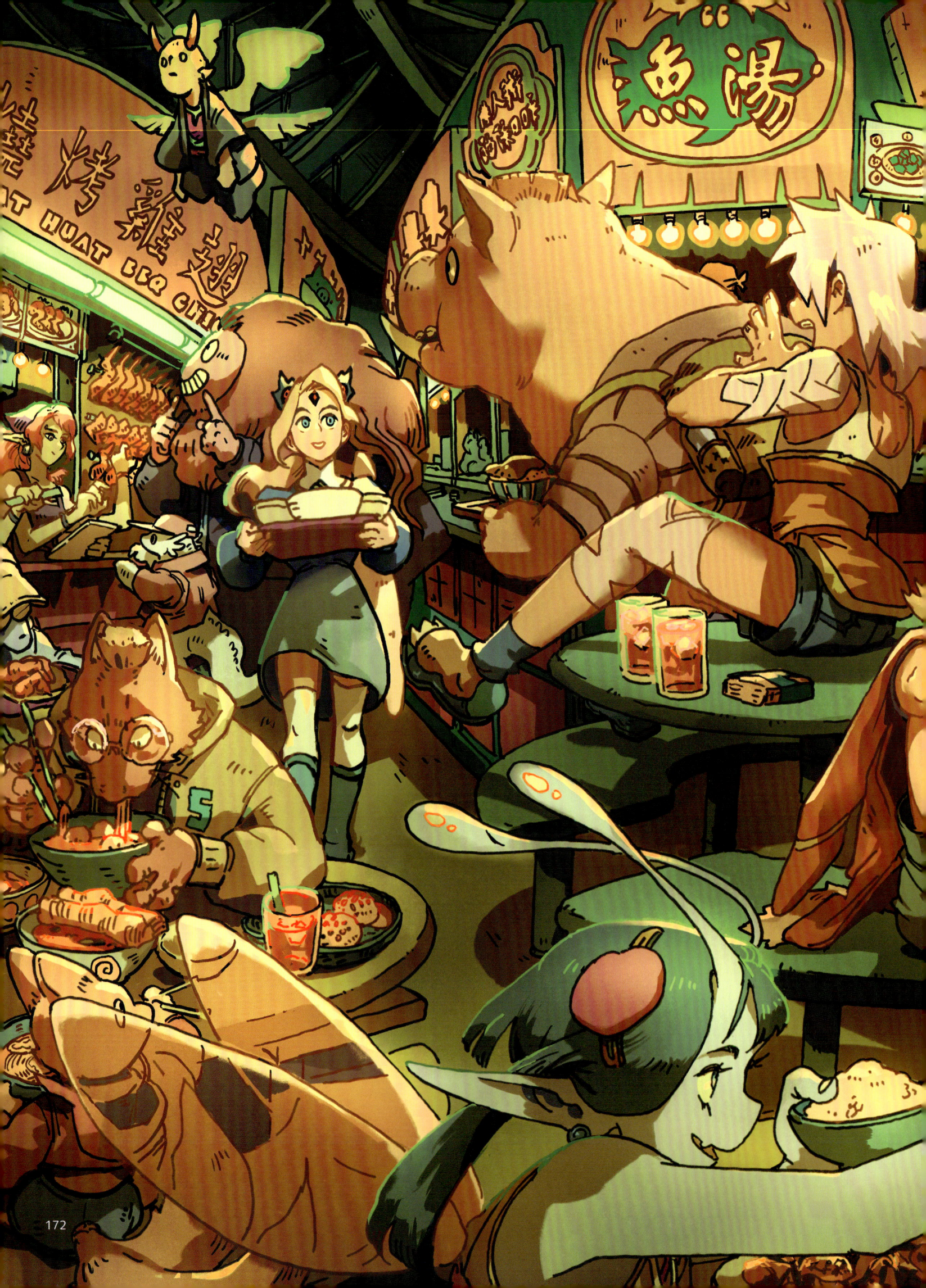

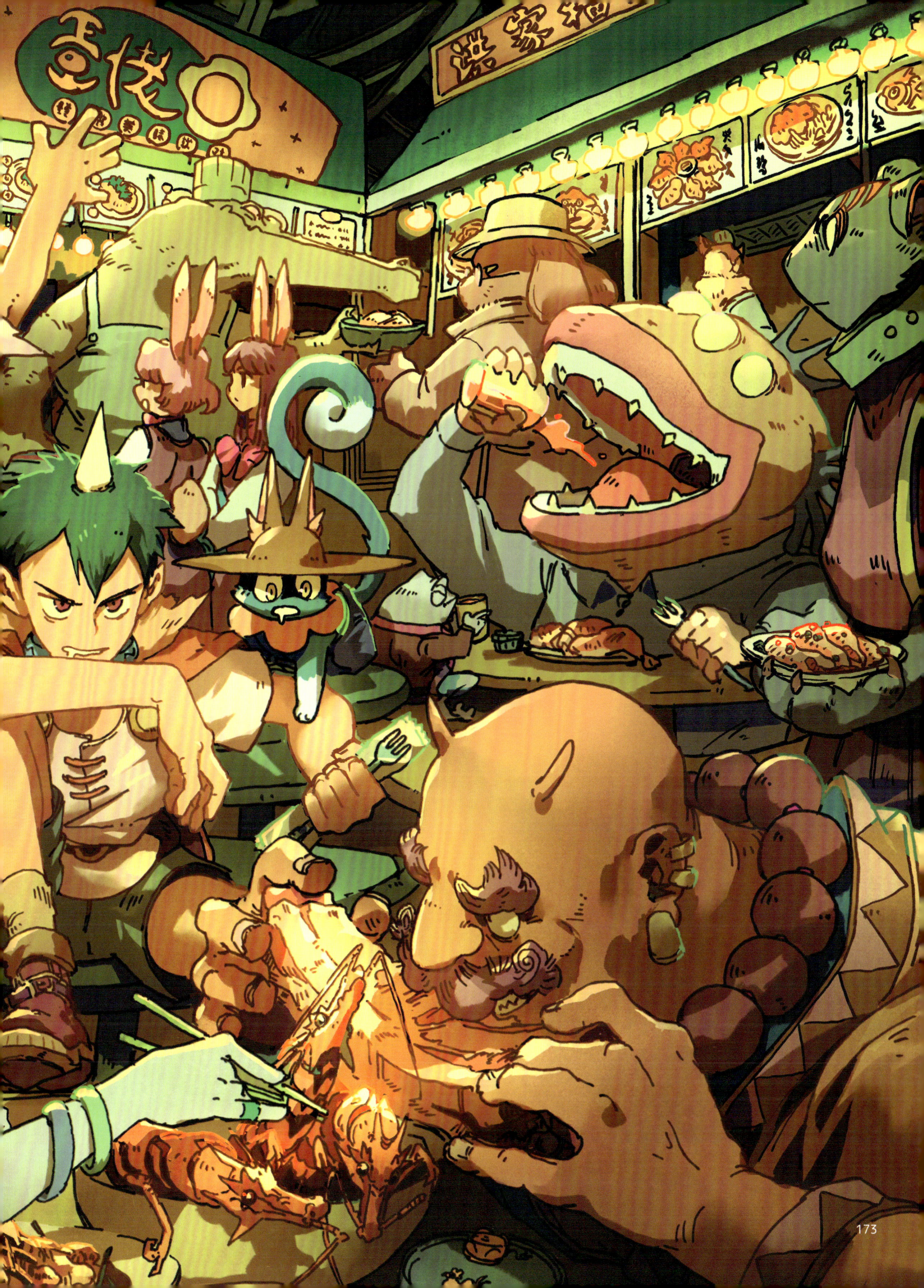

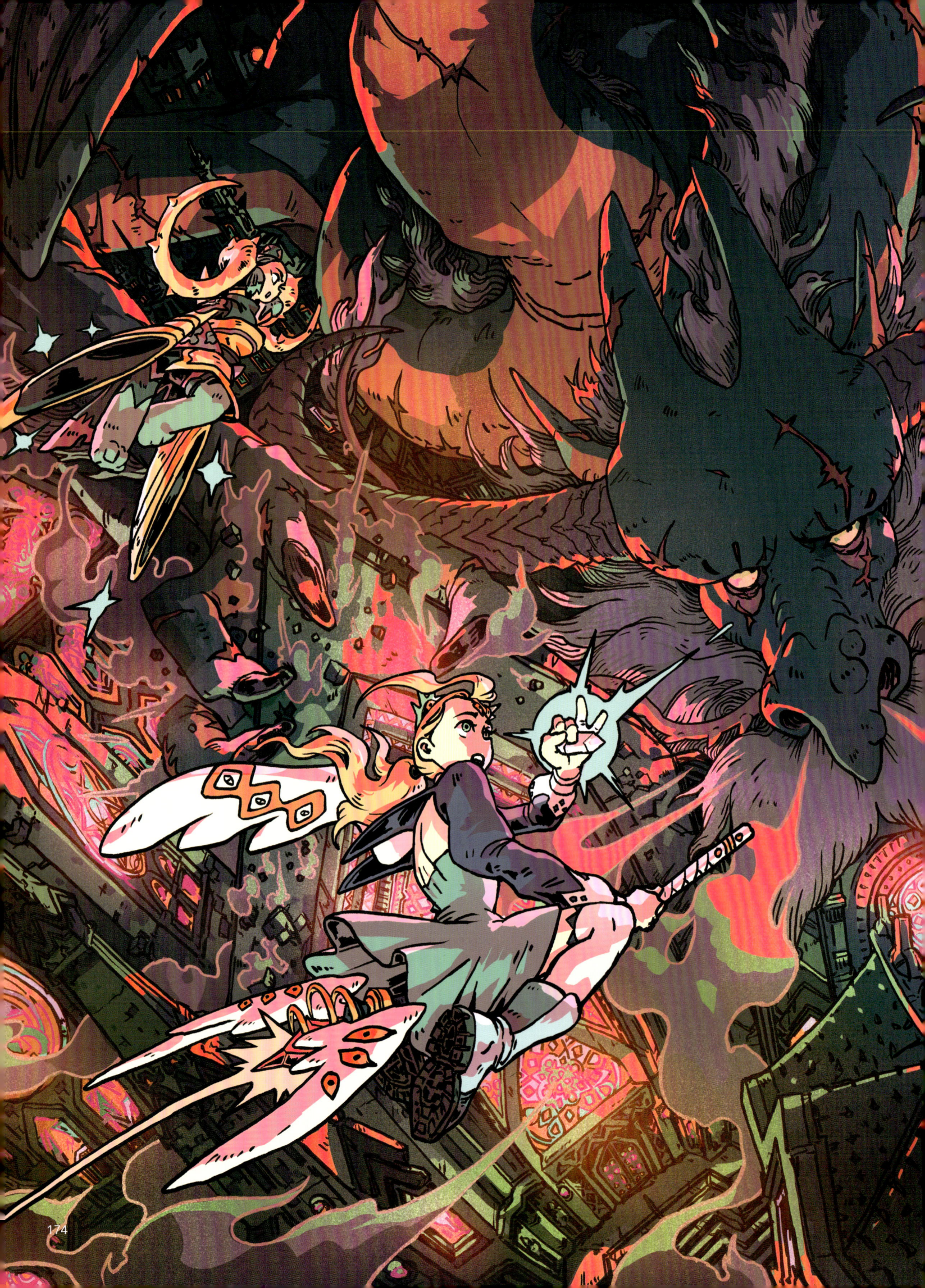

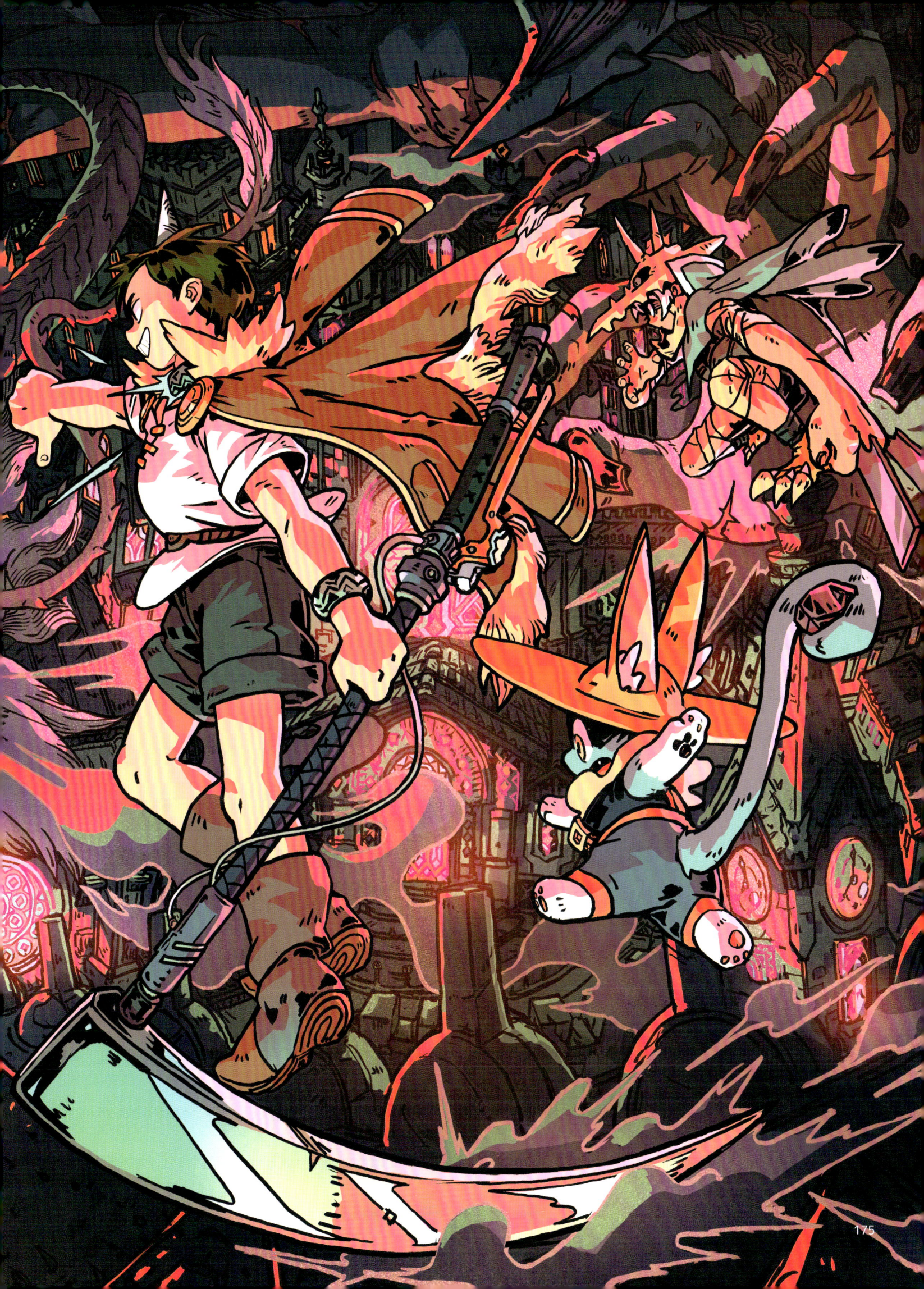

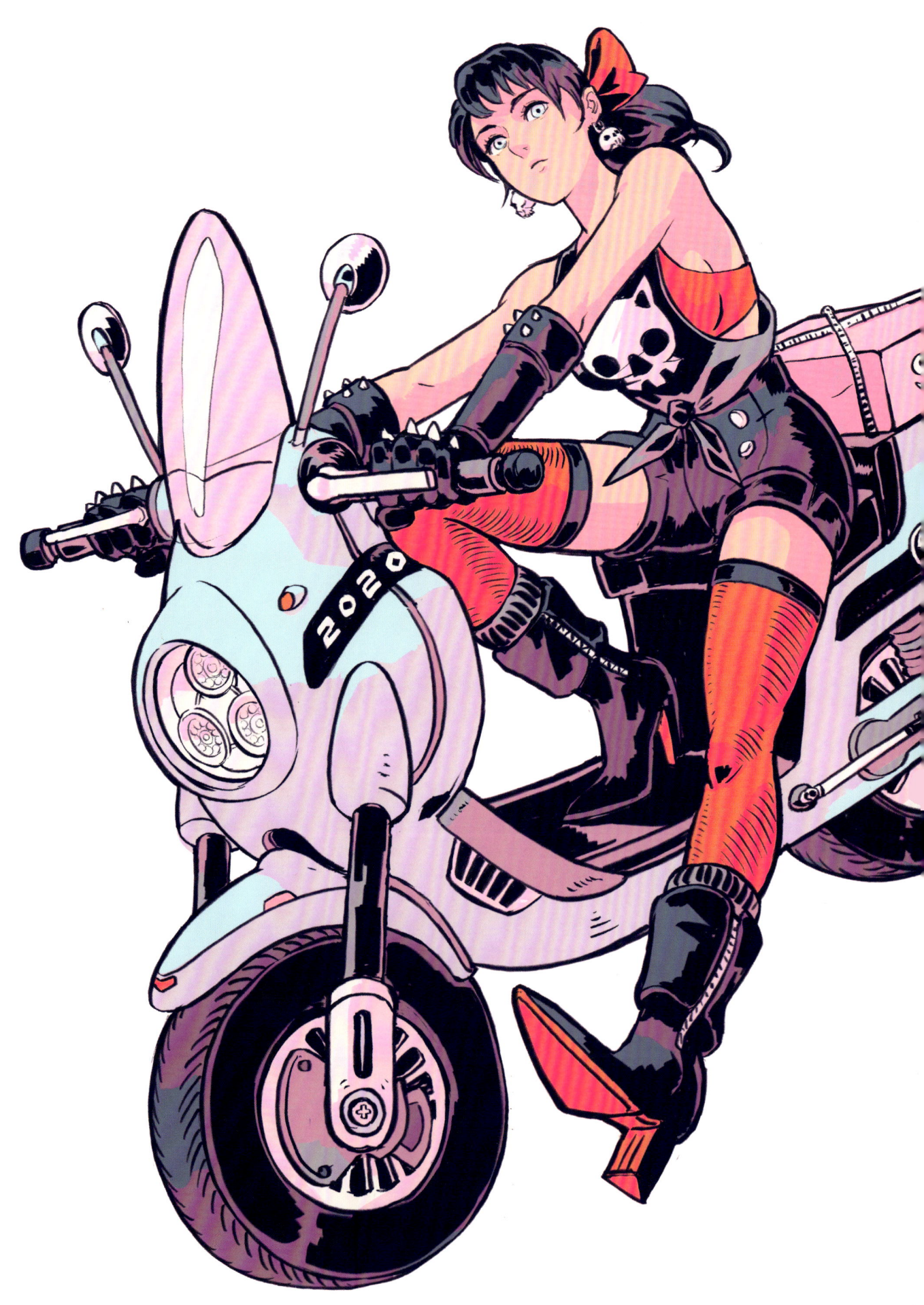

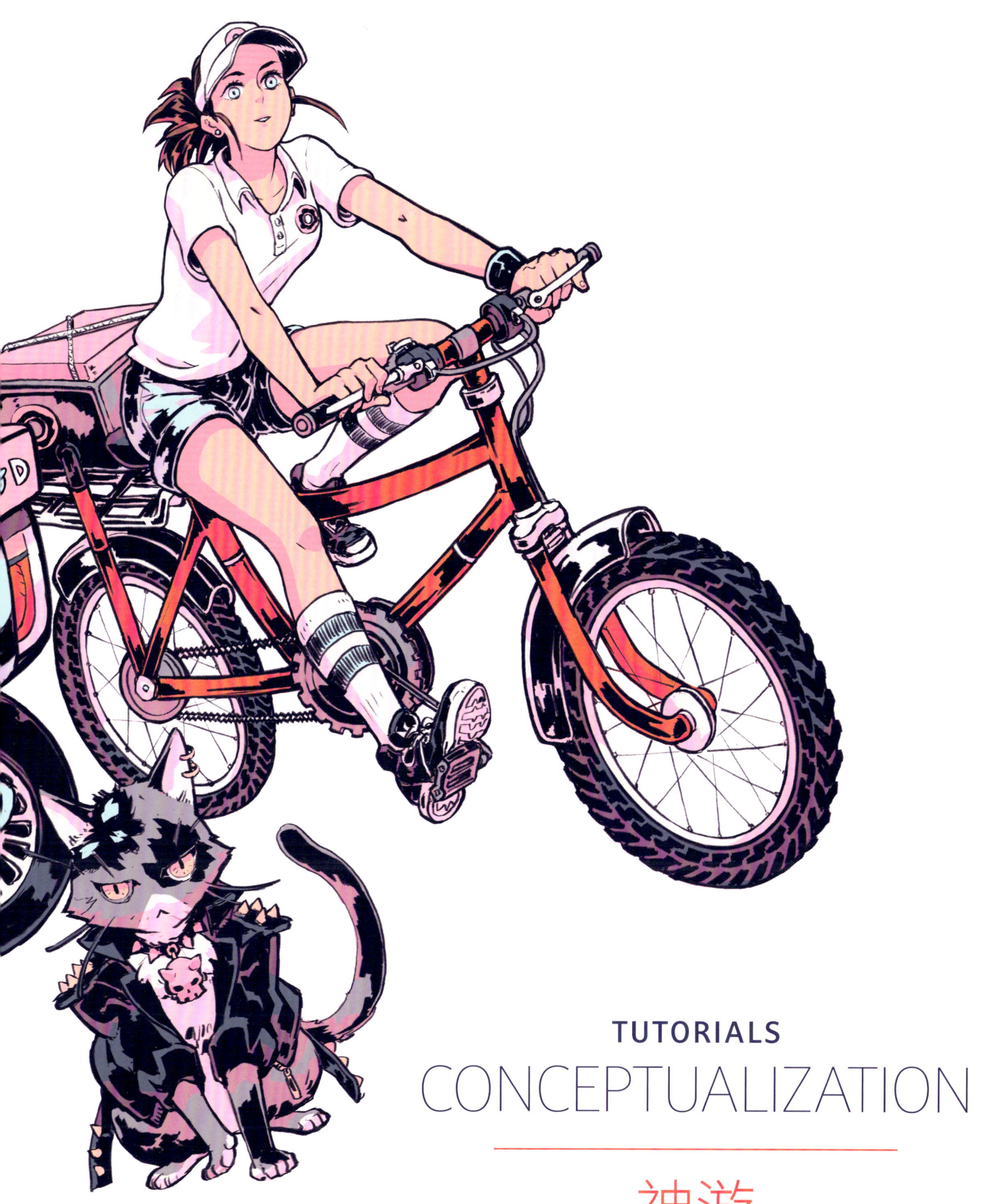

TUTORIALS
CONCEPTUALIZATION

神游

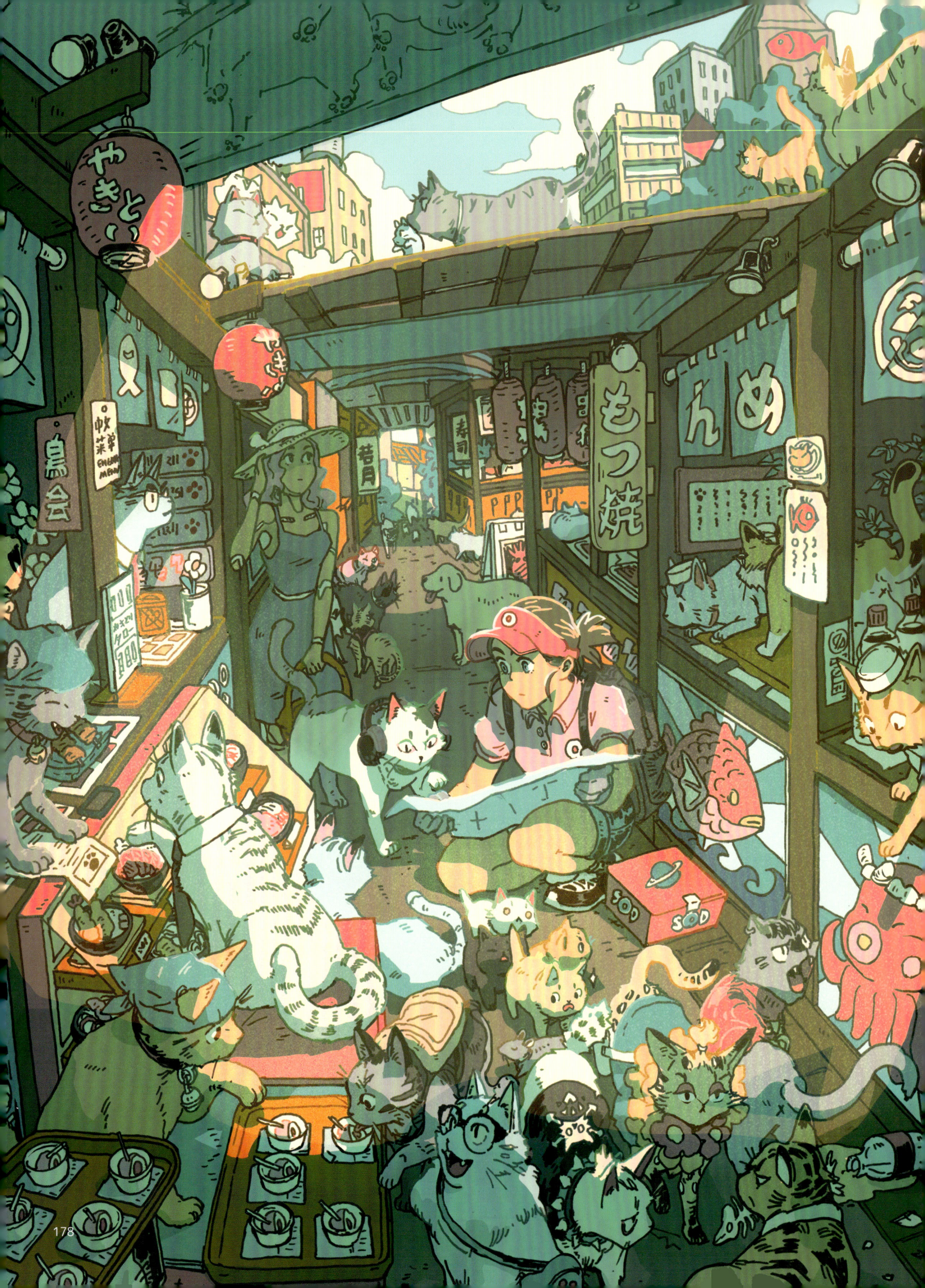

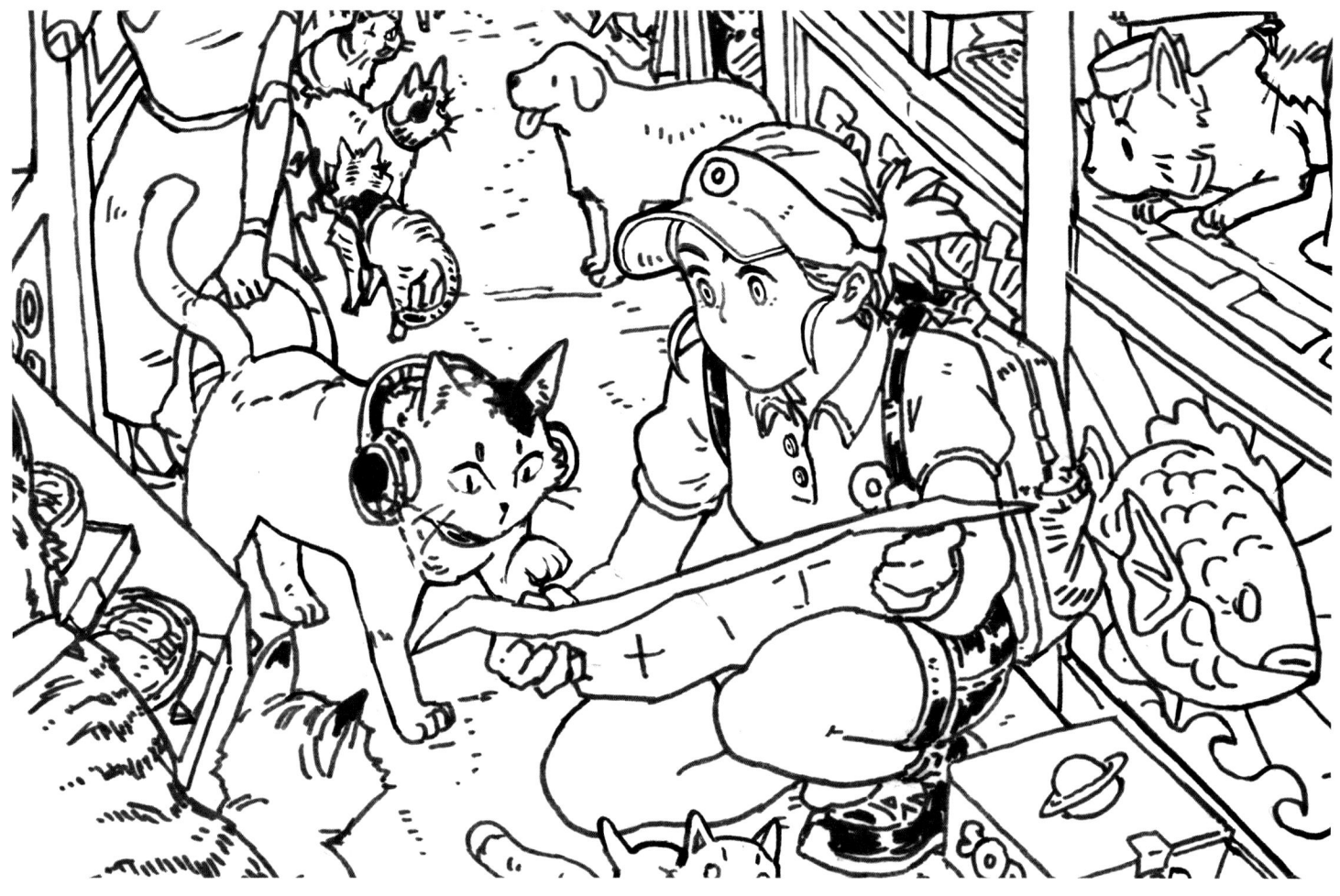

My method for coming up with an illustration idea is probably about as consistent as anyone else's – that is to say, it varies. I don't have an easy-to-follow, sure-fire methodology for coming up with a successful idea that I love, but what helps is to create a clear vision for what my work will communicate: an easily understood idea with a surprise.

Coming from a film background, I know that the best film premises are usually simple and easy to understand. However, in film you still have to have a lot of time to set up multiple ideas, and the complexity can be pretty intense. Conversely, with an illustration, you only have one snapshot to communicate everything, all at once. The story of an illustration must fit into one short sentence.

For example: 'She's lost and looking for directions.' This idea can be augmented with supporting details, but any additional pieces of information need to support that first idea: she's a delivery girl; she's delivering donuts; she's lost in a market; the market is inhabited by cats; the cats are behaving like humans; it's a busy market; the market looks appealing.

All the subsequent ideas aren't really telling a new story, but instead are servicing the first story. Often in the initial conceptualization of a piece, it's the novel combination of a simple first idea with surprising supporting details, such as the location or circumstance, that comprises my works.

Finding an idea that I think is worth drawing might sound like a lot to grapple with at first because there are so many details, but in reality, my approach is not fully formed from the beginning.

With the *Cats* illustration, for instance, I may have only had, 'She's delivering donuts to a cat universe and I'll base some of the cats and location on what it felt like to be at Nishiki Market in Kyoto.' To start, I only need to really have the focal point clear in my head. The background can be really loose blocks of space that I'll figure out later. In this case, the focal point was a girl showing a map to a helpful cat. The background was constricted by knowing what Nishiki Market looked like in real life, so the task became choosing a camera angle that would showcase the focal point while leaving space for a narrow-market scene.

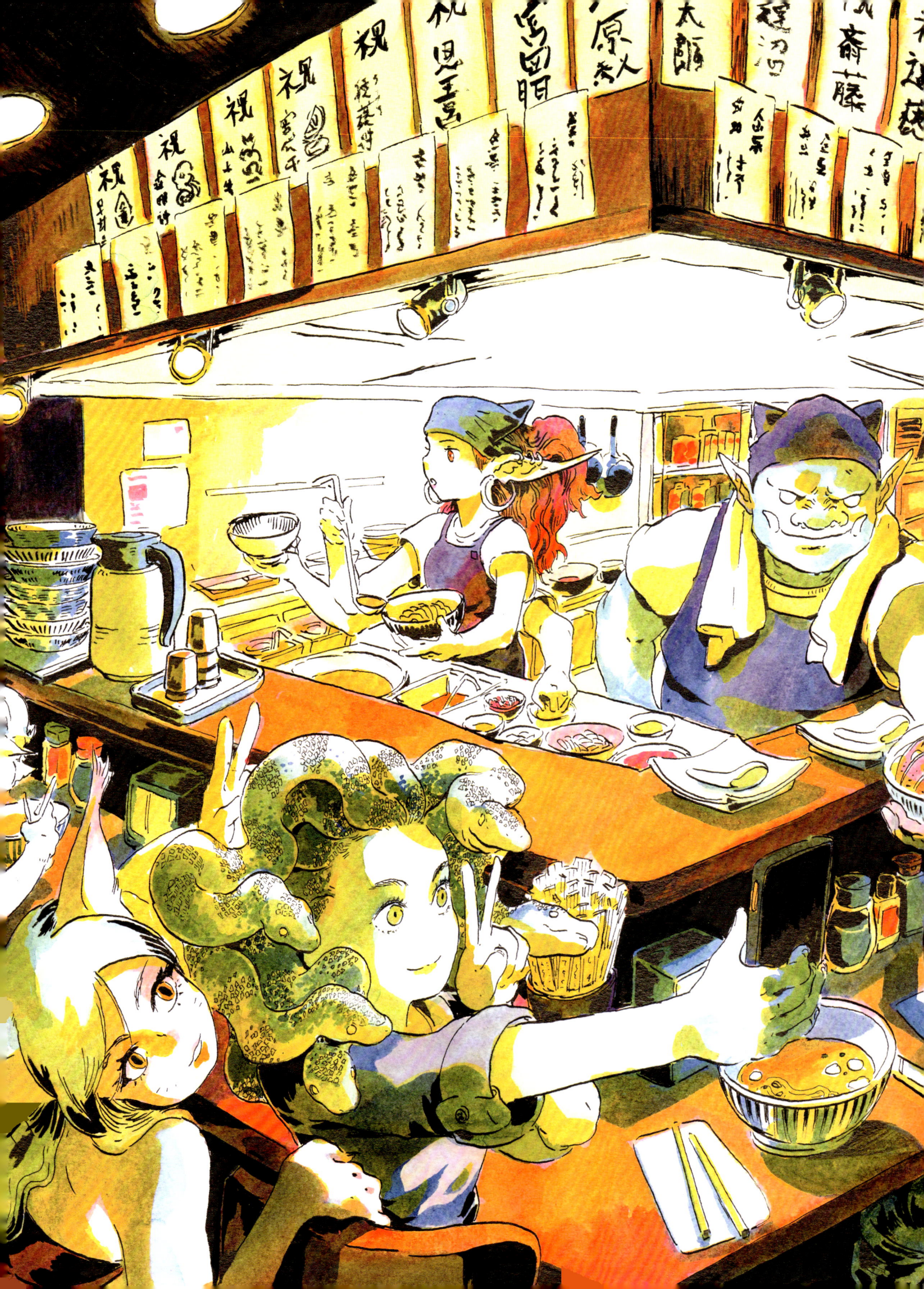

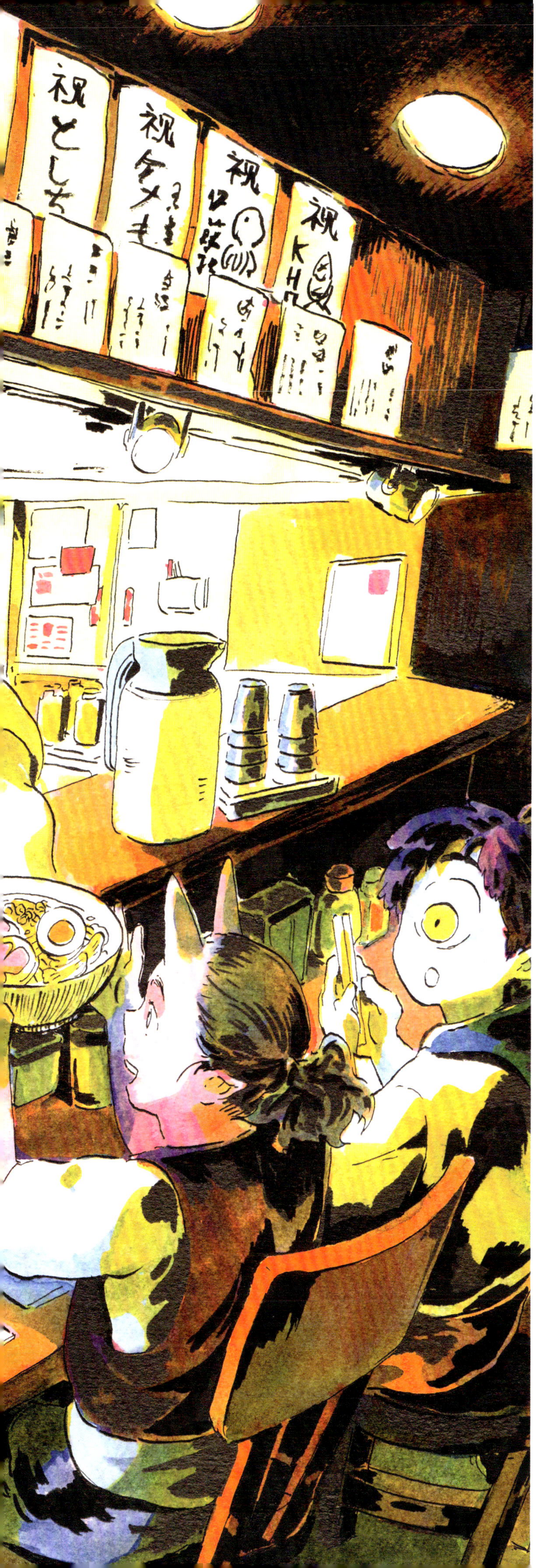

Another example: 'They're eating ramen.' Since my goal is to have an easily digestible idea, it also needs to be relatable in some way. Hence, why I draw food so often! For me, getting ramen is usually a fun and exciting experience. If I were to make a piece where regular people are eating regular ramen, there might be some audiences who find that compelling simply because they love ramen and have enough affection for that alone.

However, to satisfy my own sensibilities, I twisted that premise to be a little more surprising: 'Monsters are eating ramen; the ramen shop looks like an authentic shop in Tokyo; the monster kids are behaving like regular kids; some of them are taking selfies; one of the chefs is a monster with multiple arms and she's using all of them to cook faster.'

The supporting details in this case elevated the simple premise to be more specific, but there wasn't a new storyline. Every additional detail was still there to support the main idea: this is no ordinary ramen shop.

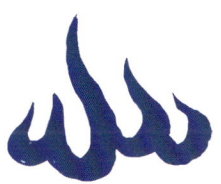

CRONUTS

It may be surprising to some that many of my most successful pieces are actually ones that are mostly improvised. For me, this often happens when I find the story so fun or silly that it's as though I'm just riffing off of the joke. Or perhaps the universe that is set forth by the premise happens to generate a lot of ideas naturally. What's important in those moments is not how well-planned something is, but how much I'm emotionally connected to it.

An example of this might be the *Cronuts* illustration, which is really just an exploration of 'bratty biker-gang girls'. I knew they were a bratty biker gang because they exist in a story where they're the polar opposite of the girl who went to extreme lengths to deliver donuts to someone in the cat universe. However, the fun exploration became 'how to make them even more bratty and irresponsible by comparison'.

The answer was: have them posing for a selfie. Make some of them pose in taunting ways. Up the recklessness by putting them in space. In fact, they've caused some sort of accident behind them. Better yet, the explosions of the accident are like flashing paparazzi cameras. Since the ideas were improvised and I didn't try to change them midway, they were also naturally drawn in order of importance.

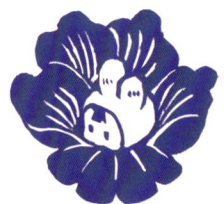

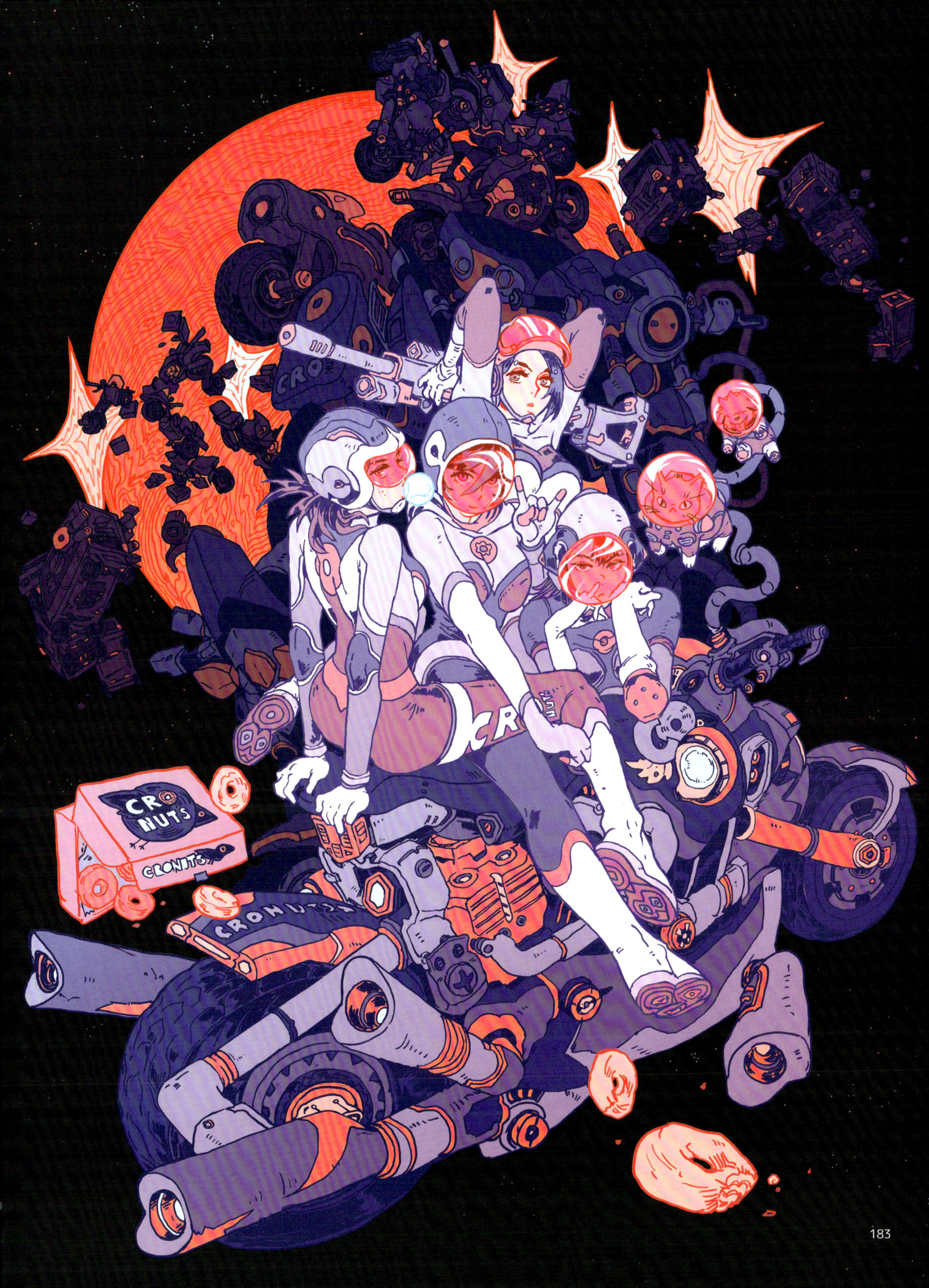

Let's talk about my process for *Qinghua Tiger Vases*. The concept for this piece came from one I made as a doodle, by which I mean a drawing that had no pre-conceptualization or story. It was purely an exploration of a visual experiment without the intent of making an illustration to communicate anything. Instead, I wanted to answer my own curiosity:

'Can I make tiger stripes look like a Qinghua blue-and-white vase pattern?'

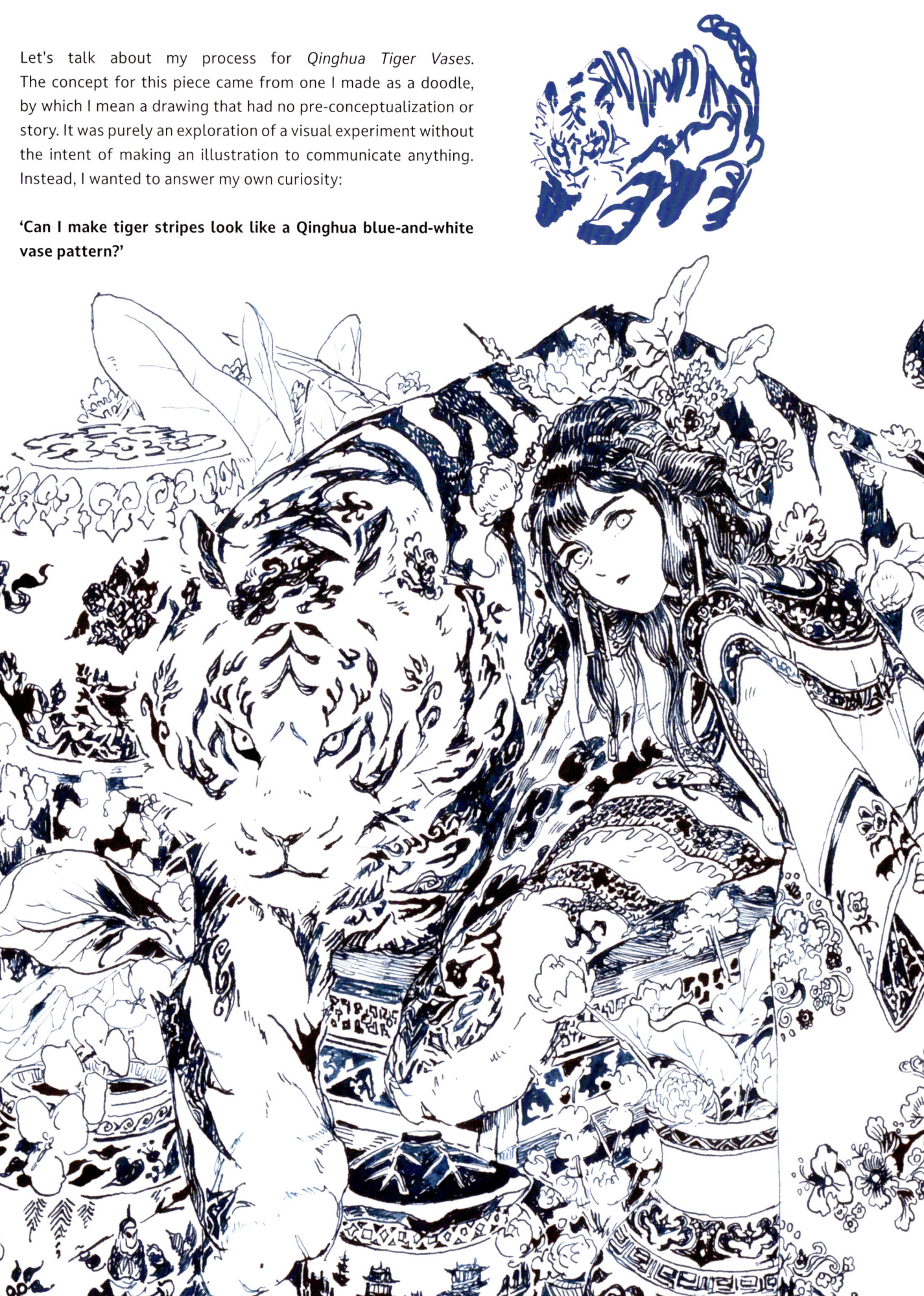

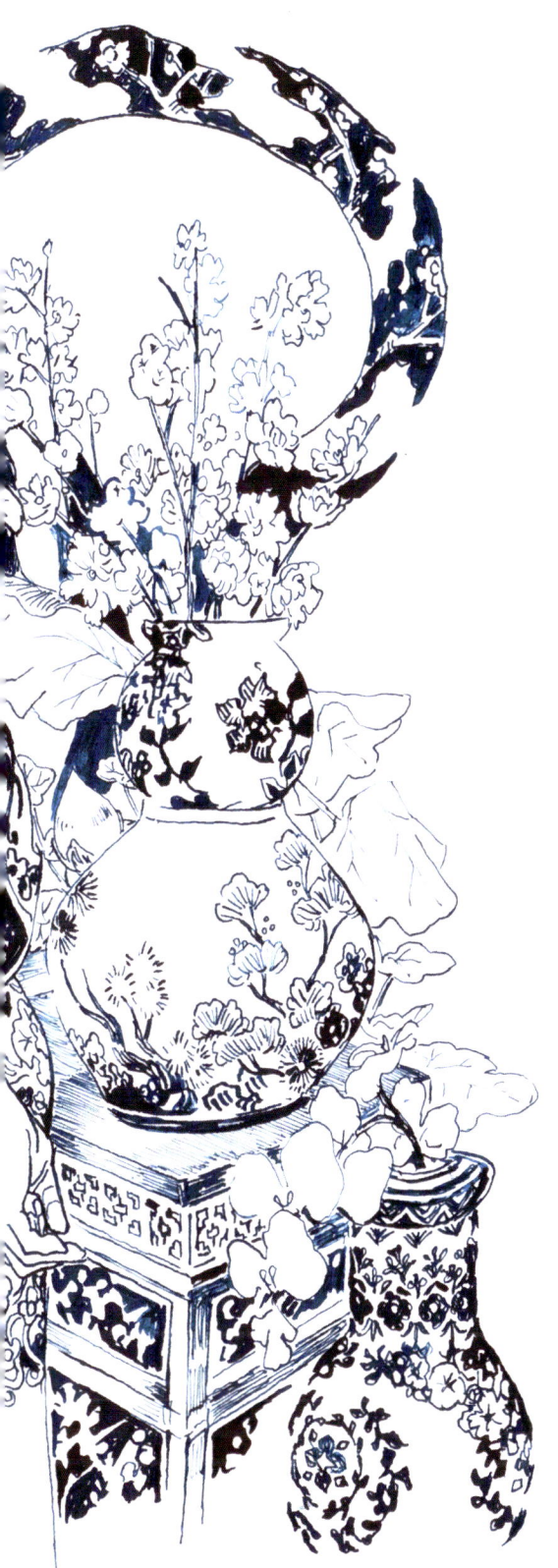

After exploring what those shapes and design patterns looked like and becoming comfortable with them, I came up with a story idea: a team of artists paint Qinghua stripes onto a tiger. To be upfront, I don't normally scaffold my ideas like this with initial test drawings, but you know what, I really should more often. I'd have a lot more to show for my work, haha.

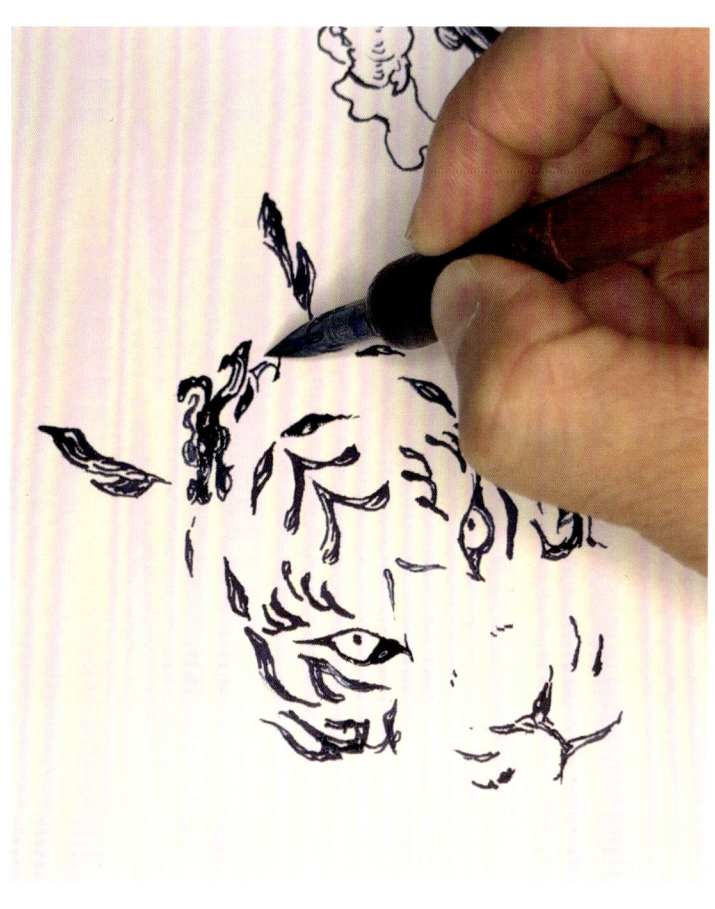

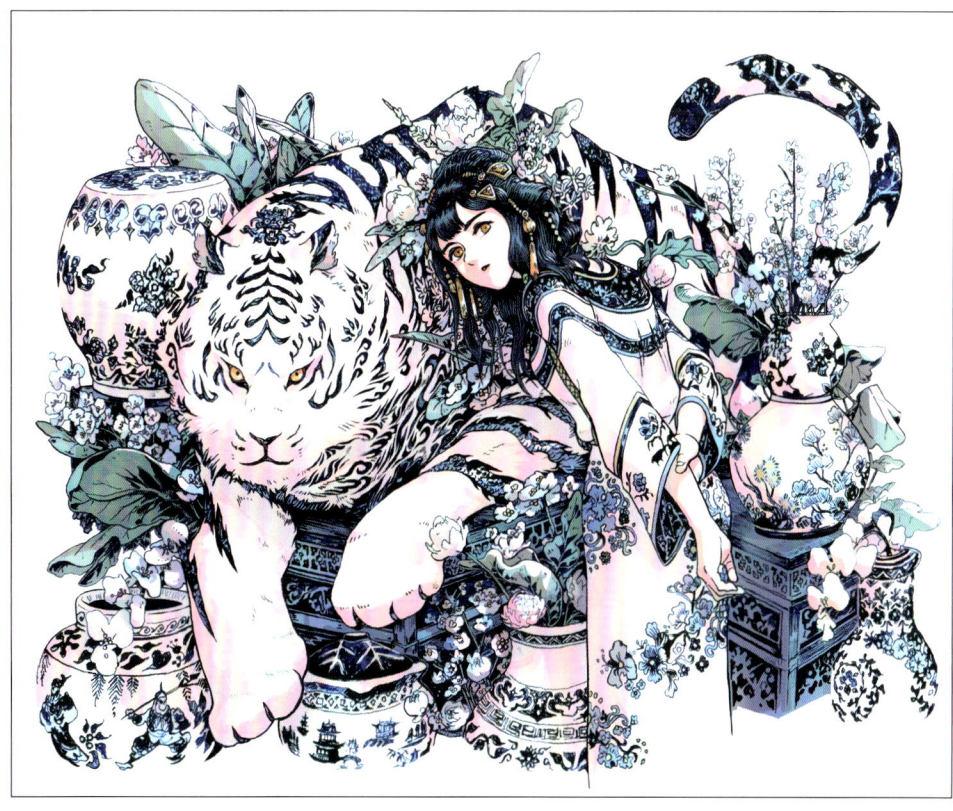

185

THUMBNAILS
BRAINSTORMING

Thumbnails are quick little drawings done to map out an idea. This is a step I don't always start with when doing personal work, but it's something I consistently do for client projects.

If I haven't got an idea yet, then this stage can be helpful for figuring out the major elements of an illustration, such as what or who the characters are, and what they're doing. In this case, I started with the premise of 'Girls paint stripes onto a tiger in a Qinghua style.' The first three thumbnails are just an exploration of how to best pose the tiger or to compose the scene so that we can see the most important part, the Qinghua stripes. The last thumbnails are an experiment: What if the girls are the same girls as *Overflow*'s cover image? In the end, I scrapped this idea because it felt too similar in setting and tone, and so I explored a different direction.

The core of this exercise is to make sure the main idea is readable, and it's also the main way I go about deciding the composition of every piece. One of the most important guiding principles for me is to make sure the audience can see what's most important, and ensure they see it first. A composition needs to read like a book – it has to guide the audience through the information so they can see what's going on. The more clear, tasteful, and novel that information is conveyed, the better the result.

Rather than focusing on the macro goal of an image's overall story and emotional resonance, what I'm thinking about on a moment-to-moment basis is: 'How will this affect where the eye moves next?' It's a simple idea and it only works if I've done the previous steps correctly, namely making sure the focal point is read first and that the poses clearly convey what's happening.

The first couple of thumbnails were drawn after I went to visit the Petersen Automotive Museum in Los Angeles, and really felt like it would be fun to draw the Qinghua girls painting an F1 car. I might still do this idea because I like it (I might use these same thumbnails even, which is a good example of not wasting effort), but at the time, I really wanted to keep improving my tiger drawings. Also, I felt like the previous Qinghua-tiger experiment was close, but not quite there. So, I returned to the same core idea on the subsequent thumbnails and finally landed on the fourth attempt in a more traditional setting.

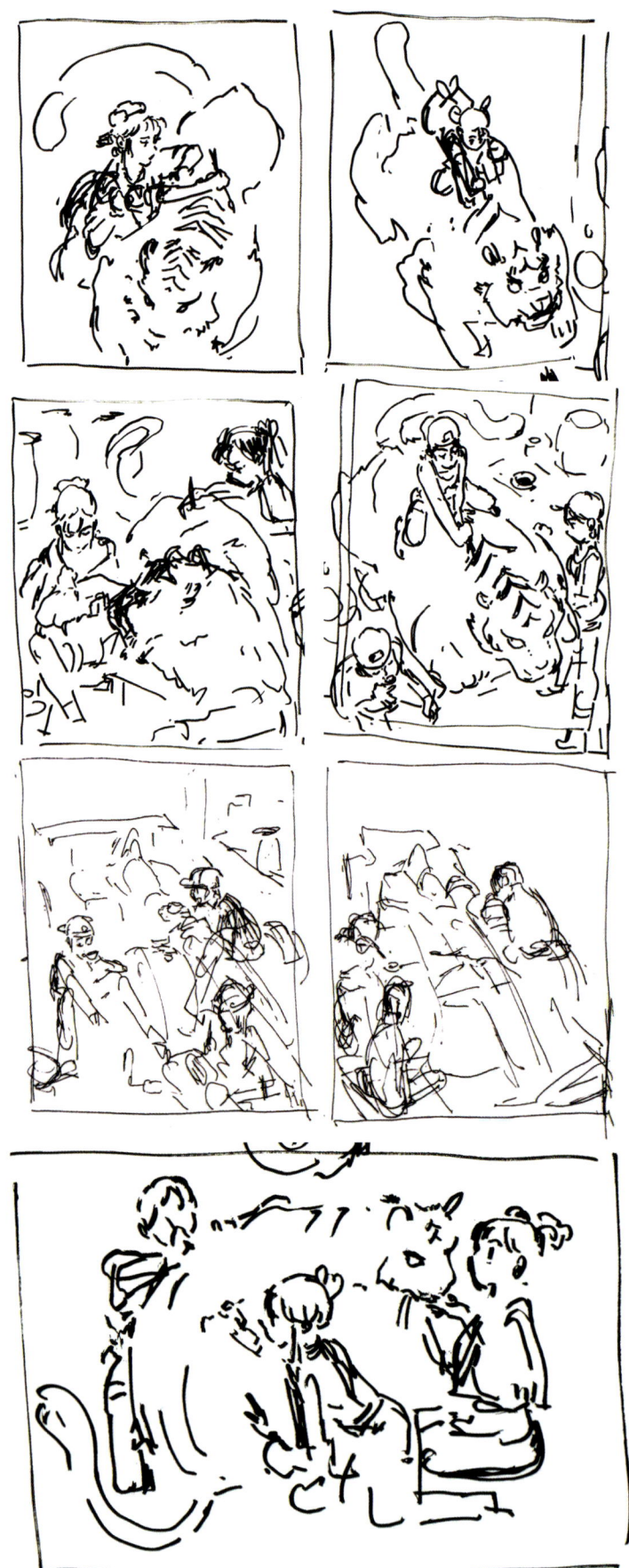

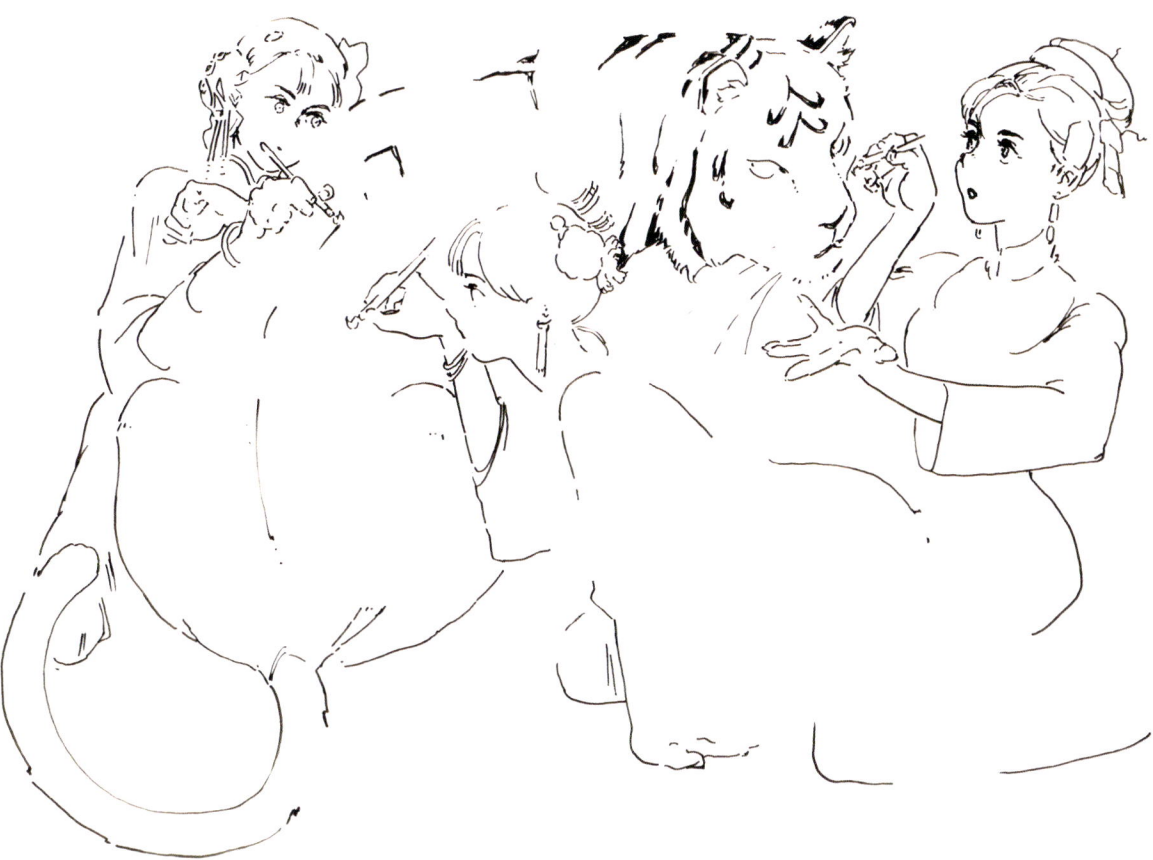

LINE ART
ATTEMPT 1

Here is the first attempt at that initial idea. It went … so-so. Initially, I was pleased with the tiger and the middle girl, but I hit a couple of issues after that. First, I felt like I goofed up the left-side girl's arm pose – her silhouette isn't clear or readable enough because her brush gets hidden inside her body, and even her second arm gets blocked inside.

Secondly, I straight-up biffed it on the eyes of the girl on the right. I had a chance to fix this, but also butterfingered my way through, resulting in eyes with much wider lines than the other girls, and it still looked a bit off. I also got confused on what pose to give her, and so she's got awkward arms as well. A swing and a miss!

However, I think it's worth noting that I felt like I learned a lot from this attempt. As an 'in-progress' drawing, I think this image reveals a bit more about how I think and draw. I am often asked how I draw with a pen, and there are many strategies I use that might be hard to see in the finished product. In this example, in which I've got a particular composition in mind, I incorporate a lot of steps that I feel are very similar to ones that other artists use when drawing with a pencil.

More specifically, in order to map out the space that a subject might occupy in the drawing, I very carefully choose to draw the safest and most important lines that can help me indicate those elements. This requires a muscle that I think everyone has to flex when it comes to drawing things like overlap or foreshortening – you have to take a leap of faith and trust your ability to visualize what's going where on the page, just with your mind's eye.

This is a method that I've since adapted and use regularly in many places, even when it's not for overlap. In this case, as soon as I've indicated enough information for my own understanding of what's clearly happening on the page, I move on to other elements that might not be as clear to me. If you look at my figure drawing, you'll see me use this technique a lot. That's because it's a habit that I learned during those live sessions that only allow for a few minutes of drawing time. Time is of the essence, so it's much more important to focus on what's really worthwhile to you.

Skip the parts you already feel comfortable with and focus on what's interesting, whether it's to learn more about strengthening your weaknesses or just to enhance some sort of emotion you're trying to evoke.

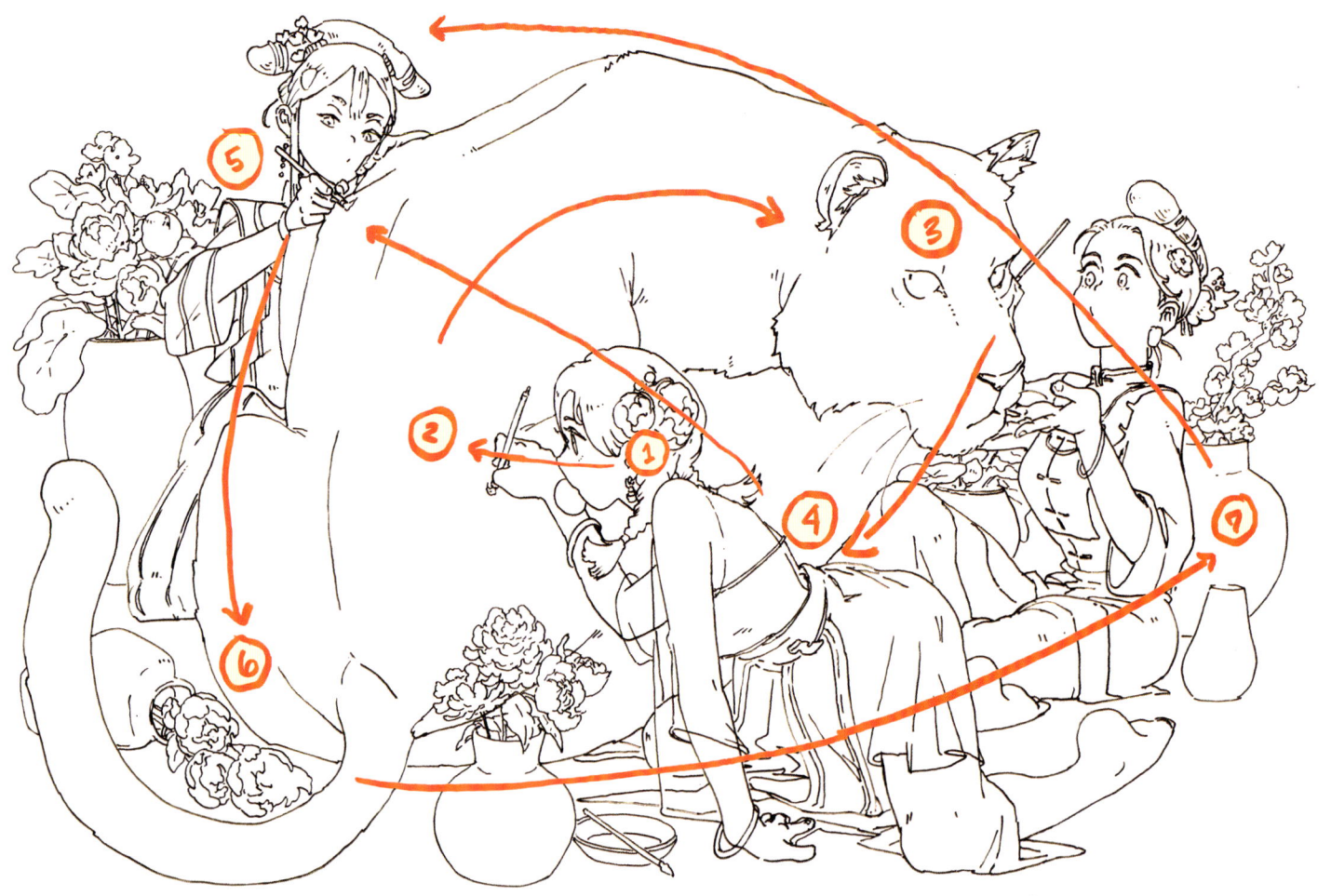

ATTEMPT 2

The second attempt went a lot better. I especially felt that positioning the left-hand girl higher in the frame helped with then guiding the viewer's eye down towards the right. Similarly, I placed the other characters in such a way that the most interesting information was paced more evenly throughout the piece, almost creating a sort of figure of eight to move you continuously through it.

As far as deciding the order of what to draw, it basically goes something like this: focal point/character's face > elements in front of the focal point > secondary characters > background.

This feels very straightforward to me, but I'll try to explain more about why I feel this is important, since it can be easy to forget, and instead you could just start drawing things that feel interesting in the moment.

Basically, if your image is about the focal point, it's important for that to get priority when it comes to placement and even overlap. Even if you want something to be in the very front, such as a hand or intense foreground elements like leaves, those elements are never as important as the overall readability of the focal point. We need to know what's going on. So, draw the parts you absolutely need to see in order to comprehend the central idea to ensure they aren't compromised.

The biggest challenge at this point was deciding whether to leave the stripes for the colour stage. I also wasn't sure whether to make a background or not. To me, so much of drawing feels like an internal battle – so many dangling possibilities can become overwhelming to the point of paralysis. During those times, I follow the same logic I use to handle line art: find the elements that I'm most sure about and do those first. In this case, I absolutely knew that the vases needed Qinghua-style paintings on them, and that the tiger's stripes would as well. So, at least that was a safe next step!

Although I used colour here, I still technically considered this part of the line-art stage. Admittedly, this phase started out shaky. I felt like I didn't think enough about how to convey the flatness of the tiger's front plane while I was drawing the initial marks. The struggle is definitely finding the willpower to soldier on, even when self-doubt starts to make me second-guess my decisions, such as whether I've messed up enough to warrant a retry.

At this point, my strategy was to try to overpower such thoughts with positive thinking. *Might as well see if I can save this. Maybe it's not so bad. Those issues won't matter once you add something else.* It doesn't always work, but it sure helps me finish more drawings!

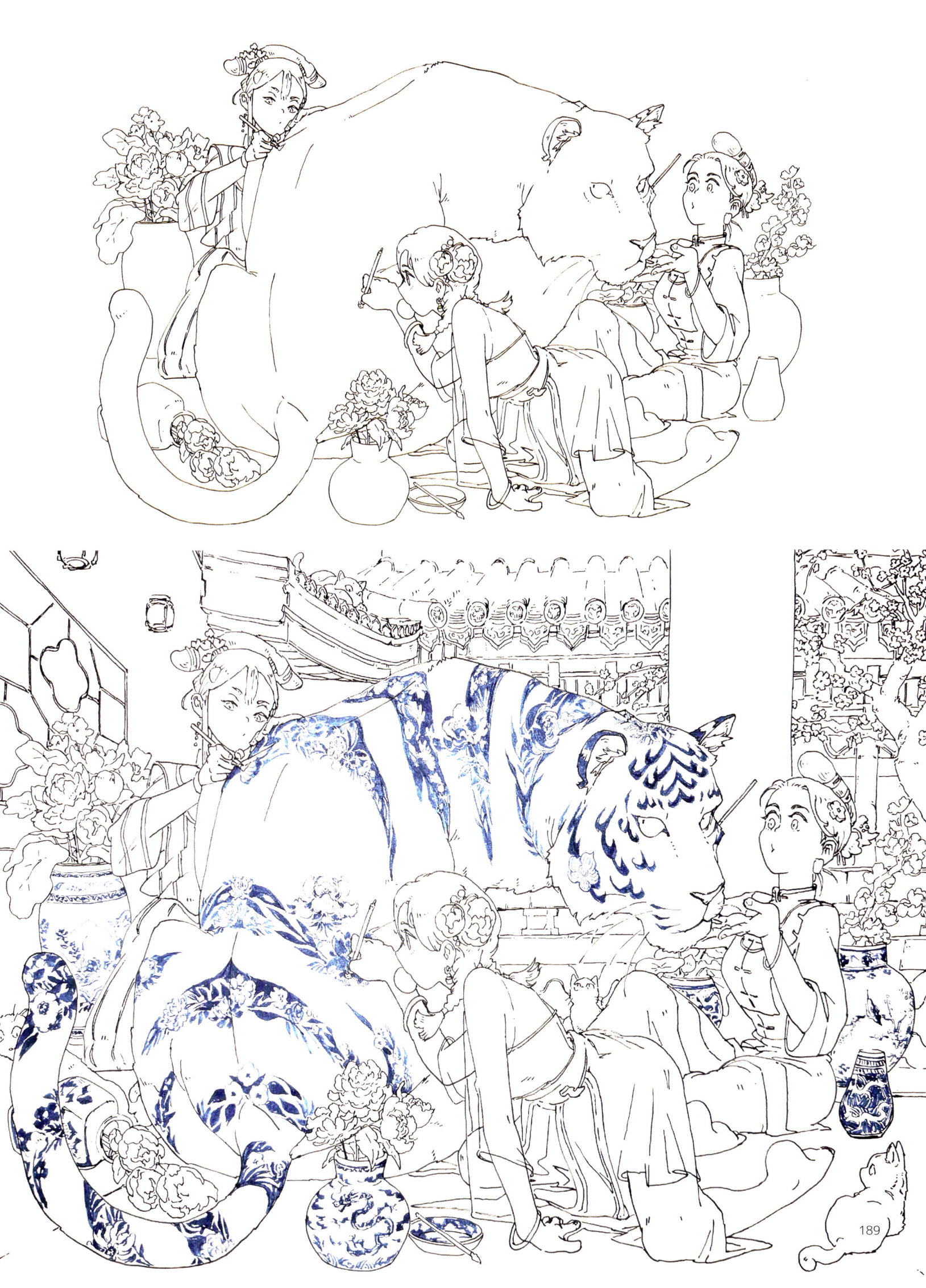

COLOUR

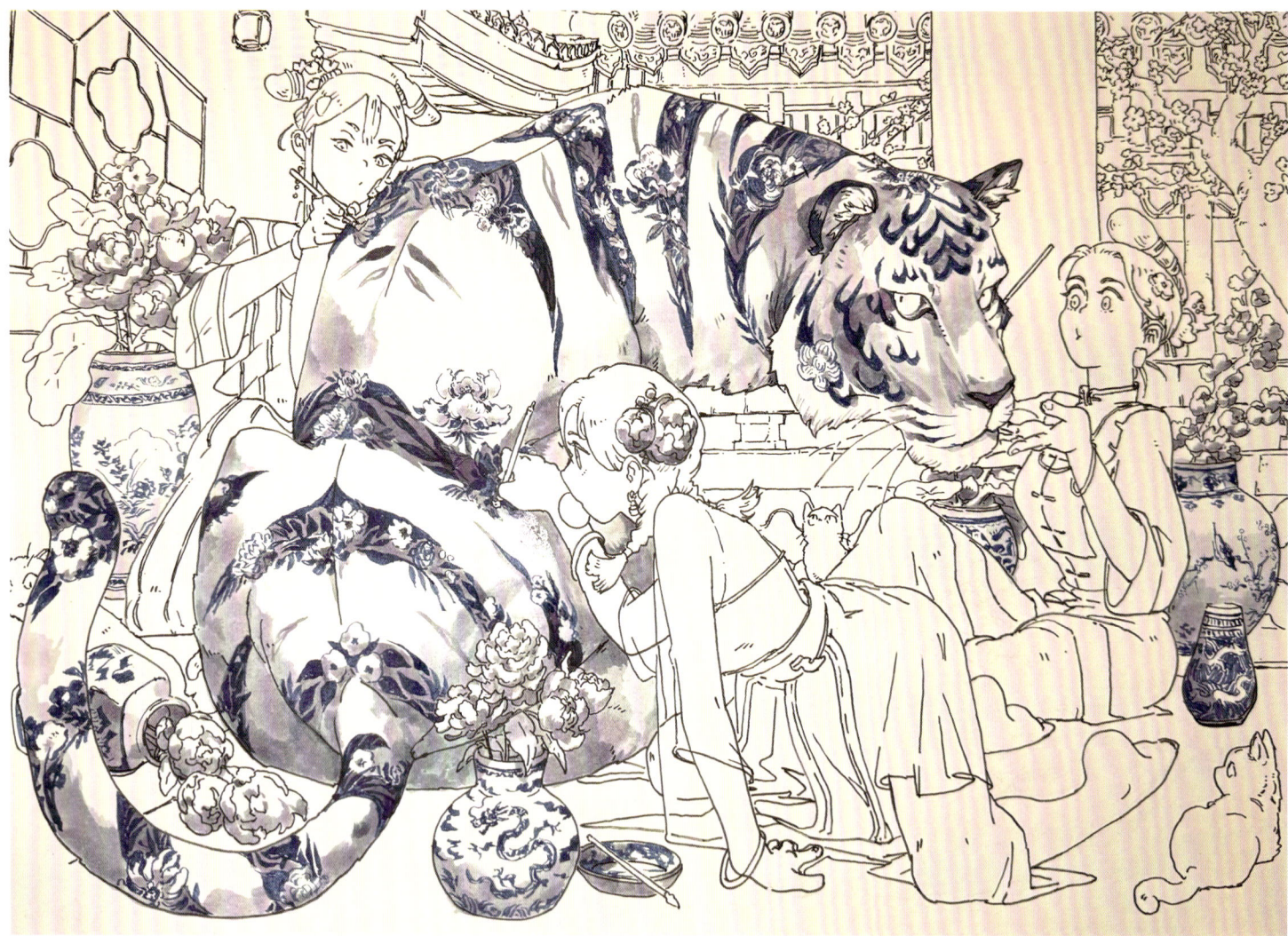

SHADING

The rule for the focal point also applies to colour: you don't want to colour the secondary elements in a way that competes with the central focus. So again, start with the most important components of the drawing, whoever or whatever that is, and balance the rest of the image accordingly. That is the safest and easiest way to proceed. In this case, the focal point is the tiger.

For this drawing, I also wanted to try out a new medium – dual-colour inks from Pilot. It took me a while to figure them out, but the more value you put down, the more it veers towards the second colour; in this case, from green to purple. This became more apparent as I worked on the background and loaded up lots more ink.

I think it's imperative that I continue to explore new mediums and subject matter in order to maintain the sense of play that I find so important. It infuses artwork with genuine joy. If I'm not pushing myself in some regard, then I'm probably repeating myself, which can quickly become boring. Of course, there's a multitude of ways to push yourself. Perhaps it's just by tapping

into a different emotion you'd like to channel and it has nothing to do with the practice of art itself. But you have to feel at ease while drawing and not be overly precious about the result, and so having fun by playing with mediums can be a big part of that.

Truthfully, in between this image and the last, I made a big mistake. I saw some Hanfu outfits that combined pink along with a white and blue Qinghua colour scheme, and originally, I wanted to have a white tiger where some of the lighting made portions of the fur turn pink. But – and I should have seen this coming – the pink just made it look like a normal orange tiger. Welp! That wasn't necessarily a bad thing, and so I thought I'd see what would happen if I used the same tone to colour the next most important element: the girls' skin tones. Although this feels like an issue that might be tied to traditional mediums, I follow a similar approach with digital tools: the way I discover the overall palette is by using the same handful of colours throughout the entire piece.

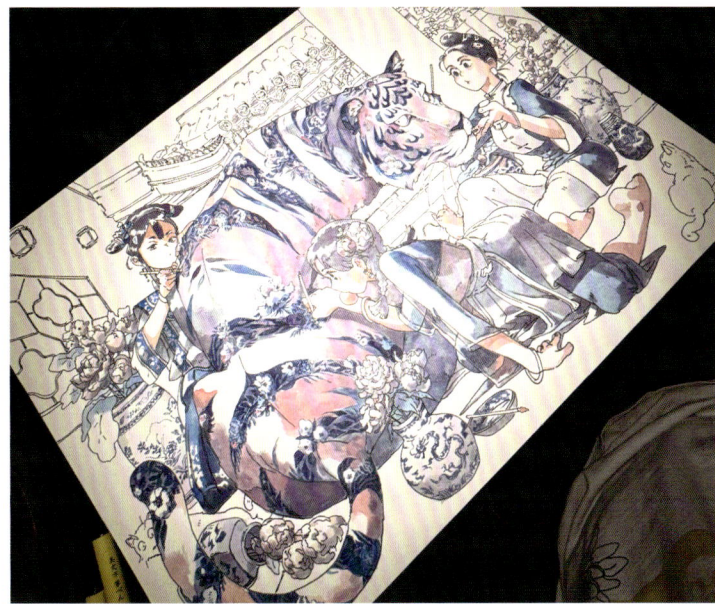

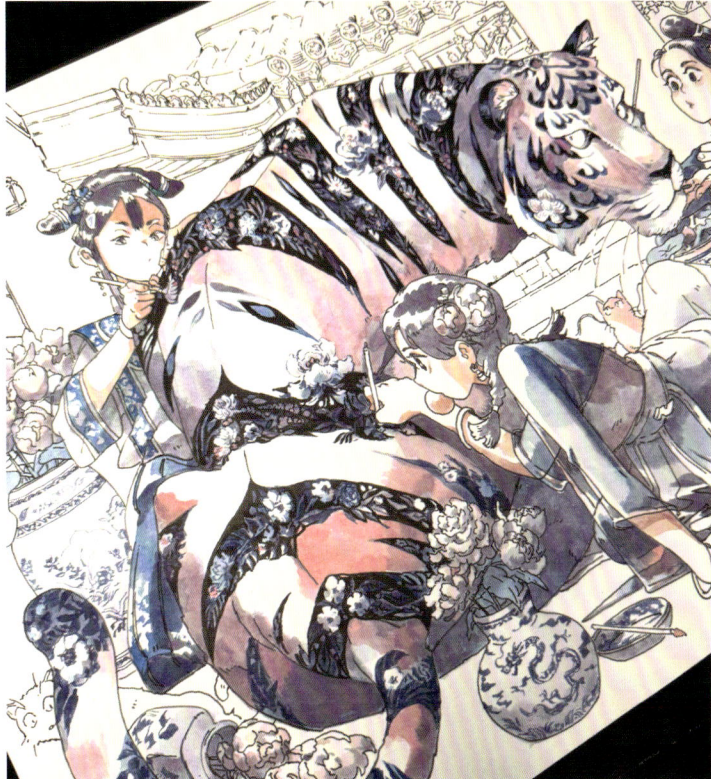

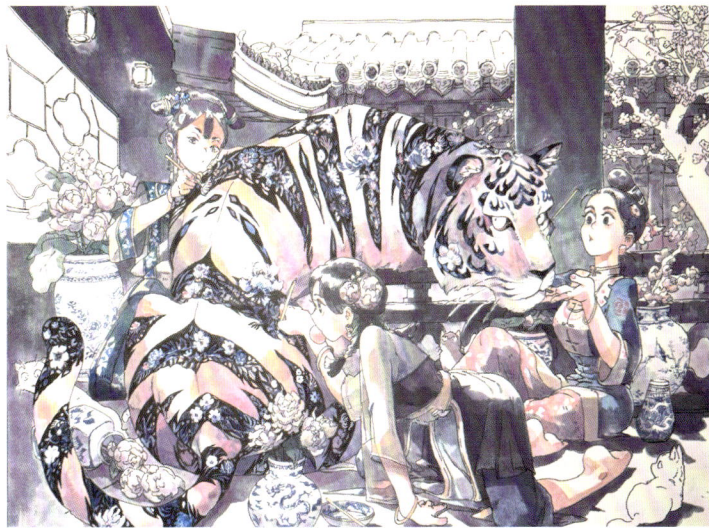

This approach to colour helps me unify a piece and removes the issue of too many competing colour combinations. It is a theory and technique I learned by using a CMYK approach. This means painting in one pass of cyan, then yellow, then magenta, with 'K' being the black lines. No matter how I combined those three colours, the result was always within the same colour story, so it basically always looked pleasing, even if it meant I had pushed some colours to be less accurate to their real-world counterparts.

One of the most frustrating yet satisfying things about my process is the patience required to avoid certain parts of the image until the proper prerequisite steps have been completed. In this case, the thing I had to wait to do was colour in the background. I had many thoughts and ideas while painting the tiger, one of them being to make the background a really intense solid black to make the tiger pop. But I also knew the important competing element would be the stripes, and as I didn't know how boldly I'd be able to make them stand out using the blue inks and pink accent colours, I didn't want the weight to be pulled towards the background.

After my first go at the Qinghua stripes, I felt it was necessary to introduce some black to the stripes so they could read more clearly. After doing so, I realized they worked well as the most visually dominant source of black. Also, I became more comfortable with the dual-coloured inks while painting the girls, and decided they could add some interesting variations to the background's large shadowed areas. Long story short, it was satisfying to finally fill in the background because I spent so long imagining what it would do to the piece.

After doing a pass for all the background shadows, I was pleased with the nice gradation from the dual inks. Value wise, things were in a good place, but the hue was slightly out of line with where I wanted the overall colour scheme to be. Basically, the background shadows were so purple and green that they were competing with the blues and pinks on the tiger and girls. To counter this, and to enhance the contrast, I added some more blue tones to the shadows.

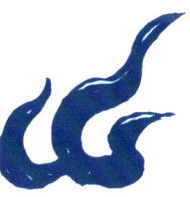

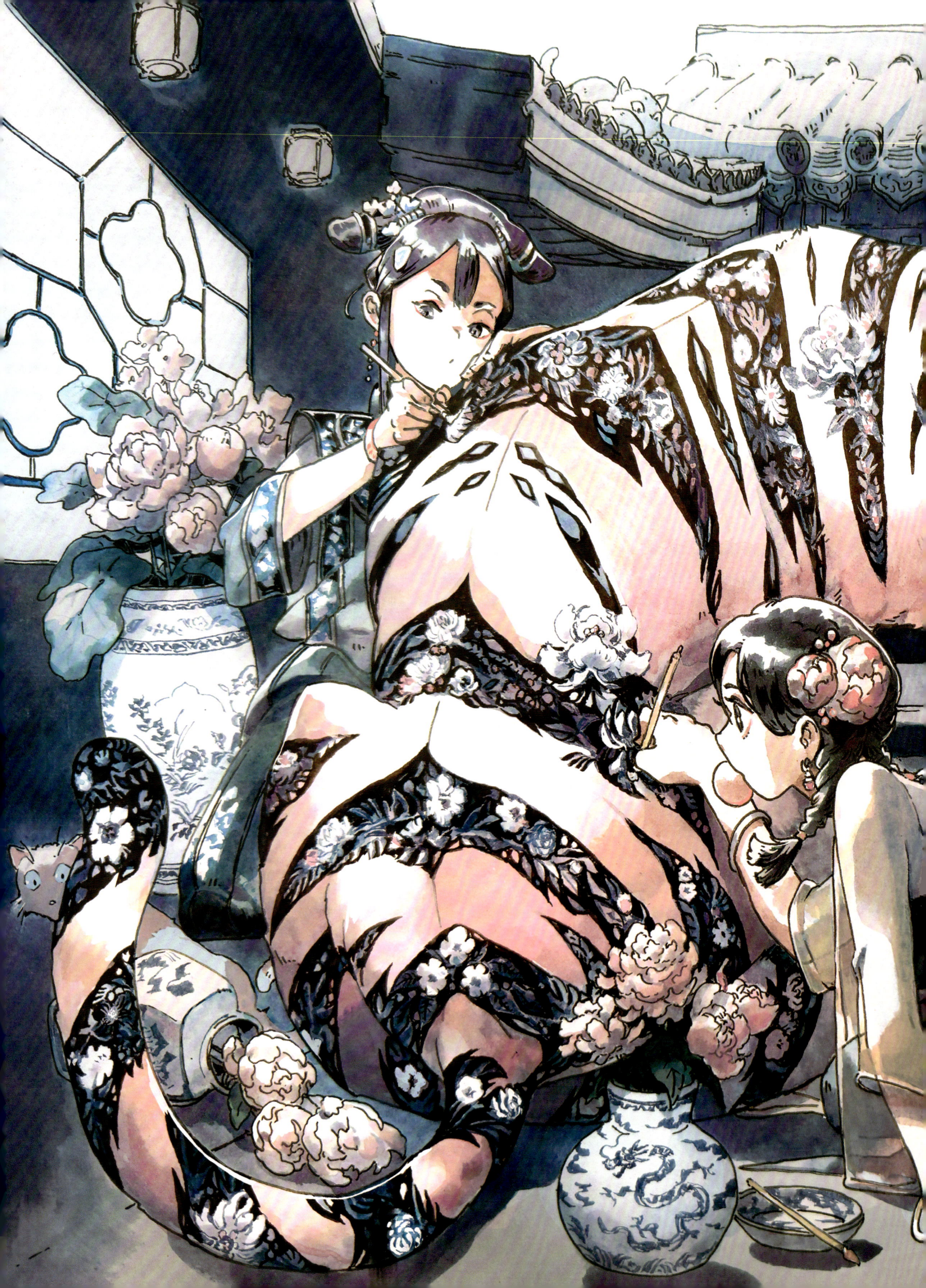

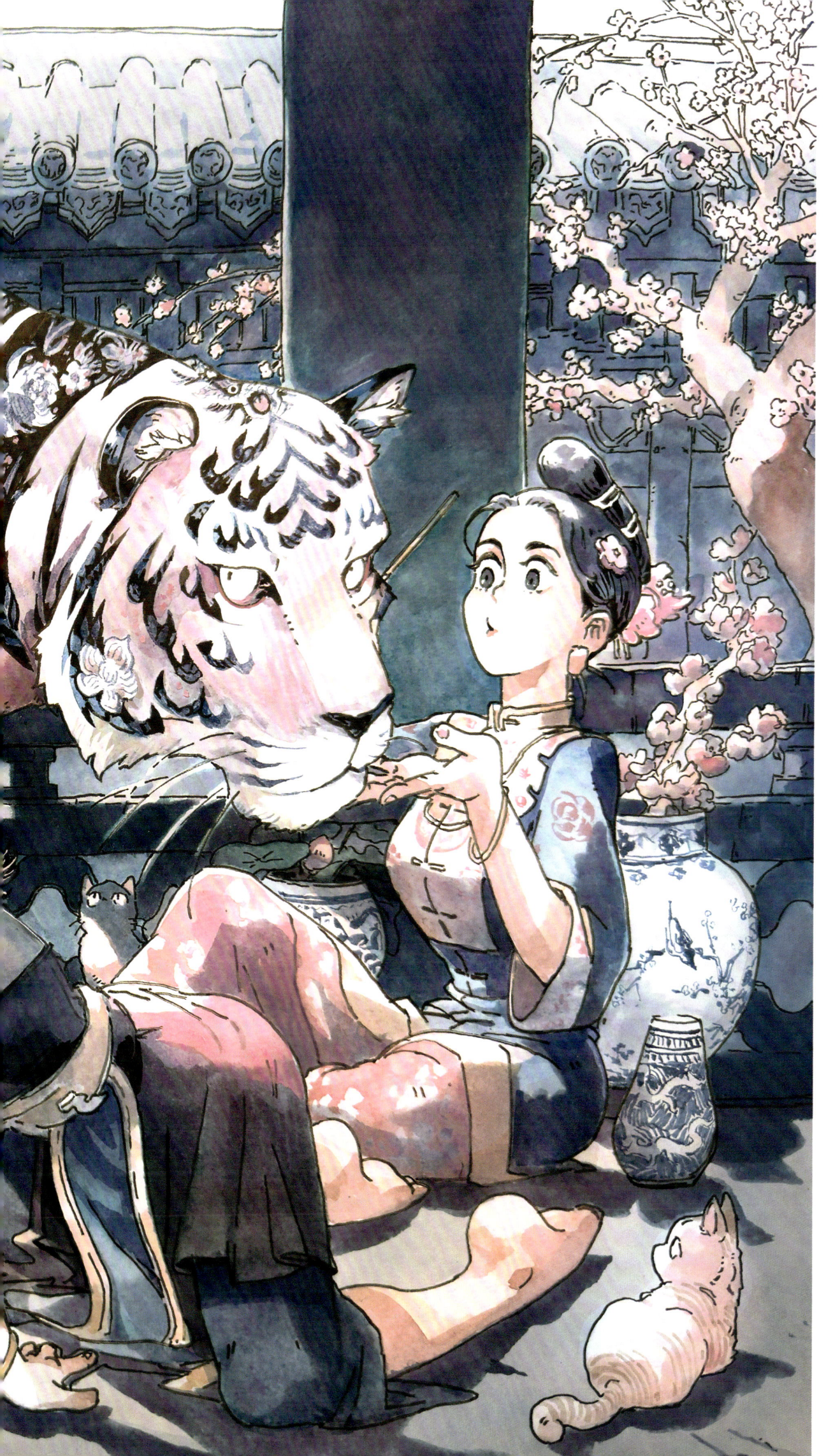

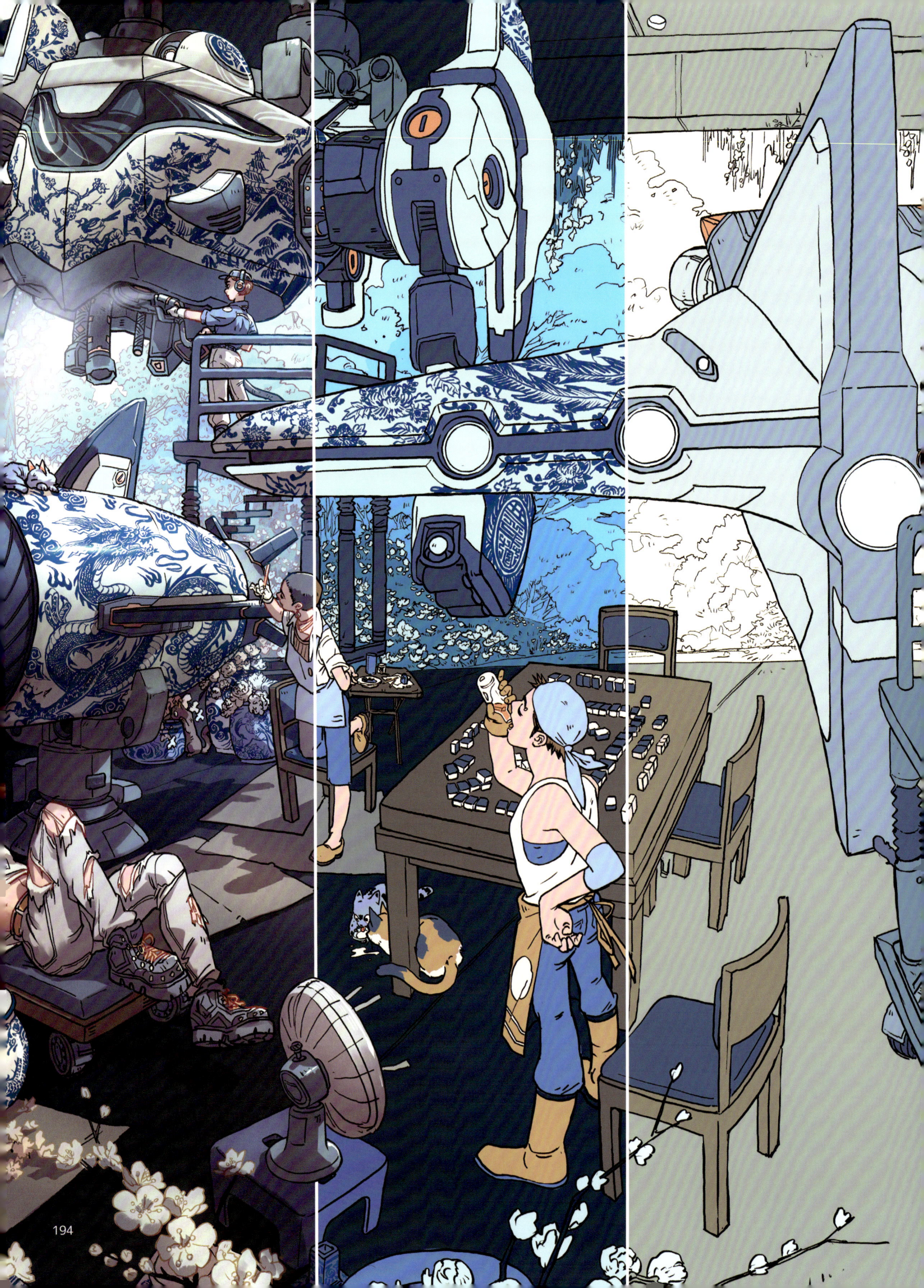

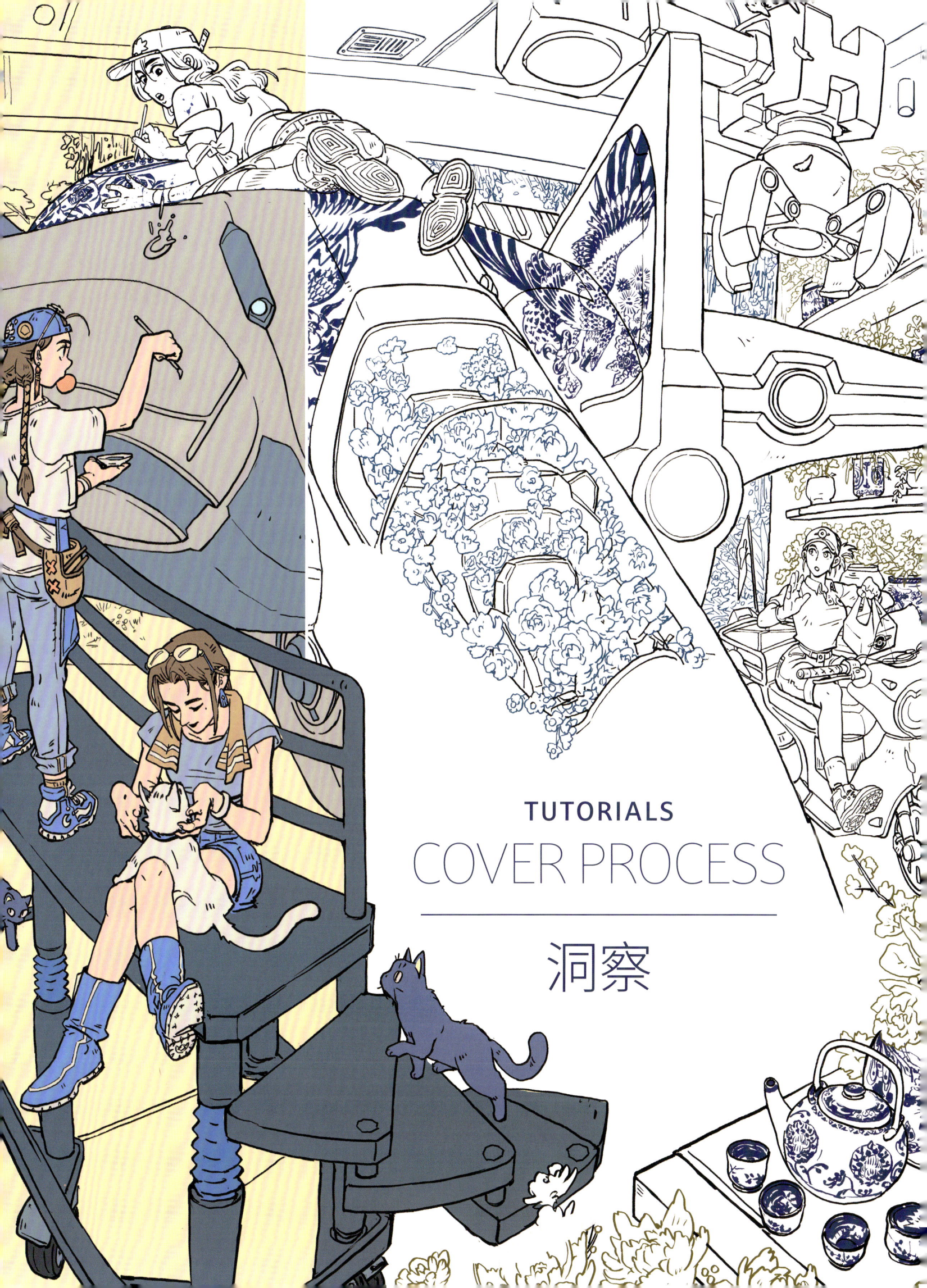

TUTORIALS

COVER PROCESS

洞察

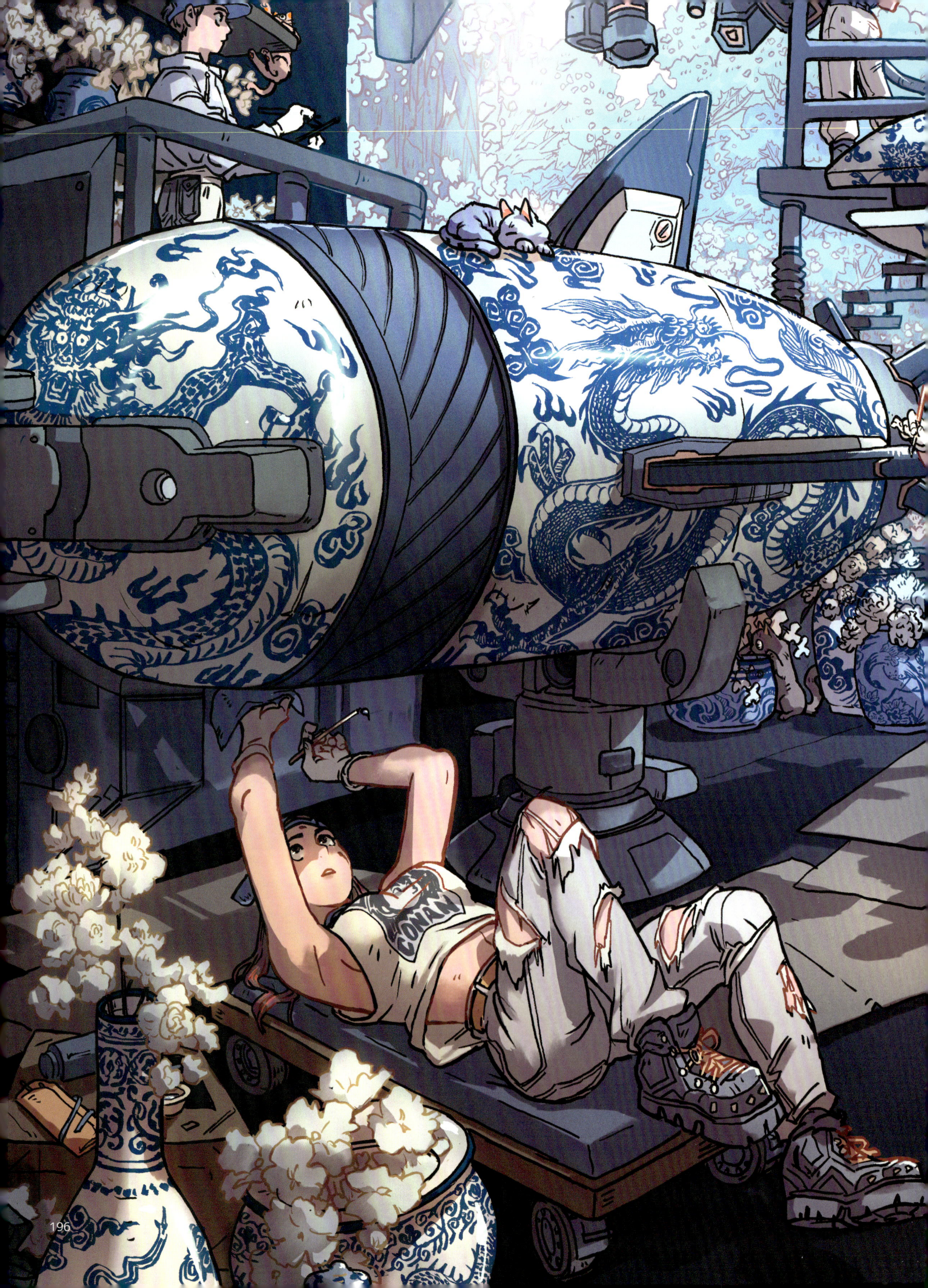

COVER PROCESS

Although I prefer to work from a traditional drawing using an ink pen, the *Overflow* cover image was digital from start to finish. I got the idea while travelling with my one-year-old son to visit his grandparents, so I had to draw on the go with my iPad. I worked while he napped or played at the park, and I'm oddly okay with drawing inside of a car if it's too bright outside.

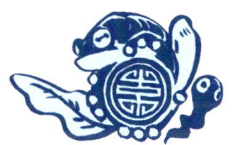

THUMBNAILS

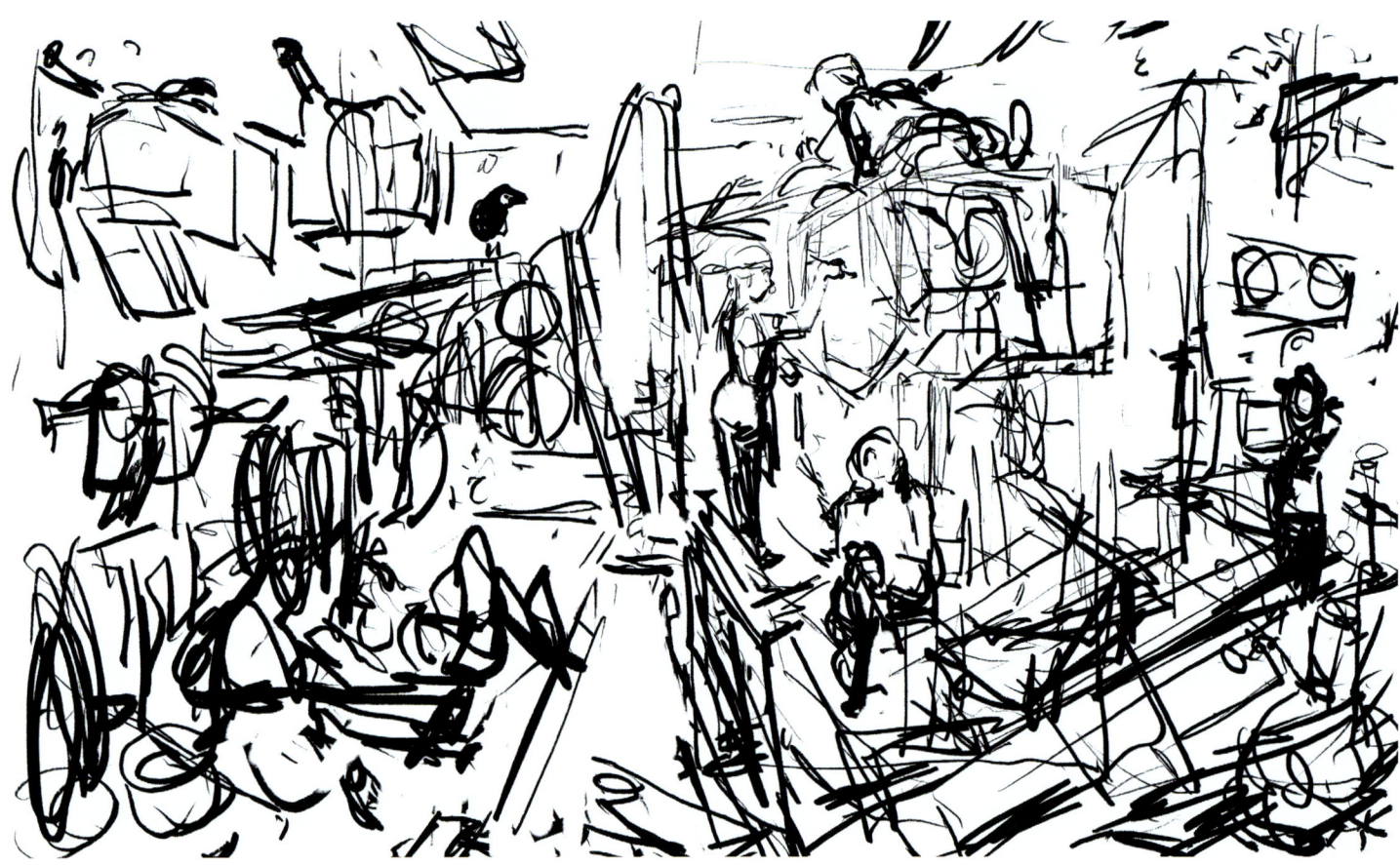

BRAINSTORMING

The thumbnails for this piece were unique in that they all expressed slightly different moments and almost all made it into the final image. I originally envisioned the piece as a vertically oriented poster, not as the cover for the book. As such, even after I decided on the primary image, I later realized that if I wanted to do a wrap-around cover, I would need to draw much more anyway.

To break down the process a bit further, the first thing for me to figure out was how to balance relatable characters with fantastical, Qinghua-patterned vehicles. **The question that I asked here was, 'What is the best way to show the most interesting aspects of this scene?'**

The first thumbnail with the girl painting tells that baseline story, but what it lacked for me was the human qualities that would make the scene feel lived-in.

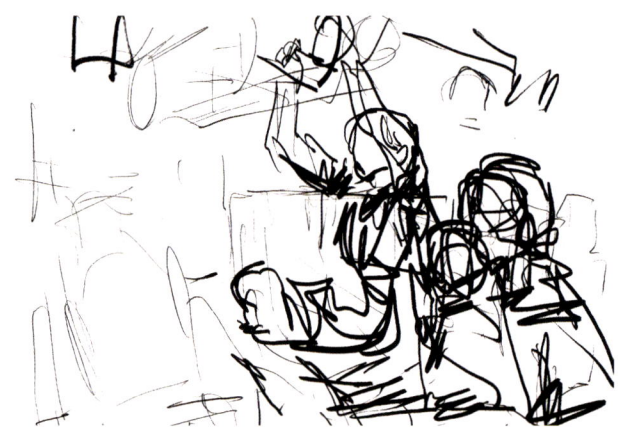

I wanted to distinguish that the artists painting these vehicles were doing this work without too much thought, despite how impressive it looks. It is commonplace for them because they are true masters of their craft, simply doing what they do. In other words, they should be experiencing the sort of flow state that the book is all about.

In the next set of thumbnails, I continued to explore moments that I thought could carry an illustration – namely, a tea break between work, casual banter between the painters, and poses that highlighted the peculiarity of painting such unique objects.

If you look closely, you'll also notice how I started to think about having a variety of fantasy vehicles, mechs, and cars to further demonstrate that this was a paint shop first, rather than a machine factory.

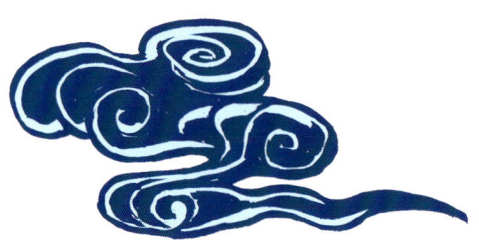

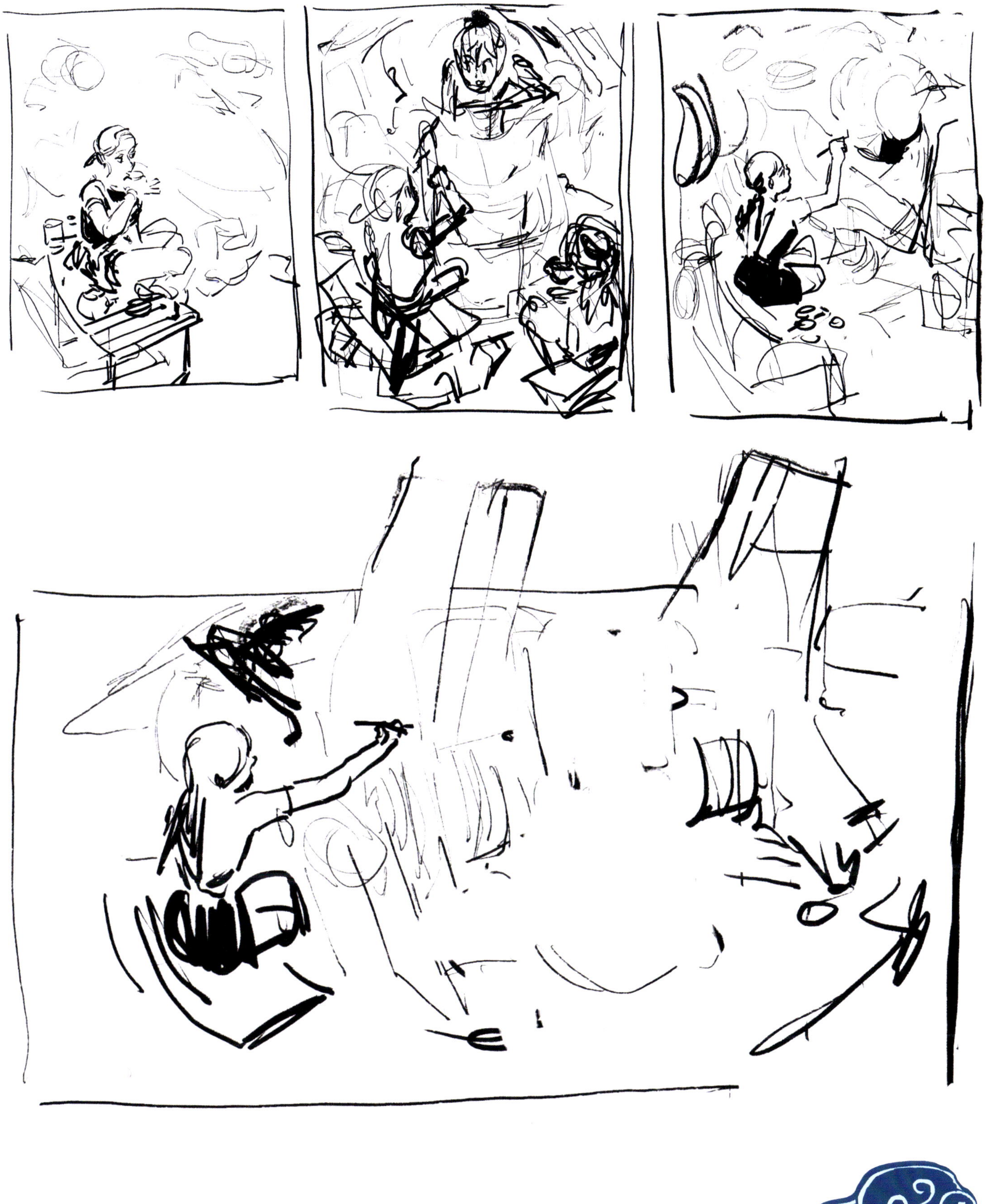

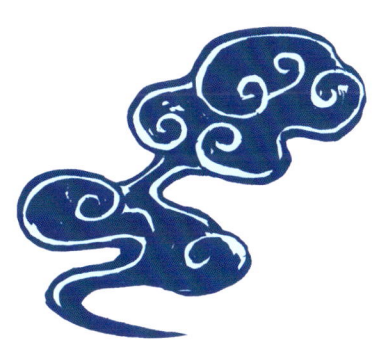

WHAT IS THE BEST WAY TO SHOW THE MOST INTERESTING ASPECTS OF THIS SCENE?

LINE ART

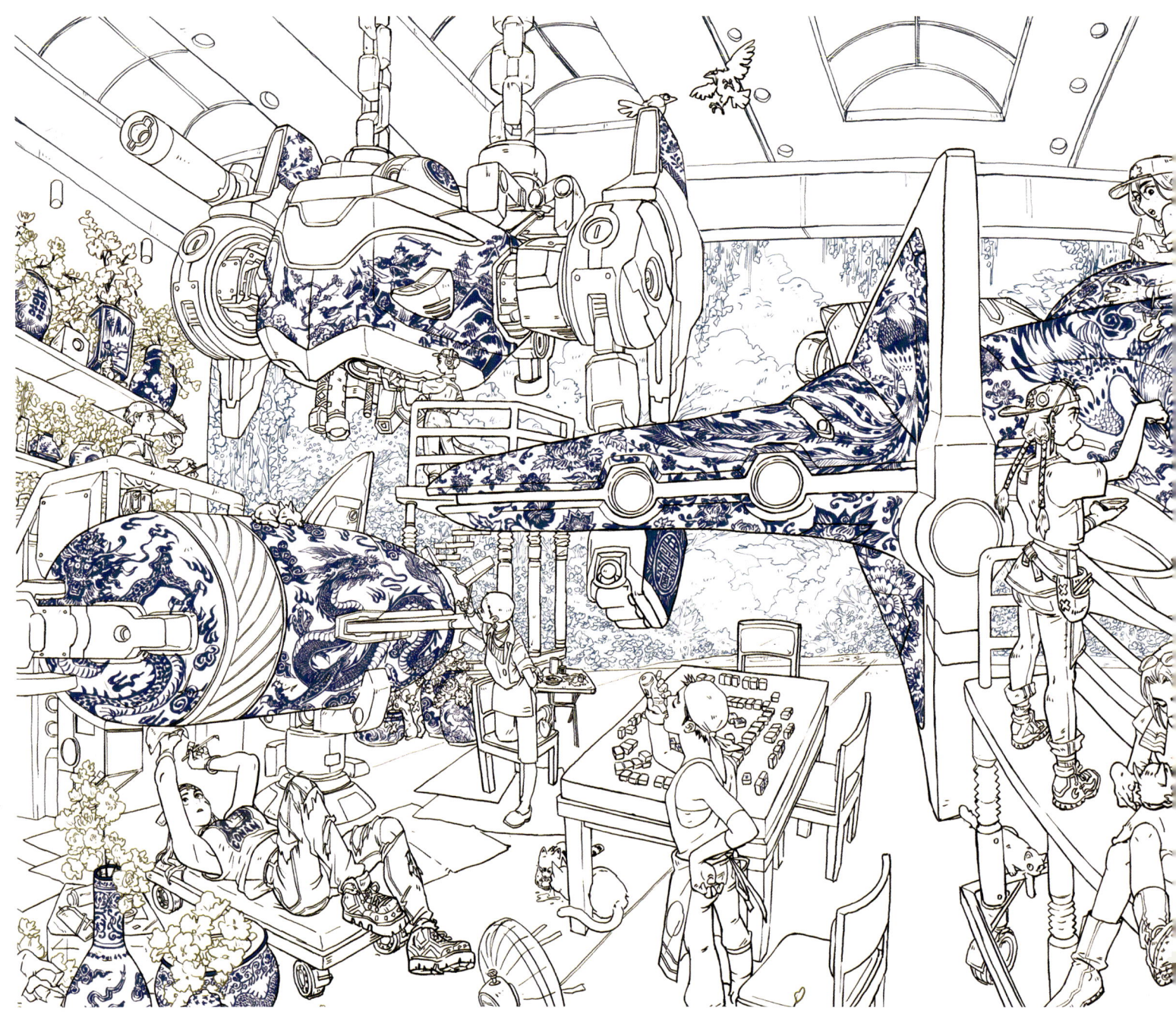

LINE-ART PROCESS

One unique experience for me during the making of this piece was combining my figure drawing, or 'copy from life' attitude, with drawing from the imagination. I know that might be hard to understand, so I'll try to unpack it a bit more. For me, figure drawing is almost a habitual act, where a large portion of the time is spent copying exactly what you're seeing in front of you onto the paper. There are times when you can challenge yourself to increase the emotion, add fun imaginative elements, or even manipulate what you're seeing in your head altogether, but what you'll mainly be doing is taking what you see and distilling those observations into your drawing.

I should mention that I feel this is slightly separate from the flow state I previously described, where your own understanding of what you want to draw is so clear that you're able to draw without encountering too much resistance. This time, I tapped into a *different* flow state where, rather than having to imagine and then project one shape at a time, I felt like I was acting with the sort of assuredness I'd only normally feel while live-drawing in person. Anyone who's drawn from both a video and a live model might know what I'm talking about. The sensation is different. Your presence in the room makes the 'same' information much more valuable. You can feel weight, muscles, and volume.

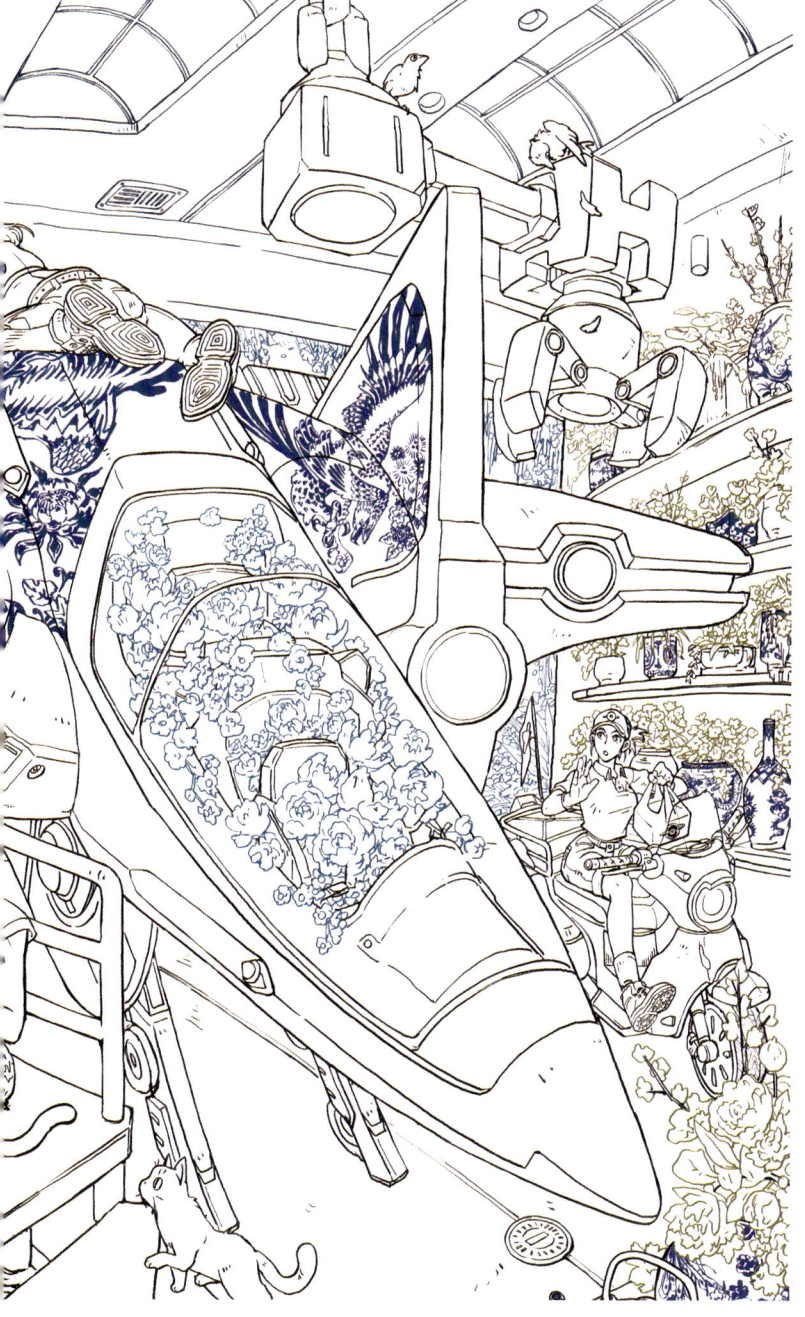

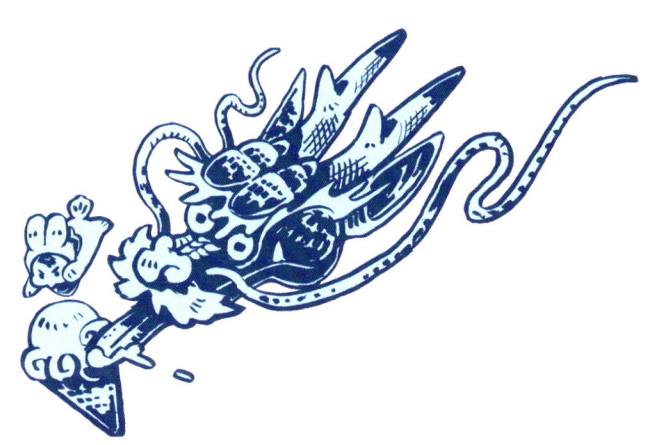

The title of this book, *Overflow*, stems from this experience. Flow does much more than just allow me to project onto the page. The feeling is almost like having access to a lucid dream that is vivid enough to reference. To nerd out about it further, it's like bridging the experience of drawing from the imagination with how I normally approach figure drawing. As I'm sure is the case for many other artists, the two types of drawing have always felt worlds apart for me. Drawing from life is so much easier and so much faster because the answers are alive and right in front of you.

Drawing from the imagination can be painstaking, requiring endless Google tabs full of references. Answers don't exist anywhere else (unless you're just copying, which never feels as rewarding). The first time I combined the two experiences, even if it was only temporary, felt like a breakthrough.

Aside from loving the result of this piece, I'm excited by the prospect of getting better at drawing in order to experience this sensation more. Whereas before I just wanted to tap into a flow state, I now feel like I have decent control over this aspect of myself. Now I'm chasing this overflow.

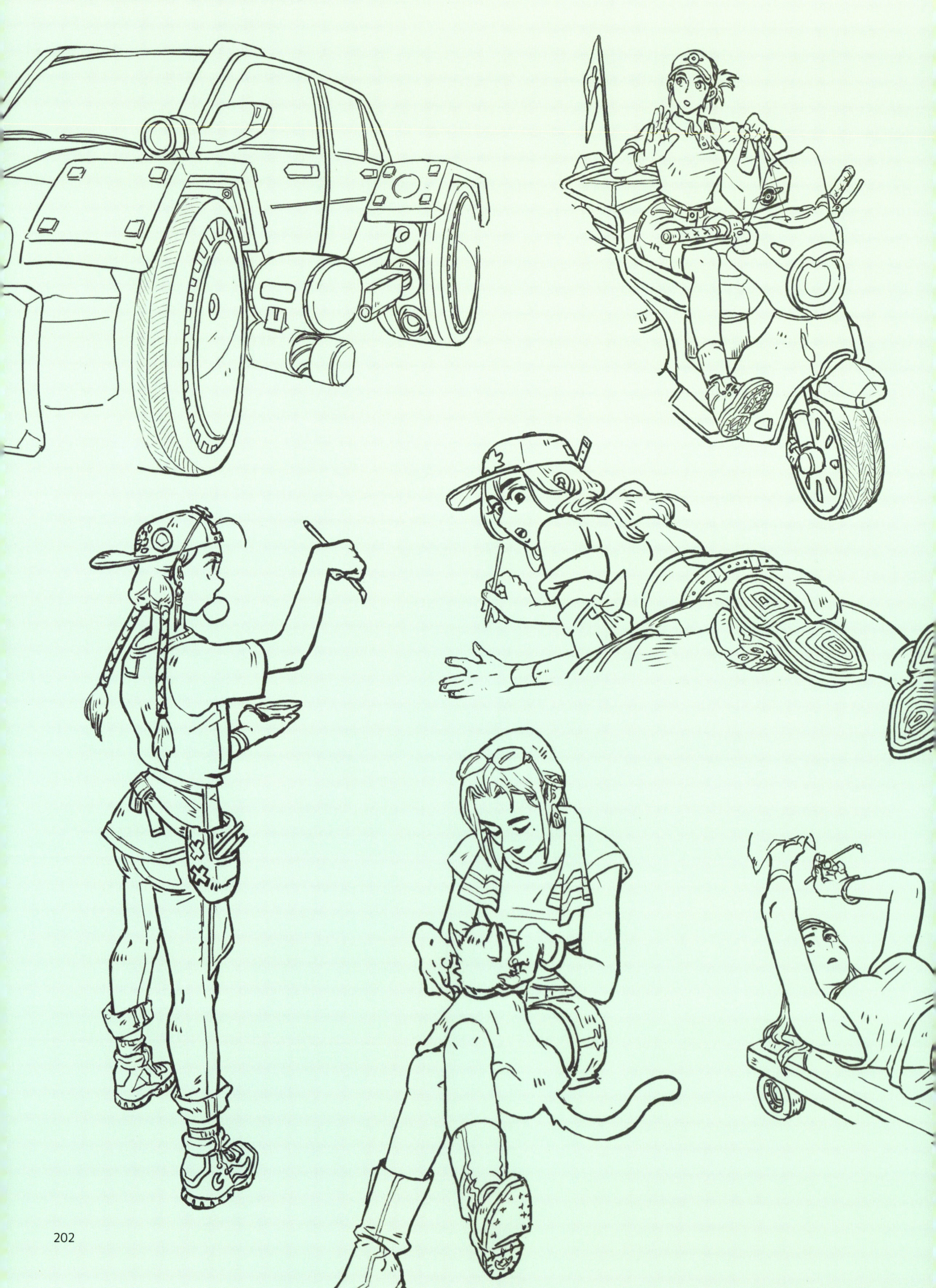

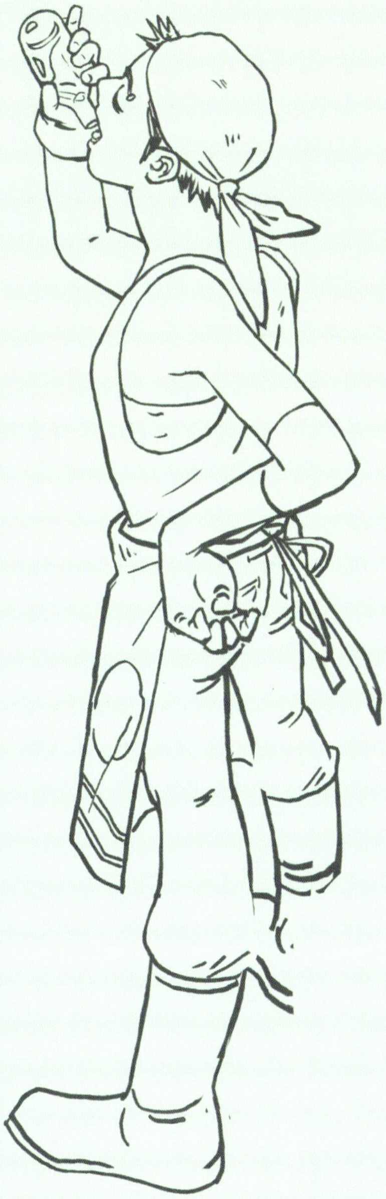

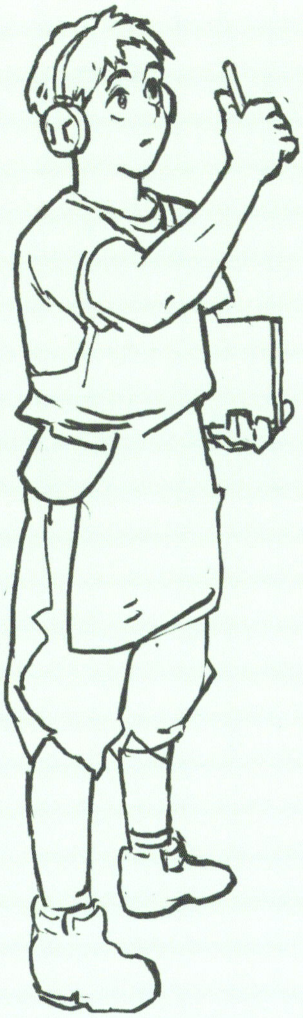

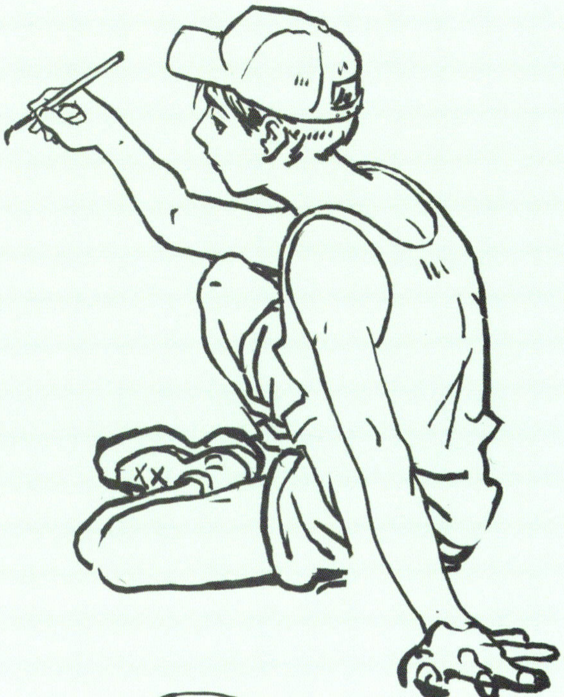

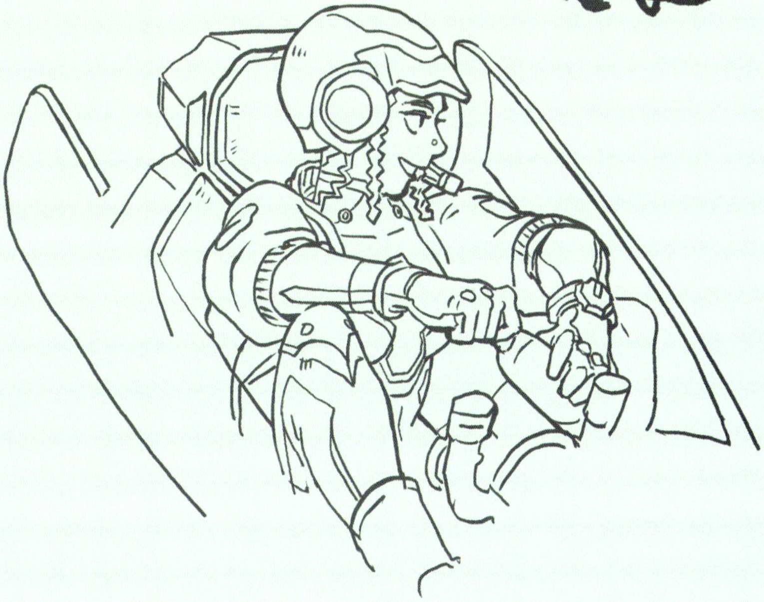

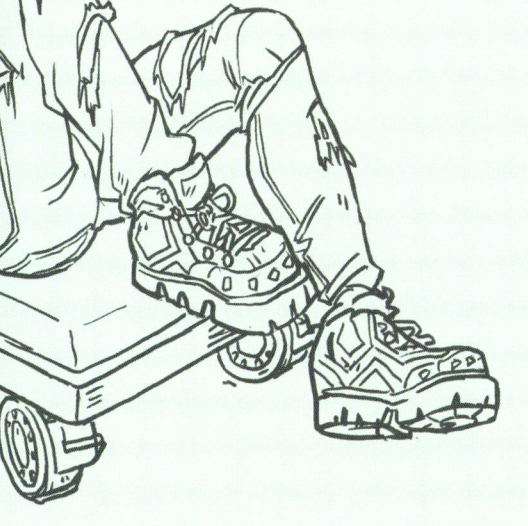

LINE ART

Here's a collection of the other characters and poses that I drew before axing them, the most notable being my own cameo and changing the car into a giant bomb/rocket.

Since this piece is entirely digital, it's unique in comparison to my other work because I was able to draw over the final thumbnail. However, you will notice several changes, and the digital medium also allowed me to rewind a few times.

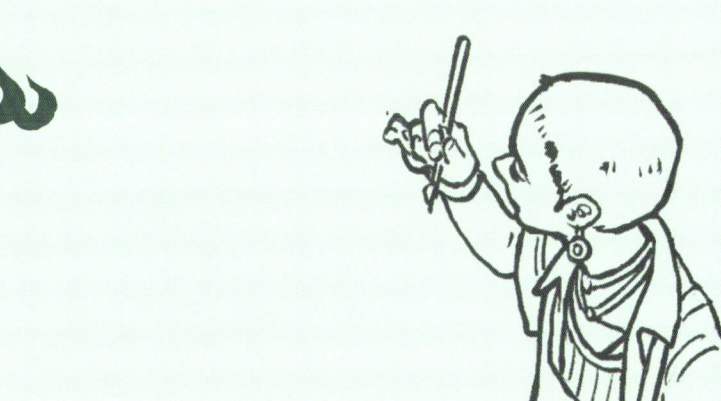

FLATS

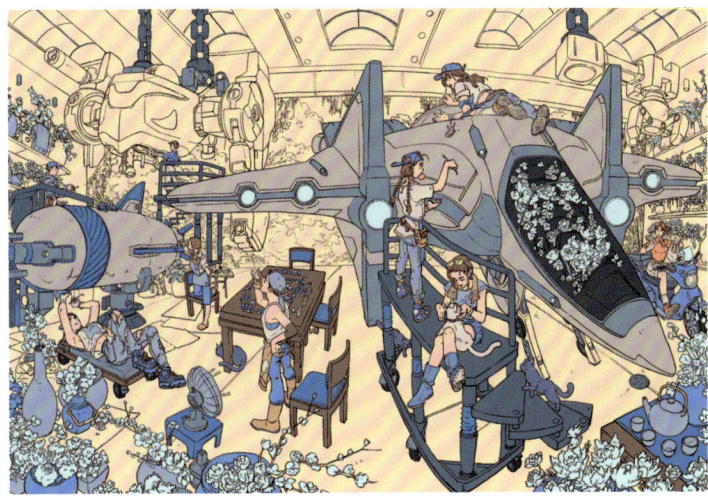

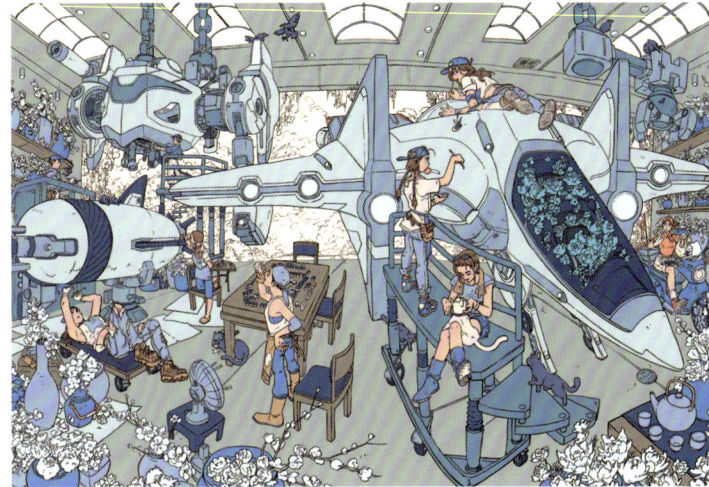

FLATS STAGE I

From here, I'd like to use several pieces at once to talk more about the range of approaches and how different things can look in different contexts. For me, flats went from the most boring, mindless activity to one of the most important parts of the process. They are often the keys to understanding the core appeal and balance of the overall image.

Full disclosure, this philosophy stems from the fact that I started asking my convention assistants to help me speed up the process of making illustrations by completing the flats for me. The rules I gave them were simple at first:

'Go from light to dark, warm to cool. Practically, this means colour in the eye-whites first and other white areas in the piece should also be on the same layer. Then go from white to warmer colours, such as off-white to yellows, pinks, and reds before gradually moving to purples, blues, and greens, and finally, darker colours like black. Use as few colours as possible. If the piece calls for four-to-five different shades of red, use the bare minimum and avoid too much overlap of the same colour on different objects in the same scene. In reality, this usually means at least eight layers, maybe up to twenty if the piece is super complicated.'

FLATS STAGE II

The goal of this approach is to make it easier to alter an image later. It also clarifies what the dominant colours have to be, given the relative materials that appear in the image. Basically, it gives you more powerful knobs to turn when honing a digital artwork, since adjusting the hue and saturation has a ubiquitous effect on the entire composition.

I know this sounds simple and straightforward enough, but in my experience flats are nearly impossible to follow well if you are not the primary artist. Only the artist knows the colour layers that materials will fall into.

For example, when an off-white colour could be pink or yellow, that choice is important for pushing the piece towards one direction or another. The sum of these micro decisions is the first and most pivotal step towards building up the colour identity of a piece. Even in this seemingly mindless phase where all you do is colour within the lines for what feels like forever, you are making important decisions.

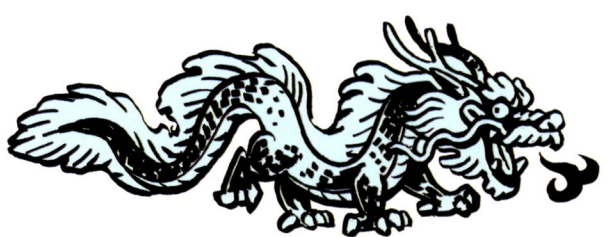

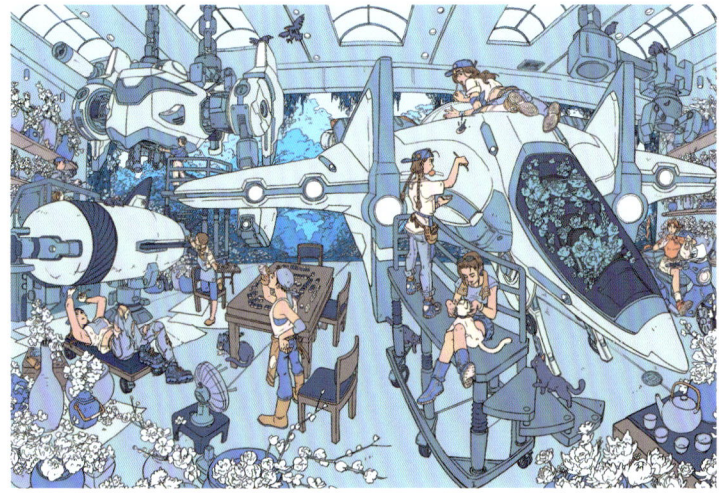

FLATS STAGE III

In short, flats are where you can find the fundamental identity of a piece. I also followed the same methodology that I've expressed previously in this book: it's all about making the focal point stand out. So, I started with those elements first just to make sure that the colours within them became the throughline and that everything else in the piece aligned with them. The biggest challenge was maintaining this focus and not getting lost in beautiful colour combinations or realistic colour choices that didn't serve the central idea.

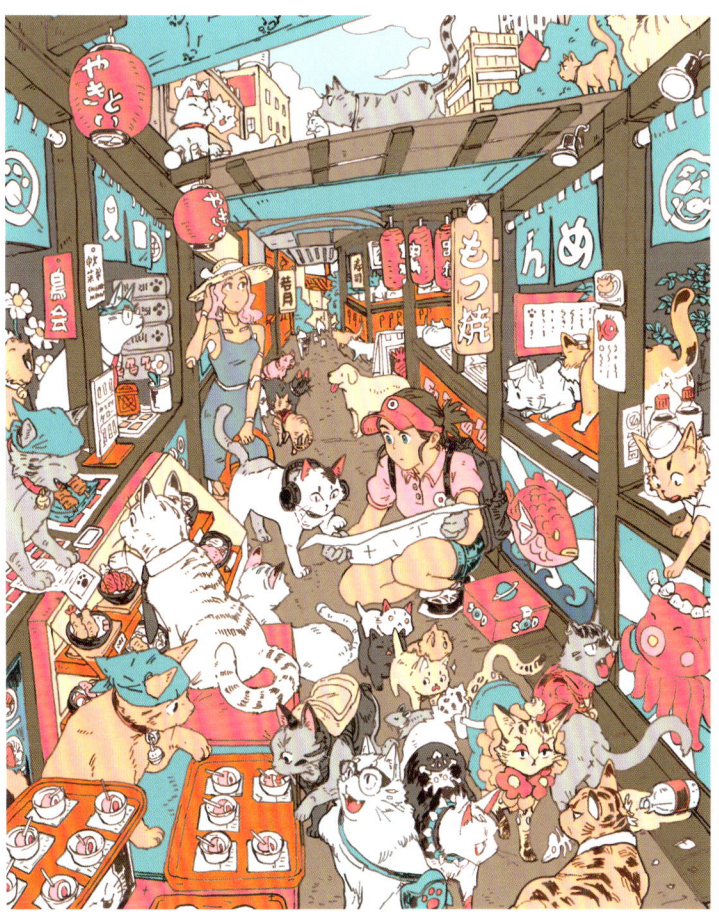

FLATS EXAMPLE I: BUTCHER

For the piece above, notice how the blue is reserved for the most important story elements. The dragon gets the brightest, loudest blue while the butcher's eyes and apron get the second look.

I also wanted the warm mustard yellow exclusively for the human characters, gently guiding you towards them. The rest of the meat in the piece is almost just a textural pattern of red so these elements can stand out.

FLATS EXAMPLE II: CATS

The goal for this piece was to make sure the central character would pop. I knew I would have to use pink on the main character's shirt, so to make sure she would stand out in the crowd I used pink as sparingly as possible everywhere else. This hero colour dictates the balance for the rest of the piece.

Pink still needs to be present throughout, but because it would lose its efficacy for directing the eye if overused, it's just used as a highlight and accent colour. I also thought about how white would be the loudest in the middle, but because it was used in the flats, I needed to rely on shading to push back its presence elsewhere.

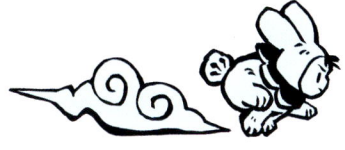

SHADING

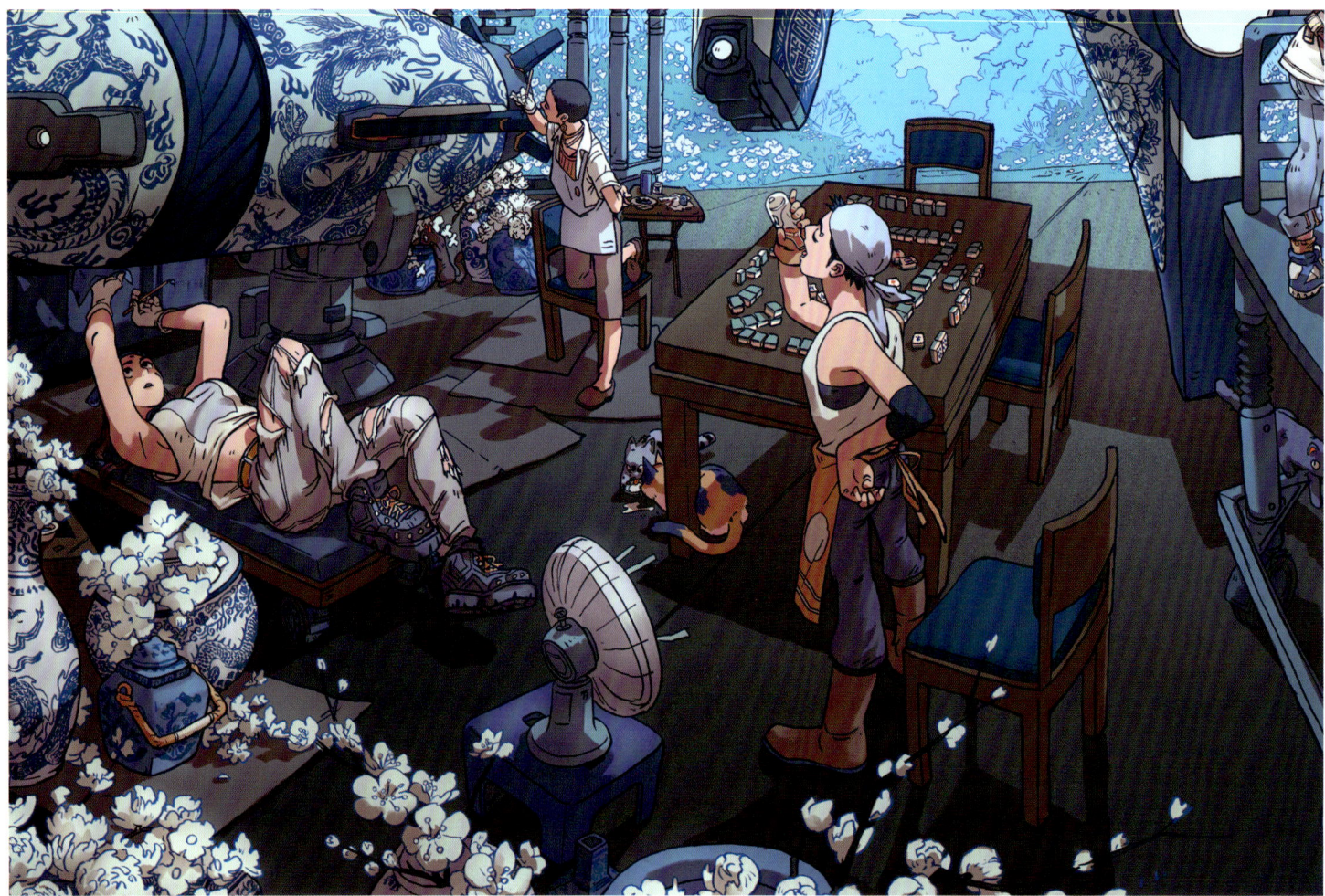

After labouring so much over the flats, I'm often dying for the next step of shading because I know the way that lighting can drastically affect how the eye moves through a piece. I usually rely on shading to push back elements that don't really deserve as much spotlight, and this is particularly obvious when it comes to artwork with detailed lines.

There's no problem with having them there, but the volume needs to be turned way down so they don't compete with the focal point.

Practically speaking, I accomplish my shading with a Multiply layer style containing a single colour. This option is available in Photoshop (a software I've been using since fifth grade) and Procreate. I constantly adjusted the hue and saturation on this layer to discern the room's quality of light – is it casting a cool or warm shadow? I find that more decisive shadows usually result from changing the colour of the shadow, more so than tweaking the layer's opacity. But I definitely use both to fine-tune the degree of prominence. This usually means somewhere between 50–80% opacity with a very bright colour.

For a borderline-panoramic illustration with a lot going on, I had to first put everything in shadow that wasn't worth seeing. If the Qinghua painting wasn't the most interesting, it could be in shadow. The hidden details would still be there for the audience to discover, but it isn't crucial to immediately understand the piece's intent and atmosphere.

Another element of this piece that was different for me was wanting to experiment with gradient contour shading, as opposed to the simpler hard-edge shading I normally do. Contour shading is where a shadow gradually occurs because the form of an object slowly curves away from the light source, just like a ball might under a spotlight. This is different from the shadow that might be cast underneath a ball on the floor, which is caused by an object blocking the light from hitting something else.

If you want to see what I mean, look at the slight gradients and smudging around the knees of the two girls in the middle and on the rounder surfaces of the mechanical objects. There's something really satisfying about correctly distinguishing between the two types of shadows. It's something I want to get better at!

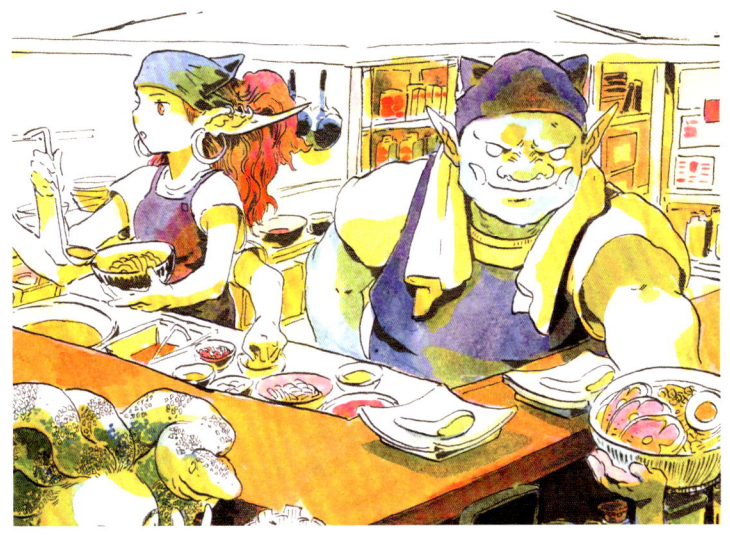

RAMEN SHOP

Although this is a traditional ink piece, the approach to shading follows the same principle, maybe even more so as there's no way to add light unless you use mixed media. This work was done in passes of CMYK shading, in which every pass must accomplish two things at once: place hues where they need to be and shade objects with a unified lighting scheme.

In line with colour theory, by combining all three colours, you get grey, and the more you add the darker it gets. Therefore, I shaded everything that was not hit by the light, completing multiple passes on whatever needed to be pushed away from the viewer's attention.

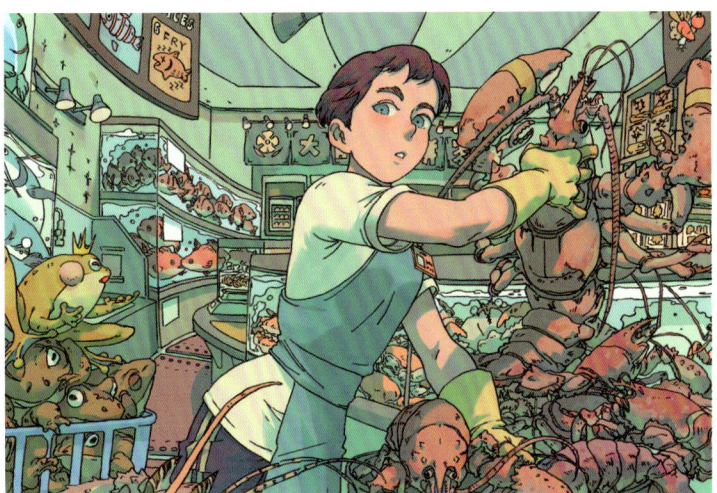

FROG PRINCE

The *Frog Prince* piece is a great example of how the shading had a lot of heavy lifting to do. With so much competing visual information, it was important that the frog could be seen among so many similarly sized creatures.

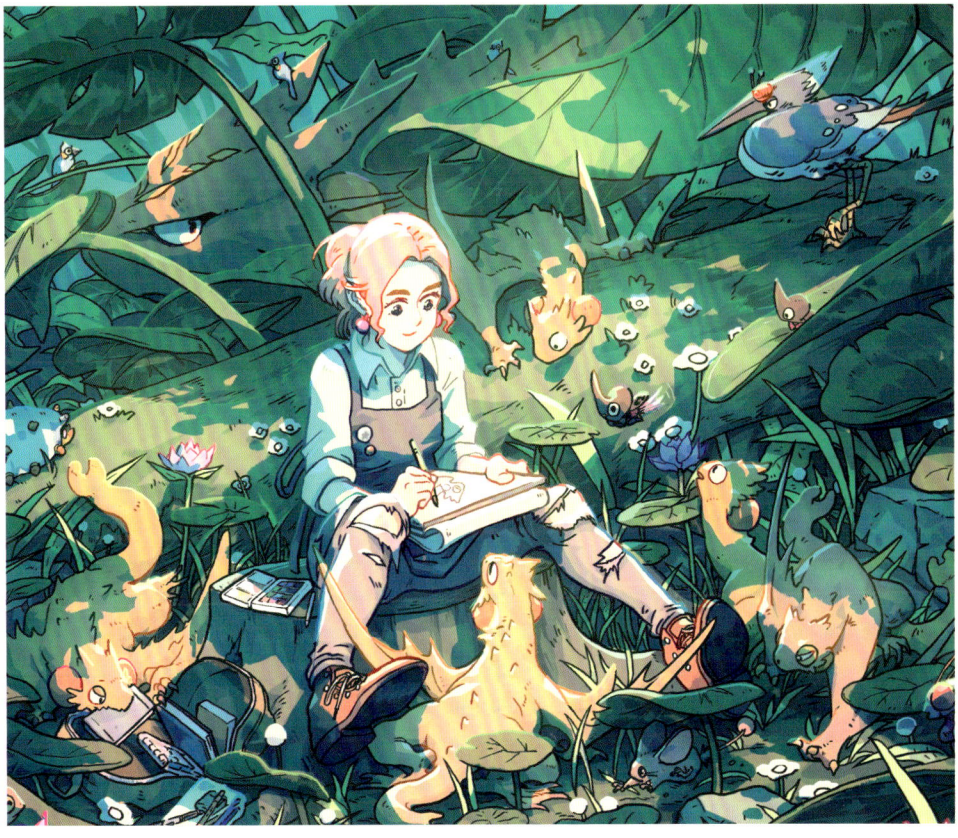

DRAGON DOODLER

In this piece, I wanted the viewer to experience the girl first, then the dragons in the foreground, followed by the mother dragon in the background.

What has been shaded in and the degree to which they've been shaded has a very direct relationship with the order of how I reveal the story.

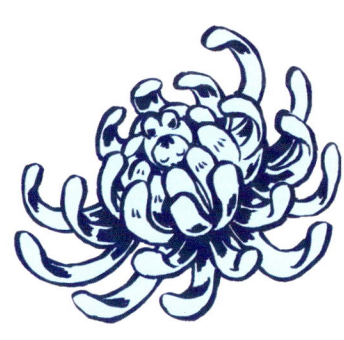

HIGHLIGHTS

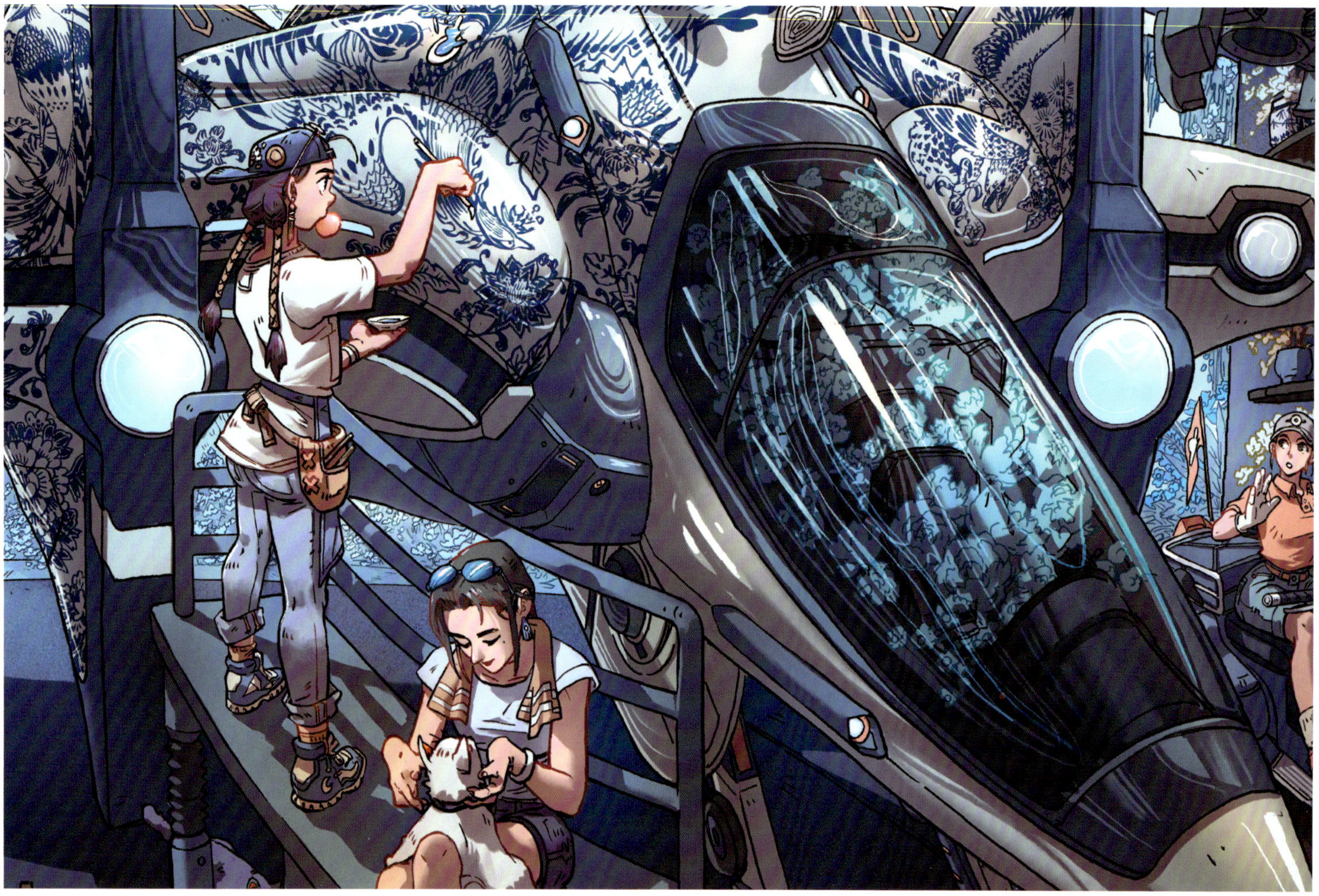

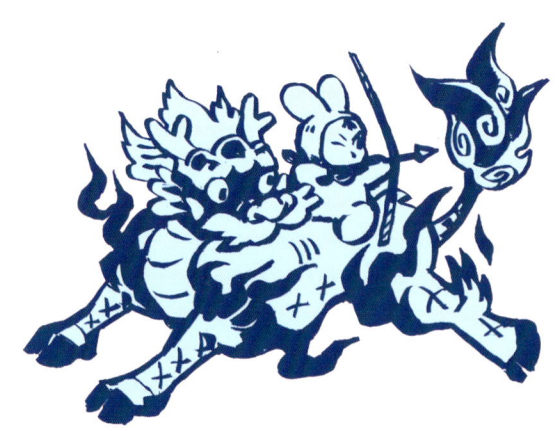

As much as shading was something I was looking forward to, highlighting was actually the step that interested me the most. This is because my goal was to practise vehicle reflections, which is part of the highlights phase. Recently, I've been inspired by illustrations that feature realistic vehicles. The way light tends to bend on them is something I have a hard time understanding, but I really want to improve.

As far as my normal approach goes, painting highlights is like adding a cherry on top of an ice-cream sundae. Generally speaking, they aren't the point and can't fix anything too major. Yet, they really add a sort of flair that can elevate a work's dynamism.

The math is pretty straightforward to explain, at least for my approach: add a bright colour (close to white) to a surface that most directly receives light. For this piece, I really tried to reserve highlights for the mechanical objects I wanted to stand out. Rather than adding them to every object, where it might make more physical, real-world sense, I chose to follow more story-oriented guidelines. For brighter colours, the usual way I set up highlights is with a normal-layer style.

However, I'm also a big fan of using clipping masks to home in on the exact colour I want, meaning the base layer is mostly used to help me mask out where the highlights should go. I will occasionally try adjusting my highlight layers to be in a soft light, hard light, or overlay layer style, but I usually reserve those styles for softer adjustments later.

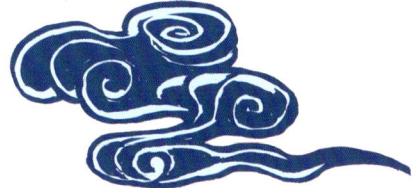

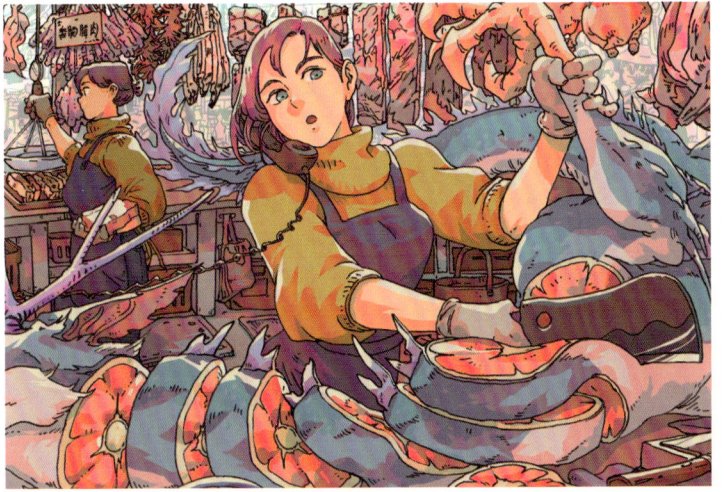

THE BUTCHER

Doing hair highlights and adding a back-rim light is a great way to stop a character from blending into a dark background. The choice between realism and story focus is also prominent in this piece. If I had chosen to to make the meat super shiny with lots of highlights then it would look very appetizing, which sounds like a potentially good idea.

However, that choice would have changed the focus of the story. For me, the piece was about the butcher being a badass who could cut through a dragon with one hand, not how great the meat is.

DEMON KING

For images with super-intense lighting schemes, such as cityscapes at night, highlights can become the star of the show. In this case, I knew the background buildings were light-pink from the inside, but I had to be patient and wait to extend that pink onto the characters as a backlit highlight.

Notice how there's also a green under-light near the bottom. Although it isn't motivated by any in-scene light source, I added the lights to give more definition to the forms, especially on the minor characters and props, which would have otherwise blended into the background.

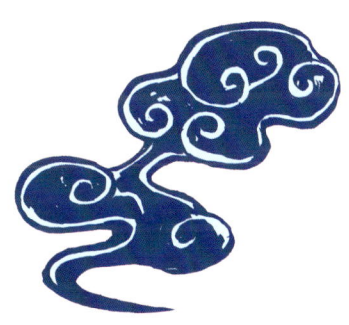

FINISHING TOUCHES

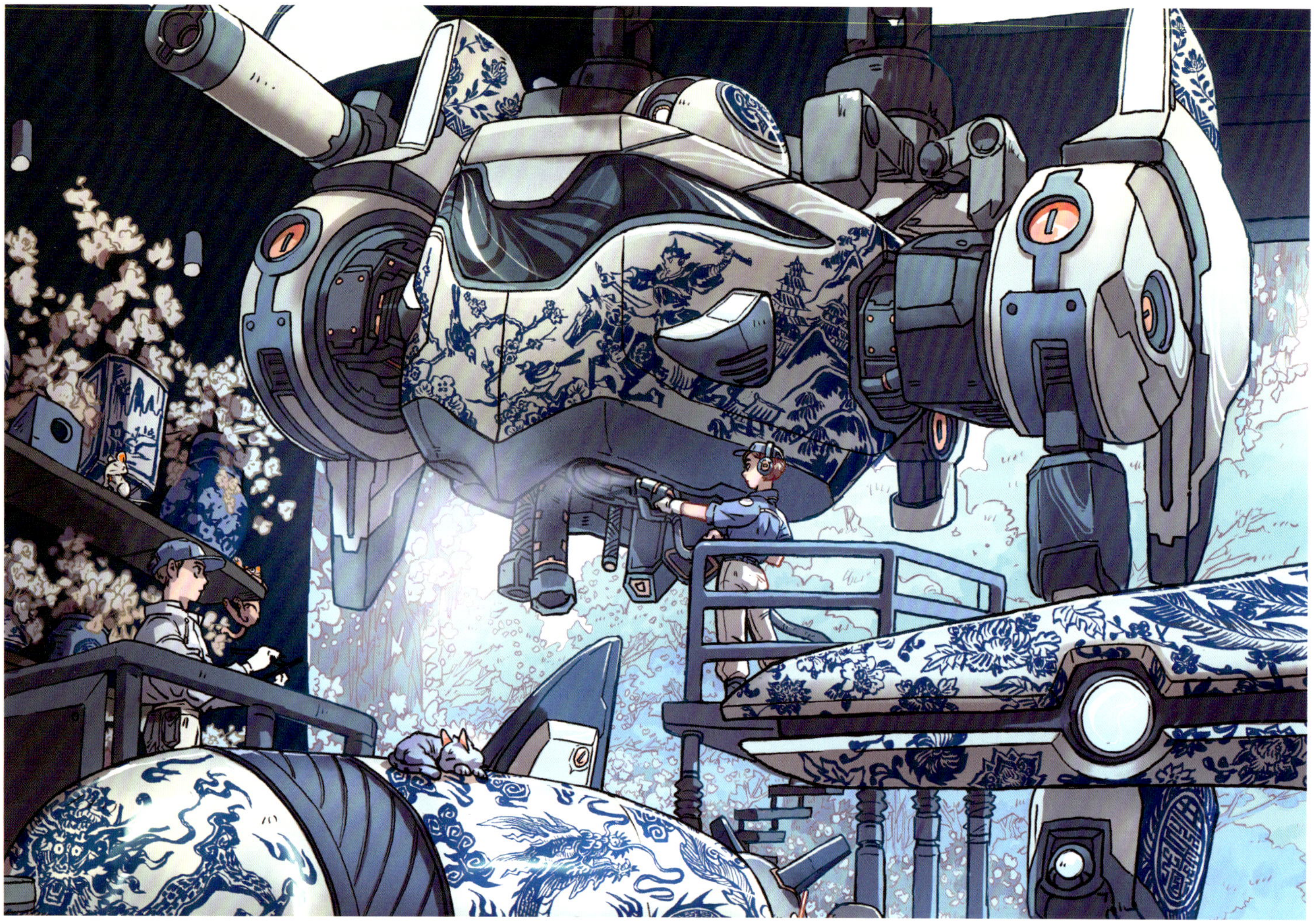

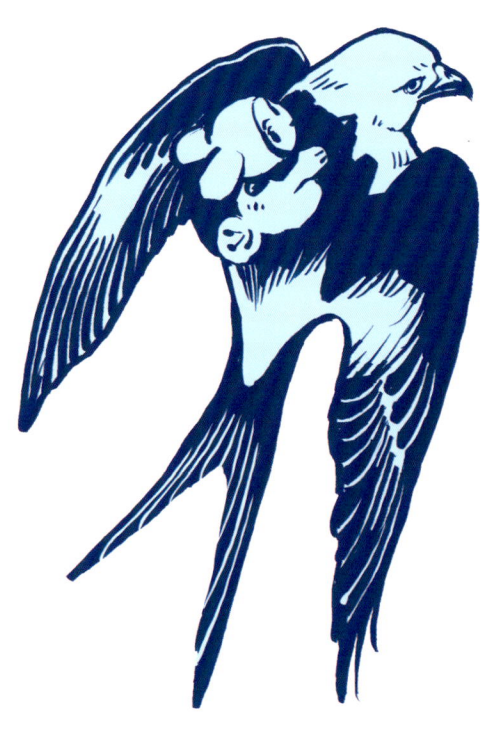

In my own personal digital workflow, the finishing touches are anything that occurs on top of the line layer – things like adjustment layers for levels, soft-brush touch-ups, or maybe an overall noise layer.

For this piece, there weren't too many big changes. They were mostly soft glows added to the background, creating the illusion of distance that comes from atmospheric diffusion. I also often colour in the lines to further accentuate highlights on any elements that deserve a pop.

The bigger challenge for this piece was finding the balance between wanting things to feel bright, while needing it to be dark enough for gold-foil text to sit on. It is a unique challenge that I don't usually have to consider. As such, I finished the piece as a print in its own right, then, after mocking up the additional text on top, I decided I needed to find a middle ground and not have two different versions of the same artwork.

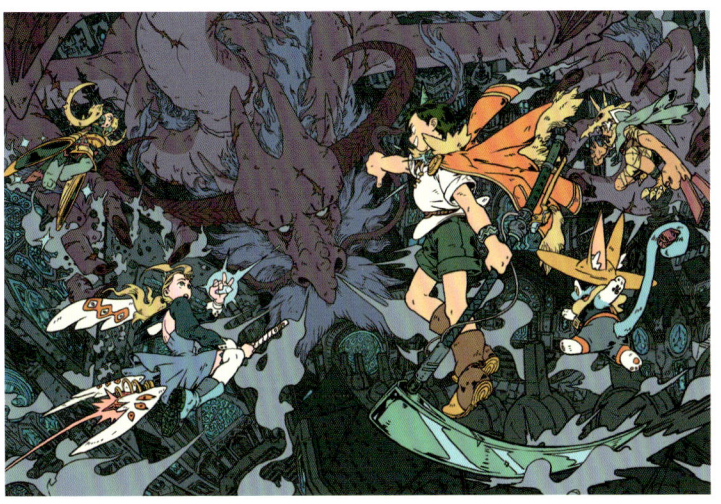
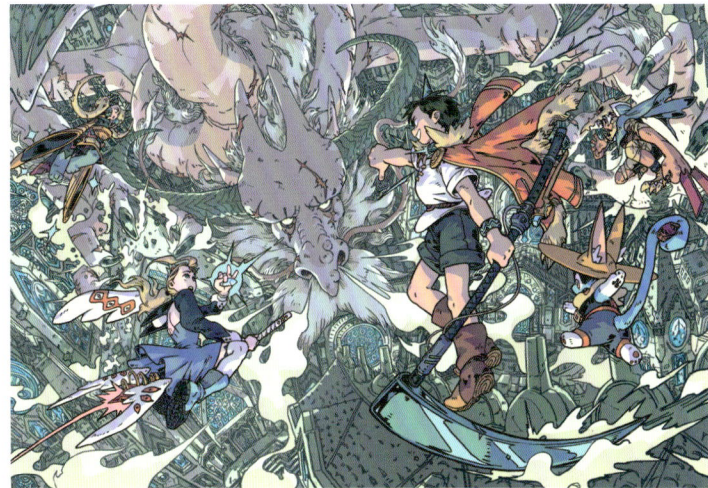

BAD BOY JUJU: CATHEDRAL

Sometimes, I'll get to this point and still feel like I haven't figured out a drawing. That's the case with this piece; the crushing number of controls and levers provided by the digital medium had smashed my own sense of figuring out the work's colour story.

The struggle was that there were some canvas-wide adjustments like a solid colour overlaid on top of everything that could drastically alter a piece's tone. I call this situation, which I have found myself in many times, hue-and-saturation hell because it's exactly that: I'm stuck in a never-ending struggle with the hue/ saturation adjustments tool, unsure of what colour combination looks best.

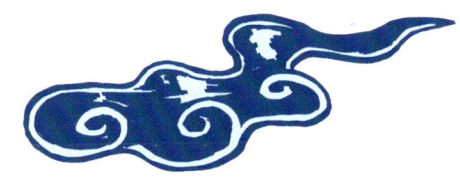

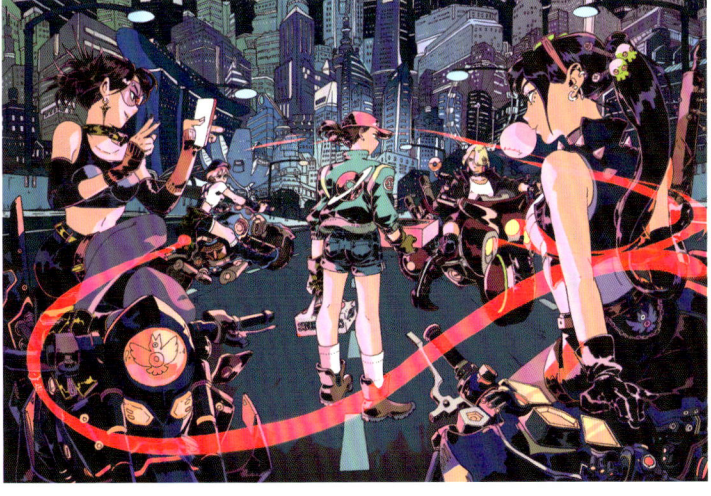

NEO

This is a piece that was based on the concept of motorcycle light trails sweeping through the image. I couldn't wait until the end to add them because things needed to be balanced in line with their presence, so I made a rough mock-up of how they would look at the beginning. I still consider it a finishing touch, however, and made sure the image still worked without them.

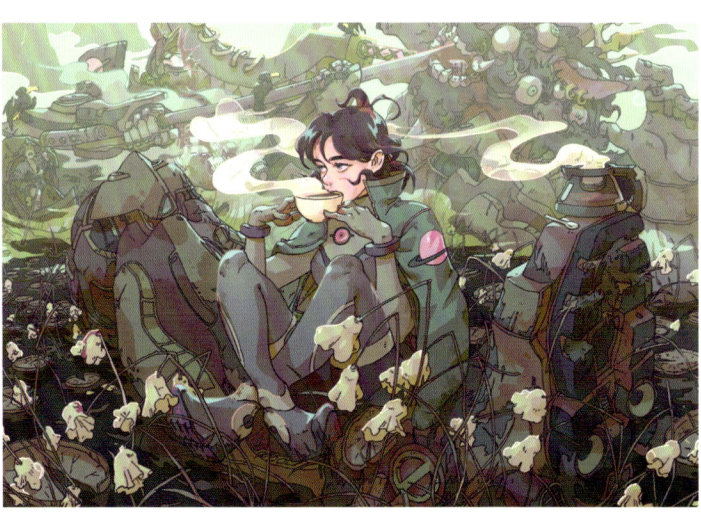

MONDAY

The biggest issue I had with this piece was the background taking up a lot of space in close proximity to the central character. In order to make the piece read at my desired pace, first wanting the viewer to take in the character's jaded attitude while drinking their Monday morning coffee, I needed to use fog to push the background away. Since the lighting scheme was daytime, I couldn't use shadow to do this, so I waited until the end to add some white, low-opacity fog.

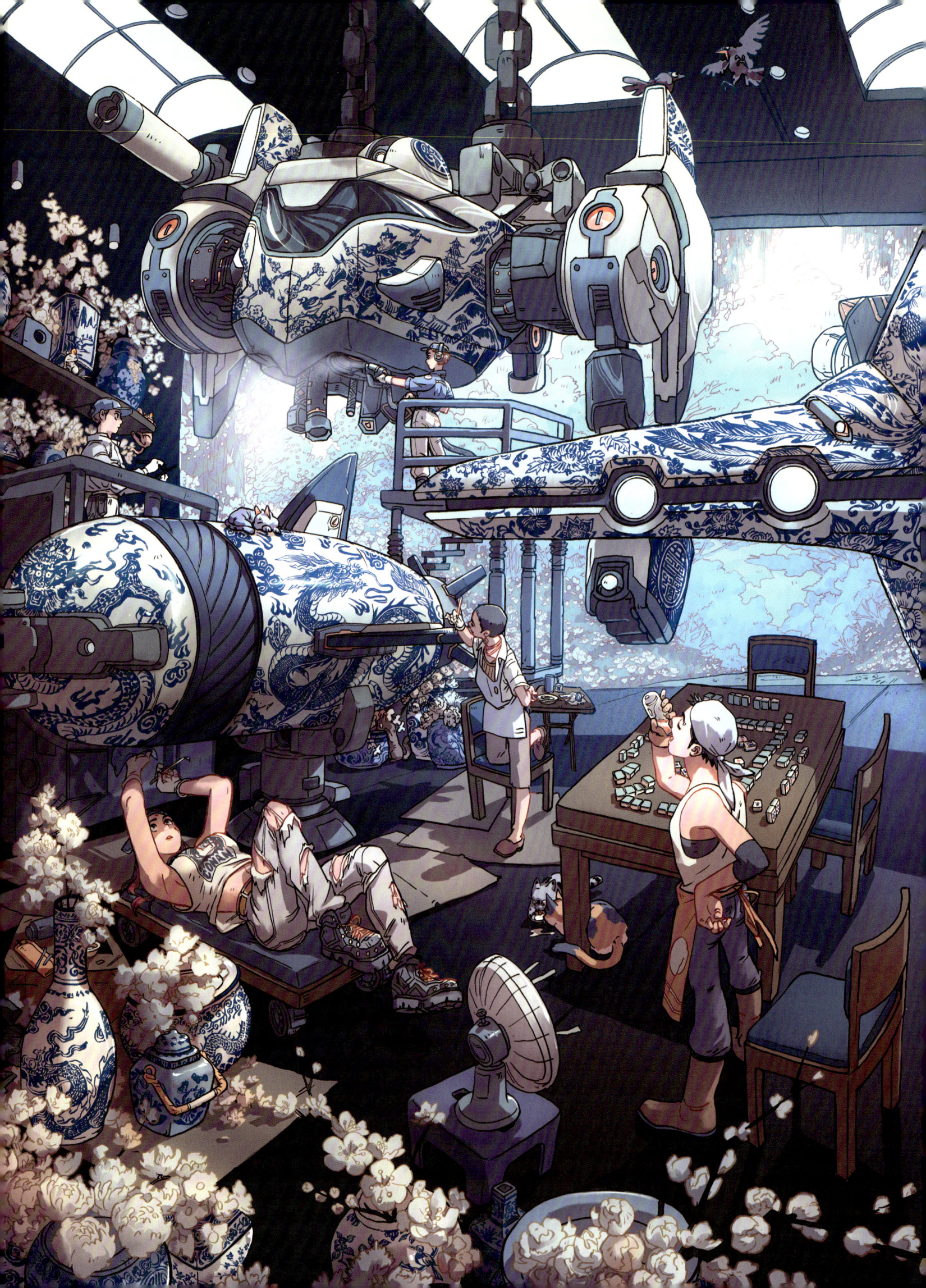

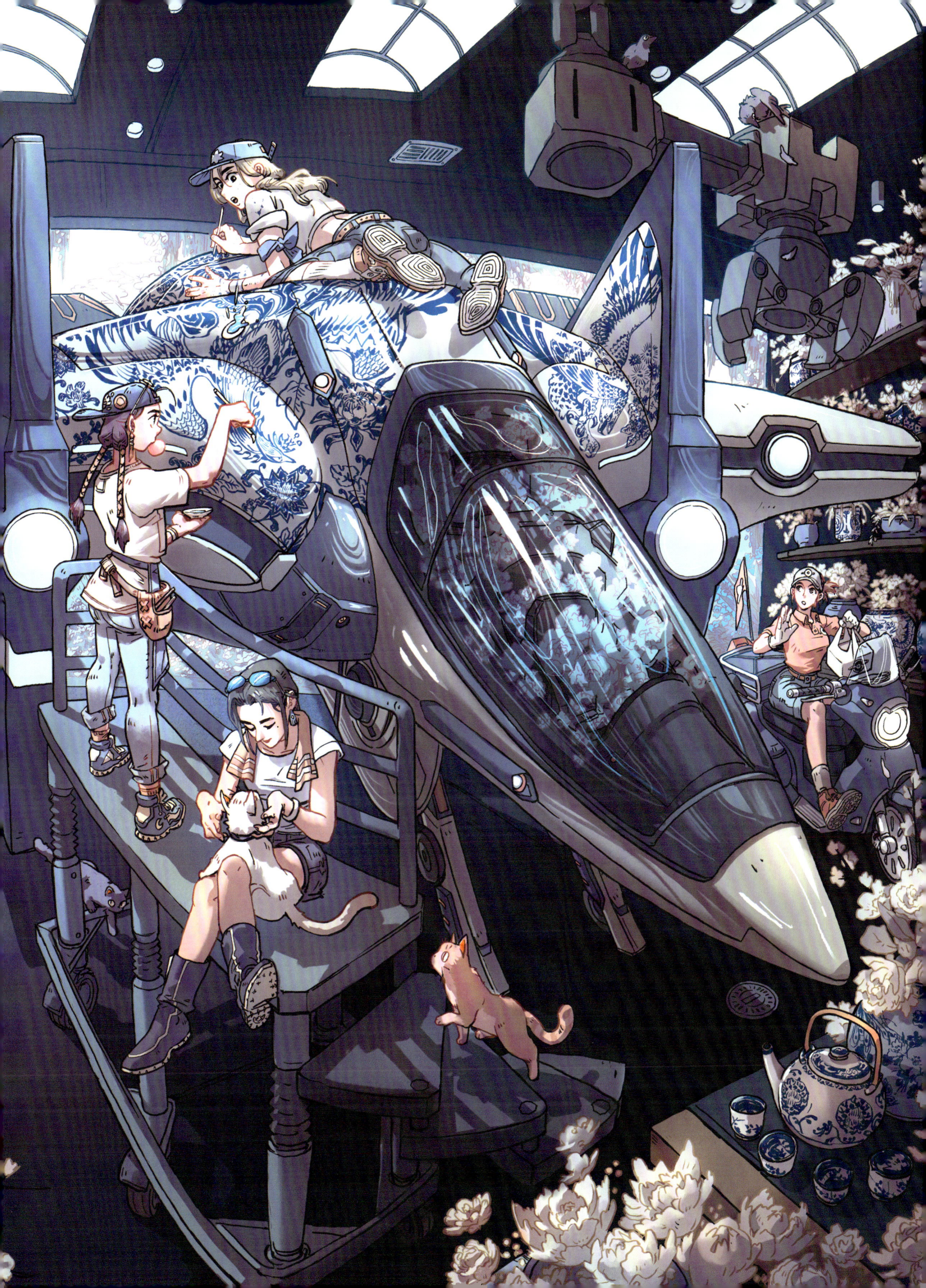

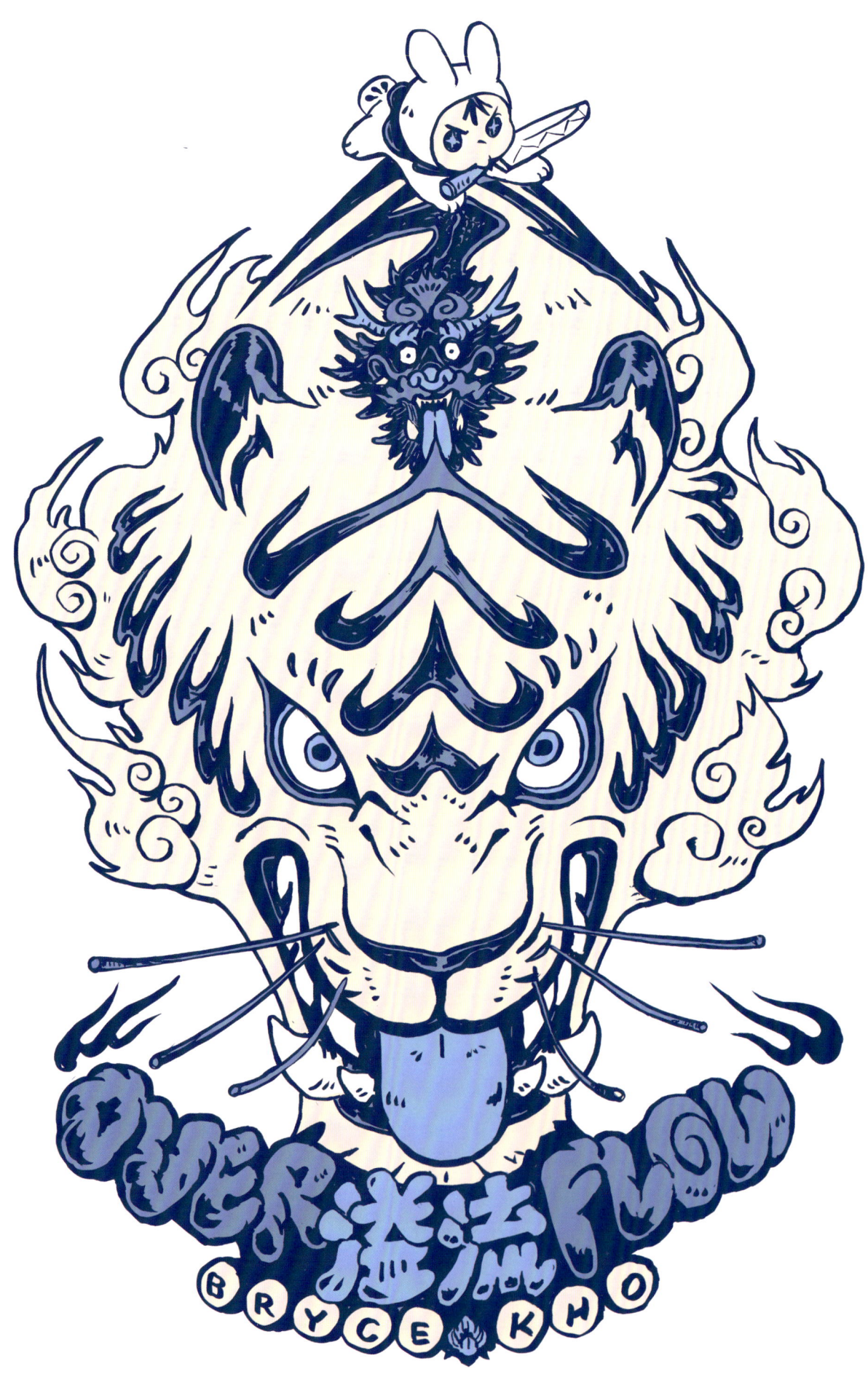

ACKNOWLEDGEMENTS

I cannot overstate how much more exhausting it is to be a parent than it is to work on drawings all day, so my biggest thank you goes to my wife Lai Xu for taking care of our son, Conan, while I was working my hardest to make this book a reality. My parents and Lai's parents deserve a big thank you for helping out during this time as well. I'd also like to thank my editor Rhee for guiding me through the process; Jeffrey and Sara for scanning hundreds of pieces; Sabrina for designing and then redesigning so many pages; and Thierry for allowing me to take time off to pursue this book while still working for Sabotage.

Lastly – Conan, you may not have been old enough to realize it, but you helped out so much by being a source of constant joy and inspiration, so thank you for being my good little guy.

3dtotal Publishing

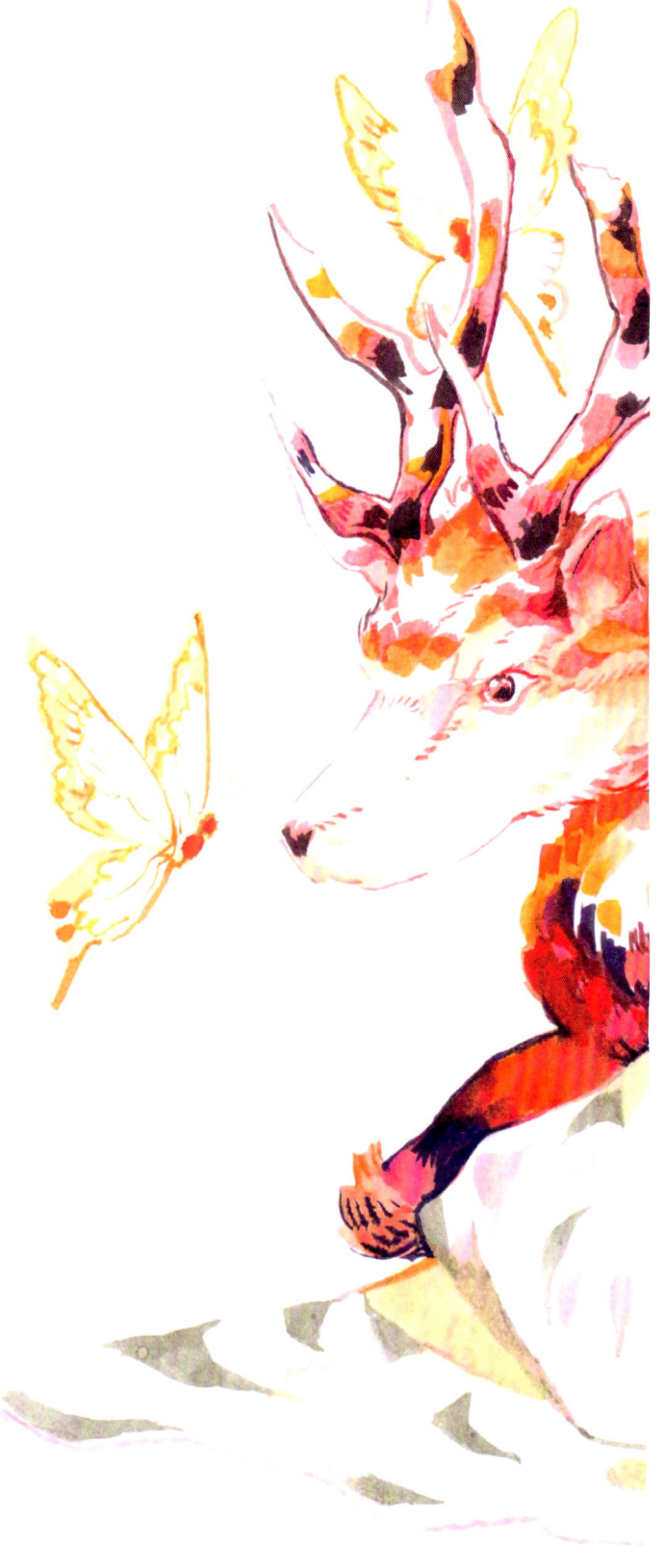

3dtotal Publishing is a trailblazing, creative publisher specializing in inspirational and educational resources for artists.

Our titles feature top industry professionals from around the globe who share their experience in skilfully written step-by-step tutorials and fascinating, detailed guides. Illustrated throughout with stunning artwork, these bestselling publications offer creative insight, expert advice, and essential motivation. Fans of digital art will enjoy our comprehensive volumes covering Adobe Photoshop, Procreate, and Blender, as well as our superb titles based around character design, including *Fundamentals of Character Design* and *Creating Characters for the Entertainment Industry*. The dedicated, high-quality blend of instruction and inspiration also extends to traditional art. Titles covering a range of techniques, genres, and abilities allow your creativity to flourish while building essential skills.

Well-established within the industry, we now offer over 100 titles and counting, many of which have been translated into multiple languages around the world. With something for every artist, we are proud to say that our books offer the 3dtotal package:

LEARN • CREATE • SHARE

Visit us at store.3dtotal.com
3dtotal Publishing is part of 3dtotal.com, a leading website for CG artists founded by Tom Greenway in 1999.

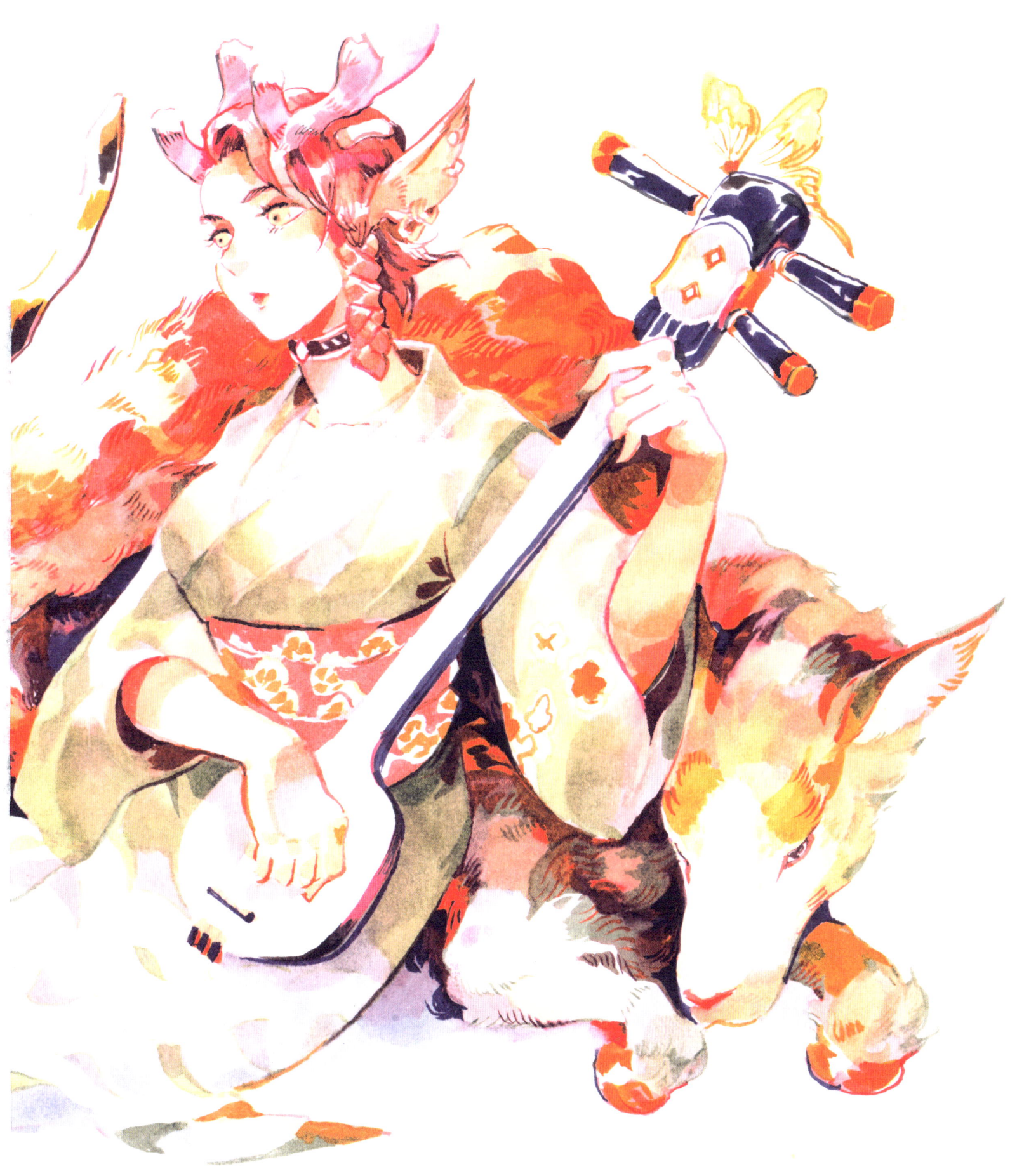

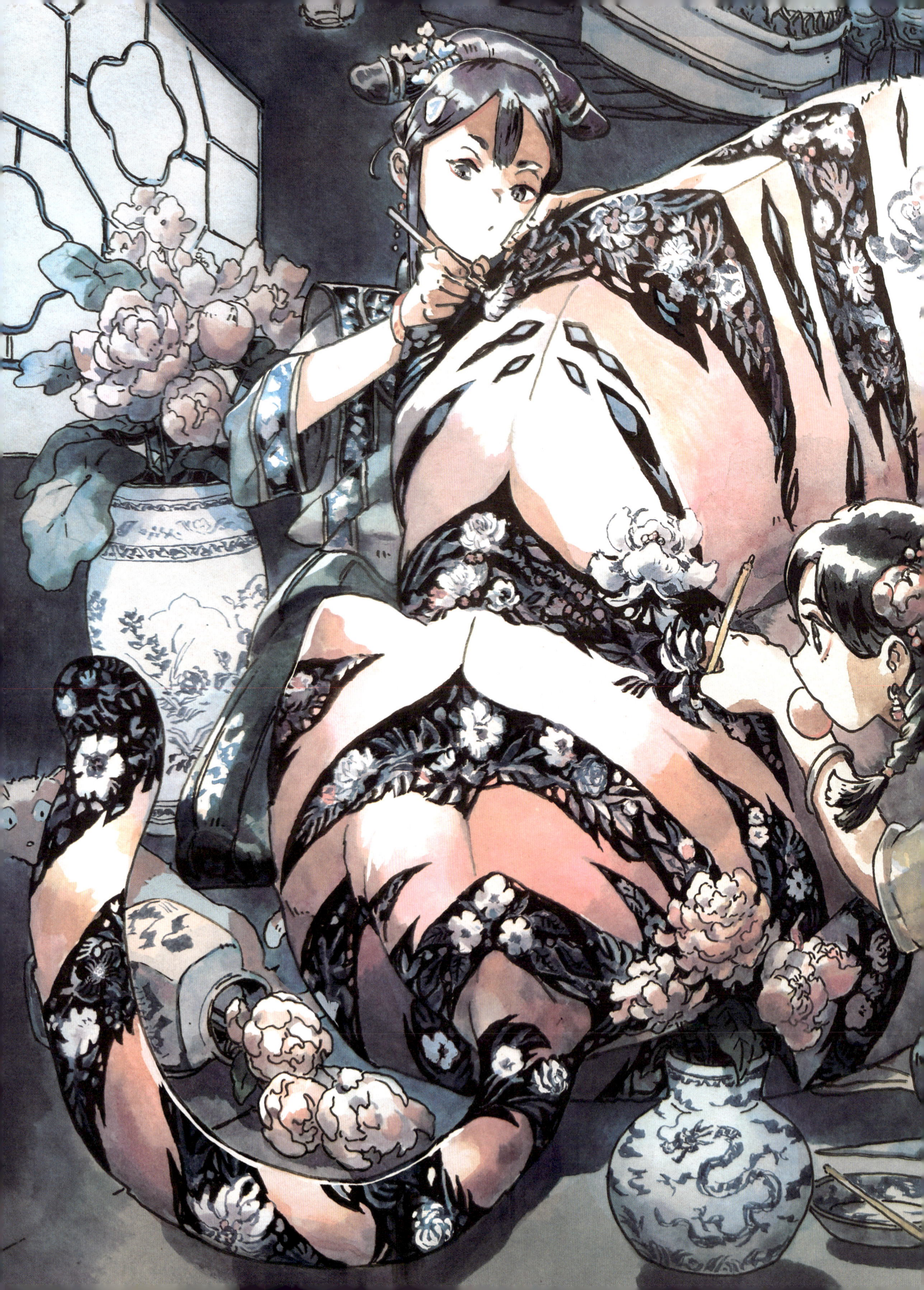